Lecture Notes in Computer Science 1636

Edited by G. Goos, J. Hartmanis and J. van Leeuwen

Springer

Berlin
Heidelberg
New York
Barcelona
Hong Kong
London
Milan
Paris
Singapore
Tokyo

Lars Knudsen (Ed.)

Fast Software Encryption

6th International Workshop, FSE'99
Rome, Italy, March 24-26, 1999
Proceedings

Springer

Series Editors

Gerhard Goos, Karlsruhe University, Germany
Juris Hartmanis, Cornell University, NY, USA
Jan van Leeuwen, Utrecht University, The Netherlands

Volume Editor

Lars Knudsen
University of Bergen, Department of Informatics
N-5020 Bergen, Norway
E-mail: lars.knudsen@ii.uib.no

Cataloging-in-Publication data applied for

Die Deutsche Bibliothek - CIP-Einheitsaufnahme

Fast software encryption : 6th international workshop ;
proceedings / FSE '99, Rome, Italy, March 24 - 26, 1999. Lars
Knudsen (ed.). - Berlin ; Heidelberg ; New York ; Barcelona ; Hong
Kong ; London ; Milan ; Paris ; Singapore ; Tokyo : Springer, 1999
  (Lecture notes in computer science ; Vol. 1636)
  ISBN 3-540-66226-X

CR Subject Classification (1998): E.3, F.2.1, E.4, G.4

ISSN 0302-9743
ISBN 3-540-66226-X Springer-Verlag Berlin Heidelberg New York

This work is subject to copyright. All rights are reserved, whether the whole or part of the material is
concerned, specifically the rights of translation, reprinting, re-use of illustrations, recitation, broadcasting,
reproduction on microfilms or in any other way, and storage in data banks. Duplication of this publication
or parts thereof is permitted only under the provisions of the German Copyright Law of September 9, 1965,
in its current version, and permission for use must always be obtained from Springer-Verlag. Violations are
liable for prosecution under the German Copyright Law.

© Springer-Verlag Berlin Heidelberg 1999
Printed in Germany

Typesetting: Camera-ready by author
SPIN: 10703422   06/3142 – 5 4 3 2 1 0   Printed on acid-free paper

Preface

The Fast Software Encryption Workshop 1999 is the sixth in a series of workshops starting in Cambridge in December 1993.

The workshop was organized by General Chair William Wolfowicz, Fondazione U. Bordoni, and Programme Chair Lars Knudsen, University of Bergen, Norway, in cooperation with Securteam, as far as local arrangements were concerned. The workshop was held March 24-26, 1999 in Rome, Italy.

The workshop concentrated on all aspects of fast secret key ciphers, including the design and cryptanalysis of block and stream ciphers, as well as hash functions.

There were 51 submissions, all of them submitted electronically. One submission was later withdrawn by the authors, and 22 papers were selected for presentation. All submissions were carefully reviewed by at least 4 committee members. At the workshop, preliminary versions of all 22 papers were distributed to all attendees. After the workshop there was a final reviewing process with additional comments to the authors.

It has been a challenge for me to chair the committee of this workshop, and it is a pleasure to thank all the members of the programme committee for their hard work. The committee this year consisted of, in alphabetic order, Ross Anderson (Cambridge, UK), Eli Biham (Technion, Israel), Don Coppersmith (IBM, USA), Cunsheng Ding (Singapore), Dieter Gollmann (Microsoft, UK), James Massey (Denmark), Mitsuru Matsui (Mitsubishi, Japan), Bart Preneel (K.U. Leuven, Belgium), Bruce Schneier (Counterpane, USA), and Serge Vaudenay (ENS, France).

It is a great pleasure to thank William Wolfowicz for organising the workshop. Also, it is a pleasure to thank Securteam for the logistics and Telsy and Sun for supporting the conference. Finally, a big thank you to all submitting authors for their contributions, and to all attendees (approximately 165) of the workshop. Finally, I would like to thank Vincent Rijmen for his technical assistance in preparing these proceedings.

April 1999   Lars Knudsen

Table of Contents

Advanced Encryption Standard

Remotely Keyed Encryption

Analysis of Block Ciphers I

Miscellaneous

Modes of Operation

Analysis of Block Ciphers II

Stream Ciphers

Improved Analysis of
Some Simplified Variants of RC6

Scott Contini[1], Ronald L. Rivest[2], M.J.B. Robshaw[1], and Yiqun Lisa Yin[1]

[1] RSA Laboratories, 2955 Campus Drive
San Mateo, CA 94403, USA
{scontini,matt,yiqun}@rsa.com
[2] M.I.T. Laboratory for Computer Science, 545 Technology Square
Cambridge, MA 02139, USA
rivest@theory.lcs.mit.edu

Abstract. RC6 has been submitted as a candidate for the Advanced Encryption Standard (AES). Two important features of RC6 that were absent from its predecessor RC5 are a *quadratic function* and a *fixed rotation*. By examining simplified variants that omit these features we clarify their essential contribution to the overall security of RC6.

1 Introduction

RC6 is an evolutionary improvement of the block cipher RC5 [9] that was designed to meet the requirements of the Advanced Encryption Standard (AES). Like RC5, RC6 makes essential use of data-dependent rotations, but it also includes new features such as the use of four working registers instead of two, and the inclusion of integer multiplication as an additional primitive operation. Two components of RC6 that were absent from RC5 are a *quadratic function* to mix bits in a word more effectively and a *fixed rotation* that is used both to hinder the construction of good differentials and linear approximations and also to ensure that subsequent data dependent rotation amounts are more likely to be affected by any ongoing avalanche of change.

An initial analysis of the security of RC6 and its resistance to the basic forms of differential and linear cryptanalysis was given in [3]. Here we further illustrate how these new operations contribute to the security of RC6 by studying simplified variants (that is, intentionally weakened forms) of RC6. In particular, our approach is to find the best attack on the weakened forms and then try to adapt the attack to the full cipher. Since one of the design principles of RC6 was to build on the experience gained with RC5, the focus of our analysis will be in assessing the relevance to RC6 of the best existing cryptanalytic attacks on RC5. We will often refer to the work of Knudsen and Meier [8] and that of Biryukov and Kushilevitz [2]. These authors in particular have made very significant advances in understanding the security of RC5.

Our work splits naturally into two parts. The first focuses on the usefulness of the fixed rotation and the second on the quadratic function. While our analysis is targeted at RC6 and its simplified variants, some of the results might well be of independent interest. Our analysis starts by considering some of the weakened variants of RC6 that were introduced in [3]. More specifically, by dropping the fixed rotation we derive a cipher that we will denote by RC6-NFR (where NFR stands for no fixed rotation), by dropping the quadratic function we obtain RC6-I (where I stands for the identity function), and by dropping both operations we have RC6-I-NFR.

We will consider characteristics and differentials for RC6-I-NFR and RC6-NFR that have already been described in [3]. We study the relations between certain values of the subkeys and the probability of a characteristic and/or differential. Such phenomena are similar to the "differentially-weak keys" of RC5 observed by Knudsen and Meier [8]. We describe our observations and provide a thorough analysis which suggests that inclusion of the fixed rotation destroys the structure required for such dependencies to form. As a consequence RC6-I and RC6 itself seem to be immune from any direct extension of the results previously obtained on RC5.

Second, we examine the diffusive properties of the quadratic function and other operations that are used in RC6. In this analysis we track the Hamming weight (the number of 1's) of the exclusive-or difference between two quantities as they are encrypted. Quite naturally this leads to the idea of differentials that are constructed using such a measure of difference and this notion is very similar in spirit to earlier work on RC5 [2, 8]. We show that the quadratic function drastically increases the Hamming weight of some input difference when the Hamming weight of an input difference is small. This indicates that the use of both the quadratic function and data-dependent rotations in RC6 make it unlikely that differential attacks similar to those that were useful for RC5 [2, 8] can be effectively extended to RC6.

2 Description of RC6 and variants

A version of RC6 is specified as RC6-$w/r/b$ where the word size is w bits, encryption consists of a nonnegative number of rounds r, and b denotes the length of the encryption key in bytes. Throughout this paper we will set $w = 32$, $r = 20$, $b = 16$, 24, or 32 and we will use RC6 to refer to this particular version. The base-two logarithm of w will be denoted by $\lg w$ and RC6 uses the following six basic operations:

$a + b$	integer addition modulo 2^w
$a - b$	integer subtraction modulo 2^w
$a \oplus b$	bitwise exclusive-or of w-bit words
$a \times b$	integer multiplication modulo 2^w
$a \lll b$	rotate the w-bit word a to the left by the amount given by the least significant $\lg w$ bits of b
$a \ggg b$	rotate the w-bit word a to the right by the amount given by the least significant $\lg w$ bits of b

The user supplies a key of length k bytes which is then expanded to a set of subkeys. The key schedule of RC6 is described in [10]. Since here we are only concerned with encryption, we will assume that the subkeys $S[0], \ldots, S[43]$ are independent and chosen at random. RC6 works with four w-bit registers A, B, C, D which contain the initial input plaintext as well as the output ciphertext at the end of encryption. We use $(A, B, C, D) = (B, C, D, A)$ to mean the parallel assignment of values on the right to registers on the left.

Encryption with RC6-$w/20/b$

Input: Plaintext stored in four w-bit input registers A, B, C, D
                     w-bit round keys $S[0, \ldots, 43]$

Output: Ciphertext stored in A, B, C, D

Procedure: $B = B + S[0]$
                 $D = D + S[1]$
                 for $i = 1$ **to** 20 **do**
                    {
                           $t = (B \times (2B + 1)) \lll \lg w$
                           $u = (D \times (2D + 1)) \lll \lg w$
                           $A = ((A \oplus t) \lll u) + S[2i]$
                           $C = ((C \oplus u) \lll t) + S[2i + 1]$
                           $(A, B, C, D) = (B, C, D, A)$
                    }
                 $A = A + S[42]$
                 $C = C + S[43]$

The three simplified variants of RC6 that we will consider throughout the paper are distinguished from RC6 in the way the values of t and u are assigned. These differences are summarized in the following table.

The assignment of t and u in RC6 and some weakened variants			
	RC6-I-NFR	RC6-I	RC6-NFR	RC6
$t =$	B	$B \lll \lg w$	$B \times (2B + 1)$	$(B \times (2B + 1)) \lll \lg w$
$u =$	D	$D \lll \lg w$	$D \times (2D + 1)$	$(D \times (2D + 1)) \lll \lg w$

3 The fixed rotation

In [8] Knudsen and Meier show that the values of some of the subkeys in RC5 can have a direct effect on the probability of whether some differential holds. In this section we show that a similar phenomenon can be observed in weakened variants of RC6 that do not use the fixed rotation. This should perhaps come as little surprise since while the structure of RC6-I-NFR is very different to that of RC5, it uses the same operations and might be expected to have similar behavior at times. We will then consider the role of the fixed rotation used in RC6 and we will demonstrate by analysis and experimentation that the effects seen in RC5 and some simplified variants of RC6 do not seem to exist within RC6 itself.

3.1 Existing analysis on RC6-I-NFR and RC6-NFR

In [3] one potentially useful six-round iterative characteristic was provided for attacking both RC6-I-NFR and RC6-NFR. This is given in Table 1. Here e_t is used to denote the 32-bit word that has all bits set to zero except bit t where $t = 0$ for the least significant bit. We use A_i (respectively B_i, C_i and D_i) to denote the values of registers A (respectively B, C, and D) at the beginning of round i. As an example, A_1, B_1, C_1, and D_1 contain the plaintext input after pre-whitening and for the six-round variants of the cipher, A_7, B_7, C_7 and D_7 contain the output prior to post-whitening. According to [3], when averaged over all possible subkeys, the expected probability that this characteristic holds is 2^{-30} for both RC6-I-NFR and RC6-I.

3.2 Refined analysis of RC6-I-NFR and RC6-NFR

Closer analysis of the characteristic probabilities for RC6-I-NFR and RC6-NFR suggests that the values of some of the subkeys during encryption are important. In particular, the characteristic of interest for RC6-I-NFR and RC6-NFR given in Table 1 can only occur if certain subkey conditions are met. Further, once these subkey conditions hold then the characteristic occurs with probability 2^{-20}, which is much higher than the initial estimate of 2^{-30} that was obtained by averaging over all subkeys.

i	A_i	B_i	C_i	D_i
1	e_{31}	e_{31}	0	0
		$\downarrow$		
2	e_{31}	0	0	0
		$\downarrow$		
3	0	0	0	e_{31}
		$\downarrow$		
4	0	e_{31}	e_{31}	0
		$\downarrow$		
5	e_{31}	e_{31}	0	e_{31}
		$\downarrow$		
6	e_{31}	e_{31}	e_{31}	0
		$\downarrow$		
7	e_{31}	e_{31}	0	0

Table 1. A characteristic for RC6-I-NFR and RC6-NFR.

In the analysis that follows we will concentrate on RC6-NFR. The same arguments and results can be applied to RC6-I-NFR by replacing $f(x) = x \times (2x+1)$ with the identity function $f(x) = x$. We will use the fact that $x \bmod 2^i$ uniquely determines $(x \times (2x+1)) \bmod 2^i$. Furthermore, the notation "$=_{32}$" will be used to indicate when two values are congruent modulo 32.

5

Lemma 1. *If the characteristic given in Table 1 holds for RC6-NFR, then the following two conditions on the subkeys must hold:*

$$f(-S[9]) =_{32} -S[7],$$
$$f(S[8]) =_{32} -S[11].$$

Proof. First we observe that if the characteristic is to hold, then certain rotation amounts derived from the B and D registers must be zero. Note that we always have that $B_i = A_{i+1}$ and that $D_i = C_{i+1}$. As a consequence, for the characteristic to hold we must have

$$D_2 =_{32} C_3 =_{32} 0, \qquad B_3 =_{32} A_4 =_{32} 0,$$
$$B_4 =_{32} A_5 =_{32} 0, \qquad D_4 =_{32} C_5 =_{32} 0,$$
$$B_5 =_{32} A_6 =_{32} 0, \qquad B_6 =_{32} A_7 =_{32} 0.$$

Using the fact that the rotation amounts are 0, we get the following two equations from rounds three and four and rounds four and five.

$$B_4 = (C_3 \oplus f(D_3)) + S[7], \qquad (1)$$
$$B_5 = (C_4 \oplus f(D_4)) + S[9]. \qquad (2)$$

Since $B_4 =_{32} 0$, $C_3 =_{32} 0$, $B_5 =_{32} 0$ and $D_4 =_{32} 0$, we have $S[7] =_{32} -f(D_3)$ and $C_4 =_{32} -S[9]$. Since $C_4 = D_3$, we obtain the first condition on subkeys $S[7] =_{32} -f(-S[9])$.

Similarly, looking at the computation from rounds four and five and rounds five and six, we get the following two equations.

$$D_5 = A_4 \oplus f(B_4) + S[8], \qquad (3)$$
$$B_6 = C_5 \oplus f(D_5) + S[11]. \qquad (4)$$

Since $A_4 =_{32} 0$, $B_4 =_{32} 0$, $B_6 =_{32} 0$ and $C_5 =_{32} 0$, we have $D_5 =_{32} S[8]$ and $S[11] =_{32} -f(D_5)$, and so $S[11] =_{32} -f(S[8])$. $\square$

The subkey dependencies in Lemma 1 were obtained using only four equations (those for B_4, B_5, D_5 and B_6). In total, one could write down 12 equations of the form $B_{i+1} = (((C_i \oplus f(D_i)) \lll f(B_i)) + S[2i+1]$ and $D_{i+1} = (((A_i \oplus f(B_i)) \lll f(D_i)) + S[2i]$ for this characteristic. Although there might be dependencies involving other equations, the four given above will be the focus of the rest of this section. Essentially, each equation involves four variables and the aim is to combine equations to obtain two expressions with a single variable. If the two expressions involve the same variable then we can obtain conditions on the subkeys involved. The four equations we use are the only ones from the set of twelve that allow us to do this.

It is worth noting that given such conditions on the subkeys involved not only does the characteristic hold, but it does so with a higher probability than the expected value given in [3].

Lemma 2. *Assume that the characteristic given in Table 1 holds up to round five. Furthermore suppose that $f(-S[9]) =_{32} -S[7]$ and $f(S[8]) =_{32} -S[11]$. Then $B_5 =_{32} 0$ and $B_6 =_{32} 0$.*

Proof. From Lemma 1, we have that $S[7] =_{32} -f(D_3)$. This is equivalent to $-S[7] =_{32} f(C_4)$. Also, we have that $B_5 =_{32} C_4 + S[9]$. So, if $-S[7] =_{32} f(-S[9])$ then $f(C_4) =_{32} f(-S[9])$ which implies that $C_4 =_{32} -S[9]$ and so $B_5 =_{32} 0$. A similar argument can be used to show that $B_6 =_{32} 0$. □

Lemma 2 shows that when the subkey conditions hold, $B_5 =_{32} 0$ and $B_6 =_{32} 0$. In this case the probability of the characteristic will be $2^{-30} \times 2^5 \times 2^5 = 2^{-20}$, since two of the rotation amounts are always zero. Recall that the estimated probability for the characteristic when averaged over all keys is 2^{-30} [3]. Here we have shown (Lemmas 1 and 2) that there is some irregularity in the distribution of the probability: For a fraction of 2^{-10} keys the probability is 2^{-20}, and for the rest of the keys the probability is much smaller than 2^{-30}. This kind of irregular distribution can sometimes be exploited as was demonstrated by Knudsen and Meier with RC5 [8] who showed some techniques for using it in a differential attack. We would expect the same to apply here. Similar subkey dependencies can be observed for some of the other characteristics for RC6-I-NFR and RC6-NFR given in [3]. However in some cases the characteristic must be iterated more than once before dependencies exist.

Note that the behavior of the differential associated with some characteristic is typically of more importance in a differential attack. For RC6-I-NFR, while the characteristic displays the irregular behavior already described, the associated differential has been experimentally verified to hold with the expected probability [3]. However the associated differential for RC6-NFR appears to have the same irregular behavior as the characteristic. Why is there this discrepancy? In [3] it is shown how the introduction of the quadratic function helps to reduce the additional effect of differentials. In short, for RC6-I-NFR there are many equally viable paths that match the beginning and end-points of the characteristic. If the characteristic fails to hold because of some choice of subkey values, other characteristics hold instead thereby maintaining the probability of the differential. However, with RC6-NFR we introduce the quadratic function and this typically reduces differentials to being dominated by the action of a single characteristic. Irregular behavior in the characteristic will therefore manifest itself as irregular behavior in the differential.

3.3 Differential characteristics in RC6-I and RC6

Let us now consider the role of the fixed rotation that was omitted in RC6-I-NFR and RC6-NFR. We will find that this single operation removes the kind of subkey dependencies that occurred in these two variants.

We will focus on RC6-I in the analysis for simplicity, and the same arguments also apply to the full RC6. We will need to make some heuristic assumptions to make headway with our analysis. Nevertheless our experimental results confirm that the differential behavior of RC6-I is pretty much as expected. It also closely matches the behavior described in [3].

Consider the characteristic given in Table 2. This is the characteristic which seemed to be one of the most useful for attacking RC6-I [3]. We first argue that there are no subkey dependencies of the form we described in Section 3.2 for this characteristic and we then broaden our discussion to include other, more general, characteristics.

i	A_i	B_i	C_i	D_i
1	e_{16}	e_{11}	0	0
		↓		
2	e_{11}	0	0	0
		↓		
3	0	0	0	e_{26}
		↓		
4	0	e_{26}	e_{26}	0
		↓		
5	e_{26}	e_{21}	0	e_{26}
		↓		
6	e_{21}	e_{16}	e_{26}	0
		↓		
7	e_{16}	e_{11}	0	0

Table 2. A useful characteristic for RC6-I.

At this stage we need some new notation and the exponent n will be used to denote when some quantity has been rotated to the left by n bit positions. For example, $D_2^5 =_{32} 15$ means that when D_2 is rotated five bits to the left, then the decimal value of the least significant five bits is 15. Of course, this is the same as saying that the most significant five bits of D_2 take the value 15.

For simplicity, we will assume that $(x + y)^j = x^j + y^j$ where j denotes a rotation amount. This is true if, and only if, there is no carry-out when adding the top j bits and no carry-out when adding the bottom $32 - j$ bits. For the sake of our analysis however we make this assumption, since it should actually facilitate the construction of any potential subkey dependencies!

Following the arguments in Lemma 1, for the characteristic in Table 2 to hold the following rotation amounts must take the values indicated:

$$D_2^5 =_{32} C_3^5 =_{32} 15, \qquad B_3^5 =_{32} A_4^5 =_{32} 27,$$
$$B_4^5 =_{32} A_5^5 =_{32} 27, \qquad D_4^5 =_{32} C_5^5 =_{32} 27,$$
$$B_5^5 =_{32} A_6^5 =_{32} 17, \qquad B_6^5 =_{32} A_7^5 =_{32} 17.$$

We wish to write down four equations similar to Equations (1), (2), (3) and (4) which cause subkey dependencies in RC6-NFR. From round three to four, the difference e_{26} is copied from register D_3, is changed to e_{31} by the action of the fixed rotation, and then exclusive-ored into the C strand. For it to become the e_{26} that appears in B_4, the data dependent rotation B_3^5 must have the value 27. Hence, we must have $B_3^5 =_{32} 27$ and $B_4 = (C_3 \oplus D_3^5)^{27} + S[7] = C_3^{27} \oplus D_3 + S[7]$.

In a similar way other equations can be derived:

$$B_4 = C_3^{27} \oplus D_3 + S[7], \tag{5}$$
$$B_5 = C_4^{27} \oplus D_4 + S[9], \tag{6}$$
$$D_5 = A_4^{27} \oplus B_4 + S[8], \tag{7}$$
$$B_6 = C_5^{17} \oplus D_5^{22} + S[11]. \tag{8}$$

In Lemma 1 we observed a subkey dependency by combining the analogous equations to (5) and (6), and another dependency from combining the analogous equations to (7) and (8). In the case of RC6-I we can demonstrate that neither approach now works.

We first consider Equations (5) and (6). For Equation (6) we know that the values of $B_5^5 \bmod 32$, $D_4^5 \bmod 32$, and $S[9]^5 \bmod 32$ are fixed. This implies a condition on the least significant five bits of C_4. Since C_4 is the same as D_3, we have a condition on $D_3 \bmod 32$. We now have conditions on all the registers in Equation (5), namely, $B_4^5 \bmod 32$, $C_3^5 \bmod 32$, and $D_3 \bmod 32$. However the bits from different words involved in this equation are from different positions. They don't lead to any constraints on $S[9]$, and there appear to be no subkey dependencies as a result.

Similarly arguments also apply to Equations (7) and (8). One may also try to combine Equations (5) and (7), since they have the quantity B_4 in common, or Equations (6) and (8), since they have $C_5 = D_4$ in common. However, these combinations once again fail to give any subkey dependencies.

We performed experiments on RC6-I to assess the probability of the characteristics given in Table 2. These results confirmed that the distribution of the characteristic probability was as expected, and there was no indication of any subkey dependencies for the characteristic.

i	A_i	B_i	C_i	D_i
1	e_{t+5}	e_t	0	0
		$\downarrow$		
2	e_t	0	0	0
		$\downarrow$		
3	0	0	0	e_s
		$\downarrow$		
4	0	e_u	e_s	0
		$\downarrow$		
5	e_u	e_{u-5}	0	e_v
		$\downarrow$		
6	e_{u-5}	e_{u-10}	e_v	0
		$\downarrow$		
7	e_{u-10}	e_{u-15}	0	0

Table 3. A generalized characteristic for RC6-I.

More generally, we might consider characteristics of the form given in Table 3. The values which we need to fix if the characteristic is going to hold are

$$D_2^5 =_{32} C_3^5 =_{32} s - t, \qquad B_3^5 =_{32} A_4^5 =_{32} u - 5 - s,$$
$$B_4^5 =_{32} A_5^5 =_{32} u - 5 - s, \qquad D_4^5 =_{32} C_5^5 =_{32} v - u - 5,$$
$$B_5^5 =_{32} A_6^5 =_{32} u - 15 - v, \qquad B_6^5 =_{32} A_7^5 =_{32} u - 15 - v.$$

Let $r_1 = u - 5 - s$, $r_2 = v - u - 5$, and $r_3 = u - 15 - v$. Then the subkey dependencies we observed would be produced by the following equations:

$$B_4 = C_3^{r_1} \oplus D_3^{5+r_1} + S[7],$$
$$B_5 = C_4^{r_1} \oplus D_4^{5+r_1} + S[9],$$
$$D_5 = A_4^{r_2} \oplus B_4^{5+r_2} + S[8],$$
$$B_6 = C_5^{r_3} \oplus D_5^{5+r_3} + S[11].$$

Following similar arguments to those presented earlier, it can be verified that there is no choice for r_1, r_2, and r_3 that makes the characteristic depend upon the values of the subkeys. In particular, the most promising values to try are $r_1 = 0$; $r_1 = 27$; $r_3 = 0$ and $r_2 = 22$; and $r_3 = 0$, $r_2 = 27$, and $r_1 = 27$.

The fixed rotation is an important component of RC6. Not only does it help to hinder the construction of good differentials and linear approximations [3] but it helps to disturb the build-up of any inter-round dependencies. Here the fixed rotation ensures that equations can simultaneously hold without forcing any restriction on the values of the quantities involved.

4 The quadratic function

In this section, we examine the diffusive properties of the quadratic function and other operations used in RC6. Both the work of Knudsen and Meier [8] and that of Biryukov and Kushilevitz [2] rely on the following fact about RC5: It has a relatively slow avalanche of change from one round to the next, unless the difference in two words is in the bits used to determine a data-dependent rotation. When that happens, the amount of change in one round to the other can be dramatic, but until then the rate of change tends to be rather modest. This can be exploited to a limited degree in attacks on RC5 [2, 8].

We will choose a measure of diffusion that complements naturally the work given in [2, 8]. We will use the Hamming weight of the exclusive-or difference between two words as a measure of the difference, rather than the actual value of the difference as we would in differential cryptanalysis [1] or part of the difference as we would in truncated differential cryptanalysis [7]. It is straightforward to envisage using this notion of difference in a differential-style attack, something we call *Hamming weight differentials*, and this is very similar to some of the earlier analysis of RC5 [2, 8]. While this earlier work focused on how to effectively use such differentials to attack RC5, the focus of our work will be on assessing the likely impact of the quadratic function in thwarting such attacks.

Even for a simple operation it can be difficult to fully characterize the probability distribution of the Hamming weight of some output difference given the Hamming weight of the input differences. We will study the problem by analyzing the *expected* Hamming weight of such an output difference and it turns out that such an approach provides a good insight into the role of the different operations.

Our analysis shows that the quadratic function drastically increases the Hamming weight of some difference especially when the Hamming weight of the input difference is small. This illustrates a nice effect whereby the use of the quadratic function complements that of the data-dependent rotation. As we have mentioned, the data-dependent rotation becomes an effective agent of change only when there is a difference in the rotation amount. With a small Hamming weight difference, it is less likely that non-zero difference bits appear in positions that affect a rotation amount. However, the quadratic function helps to drastically increase the avalanche of change so that the full benefit of the data-dependent rotations can be gained as soon as possible.

4.1 Definitions and assumptions

We introduce some useful notation and definitions. For a w-bit binary vector X, let $|X|$ denote the *Hamming weight* of X, i.e., $|X|$ is the number of 1's in X. Throughout this paper we will be continually referring to RC6 and so we will assume that the word size $w = 32$. We will let $X' = X_1 \oplus X_2$, $Y' = Y_1 \oplus Y_2$, and $Z' = Z_1 \oplus Z_2$ and we use x, y, z to denote the Hamming weight of the differences $|X'|, |Y'|, |Z'|$, respectively.

Let us consider the following two conditions that may be imposed on some difference that has Hamming weight x.

A: There is a single block of consecutive 1's of length x, and the block is distributed randomly at some position in the input difference.

B: There are $t > 1$ blocks of consecutive 1's of length $x_1, x_2, ..., x_t$ such that $x_1 + x_2 + \cdots + x_t = x$. In addition, each block is distributed randomly across the input difference.

Condition B is actually a good characterization for the differences in the intermediate rounds of RC6 and its variants. In each round (of RC6 or its variants) any difference in the A and C strands are rotated by a random amount due to the data-dependent rotations. Hence each block of 1's within the differences is distributed randomly. Condition A is a special case of Condition B. In the next two sections when we examine the diffusive properties of individual operations, we will first consider the special case Condition A and then generalize the results to Condition B.

4.2 Diffusive properties of the basic operations

Here we analyze the basic operations of exclusive-or, addition, and rotation. The more complicated quadratic function will be considered in the next section.

Lemma 3. (exclusive-or) *For $i = 1, 2$ let $Z_i = X_i \oplus Y_i$. If X' and Y' satisfy Condition A, then $E(z) = x + y - \frac{2xy}{w}$.*

Proof. Since the block of 1's in X' and Y' is distributed randomly, each bit "1" in X' overlaps with each bit "1" in Y' with probability $\frac{1}{w}$. So the expected length of overlap in the output difference is $\frac{xy}{w}$, implying that the expected Hamming weight of the output is $x + y - \frac{2xy}{w}$. $\square$

Corollary 4. (exclusive-or) *For $i = 1, 2$ let $Z_i = X_i \oplus Y_i$. If X' and Y' satisfy Condition B then $E(z) = x + y - \frac{2xy}{w}$.*

Proof. Follows directly from the proof of Lemma 3. $\square$

Note that the expected overlap between the quantities X' and Y' is similar to the number of "corrections" used by Biryukov and Kushilevitz in their analysis of *corrected Fibonacci sequences* [2]. There an explicit formula was not provided [2] but all sequences with a "reasonable" number of corrections were experimentally generated and this was used as an estimate in their work.

Lemma 5. (addition) *For $i = 1, 2$ let $Z_i = X_i + S$, where S is the subkey. If X' satisfies Condition A then averaging over all possible X_1, X_2, S, $E(z) = c + \frac{x+1}{2}$ where $c \in [0, 1]$ and depends on X'.*

Proof. We start with the special case where $|X'| = w$, that is, X_1 and X_2 differ in all bits. We first prove that when averaging over all possible X_1, X_2, S,

$$prob(X_1 + S < 2^w \text{ and } X_2 + S \geq 2^w) = \frac{1}{4}. \tag{9}$$

Given any $X_1 \in \{0, 1\}^w$, we define

$$d(X_1) = |S : S \in \{0, 1\}^w, \text{s.t. } X_1 + S < 2^w \text{ and } X_2 + S \geq 2^w|.$$

If $X_1 < 2^{w-1}$, we have $d(X_1) = X_2 - X_1 = (X_1 \oplus (2^w - 1)) - X_1 = 2^w - 1 - 2X_1$. (If $X_1 \geq 2^{w-1}$, $d(X_1) = 0$.) Hence,

$$prob(X_1 + S < 2^w \text{ and } X_2 + S \geq 2^w) = \frac{\sum_{X_1=0}^{2^{w-1}-1} d(X_1)}{2^w \times 2^w} = \frac{1}{4}.$$

Note that for Equation 9 the particular value of w is unimportant. So we can consider the least significant j bits of X_1, X_2, S. More precisely, for $1 \leq j \leq w$, define $X_1(j) = X_1 \bmod 2^j, X_2(j) = X_2 \bmod 2^j, S(j) = S \bmod 2^j$. Then,

$$prob(X_1(j) + S(j) < 2^j \text{ and } X_2(j) + S(j) \geq 2^j) = \frac{1}{4}. \tag{10}$$

By symmetry,

$$prob(X_1(j) + S(j) \geq 2^j \text{ and } X_2(j) + S(j) < 2^j) = \frac{1}{4}. \tag{11}$$

From Equations 10 and 11, we know that with probability $1/2$, exactly one of the two addition operations ($X_1 + S$ and $X_2 + S$) produces a carry into bit j. If this happens, Z_1 and Z_2 will be the same in bit j. Therefore, with probability $1/2$, the jth bit ($j \geq 1$) of $Z' = Z_1 \oplus Z_2$ is 1. Since bit 0 of Z' is always 1, the expected Hamming weight of Z' is $\frac{w-1}{2} + 1 = \frac{w+1}{2} = c + \frac{w+1}{2}$ for $c = 0$. We have proved the Lemma for the special case where $|X'| = w$.

Let us now consider the general case where $|X'| = x$ for some $1 \leq x \leq w$. Let v be the index of the most significant 1 in X'. So X_1 and X_2 are the same in bits $v + 1$ through $w - 1$. When computing $Z_1 = X_1 + S$ and $Z_2 = X_2 + S$, it is possible that one or both of the carries will propagate into bits $v + 1$ and higher. It is not hard to show that the "extra" number of bit differences between Z_1 and Z_2 due to this carry effect has an expectation c for some $0 \leq c \leq 1$. So the expected Hamming weight of the output difference is $c + \frac{x+1}{2}$. $\qquad\square$

Corollary 6. (addition) *For $i = 1, 2$ let $Z_i = X_i + S$, where S is the subkey. Suppose that X' satisfies Condition B and there are t blocks of 1's in X'. Then averaging over all possible keys S, $E(z) \leq t + \frac{x+t}{2}$.*

Proof. Follows from Lemma 5. $\qquad\square$

The fixed rotation $Z = X \lll \lg w$ always preserves the Hamming weight of the input difference in the output difference. For data-dependent rotations, it is straightforward to see that provided the input difference does not affect the rotation amount, then the Hamming weight of the difference is preserved. We can state this simple fact in the following lemma.

Lemma 7. (data-dependent rotation) *For $i = 1, 2$ let $Z_i = X_i \lll Y_i$. If $Y' =_w 0$, then $z = x$.*

The more interesting case is when $Y' \neq_w 0$. It has previously been shown [4, 6] that once a difference in the amount of rotation is experienced then the output difference is distributed in an essentially random manner over a very large set. This essentially makes any differential-style attack impossible since in this case there is a very substantial diffusive effect. So depending on the difference Y', a data-dependent rotation can either preserve the Hamming weight or increase the Hamming weight by a significant amount. The probability of the latter case occurring is closely related to the Hamming weight of Y' and we have the following lemma that characterizes such a relation for the special case.

Lemma 8. *Let $y = |Y'|$ and let p be the probability that $Y' \neq_w 0$. If Y' satisfies Condition A then $p = \min\left(\frac{y + \lg w - 1}{w}, 1\right)$.*

For the more general case when Y' satisfies Condition B it is not so simple to derive a precise formula similar to the one given above. However it is clearly the case that the heavier the Hamming weight of Y', the larger the probability that some part of the non-zero input difference will have an effect on the rotation amount.

4.3 Diffusive properties of the quadratic function

Here we consider the diffusive properties of the quadratic function $Z = f(X)$, an important new operation in RC6. First, we restate a lemma regarding the quadratic function that first appeared in [3]. This lemma characterizes the behavior of the output when a single bit of some input is flipped.

Lemma 9. **[3]** *Given an input X_1 chosen uniformly at random from $\{0, 1\}^{32}$, let $g_{i,j}$ denote the probability that flipping bit i of X_1 will flip bit j of $Z_1 = f(X_1)$. Then,*

$$g_{i,j} = \begin{cases} 0 \ for \ j < i, \\ 1 \ for \ j = i, \\ 1 \ for \ j = 1 \ and \ i = 0, \ and \end{cases}$$

$$g_{i,j} \in [1/4, 3/4] \ for \ j > i \geq 1 \ or \ j \geq 2 \ and \ i = 0.$$

For the last case, $g_{i,j}$ is close to $3/4$ if $j = 2i + 2$, and for most of the other i, j pairs $g_{i,j}$ is close to $1/2$.

Put descriptively this lemma shows that flipping bit i of some input X will always flip bit i of the output and will, in most cases, also flip bit j where $j > i$ of the output with probability around $1/2$.

We can extend the lemma to the more general case where multiple bits of the input are flipped and we obtain a similar result: Let i be the bit position of the least significant 1 in X'. Then flipping bit i of the input X_1 will always flip bit i of the output and will, in most cases, flip bit j for $j > i$ of the output with probability around $1/2$. Experiments confirm both this intuition and also the following, perhaps surprising, result.

Lemma 10. (quadratic function) *For $i = 1, 2$ let $Z_i = f(X_i)$. Let $x = |X'|$ and $z = |Z'|$. If X' satisfies Condition A then $E(z) \approx 1 + \frac{x+w-2}{4}$.*

Proof. Let i be the index of the least significant 1 in X'. For a fixed i, the expected value of z is roughly $1 + (w - 1 - i)/2$. If X' satisfies Condition A then i is uniformly distributed between 0 and $(w - x)$. Hence,

$$E(z) \approx \frac{1}{(w - x) + 1} \sum_{i=0}^{w-x} \left(1 + \frac{w - 1 - i}{2}\right) = 1 + \frac{x + w - 2}{4}.$$

$\square$

Corollary 11. (quadratic function) *For $i = 1, 2$ let $Z_i = f(X_i)$. Let $x = |X'|$ and $z = |Z'|$. If X' satisfies Condition B and there are t blocks of 1's in X', then $E(z) \geq 1 + \frac{x+w+t-3}{4}$.*

Proof. Similar to the proof of Lemma 10. $\square$

Lemma 10 shows that even when the difference in some input to the quadratic function has Hamming weight 1, the average Hamming weight of the difference in the output is 8.75. This is a very important result. All the other basic operations in RC6, as well as those used in RC5, generally provide little or no additional change to the output difference if the Hamming weight of the input difference is very low.

We can illustrate the effect of including the quadratic function in the following way. We experimentally measure the probability that the rotation amounts[3] at the end of a given number of rounds are unaffected by a single bit change in the first word of the input to the cipher. We consider rotation amounts in this exercise because current differential-style attacks on RC5 and RC6 require any difference propagating through the cipher to leave the rotation amounts unchanged. We use "-" to indicate that experimentally the probability is approximately (2^{-20}), which is indistinguishable from random noise.

Rounds	RC6-I-NFR	RC6-I	RC6-NFR	RC6
2	$2^{-0.54}$	$2^{-0.64}$	$2^{-1.32}$	$2^{-10.27}$
4	$2^{-2.15}$	$2^{-2.45}$	$2^{-6.27}$	-
6	$2^{-6.14}$	$2^{-7.04}$	$2^{-14.30}$	-
8	$2^{-12.76}$	$2^{-14.97}$	-	-
10	$2^{-19.07}$	-	-	-

For an increased number of rounds, the probability of unchanged rotation amounts gives a good illustration of the relative diffusive effect of RC6 and its weakened variants. It also illustrates the role of the quadratic function in the security of RC6.

Basic differential-style attacks attempt to predict and control the change from one round to the next during encryption [5]. Improved attacks on RC5 [2, 8] do not attempt to predict the difference quite so closely. Instead, they rely on the relatively slow diffusive effect of RC5 to ensure that any change propagating through the cipher remains manageable and to some extent predictable. Even though single-bit starting differences might be used, differentials with an ending difference of Hamming weight 15, for example, can still be useful [2, 8].

The quadratic function was added to RC6 to address this particular shortcoming of RC5 and our work suggests that the quadratic function is likely to hinder attacks that rely on a modest avalanche of change from one round to the next.

5 Conclusions

In this paper we have considered the role of two operations in RC6 that differentiate it from RC5. Both operations are essential to the security of RC6. It is interesting to observe that RC6-I-NFR, a simplified variant of RC6 without either of these operations, has some of the behavior of RC5. RC6-I-NFR tends

---

[3] By "rotation amounts" we mean the low five bits of the registers for RC6-I-NFR and RC6-NFR, the high five bits of the registers for RC6-I, and the high five bits of the output of $f(x)$ for RC6.

to have a slow rate of diffusion thereby potentially providing opportunities to mount differential attacks similar to those described for RC5 [2, 8]. Further, RC6-I-NFR demonstrates some of the differentially-weak key phenomena that has also been observed in RC5 [8]. The introduction of both the fixed rotation and the quadratic function makes RC6 resistant to such shortcomings.

We stress the importance of simplicity when designing a cipher. Unnecessary complexity makes it hard to perform a systematic examination of the true security offered. By contrast, the exceptional simplicity of RC5 invites others to assess its security. This tradition continues with RC6 with a design that encourages the researcher and aims to facilitate a deep understanding of the cipher.

Acknowledgements

We would like to thank Yuan Ma for his insightful contributions.

References

1. E. Biham and A. Shamir. *Differential Cryptanalysis of the Data Encryption Standard*. Springer-Verlag, New York, 1993.
2. A. Biryukov and E. Kushilevitz. Improved cryptanalysis of RC5. In K. Nyberg, editor, *Advances in Cryptology — Eurocrypt '98*, volume 1403 *Lecture Notes in Computer Science*, pages 85–99, 1998. Springer Verlag.
3. S. Contini, R.L. Rivest, M.J.B. Robshaw and Y.L. Yin. The Security of the RC6 Block Cipher. v1.0, August 20, 1998. Available at www.rsa.com/rsalabs/aes/.
4. S. Contini and Y.L. Yin. On differential properties of data-dependent rotations and their use in MARS and RC6. *To appear*.
5. B.S. Kaliski and Y.L. Yin. On differential and linear cryptanalysis of the RC5 encryption algorithm. In D. Coppersmith, editor, *Advances in Cryptology — Crypto '95*, volume 963 of *Lecture Notes in Computer Science*, pages 171–184, 1995. Springer Verlag.
6. B.S. Kaliski and Y.L. Yin. On the Security of the RC5 Encryption Algorithm. RSA Laboratories Technical Report TR-602. Available at www.rsa.com/rsalabs/aes/.
7. L.R. Knudsen. Applications of higher order differentials and partial differentials. In B. Preneel, editor, *Fast Software Encryption*, volume 1008 of *Lecture Notes in Computer Science*, pages 196–211, 1995. Springer Verlag.
8. L.R. Knudsen and W. Meier. Improved differential attacks on RC5. In N. Koblitz, editor, *Advances in Cryptology — Crypto '96*, volume 1109 of *Lecture Notes in Computer Science*, pages 216–228, 1996. Springer Verlag.
9. R.L. Rivest. The RC5 encryption algorithm. In B. Preneel, editor, *Fast Software Encryption*, volume 1008 of *Lecture Notes in Computer Science*, pages 86–96, 1995. Springer Verlag.
10. R.L. Rivest, M.J.B. Robshaw R. Sidney and Y.L. Yin. The RC6 Block Cipher. v1.1, August 20, 1998. Available at www.rsa.com/rsalabs/aes/.

Linear Cryptanalysis of RC5 and RC6

Johan Borst, Bart Preneel, Joos Vandewalle

K.U. Leuven, Dept. Elektrotechniek-ESAT/COSIC
Kardinaal Mercierlaan 94, B-3001 Heverlee Belgium
Johan.Borst@esat.kuleuven.ac.be

Abstract. In this paper we evaluate the resistance of the block cipher RC5 against linear cryptanalysis. We describe a known plaintext attack that can break RC5-32 (blocksize 64) with 10 rounds and RC5-64 (blocksize 128) with 15 rounds. In order to do this we use techniques related to the use of multiple linear approximations. Furthermore the success of the attack is largely based on the linear hull-effect. To our knowledge, at this moment these are the best known plaintext attacks on RC5, which have negligible storage requirements and do not make any assumption on the plaintext distribution. Furthermore we discuss the impact of our attacking method on the AES-candidate RC6, whose design was based on RC5.

1 Introduction

The iterated block cipher RC5 was introduced by Rivest in [Riv95]. It has a variable number of rounds denoted with r and key size of b bytes. The design is word-oriented for word sizes $w = 32, 64$ and the block size is $2w$. The choice of parameters is usually denoted by RC5-w, RC5-w/r, or RC5-$w/r/b$. Currently RC5-32/16 is recommended to give sufficient resistance against linear and differential attacks [KY98].

RC5 has been analyzed intensively. For an overview we refer to the report by Kaliski and Yin [KY98]. Currently the best published attack can be found in [BK98]. There a chosen plaintext attack is described for which we summarize the complexities for different round versions of RC5[1] in the second column of Table 1. As this is a differential attack, it yields a known plaintext attack for a larger amount of known plaintexts [BS93]. We give the estimated required amount of known plaintexts in the third column of Table 1. The known plaintext attack however needs a storage capacity for all the required plaintexts, i.e., the attack can not be mounted in a way that the attacker obtains and analyzes the plaintexts one by one. We give the estimated required storage capacity of the known plaintext-version in the fourth column. For example, to mount this attack for 4 rounds one would need to store 2^{36} plaintexts with corresponding ciphertexts, which is about 1 GByte. In this paper we present an attack that

---

[1] Although the attack of [BK98] makes use of very sophisticated techniques, according to the authors the required amount of chosen plaintexts for the attack on 12 rounds might be reduced to 2^{38}.

requires a negligible storage capacity. We give the required amount of plaintexts in the fifth column of Table 1.

Table 1. Complexities (lg) of the attacks on RC5-32.

Rounds	Biryukov/Kushilevitz			Our attack	
	Chosen plaintexts	Known plaintexts	Storage	Known plaintexts	Storage
4	7	36	36	28	negligible
6	16	40.5	40.5	40	negligible
8	28	46.5	46.5	52	negligible
10	36	50.5	50.5	64	negligible
12	44	54.5	54.5	–	–

Our attack is a linear attack, whose high success rate is based on a large linear hull-effect [Nyb94]. To our knowledge it is the first time that this effect has significant consequences in the evaluation of the resistance of a cipher against linear attacks. Furthermore we use techniques closely related to multiple linear approximations to set up a practical attack.

Recently RC6 [RC6.1] has been submitted to NIST for the AES-Development Effort as a candidate to replace the DES as block cipher standard. The design of RC6 is based on RC5 and its public security analysis. Special adjustments were done to make RC6 resistant against the successful differential attacks on RC5. In this paper we also address the consequences for RC6 of our linear attack on RC5.

The remainder of this paper is organized as follows. In Sect. 2 we describe some techniques from linear cryptanalysis and show their merits and limitations when applied to RC5 in Sect. 3. In Sect. 4 we describe our attack on RC5 and we give experimental results on RC5-32 and RC5-64. We discuss the consequences for RC6 in Sect. 5 and conclude in Sect. 6.

2   Linear Cryptanalysis

Linear cryptanalysis was introduced and developed by Matsui in [Mat93,Mat94]. Additional advanced techniques, which are relevant for this paper can be found in [KR94,Nyb94,Vau96]. A basic linear attack makes use of a linear approximation between bits of the plaintext P, bits of the plaintext C and bits of the expanded key K. Such a linear approximation is a probabilistic relation that can be denoted as

$$\alpha \cdot P \oplus \beta \cdot K = \gamma \cdot C, \tag{1}$$

where α, β and γ are binary vectors and $\chi \cdot X = \bigoplus_i \chi_i X_i$ for $\chi = (\chi_0, \chi_1, \ldots)$. Instead of P or C one can use intermediate computational values that can be computed from P or C under the assumption of a key value. If a linear approximation holds with probability $p = \frac{1}{2} + \delta$ with $\delta \neq 0$, a linear attack can be mounted which needs about $c|\delta|^{-2}$ plaintexts. The value of c depends on the attacking algorithm that is used. Here δ is called the deviation and $|\delta| = \epsilon$ is called the bias.

Since the key K is fixed, (1) can be transformed into (2) without changing the bias.

$$\alpha \cdot P = \gamma \cdot C, \tag{2}$$

We say that *for certain values $\tilde{P}$ and $\tilde{C}$, (2) behaves in the deviation direction* if $\alpha \cdot \tilde{P} \oplus \gamma \cdot \tilde{C} = b$ and $\alpha \cdot P \oplus \gamma \cdot C = b$ has a positive deviation.

A linear approximation for the whole cipher can be derived by 'chaining' linear approximations between intermediate values. If the probabilities of these approximations are *independent*, the value of the deviation of the derived approximation can be computed with Matsui's Piling Up Lemma [Mat93]. This states that the deviation δ of n chained approximations with deviations δ_i is given by

$$\delta = 2^{n-1} \prod_{i=1}^{n} \delta_i.$$

3 RC5 and Linear Cryptanalysis

RC5 is defined as follows. First $2r + 2$ round keys $S_i \in \{0,1\}^w$, $i = 0, \ldots, 2r+1$, are derived from the user key.[2] If $(L_0, R_0) \in \{0,1\}^w \times \{0,1\}^w$ is the plaintext, then the ciphertext (L_{2r+1}, R_{2r+1}) is computed iteratively with:

$$L_1 = L_0 + S_0 \tag{3}$$
$$R_1 = R_0 + S_1 \tag{4}$$
$$U_i = L_i \oplus R_i \tag{5}$$
$$V_i = U_i \lll R_i \tag{6}$$
$$R_{i+1} = V_i + S_{i+1} \tag{7}$$
$$L_{i+1} = R_i \tag{8}$$

for $i = 1, \ldots, 2r$. Here $+$ denotes addition modulo 2^w and $x \lll y$ rotation of w-bit word x to the left over $y \bmod w$ places. The computation of (L_{i+2}, R_{i+2}) from (L_i, R_i) with i odd is considered as one round of RC5. In Fig. 1 a graphical representation of one round is given.

3.1 Linear Approximations

We shall consider the following linear approximations for xor, data-dependent rotation and addition. We only look at approximations that consider one bit of

---

[2] As the key schedule of RC5 has no relevance for our analysis we refer to [Riv95] for a description. However for our experiments we have used the key schedule.

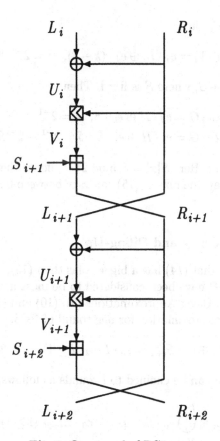

Fig. 1. One round of RC5.

each term of the equation. The binary vector that has a 1 on position i and is 0 everywhere else, will be denoted with e_i. Let $A = B \oplus C$. Then:

$$e_i \cdot A = e_i \cdot B \oplus e_i \cdot C, \quad \delta = 2^{-1} \tag{9}$$

for $i \in \{0, \ldots, w - 1\}$. Let $D = E \lll F$. Then:

$$e_i \cdot D = e_j \cdot E \oplus e_k \cdot F \oplus e_k \cdot (i - j), \quad \delta = 2^{-\lg w - 1} \tag{10}$$

for $i, j \in \{0, \ldots, w - 1\}$ and $k \in \{0, \ldots, \lg w - 1\}$. (Here we have abused the ".''-notation slightly to denote the k-th bit in the binary representation of $i - j$.) If one is only interested in the bias of (10), one can leave out the term $e_k \cdot (i - j)$ or even $e_k \cdot F$, see for example [KY98]. We use (9) and (10) to pass the xor and rotation in RC5 as follows. Let $j, k \in \{0, \ldots, \lg w - 1\}$. Then

$$e_j \cdot U_i = e_j \cdot L_i \oplus e_j \cdot R_i, \quad \delta = 2^{-1} \tag{11}$$

$$e_k \cdot V_i = e_j \cdot U_i \oplus e_j \cdot R_i \oplus e_j \cdot (k - j), \quad \delta = 2^{-\lg w - 1}. \tag{12}$$

Chaining these two yields:

$$e_k \cdot V_i = e_j \cdot L_i \oplus e_j \cdot (k-j), \quad \delta = 2^{-\lg w - 1}. \tag{13}$$

Finally, let $G = H + S$, where S is fixed. Then:

$$e_0 \cdot G = e_0 \cdot H \oplus e_0 \cdot S, \quad \delta = 2^{-1} \tag{14}$$

$$e_i \cdot G = e_i \cdot H \oplus e_i \cdot S, \quad \delta = 2^{-1} - 2^{-i} S[i] \tag{15}$$

for $i \in \{1, \ldots, w-1\}$. Here $S[x] = S \bmod 2^{x+1}$, hence the x LSB's of S. Hence, depending on the key, the bias of (15) can vary between 0 and $\frac{1}{2}$. On the average it is $\frac{1}{4}$.

3.2 Key Dependency and Piling-Up

Because of the fact that (14) has a bigger bias than (15), 'traditionally' approximations on the LSB have been considered to be most useful for a linear attack (see [KY95,KY98]). Using Approximations (9), (10) and (14) one can derive the following iterative approximation for one round of RC5.

$$e_0 \cdot L_i \oplus e_0 \cdot S_{i+1} = e_0 \cdot L_{i+2} \ (i \geq 1), \quad \delta = 2^{-\lg w - 1} \tag{16}$$

This approximation can be chained to l rounds as follows.

$$e_0 \cdot L_i \oplus \bigoplus_{j=0}^{l-1} e_0 \cdot S_{i+1+2j} = e_0 \cdot L_{i+2l} \ (i \geq 1), \quad \delta = ? \tag{17}$$

According to the Piling Up Lemma (2) this approximation would have deviation $\delta = 2^{l-1} 2^{(-\lg w - 1)l} = 2^{-l \lg w - 1}$ if the chained approximations would be independent. This is however not the case.

To illustrate this consider (17) for $l = 2$. The deviation of this approximation depends on the $\lg w$ least significant bits of S_{i+2}. This can be seen as follows. The probability that (16), i.e., the approximation over the first round, holds depends on the value of $R_i \bmod w$. If $R_i \bmod w = 0$ it always holds, otherwise it holds with probability $\frac{1}{2}$. Hence, the deviation of (16) is computed under the assumption that every value of $R_i \bmod w$ is equally likely. If $R_i \bmod w = 0$ then the $\lg w$ least significant bits of L_{i+1} are known. Now consider the approximation for each possible value of R_{i+1} separately. If $R_{i+1} \bmod w \in \{0, \ldots, \lg w - 1, w - \lg w + 1, \ldots, w - 1\}$ then, depending on the value of $S_{i+2} \bmod w$, part of the $\lg w$ least significant bits of R_{i+2} can be computed. It turns out that the values of R_{i+3} are not equally likely. Hence, the Piling Up Lemma cannot be applied.

To illustrate this effect we have computed the bias of the two round approximation for RC5-32 for every value of $S_{i+2} \bmod w$. These results are given in Table 2. It can be seen that the bias can vary significantly between $\approx 2^{-10}$ and $\approx 2^{-16}$. On the other hand the average value is $\frac{1}{32} \sum_{x=0}^{31} |\delta_x| \approx 2^{-11}$. Since $\delta_x \neq 0$ for all x, the average amount of expected plaintexts needed based on

Table 2 is given by $\frac{1}{32} \sum_{x=0}^{31} \delta_x^{-2} \approx 2^{22}$. Both are in accordance with the Piling Up Lemma.

Note further that for two values of $S_{i+2} \bmod w$ the deviation is negative. For those values this means that if one would mount a basic linear attack (Algorithm 1 in [Mat93]) on four rounds using (17) to find $S_0 \oplus S_2 \oplus S_4$ based on the Piling Up Lemma, most likely one would find $S_0 \oplus S_2 \oplus S_4 \oplus 1$, given enough texts.

We can conclude that although the deviation can vary significantly, the Piling Up Lemma gives a good estimate for the average bias for RC5. We will show that this estimate can be used to compute the expected average success rate of a linear attack that does not use the sign of the deviation, but only its absolute value; the bias.

Table 2. The deviation δ_x of Approximation (17) with $l = 2$ for RC5-32, depending on $x = S_{i+2} \bmod w$.

$x = S_{i+2} \bmod w$	$10^3 \delta_x$	$\lg \|\delta_x\|$	$x = S_{i+2} \bmod w$	$10^3 \delta_x$	$\lg \|\delta_x\|$
00	0.930786	-10.07	10	0.228882	-12.09
01	0.991821	- 9.98	11	0.656128	-10.57
02	0.473022	-11.05	12	0.015259	-16
03	0.564575	-10.79	13	-0.015259	-16
04	0.595093	-10.71	14	0.137329	-12.83
05	0.686646	-10.51	15	0.534058	-10.87
06	0.473022	-11.05	16	0.503540	-10.96
07	0.503540	-10.96	17	0.717163	-10.45
08	0.595093	-10.71	18	0.625610	-10.64
09	0.564575	-10.79	19	0.778198	-10.33
0a	0.289917	-11.75	1a	0.747681	-10.39
0b	0.381470	-11.36	1b	0.839233	-10.22
0c	0.411987	-11.25	1c	0.381470	-11.36
0d	0.289917	-11.75	1d	0.381470	-11.36
0e	0.106812	-13.19	1e	0.076294	-13.68
0f	0.228882	-12.09	1f	-0.045776	-14.42

3.3 Key Dependency and Linear Hulls

The concept (approximate) *linear hull* was introduced in [Nyb94]. We will use the term linear hull in the way it was used in [RC6.2]. A linear hull is the set of all chains of linear equations over (a part of) the cipher that produce the same linear equation. The existence of this effect for RC5 was first noticed in [RC6.2,RC6.3] where also some preliminary work in determining the linear hull effects for RC6 (and some simplified versions) can be found.

The following linear hull for an approximation of two rounds (i till $i + 3$) of RC5 can be noticed. Let $j, l \in \{0, \ldots, w - 1\}$. Using (9), (10), (14) and (15) for

j the following $\lg w$ approximations for two rounds can be derived[3].

$$e_j \cdot L_i \oplus e_j \cdot (k - j) \oplus e_k \cdot S_{i+1} = e_k \cdot L_{i+2}, \quad \delta = \delta_{j,k} \qquad (18)$$

for $k = 0, \ldots, \lg w - 1$. Likewise for the next two rounds and l also $\lg w$ approximations can be derived:

$$e_k \cdot L_{i+2} \oplus e_k \cdot (l - k) \oplus e_l \cdot S_{i+3} = e_l \cdot L_{i+4}, \quad \delta = \delta_{k,l} \qquad (19)$$

for $k = 0, \ldots, \lg w - 1$. Hence, one can chain $\lg w$ pairs of (18) and (19) to obtain the two round approximation

$$e_j \cdot L_i \oplus e_k \cdot S_{i+1} \oplus e_l \cdot S_{i+3} \oplus e_j \cdot (k - j) \oplus e_k \cdot (l - k) = e_l \cdot L_{i+4}, \quad \delta = \delta_{j,k,l} \quad (20)$$

Neglecting the key-dependency of chaining and using the Piling Up Lemma one gets for this bias

$$\delta_{j,k,l} = \begin{cases} 2^{-2\lg w - 1} & k = 0, l = 0 \\ 2^{-2\lg w - 1}(1 - 2^{-k+1} S_{i+1}[k - 1]) & k \neq 0, l = 0 \\ 2^{-2\lg w - 1}(1 - 2^{-l+1} S_{i+3}[l - 1]) & k = 0, l \neq 0 \\ 2^{-2\lg w - 1}(1 - 2^{-k+1} S_{i+1}[k - 1])(1 - 2^{-l+1} S_{i+3}[l - 1]) & k \neq 0, l \neq 0 \end{cases}$$
$$(21)$$

We note two things about (20) and its deviation given in (21). Firstly it is clear from (21) that the deviation is key dependent, i.e., dependent on the $\lg w - 1$ LSB's of S_{i+1} and S_{i+3}. But we will show that because of the linear hull effect, this key dependency is negligible. Secondly, for each choice of the triple j, k, l the term $C_{j,k,l} = e_k \cdot S_{i+1} \oplus e_l \cdot S_{i+3} \oplus e_j \cdot (k - j) \oplus e_k \cdot (l - k)$ is constant, either 0 or 1. This constant actually determines the sign of the deviation of the following approximation, which can be derived from (20) by leaving out $C_{j,k,l}$.

$$e_j \cdot L_i = e_l \cdot L_{i+4}, \quad \delta = \tilde{\delta}_{j,l}. \qquad (22)$$

For the deviation the following holds:

$$\tilde{\delta}_{j,l} = \sum_{k \in V_{j,l}} \delta_{j,k,l} - \sum_{k \notin V_{j,l}} \delta_{j,k,l}, \qquad (23)$$

where $V_{j,l} = \{k \in \{0, \ldots, \lg w - 1\} | C_{j,k,l} = 0\}$.

One can extend approximation (22) to hold for r subsequent rounds. In this way one gets the following approximation for r rounds.

$$e_j \cdot L_i = e_l \cdot L_{i+2r}, \quad \delta = \tilde{\delta}_{j,l}, \qquad (24)$$

where $i, j \in \{0, \ldots, w - 1\}$. The deviation can be computed/approximated by considering the parts of the different chains, for the k-th round in the chain given by

$$e_{j_k} \cdot L_{i+2k} = e_{l_k} \cdot L_{i+2k+2}, \qquad (25)$$

---

[3] Note that in Equation (18) and others $\delta_{j,k}$ is not the Kronecker delta, but a variable δ with indices j and k.

where $k \in \{0, \ldots, r-1\}$ and

$$j_k \begin{cases} = j & \text{if } k = 0 \\ \in \{0, \ldots, \lg w - 1\} & \text{if } k \neq 0 \end{cases}$$

$$l_k \begin{cases} \in \{0, \ldots, \lg w - 1\} & \text{if } k \neq r - 1 \\ = l & \text{if } k = r - 1 \end{cases}$$

and

$$j_k = l_{k-1} \text{ for } k \in \{1, \ldots, r-1\}.$$

In this way it can be seen that Equation (24) is a linear hull that consists of $(\lg w)^{r-1}$ different chains, namely for all of the choices of j_k, l_k. When we take the average bias of $\frac{1}{4}$ for the approximation of addition on non-LSB's, we get for the bias of (24):

$$|\tilde{\delta}_{j,l}| = \begin{cases} c(r) & \text{if } l = 0 \\ \frac{1}{2}c(r) & \text{if } l \neq 0 \end{cases} \tag{26}$$

where $c(r)$ can be estimated as

$$
\begin{aligned}
c(r) &\approx \gamma \left(\sum_{k=0}^{r-1} \binom{r-1}{k} (\lg w - 1)^k 2^{(-\lg w - 1)r + r - 1 - k} \right) \\
&= \gamma \left(2^{(-\lg w - 1)r} \sum_{k=0}^{r-1} \binom{r-1}{k} (\lg w - 1)^k 2^{r-1-k} \right) \\
&= \gamma \left(2^{(-\lg w - 1)r} (\lg w - 1 + 2)^{r-1} \right) \\
&= \gamma \left(\frac{1}{2w} \left(\frac{\lg w + 1}{2w} \right)^{r-1} \right)
\end{aligned} \tag{27}
$$

where γ is a factor that accounts for the effect of different chains that cancel each others contribution. The increasement factor $c^+(r)$ of the bias is expressed as

$$c(r+1) = c^+(r) \cdot c(r), \text{ for } r = 2, \ldots \tag{28}$$

Hence, if a linear attack can be mounted on RC5 with r rounds using x known plaintexts, then this attack will have the same success probability if adapted to RC5 with $(r+1)$ rounds if $(c^+(r))^{-2}x$ known plaintexts are available. From (27) and (28) follows $c^+ = \frac{\lg w + 1}{2w}$. Now, for RC5-32 we have $c^+(r) \approx 2^{-3.4}$ and for RC5-64 we have $c^+(r) \approx 2^{-4.2}$. In Sect. 4.4 we will show that the attacks that we have implemented for RC5-32 and RC5-64 approximately behave according to the previously derived approximate expectations. Hence, we can neglect the key dependency in (24): the bias given according to (26) is a sufficient practical estimate.

4 The Attack on RC5

In this section we derive a linear attack on RC5 and present an overview of the experimental results. In Sect. 4.1 we give the linear approximation and the method that is used to guess key bits. In Sect. 4.2 we specify this method. In Sect. 4.3 we describe the search algorithm. Finally, in Sect. 4.4 experimental results of the implemented attack are given.

4.1 The Linear Approximations

We have derived and implemented a linear attack that uses approximation (24). Since this approximation does not involve any key bits, a basic linear attack is not possible. In particular for an r-round attack we will use (24) with $i = 0$ and $k = r$. The first addition, adding S_0, will be passed with an approximation on the LSB, since this has bias $\frac{1}{2}$. Therefore we take $j = 0$ in (24). We also choose $l = 0$ in (24) because then also the last key-addition in the whole approximation will be passed with bias $\frac{1}{2}$. It might be possible to further improve the attack by (also) using approximations with other values for j and l, but we have not found a method to do this.

To attack r rounds of RC5 we use the fact that each linear path that is part of the hull given by (24) is a chain of r 1-round approximations of the form (25). We will split the approximation into two parts. The first contains the approximation for the first key addition and the first round. This gives us the following $\lg w$ approximations. Each is the first part of a set of linear approximations that is contained in the linear hull of (24).

$$e_0 \cdot L_0 = e_k \cdot L_3 \text{ for } k = 0, \ldots, \lg w - 1. \tag{29}$$

The remainder of the whole approximation can be specified by the following $\lg w$ approximations, each beginning with a different bit of L_3:

$$e_k \cdot L_3 = e_0 \cdot L_{2r+1} \text{ for } k = 0, \ldots, \lg w - 1. \tag{30}$$

When for a certain plaintext encryption the intermediate value $R_1 \bmod w = k$, hence an element of $\{0, 1, \ldots, \lg w - 1\}$, then (29) behaves in the deviation direction. Hence, if also (30) behaves in the deviation direction then the whole approximation behaves in that direction. On the other hand, if $R_1 \bmod w \notin \{0, 1, \ldots, \lg w - 1\}$ then the probability that the whole approximation behaves in the direction of the deviation is much lower.

In the attack we want to check for every text if one of the approximations that correspond to (30) was followed. Since we have no information about any intermediate values we do not have a criterion that always holds. Instead we will derive a function that is expected to give higher values when one of the approximations was followed. Hence this function will have higher values for encryptions where $R_1 \bmod w \in \{0, 1, \ldots, \lg w - 1\}$ than for other R_1 values. Because $R_1 \bmod w = (R_0 - S_1) \bmod w$ and R_0 is known we can guess $S_1 \bmod w$ from this. We call this function the *non-uniformity function*. In the next section we will describe it.

We note here that the use of such a function fits in the frameworks of statistical cryptanalysis as described by Vaudenay in [Vau96] or partitioning cryptanalysis as described by Harpes and Massey in [HM97].

4.2 A Non-uniformity Function

The non-uniformity function ν computes non-uniformity values for a given set of corresponding plaintext/ciphertext pairs. This set is divided into w subsets, each set contains plaintexts with the same R_0 mod w-value. For each set a non-uniformity value can be computed.

We look at the last round of the encryption. Suppose that one approximation of the linear hull corresponding to (30) is followed up to the last round. Say that in this particular case $e_k \cdot L_{2r-1}$ was biased for some $k \in \{0, \ldots, \lg w - 1\}$. Then following the approximation to the end would mean that R_{2r-1} mod $w = (w - k)$ mod w with a higher probability than other values. As seen in Sect. 3.2 depending on the subkeys also the other possible values of R_{2r-1} mod w might not be uniformly distributed. But in any case certain values of R_{2r-1} mod w will have a higher probability when (30) behaves in the deviation direction then when it does not behave in that way.

If we would know the value of R_{2r-1} mod w it would be possible to compute $\lg w$ bits of S_{2r+1} or two possible values for those bits from the ciphertext with:

$$S_{2r+1} = R_{2r+1} - (R_{2r-1} \oplus L_{2r+1}) \lll L_{2r+1}, \qquad (31)$$

since the values of R_{2r+1} and L_{2r+1} are known from the ciphertext. We will use $S\langle n \rangle$ to denote the $\lg w$-bit string, given by the bits $(n + \lg w - 1)$ mod $w, \ldots, (n + 1)$ mod w, n of S. The value of L_{2r+1} mod w determines for which $\lg w$ bits of S_{2r+1} information can be computed, namely $S\langle L_{2r+1} \bmod w \rangle$. If L_{2r+1} mod $w = 0$ then the $\lg w$ LSB's can be computed. When L_{2r+1} mod $w \neq 0$ we can compute two values for $S\langle L_{2r+1} \bmod w \rangle$. The carry bit of the addition in (31) determines which one is the correct one.

In the attack we do not know the value of R_{2r-1} mod w or even which value would be the most probable. Instead of trying to compute $\lg w$ bits of S_{2r+1} we make a similar computation for a value which we call S'. It is computed by taking R_{2r-1} mod $w = 0$ in (31), i.e.,

$$S' = R_{2r+1} - (L_{2r+1} \lll L_{2r+1}). \qquad (32)$$

Due to the non-uniform distribution of R_{2r-1} mod w it is expected that the distribution of $S'\langle \cdot \rangle$-values will be more non-uniform for encryptions where the approximation was followed than for others.

Hence, in the attack we use a counter array $A(i, j, k)$ for $i, j, k = 0, \ldots, w - 1$, where each i corresponds to a possible value of R_0 mod w, each j to a possible value of L_{2r+1} mod w and each k to a possible value of $S'\langle L_{2r+1} \bmod w \rangle$. For each text we check if the approximation holds. If it holds, we change the counter array as follows. If L_{2r+1} mod $w = 0$, we increase $A(R_0 \bmod w, L_{2r+1} \bmod w, v)$ by 2, where v is the suggested $S'\langle L_{2r+1} \bmod w \rangle$-value. If L_{2r+1} mod $w \neq 0$, we increase $A(R_0 \bmod w, L_{2r+1} \bmod w, v_0)$ and $A(R_0 \bmod w, L_{2r+1} \bmod w, v_1)$ by 1, where v_0 and v_1 are the suggested values. If the approximation does not hold, we decrease the specific array entries accordingly.

Each $(R_0 \bmod w, L_{2r+1} \bmod w)$-combination gives a distribution of $S'\langle \cdot \rangle$-values. From Sect. 4.1 we know that the distributions corresponding to the values

$R_1 \bmod w \in \{0, \ldots, \lg w - 1\}$ will be the most non-uniform. To measure the non-uniformity we check for all w bits of our S' based on the $S'\langle \cdot \rangle$-values how many times 0 is suggested and how many times 1 and take the difference of these amounts. For each $R_0 \bmod w$ we take the sum over all possible $L_{2r+1} \bmod w$ of the absolute values of these differences. In this way the *non-uniformity function* $\nu : \{0, \ldots, w - 1\} \to \mathbf{N}$ is defined:

$$\nu(r_0) = \sum_{l_{2r+1}=0}^{w-1} \sum_{x=0}^{\lg w - 1} \Big| \sum_{v:e_x \cdot v=0} A(r_0, l_{2r+1} + x, v) - \sum_{v:e_x \cdot v=1} A(r_0, l_{2r+1} + x, v) \Big|,$$

(33)

where all indices of A are taken $\bmod w$. We call the w values that are derived in this way the *non-uniformity values*. We expect that the sum of $\lg w$ non-uniformity values will be maximal for the values corresponding to texts with $R_1 \bmod w \in \{0, \ldots, \lg w - 1\}$. The final step of the algorithm guesses the value of $S_1 \bmod w$ accordingly.

The observant reader will have noticed that according to the above description it is not necessary to have counters for the $S'\langle \cdot \rangle$-values. Instead of this one could use counters corresponding to the bits of S' and change these accordingly. The description above is used to emphasize that with the $S'\langle \cdot \rangle$-distribution also other non-uniformity measurements could be used. For example, one could look at all possible values for two subsequent bits of S'. Also it is probably possible to derive information about the actual value of S_{2r+1} from the $S'\langle \cdot \rangle$-distribution. However, this falls outside the scope of this paper.

4.3 The Algorithm

1. Acquire n known plaintext/ciphertext-pairs $(P_0, C_0), \ldots, (P_{n-1}, C_{n-1})$.
2. Initialize a counter array[4] $A(i, j, k) := 0$ for $i, j, k = 0, \ldots, w - 1$.
3. For each plaintext/ciphertext-pair do:
   If $L_{2r+1} \bmod w = 0$ then
   (a) Compute $S'\langle 0 \rangle$-guess v.
   (b) If $e_0 \cdot L_0 = e_0 \cdot L_{2r+1}$ then $A(R_0, L_{2r+1}, v) := A(R_0, L_{2r+1}, v) + 2$.
   If $e_0 \cdot L_0 = e_0 \cdot L_{2r+1} \oplus 1$ then $A(R_0, L_{2r+1}, v) := A(R_0, L_{2r+1}, v) - 2$.
   If $L_{2r+1} \bmod w \neq 0$ then
   (a) Compute $S'\langle L_{2r+1} \bmod w \rangle$-guesses v_0 and v_1.
   (b) If $e_0 \cdot L_0 = e_0 \cdot L_{2r+1}$ then $A(R_0, L_{2r+1}, v_0) := A(R_0, L_{2r+1}, v_0) + 1$
   and $A(R_0, L_{2r+1}, v_1) := A(R_0, L_{2r+1}, v_1) + 1$.
   If $e_0 \cdot L_0 \neq e_0 \cdot L_{2r+1}$ then $A(R_0, L_{2r+1}, v_0) := A(R_0, L_{2r+1}, v_0) - 1$
   and $A(R_0, L_{2r+1}, v_1) := A(R_0, L_{2r+1}, v_1) - 1$.
4. Compute w non-uniformity values $\nu(i)$ according to (33), where i corresponds with a value of $R_0 \bmod w$.
5. Find the value $x \in \{0, \ldots, w - 1\}$ for which $\sum_{i=0}^{\lg w - 1} |\nu((x + i) \bmod w)|$ is maximal.
6. Guess $S_1 \bmod w = w - x$.

---

[4] For clarity in the following description of the algorithm we have left out $\bmod w$ when referring to indices of A.

4.4 The Results

We have implemented the attack on RC5-32 and RC5-64. The results are given in Table 3 and Table 4. As can be seen in the tables, we have done tests for up to 5 rounds of RC5-32 and up to 4 rounds of RC5-64. For each number of rounds tests were performed for several amounts of plaintexts. To give an indication of the practical aspects of the experiments: with our RC5-implementation carrying out the attack on the 5-round version for 10 keys with 2^{32} plaintexts took about 21 hours on a 333 MHz Pentium. To our knowledge these are the first experimentally executed known plaintext attacks on reduced versions of RC5, which require a negligible storage.

As stated at the end of Sect. 3.3, we would expect that an attack on r rounds of RC5 with x known plaintexts should have the same success probability as an attack on $r+1$ rounds with $(c^+)^{-2}x$ texts. For RC5-32 it holds that $(c^+)^{-2} \approx 2^{6.8}$, for RC5-64 $(c^+)^{-2} \approx 2^{8.4}$. It can be seen from the tables that the results are better than expected, i.e., the factor to attack an extra round is $\approx 2^6$ for RC5-32 and $\approx 2^8$ for RC5-64. We conjecture that the reason for this is that the value of $R_{i+2} \bmod w$ depends significantly on the value of $R_i \bmod w$. We are still researching this problem, but we give some preliminary evidence in the next section, where we discuss the consequences for RC6.

Based on the experimental results and the theoretical estimation of the bias of the linear approximation we can estimate the complexity of the attack on more than 4 or 5 rounds (cf. Table 5). It follows that an attack can be mounted on RC5-32 with 10 rounds that has a success probability of 45% if 2^{62} plaintexts are available. An attack on RC5-64 with 15 rounds has a success probability of 90% if 2^{123} plaintexts are available.

5 Consequences for RC6

The block cipher RC6 [RC6.1] has been submitted to NIST as an AES-candidate. Its design was based on RC5 and the security evaluation of RC5. To meet the block size requirement of 128 bits and to keep a 32-bit processor oriented design for this block size, RC6 was designed as two RC5-32's (with some changes) in parallel that interact[5]. Hence, cryptanalysis of RC5 can mostly be adapted for analysis of RC6.

However, the RC5-structure used in RC6 differs from the original version. One of the most important differences is the following. The amount of rotation in RC5-32 was determined by taking the 5 LSB's of a 32-bit word. In RC6, the 5 bits that determine the amount of rotation depend on all 32 bits of a 32-bit word.

In the first place these changes to RC5 were made to preclude the successful differential attacks on RC5 [BK98,RC6.1]. These attacks make use of the fact

---

[5] Actually, the design of RC6 also is word oriented and the blocksize is $4w$, where w is the word size. We only discuss the 128-block size version, as it is the main object for the AES standardization process.

Table 3. Experimental results of the attack on RC5-32.

Rounds	Known plaintexts	Success rate
2	2^{13}	28/100
	2^{14}	46/100
	2^{15}	89/100
	2^{16}	92/100
3	2^{17}	7/100
	2^{18}	15/100
	2^{19}	28/100
	2^{20}	49/100
	2^{21}	69/100
	2^{22}	81/100
4	2^{24}	7/100
	2^{25}	26/100
	2^{26}	44/100
	2^{27}	77/100
	2^{28}	82/100
5	2^{32}	4/10
	2^{33}	7/10
	2^{34}	9/10

Table 4. Experimental results of the attack on RC5-64.

Rounds	Known plaintexts	Success rate
2	2^{17}	39/100
	2^{18}	82/100
	2^{19}	96/100
3	2^{25}	28/50
	2^{26}	40/50
	2^{27}	47/50
4	2^{34}	9/10

Table 5. Expected number of plaintexts needed for a known plaintext attack on $r(\geq 2)$ rounds of RC5-32 or RC5-64.

Success probability:	45%	90%
RC5-32	2^{2+6r}	2^{4+6r}
RC5-64	2^{1+8r}	2^{3+8r}

that only five LSB's determine the rotations. However, these changes also provide increased resistance to the attack method described in this paper.

To illustrate this we look at a transition version between RC5 and RC6. In the definition of RC5, replace (5) and (6) with

$$T_i = (R_i(2R_i + 1)) \lll 5 \qquad (34)$$
$$U_i = L_i \oplus T_i \qquad (35)$$
$$V_i = U_i \lll T_i \qquad (36)$$

For our theoretical analysis concerning the linear hull effect, this change makes little difference. One can still use the same linear approximations. However, the first round trick and last round trick we have used now become more complicated. To compute T_1 mod 32, one has to guess all bits of S_1 and the construction of a non-uniformity function is not obvious.

We have done tests on the above described intermediate version with the last and first round replaced with a normal RC5-round. Then the first and last round trick are straightforward. We have implemented the attack for 3 and 4 rounds of the cipher and results indicate that the increase in the number of necessary plaintexts for the same success probability was more in accordance with the theoretical results for RC5. Hence, the application of the extra function to determine the rotation amounts causes these values to be more independent.

We conclude that our attack does not give an obvious possibility to mount a realistic attack on RC6. Currently we are working on a precise evaluation of its resistance against this attack method.

6 Conclusions

In this paper we have evaluated the resistance of RC5 against linear attacks. We have taken into account the applicability of the Piling Up Lemma and the consequences of linear hull effects, both in combination with possible key dependency. This resulted in estimates for the complexity to mount a linear attack.

Furthermore we have described an attack that exploits the linear hull effect that we described and implemented it on reduced versions of RC5-32 and RC5-64. In this way we estimate that our attack can theoretically break RC5-32 with 10 rounds and RC5-64 with 15 rounds. In comparison with previous attacks on RC5, our attack needs negligible storage capacity, i.e., it could be practically implemented.

The attack method has no serious consequences for the security of RC6. Apparently the precautions that the designers made to make RC6 more resistant against differential attacks, also made RC6 more resistant against more sophisticated linear attack methods.

Acknowledgments

We would like to acknowledge Antoon Bosselaers for providing a very efficient implementation of RC5, with which most of the experiments could be done in a reasonable time. Furthermore we would like to thank Vincent Rijmen and Matt Robshaw for interesting discussions and helpful suggestions. We would also like to thank Ali Selçuk for many interesting discussions, as well as for pointing out the derivation of (27).

References

[BK98] A. Biryukov, E.Kushilevitz, "Improved Cryptanalysis of RC5," *Proc. Eurocrypt'98, LNCS 1403*, Springer-Verlag, 1998, pp. 85–99.

[BS93] E. Biham, A. Shamir, *Differential Cryptanalysis of the Data Encryption Standard*, Springer-Verlag, 1993.

[HM97] C. Harpes, J.L. Massey, "Partitioning Cryptanalysis," *Fast Software Encryption, LNCS 1267*, Springer-Verlag, 1997, pp. 13–27.

[KM96] L.R. Knudsen, W. Meier, "Improved Differential Attacks on RC5," *Proc. Crypto'96, LNCS 1109*, Springer-Verlag, 1996, pp. 216–228.

[KR94] B.S. Kaliski, M.J.B. Robshaw, "Linear Cryptanalysis Using Multiple Approximations," *Proc. Eurocrypt'94, LNCS 950*, Springer-Verlag, 1995, pp. 26–39.

[KY95] B.S. Kaliski, Y.L. Yin, "On Differential and Linear Cryptanalysis of the RC5 Encryption Algorithm," *Proc. Crypto'95, LNCS 963*, Springer-Verlag, 1995, pp. 171–184.

[KY98] B.S. Kaliski, Y.L. Yin, *"On the Security of the RC5 Encryption Algorithm,"* RSA Laboratories Technical Report TR-602, Version 1.0, September 1998, available via http://www.rsa.com/rsalabs/aes.

[Mat93] M. Matsui, "Linear cryptanalysis method for DES cipher," *Proc. Eurocrypt'93, LNCS 765*, Springer-Verlag, 1994, pp. 386–397.

[Mat94] M. Matsui, "The first experimental cryptanalysis of the Data Encryption Standard," *Proc. Crypto'94, LNCS 839*, Springer-Verlag, 1994, pp. 1–11.

[Nyb94] K. Nyberg, "Linear Approximations of Block Ciphers," *Proc. Eurocrypt'94, LNCS 950*, Springer-Verlag, 1995, pp. 439–444.

[Riv95] R.L. Rivest, "The RC5 Encryption Algorithm," *Fast Software Encryption, LNCS 1008*, Springer-Verlag, 1995, pp. 86–96.

[RC6.1] R.L. Rivest, M.J.B. Robshaw, R. Sidney, Y.L. Yin, *"The RC6 Block Cipher. v1.1,"* AES Proposal, 1998, available via http://www.rsa.com/rsalabs/aes.

[RC6.2] S. Contini, R.L. Rivest, M.J.B. Robshaw, Y.L. Yin, *"The Security of the RC6 Block Cipher. v1.0,"* 1998, available via http://www.rsa.com/rsalabs/aes.

[RC6.3] S. Contini, R.L. Rivest, M.J.B. Robshaw, Y.L. Yin, *"Linear Hulls and RC6 (DRAFT),"* September, 1998.

[Sel98] A.A. Selçuk, "New Results in Linear Cryptanalysis of RC5," *Fast Software Encryption, LNCS 1372*, Springer-Verlag, 1998, pp. 1–16.

[Vau96] S. Vaudenay, "An Experiment on DES - Statistical Cryptanalysis," *Proc. 3rd ACM Conference on Computer Security*, ACM Press, 1996, pp. 139–147.

A Revised Version of CRYPTON
- CRYPTON V1.0 -

Chae Hoon Lim

Information & Communications Research Center, Future Systems, Inc.
372-2, Yang Jae-Dong, Seo Cho-Gu, Seoul, 137-130, Korea: chlim@future.co.kr

Abstract. The block cipher CRYPTON has been proposed as a candidate algorithm for the Advanced Encryption Standard (AES). To fix some minor weakness in the key schedule and to remove some undesirable properties in S-boxes, we made some changes to the AES proposal, i.e., in the S-box construction and key scheduling. This paper presents the revised version of CRYPTON and its preliminary analysis.

1 Motivations and Changes

The block cipher CRYPTON has been proposed as a candidate algorithm for the AES [22]. Unfortunately, however, we couldn't have enough time to refine our algorithm at the time of submission. So, we later revised part of the AES proposal. This paper describes this revision and analyzes its security and efficiency.

CRYPTON v1.0 is different from the AES proposal (v0.5) only in the S-box construction and key scheduling. As we mentioned at the 1st AES candidate conference, we already had a plan to revise the CRYPTON key schedule. The previous key schedule was in fact expected from the begining to have some minor weaknesses due to its too simple round key computations (actually a slight weakness was found by Serge Vaudenay etc. at ENS (posted at NIST's AES forum) and by Johan Borst [4]). We thus made some enhancements to the original key schedule, while trying to keep changes minimal. The new key schedule now makes use of bit and word rotations, as well as byte rotations. We also used distinct round constants for each round key. This way we tried to make each byte of expanded keys used in different locations (and different bit positions within a byte) of 4×4 byte array in different rounds. The new key schedule still runs much faster than one-block encryption.

In v0.5 we used two 8×8 S-boxes constructed from 4-bit permutations using a 3-round Feistel cipher. Such S-boxes, however, turned out to have too many low-weight, high-probability characteristics that may cause weak diffusion by the linear transformation following the S-box transformation. For example, the S-boxes used in V0.5 have about 300 characteristics with probability 2^{-5} and 160 linear approximations with probability 2^{-4}. Furthermore, some of such I/O pairs turned out to have minimal diffusion under linear transformations. Though we could achieve reasonably high security bounds even with such S-boxes, we wanted to make CRYPTON more stronger for long-term security by allowing a large safety margin. We thus decided to strengthen the S-box in this opportunity.

Experiments show that most Feistel-type constructions seem to generate S-boxes with too many high-probability characteristics, so we decided to use other construction methods. We first started with a Feistel structure involving three or four 4-bit permutations and repeated modifications and testings of the structure to get better 8-bit S-boxes. In the end we arrived at the structure of a SP network described in Sect.3.2. The resulting S-boxes are much stronger against differential and linear cryptanalysis when combined with linear transformations used. We decided to use four variants of one S-box, instead of independent four S-boxes, to allow greater flexibility in memory requirements (e.g., for cost-effective implementations on smart cards).

Finally, we would like to stress that the above modifications do not require any substantial change in existing analysis on the security and efficiency. The security evaluation of the new version can be done only by replacing old figures replated to S-box characteristics with new ones and there is no change in the overall structure of key scheduling. The performance figures in software implementations remain almost the same. The hardware complexity is a little bit increased due to the increased complexity for logic implementation of S-boxes.

Throughout this paper we will use the following symbols and notation:

- A 4×4 byte array A is represented by

$$A = (A[3], A[2], A[1], A[0])^t = \begin{pmatrix} A[0] \\ A[1] \\ A[2] \\ A[3] \end{pmatrix} = \begin{pmatrix} a_{03} \ a_{02} \ a_{01} \ a_{00} \\ a_{13} \ a_{12} \ a_{11} \ a_{10} \\ a_{23} \ a_{22} \ a_{21} \ a_{20} \\ a_{33} \ a_{32} \ a_{31} \ a_{30} \end{pmatrix}.$$

- $X^{\lll n}$: left rotation of X by n-bit positions.
- $X^{\lll_b n}$: left rotation of each byte in a 32-bit number X by n-bit positions.
- $f \circ g$: composition of functions f and g, i.e., $(f \circ g)(x) = f(g(x))$.
- $\wedge, \oplus$: bit-wise logical operations for AND and XOR, respectively.

2 Algorithm Specifications

CRYPTON processes a data block of 16 bytes by representing it into a 4×4 byte array as in SQUARE [6]. The round transformation of CRYPTON consists of four parallelizable steps: byte-wise substitutions, column-wise bit permutation, column-to-row transposition, and then key addition. The encryption process involves 12 repetitions of (essentially) the same round transformation. The decryption process can be made identical to the encryption process with a different key schedule. This section presents a detailed description of CRYPTON v1.0.

2.1 Basic Building Blocks

Nonlinear Substitution γ The nonlinear transformation γ consists of byte-wise substitutions on a 4×4 byte array by using four 8×8 S-boxes, S_i ($0 \leq i \leq 3$), such that $S_2 = S_0^{-1}$ and $S_3 = S_1^{-1}$ (see Sect.3.2 for details). Two different S-box arrangements are used in successive rounds alternately; γ_o in odd rounds and γ_e in even rounds. They are defined as

$$B = \gamma_o(A) \Leftrightarrow b_{ij} = S_{i+j \bmod 4}(a_{ij}),$$
$$B = \gamma_e(A) \Leftrightarrow b_{ij} = S_{i+j+2 \bmod 4}(a_{ij}).$$

Observe that the four S-boxes are arranged so that $\gamma_o^{-1} = \gamma_e$ and $\gamma_e^{-1} = \gamma_o$. This property will be used to derive identical processes for encryption and decryption.

Bit Permutation π The bit permutation π bit-wise mixes each byte column of 4×4 byte array using four masking bytes m_i's given by

$$m_0 = \texttt{0xfc}, \ m_1 = \texttt{0xf3}, \ m_2 = \texttt{0xcf}, \ m_3 = \texttt{0x3f}.$$

We first define four column permutations π_i's ($0 \le i \le 3$) as

$$[b_3, b_2, b_1, b_0]^t = \pi_i([a_3, a_2, a_1, a_0]^t) \ \Leftrightarrow \ b_j = \oplus_{k=0}^3 (m_{i+j+k \bmod 4} \wedge a_k),$$

The b_j can be expressed alternatively using bit extraction and xoring as

$$b_j = \oplus_{k=0}^3 (\overline{m}_{i+j+k \bmod 4} \wedge a_k) \oplus a,$$

where $\overline{m}_k$ denotes bit-wise complement of m_k and $a = \oplus_{k=0}^3 a_k$.

As in γ, we use two slightly different versions of bit permutation to make encryption and decryption processes identical: π_o in odd rounds and π_e in even rounds. Let A^i be the i-th byte column of a 4×4 byte array A, i.e., $A^i = (a_{3i}, a_{2i}, a_{1i}, a_{0i})^t$. Then the bit permutations π_o and π_e are defined as

$$\pi_o(A) = (\pi_3(A^3), \pi_2(A^2), \pi_1(A^1), \pi_0(A^0)),$$
$$\pi_e(A) = (\pi_1(A^3), \pi_0(A^2), \pi_3(A^1), \pi_2(A^0)).$$

Note that $\pi_o^{-1} = \pi_o$ and $\pi_e^{-1} = \pi_e$ and that if $\pi_0([d, c, b, a]^t) = [h, g, f, e]^t$, then

$$\pi_1([d, c, b, a]^t) = [e, h, g, f]^t, \ \pi_2([d, c, b, a]^t) = [f, e, h, g]^t, \ \pi_3([d, c, b, a]^t) = [g, f, e, h]^t.$$

This property will be used to derive an efficient decryption key schedule from the encryption key schedule (see Sect.2.3).

Byte Transposition τ It simply moves the byte at the (i, j)-th position to the (j, i)-th position, i.e., $B = \tau(A) \Leftrightarrow b_{ij} = a_{ji}$. Note that $\tau^{-1} = \tau$.

Key Xoring σ For a round key $K = (K[3], K[2], K[1], K[0])^t$, $B = \sigma_K(A)$ is defined by $B[i] = A[i] \oplus K[i]$ for $0 \le i \le 3$. Obviously, $\sigma_K^{-1} = \sigma_K$.

Round Transformation ρ One round of CRYPTON consists of applying γ, π, τ and σ in sequence to the 4×4 data array. More specifically, the odd and even round functions are defined (for round key K) by

$$\rho_{oK} = \sigma_K \circ \tau \circ \pi_o \circ \gamma_o \quad \text{for odd rounds,}$$
$$\rho_{eK} = \sigma_K \circ \tau \circ \pi_e \circ \gamma_e \quad \text{for even rounds.}$$

2.2 Encryption and Decryption

Let K_e^i be the i-th encryption round key consisting of 4 words, derived from a user-supplied key K using the encryption key schedule. The encryption transformation E_K of 12-round CRYPTON under key K consists of an initial key addition and 6 times repetitions of ρ_o and ρ_e and then a final output transformation. More specifically, E_K can be described as

$$E_K = \phi_e \circ \rho_{eK_e^{12}} \circ \rho_{oK_e^{11}} \circ \cdots \circ \rho_{eK_e^2} \circ \rho_{oK_e^1} \circ \sigma_{K_e^0}, \tag{1}$$

where ϕ_e is an output transformation to make encryption and decryption processes identical and is given by $\phi_e = \tau \circ \pi_e \circ \tau$. Similarly we define $\phi_o = \tau \circ \pi_o \circ \tau$.

The corresponding decryption transformation D_K can be shown to have the same form as E_K, except for using suitably transformed round keys:

$$D_K = \phi_e \circ \rho_{eK_d^{12}} \circ \rho_{oK_d^{11}} \circ \cdots \circ \rho_{eK_d^2} \circ \rho_{oK_d^1} \circ \sigma_{K_d^0}, \tag{2}$$

where the decryption round keys are defined by

$$K_d^{r-i} = \begin{cases} \phi_e(K_e^i) & \text{for } i = 0, 2, 4, \cdots, \\ \phi_o(K_e^i) & \text{for } i = 1, 3, 5, \cdots. \end{cases} \tag{3}$$

This shows that decryption can be performed by the same function as encryption with a different key schedule.

Notice that

$$\phi_e \circ \sigma_{K_e^i} = \sigma_{\phi_e(K_e^i)} \circ \phi_e = \sigma_{K_d^{r-i}} \circ \phi_e \text{ for } i = 0, 2, 4, \cdots,$$

$$\phi_o \circ \sigma_{K_e^i} = \sigma_{\phi_o(K_e^i)} \circ \phi_0 = \sigma_{K_d^{r-i}} \circ \phi_o \text{ for } i = 1, 3, 5, \cdots.$$

Using this property, we can incorporate the output transformation ϕ_e into the final round as $\phi_e \circ \rho_{eK_e^{12}} = \sigma_{K_d^0} \circ \tau \circ \gamma_e$.

2.3 Key Scheduling

CRYPTON requires total $4 \times 13 = 52$ round keys each of which is 32 bits long. These round keys are generated from a user key of $8k$ ($k = 0, 1, \cdots, 32$) bits in two steps: first nonlinear-transform the user key into 8 expanded keys and then generate the required number of round keys from these expanded keys using simple operations. This two-step generation of round keys is to allow efficient on-the-fly round key computation in the case where storage requirements do not allow to store the whole round keys (e.g., implementation in a portable device with restricted resources). It also facilitates hardware implementations.

Generating Expanded Keys Let $K = k_{31} \cdots k_1 k_0$ be a 256-bit user key. We first split K into U and V such that $U[i] = k_{8i+6} k_{8i+4} k_{8i+2} k_{8i}$ and $V[i] = k_{8i+7} k_{8i+5} k_{8i+3} k_{8i+1}$ for $i = 0, 1, 2, 3$. Then we compute the 8 expanded keys $E_e[i]$ ($0 \le i \le 7$) using round transformations with all-zero key as

$$U' = \rho_o(U), \qquad V' = \rho_e(V),$$
$$E_e[i] = U'[i] \oplus T_1, \quad E_e[i+4] = V'[i] \oplus T_0,$$

where $T_0 = \oplus_{i=0}^3 U'[i]$ and $T_1 = \oplus_{i=0}^3 V'[i]$.

Generating encryption round keys The following 13 round-constants will be used for encryption key schedule:

$$C_e[0] = \texttt{0xa54ff53a}, \quad C_e[i] = C_e[i-1] + \texttt{0x3c6ef372} \bmod 2^{32} \quad \text{for } i = 1, 2, \cdots, 12.$$

In addition, we also use the following 4 masking constants to generate distinct constants for each round key from a given round constant:

$$MC_0 = \texttt{0xacacacac}, \quad MC_i = MC_{i-1}^{\lll b1} \text{ for } i = 1, 2, 3.$$

1. compute the round keys for the first 2 rounds as

$$K_e[i] \leftarrow E_e[i] \oplus C_e[0] \oplus MC_i,$$
$$K_e[i+4] \leftarrow E_e[i+4] \oplus C_e[1] \oplus MC_i \quad \text{for } 0 \leq i \leq 3.$$

2. for rounds $r = 2, 3, \cdots, 12$, repeat the following two steps alternately:
   2-1. even rounds:

$$\{E_e[3], E_e[2], E_e[1], E_e[0]\} \leftarrow \{E_e[0]^{\lll b6}, E_e[3]^{\lll b6}, E_e[2]^{\lll 16}, E_e[1]^{\lll 24}\},$$
$$K_e[4r+i] \leftarrow E_e[i] \oplus C_e[r] \oplus MC_i \quad \text{for } 0 \leq i \leq 3.$$

   2-2. odd rounds:

$$\{E_e[7], E_e[6], E_e[5], E_e[4]\} \leftarrow \{E_e[6]^{\lll 16}, E_e[5]^{\lll 8}, E_e[4]^{\lll b2}, E_e[7]^{\lll b2}\},$$
$$K_e[4r+i] \leftarrow E_e[i+4] \oplus C_e[r] \oplus MC_i \quad \text{for } 0 \leq i \leq 3.$$

Generating decryption round keys For efficient decryption key schedule, first observe that $\phi_o = \tau \circ \pi_o \circ \tau$ and $\phi_e = \tau \circ \pi_e \circ \tau$ can be rewritten as

$$\phi_o(A) = (\phi_3(A[3]), \phi_2(A[2]), \phi_1(A[1]), \phi_0(A[0]))^t,$$
$$\phi_e(A) = (\phi_1(A[3]), \phi_0(A[2]), \phi_3(A[1]), \phi_2(A[0]))^t.$$

Here ϕ_i is actually the same as π_i except that 4 input bytes are now arranged in a row vector (see Sect.2.1.2). Also note the shift and linear properties of ϕ_i

$$\phi_i(X^{\lll 8k}) = \phi_i(X)^{\lll 32-8k} \quad \text{for } k = 1, 2, 3,$$
$$\phi_i(X) = \phi_j(X)^{\lll 8} \quad \text{for } j = i+1 \bmod 4,$$
$$\phi_i(X^{\lll b2k}) = (\phi_i(X)^{\lll b2k})^{\lll 8k} \quad \text{for } k = 1, 2, 3,$$
$$\phi_i(A[j] \oplus C) = \phi_i(A[j]) \oplus \phi_i(C).$$

In particular, $\phi_i(C) = C$ if C consists of 4 identical bytes. Using these properties, we can design a decryption key schedule similar to and almost as efficient as the encryption key schedule as follows (Decryption round constants $C_d[i]$'s are given by $C_d[i] = \phi_2(C_e[12-i])$ for even i's and $C_d[i] = \phi_0(C_e[12-i])$ for odd i's.):

1. compute the expanded keys and round constants for decryption as follows:

$$\{E_d[3], E_d[2], E_d[1], E_d[0]\} \leftarrow \{\phi_0(E_e[1])^{\lll b2}, \phi_1(E_e[0]), \phi_1(E_e[3])^{\lll b2}, \phi_2(E_e[2])^{\lll b4}\},$$
$$\{E_d[7], E_d[6], E_d[5], E_d[4]\} \leftarrow \{\phi_2(E_e[6])^{\lll b4}, \phi_0(E_e[5])^{\lll b4}, \phi_1(E_e[4])^{\lll b6}, \phi_0(E_e[7])^{\lll b6}\},$$

2. compute the first 8 round keys as

$$K_d[i] \leftarrow E_d[i] \oplus C_d[0]^{\lll 32-8i} \oplus MC_i,$$
$$K_d[i+4] \leftarrow E_d[i+4] \oplus C_d[1]^{\lll 32-8i} \oplus MC_i \quad \text{for } 0 \le i \le 3.$$

3. for rounds $r = 2, 3, \cdots, 12$, repeat the following two steps alternately:
   3-1. even rounds:

$$\{E_d[3], E_d[2], E_d[1], E_d[0]\} \leftarrow \{E_d[2]^{\lll b2}, E_d[1]^{\lll 8}, E_d[0]^{\lll 16}, E_d[3]^{\lll b2}\},$$
$$K_d[4r+i] \leftarrow E_d[i] \oplus C_d[r]^{\lll 32-8i} \oplus MC_i \quad \text{for } 0 \le i \le 3.$$

   3-2. odd rounds:

$$\{E_d[7], E_d[6], E_d[5], E_d[4]\} \leftarrow \{E_d[4]^{\lll b6}, E_d[7]^{\lll 24}, E_d[6]^{\lll 16}, E_d[5]^{\lll b6}\},$$
$$K_d[4r+i] \leftarrow E_d[i+4] \oplus C_d[r]^{\lll 32-8i} \oplus MC_i \quad \text{for } 0 \le i \le 3.$$

3 Security Analysis

3.1 Diffusion Property of Linear Transformations

Due to memory requirements, small size S-boxes are commonly used in most block cipher designs and thus effective diffusion of S-box outputs by linear transformations plays an important role for resistance against various attacks such as differential and linear cryptanalysis (DC and LC for short) [3,23]

From Sect.2.1.2, we can see that it suffices to consider any one component transformation π_i of π to examine the diffusion property of π, since π acts on each byte column independently. It is also easy to see that any column vector with n ($n < 4$) nonzero bytes is transformed by π_i into a column vector with at least $4 - n$ nonzero bytes (we call this number 4 the diffusion order of π_i). This is due to the operation of exclusive-or sum in π. More important is that the number of such input vectors giving minimal diffusion is very limited. This is due to the masked bit permutation. Table 1 shows the distribution of diffusion orders by π_i over all 32-bit numbers. We can see that there are only 204 values achieving the minimum diffusion order 4 and about 99.96 % of 32-bit numbers have diffusion order 7 or 8. This shows the effectiveness of diffusion by our combined linear transformation $\tau \circ \pi$ in successive rounds.

diffusion order	4	5	6	7	8
no. elements	204	13464	1793364	130589784	4162570479
ratio	4.75×10^{-8}	3.13×10^{-6}	4.18×10^{-4}	3.04×10^{-2}	96.92×10^{-2}

Table 1. Distribution of diffusion orders under π_i

Let us examine in more detail the set of 32-bit numbers giving minimal diffusion. For this, we define two sets of byte values, Ω_x and Ω_y, as

$$\Omega_x = \{0x01, 0x02, 0x03, 0x04, 0x08, 0x0c, 0x10, 0x20, 0x30, 0x40, 0x80, 0xc0\},$$
$$\Omega_y = \{0x11, 0x12, 0x13, 0x21, 0x22, 0x23, 0x31, 0x32, 0x33, 0x44, 0x48, 0x4c,$$
$$0x84, 0x88, 0x8c, 0xc4, 0xc8, 0xcc\} \cup \Omega_x.$$

Let I_j be a set of input vectors with j nonzero bytes which are transformed by π_i into output vectors with $4 - j$ nonzero bytes. Then all possible 32-bit values with minimum diffusion can be obtained as: for each x in Ω_x and y in Ω_y,

$$I_1 = \{(0,0,0,x)^t, (0,0,x,0)^t, (0,x,0,0)^t, (x,0,0,0)^t\},$$
$$I_2 = \{(0,0,x,x)^t, (0,x,x,0)^t, (x,x,0,0)^t, (x,0,0,x)^t, (0,y,0,y)^t, (y,0,y,0)^t\},$$
$$I_3 = \{(0,x,x,x)^t, (x,0,x,x)^t, (x,x,0,x)^t, (x,x,x,0)^t\}.$$

Therefore, we can see that there are only 204 vectors with minimum diffusion: 48 from $\pi_i(I_1) = I_3$, 108 from $\pi_i(I_2) = I_2$ and 48 from $\pi_i(I_3) = I_1$. Observe that the nonzero bytes in each input vector should have the same value to achieve minimum diffusion. Also note that the 18 values in $\Omega_y - \Omega_x$ can only occur for inputs with two separated nonzero bytes (the last two cases in I_2).

Now let us examine the diffusion effect of $\tau \circ \pi$ through consecutive rounds. This analysis can be done by assuming that in each round the S-box output can take any desired value, irrespective of the input value. This assumption is to maximally take into account the probabilistic nature of S-box transformation without details of the S-box characteristics. Since it suffices to consider worst-case propagations, we only examine inputs with 1, 2, or 3 nonzero bytes in any one column vector of a 4×4 byte array, say the first byte column. The result is shown in Table 2, where we only showed the nonzero column vector in the starting 4×4 byte array. The sum of the number of nonzero bytes throughout the evolution is of great importance to ensure resistance against differential and linear cryptanalysis. Table 2 shows that the number of nonzero bytes per round is repeated with period 4 and their sum up to round 8 is at least 32.

starting nonzero vector \ round	1	2	3	4	5	6	7	8
I_{1j} $(0 \le j \le 3)$	1	3	9	3	1	3	9	3
I_{2j} $(0 \le j \le 5)$	2	2	6	6	2	2	6	6
I_{3j} $(0 \le j \le 3)$	3	1	3	9	3	1	3	9

Table 2. Minimum possible no. of active bytes (without considering S-box char.)

3.2 S-boxes Construction and their Property

The S-box for a block cipher should be chosen to have two important requirements: differential uniformity and nonlinearity. Combined with the diffusion effect of linear transformations used, they directly determine the security level of the block cipher against DC and LC.

The maximum differential and linear approximation probabilities for an $n \times n$ S-box S (δ_S and λ_S for short) can be defined as follows. Let X and Y be a set of possible 2^n inputs/outputs of S, respectively. Then δ_S and λ_S are defined by

$$\delta_S \stackrel{\text{def}}{=} \max_{\Delta x \neq 0, \Delta y} \frac{\#\{x \in X | S(x) \oplus S(x \oplus \Delta x) = \Delta y\}}{2^n}, \tag{4}$$

$$\lambda_S \stackrel{\text{def}}{=} \max_{\Gamma x, \Gamma y \neq 0} \left(\frac{|\#\{x \in X | x \bullet \Gamma x = S(x) \bullet \Gamma y\} - 2^{n-1}|}{2^{n-1}} \right)^2, \tag{5}$$

where $a \bullet b$ denotes the parity of bit-wise product of a and b.

The nonlinear transformation adopted in CRYPTON is byte-wise substitutions using four 8×8 S-boxes, S_i $(i = 0, 1, 2, 3)$. We first constructed an 8×8 involution S-box S from two 4-bit permutations (P-boxes, for short), P_0 and P_1, using a SP network, as shown in Fig.1. Then the actual four S-boxes were derived from S as follows: for each $x \in [0, 256)$,

$$S_0(x) = S(x)^{\lll 1}, \quad S_1(x) = S(x)^{\lll 3}, \quad S_2(x) = S(x^{\lll 7}), \quad S_3(x) = S(x^{\lll 5}).$$

It is easy to see that these S-boxes satisfy inverse relationships such that $S_0^{-1} = S_2$ and $S_1^{-1} = S_3$. We decided to use four variants of S, rather than just one involution S-box or four independent S-boxes, because this will make iterative characteristics harder to occur while reducing the storage required in some limited computing environments (e.g., low-cost smart cards).

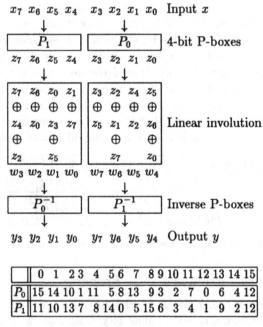

Fig.1 The selected 8×8 involution S-box S

	0	1	2	3	4	5	6	7	8	9	10	11	12	13	14	15
P_0	15	14	10	1	11	5	8	13	9	3	2	7	0	6	4	12
P_1	11	10	13	7	8	14	0	5	15	6	3	4	1	9	2	12

The involution S-box S was searched for, over some limited space of good 4-bit P-boxes and linear involutions, in such a way that it has best possible differential and linear characteristics. Moreover, among such a set of candidate involution S-boxes, we selected the final S-box S considering the following two additional requirements:

1. The high-probability I/O difference pairs (selection patterns, resp.) in S should have as high Hamming weights as possible.

2. The number of high-probability difference pairs (selection patterns, resp.) in the resulting 8×8 S-boxes S_i's should be as small as possible when the input is restricted to the minimal diffusion set Ω_y.

These requirements are to ensure that high-probability differences/selection patterns should be more rapidly diffused by linear transformations and that it should be more difficult to form a chain of high-probability S-box characteristics/linear approximations through consecutive rounds.

Table 3 shows their statistics on the distribution of input-output difference/linear approximation pairs, where the entry values are computed by the numerator of equations (4) and (5).

D	entry value	0	2	4	6	8	10			
C	no of entries	39584	20158	4976	749	62	7			
L	entry value	0	4	8	12	16	20	24	28	32
C	no of entries	13927	22058	15948	8460	3731	1094	276	36	6

Table 3. Distribution of difference/linear approx. pairs for S_i

From the table, we can see that for each i,

$$p_d \stackrel{\text{def}}{=} \delta_{S_i} = \frac{10}{256} = 2^{-4.68}, \quad p_l \stackrel{\text{def}}{=} \lambda_{S_i} = \left(\frac{32}{128}\right)^2 = 2^{-4},$$

and that there are only 7 difference pairs achieving the best characteristic probability p_d (6 selection patterns achieving the best linear approximation probability p_l). As we aimed at the S-box selection process, these high-probability characteristics have fairly heavy Hamming weights. E.g., for the characteristics with top two high probabilities (69 pairs for DC and 42 pairs for LC), the sum of input and output Hamming weights are at least 4 and larger than 8 on average.

	DC(6)				LC(24)
S_0	(11, c0)	(22, 8c)	(32, cc)	(88, 11)	(88, 11)
S_1	(11, 3)	(22, 32)	(32, 33)	(88, 44)	(88, 44)
S_2	(c0, 11)	(11, 88)	(8c, 22)	(cc, 32)	(11, 88)
S_3	(3, 11)	(32, 22)	(33, 32)	(44, 88)	(44, 88)

Table 4. The most probable characteristics over the restricted set Ω_y

More importantly, if the input is restricted to the minimal diffusion set Ω_y, the maximum entry values are at most 6 and 24 for differential and linear characteristics, respectively. There are only 4 such difference pairs and 1 such selection pattern in each S-box, as shown in Table 4. Note that even the pairs in the table belong to the more restricted set $\Omega_y - \Omega_x$. Since they are more important for worst-case analysis of DC and LC, we define these probabilities as

$$p_d' \stackrel{\text{def}}{=} \delta_{S_i}^{\Omega_y} = \frac{6}{256} = 2^{-5.42}, \quad p_l' \stackrel{\text{def}}{=} \lambda_{S_i}^{\Omega_y} = \left(\frac{24}{128}\right)^2 = 2^{-4.83}.$$

3.3 Differential Cryptanalysis

Let us first evaluate the best r-round characteristic probability for CRYPTON. In the following we only consider characteristics up to 8 rounds since that will be sufficient to show the resistance of CRYPTON to differential cryptanalysis.

First note that the probability of any characteristic in CRYPTON can be completely determined by the number of active S-boxes and their char. probabilities (e.g., see [10]). Since the number of active S-boxes involved in any 8-round characteristic is at least 32, we can obtain the most rough upper bound for the best 8-round char. probability as $p_{C_8} = p_d^{32} = 2^{-149.7}$ under the assumption of independent and uniform distribution for plaintexts and round keys, where we assumed that all the S-boxes involved have the best char. probability p_d.

However, as can be seen from Table 4, the minimum number of active S-boxes shown in Table 2 can not be achieved even with S-box characteristics with probability p_d'. Moreover, if we allow intermediate S-box output differences with larger diffusion orders, then the number of active S-boxes up to round 8 will grow much larger than the bound 32. Considering the rapid diffusion by linear transformations, we can reasonably assume that a characteristic involving a smaller number of active S-boxes with smaller S-box char. probabilities should give better overall probability than a characteristic involving a larger number of active S-boxes with larger S-box char. probabilities. Therefore, we can obtain a tighter bound for the 8-round char. probability as $p_{C_8} < (p_d')^{32} = 2^{-173.3}$. The actual probability will be much lower than this bound, but we do not proceed any more since this bound is lower enough to show the strong resistance of CRYPTON against DC based on the best characteristic.

Given a pair of input and output differences, there may be a relatively large number of characteristics starting with the input difference and ending with the output difference. It is not easy to estimate the number of such characteristics that can reside in a differential. However, the estimated 8-round char. probability, together with a rough analysis solely based on the diffusion property of linear transformations, shows that no 8-round differential can have probability significantly larger than 2^{-128}. Therefore, we believe that CRYPTON with 9 or more rounds is far secure against the basic differential attack.

3.4 Linear Cryptanalysis

An r-round linear approximation involves a number of S-box linear approximations and, as in differential cryptanalysis, the number of such S-boxes (i.e., active S-boxes) determines the complexity of linear cryptanalysis. Much the same way as DC, we can obtain a rough bound for the best 8-round linear approximation probability p_{L_r} as $p_{L_r} < (p_l')^{32} = 2^{-154.6}$. Again this value is a very loose upper bound. Actually there will be no linear approximation achieving this probability, considering the linear characteristic of S-boxes and the linear transformation involved.

As in the differential attack, we may use multiple linear approximations to improve the basic linear attack [17,18]. Suppose that one can derive N linear approximations involving the same key bits with the same probability. Then the complexity of a linear attack can be reduced by a factor of N, compared to a linear attack based on a single linear approximation [17]. However, a large number of linear approximations involving the same key bits are unlikely to be found in most ciphers, in particular in CRYPTON. Multiple linear approximations involving different key bits may be used to derive the different key bits in the different linear approximations simultaneously with almost the same complexity [18]. However, this will be of little help to improve the basic linear attack, since we already have a linear approximation probability far beyond any practical attack. Therefore, we believe that there will be no linear attack on CRYPTON with 9 or more rounds with a complexity lower than 2^{128}.

3.5 Security against Other Possible Attacks

There are some variants to the basic differential attack discussed above. Knudsen introduced the idea of a *truncated differential* [15], i.e., a differential that predicts only part of the difference (not the entire value of difference), and demonstrated that this variant may be more effective against some ciphers than the basic differential attack and may be independent of the S-boxes used [16]. Due to the fairly uniform diffusion by bit-wise permutations, we believe that truncated differentials will not be much useful in CRYPTON compared to ordinary differentials.

The *higher order differential* attack was first considered by Lai [20] and further investigated in [15,12]. Let d be the poly. degree of $(r-1)$-round output bits expressed as polynomials of plaintext bits. Then the higher order DC can find some key bits of the last round for an r-round cipher using about 2^{d+1} chosen plaintexts [12]. Obviously the success of this attack depends on the nonlinear order of S-box outputs. Since CRYPTON uses S-boxes with nonlinear order 6, the poly. degree of output bits after 3 rounds increases to $6^3 \gg 128$. Therefore, the higher order DC on CRYPTON will be completely infeasible after 4 rounds.

There also exist some algebraic attacks using polynomial relations between ciphertexts and plaintexts. The *interpolation attack* [12] proposed by Jakobsen and Knudsen is applicable if the number of coefficients in the polynomial expression of the ciphertext is less than the size of ciphertext space. Its probabilistic variant allows to use some probabilistic non-linear relations with increased complexity [11]. The S-boxes used in CRYPTON do not allow any simple algebraic description and the bit permutation π in each round further complicates algebraic relations between S-box outputs. We thus believe that this kind of algebraic attacks cannot be applied to CRYPTON.

Another notable attack is the differential attack based on *impossible differentials* recently introduced by Biham et al. [1,2]. It seems not easy to systematically find some impossible events in block ciphers based on the SP network. Thus the applicability of this attack to CRYPTON should be further investigated in the future. Other variants of differential attacks, such as the differential-linear attack [9] and the *boomerang attack* (differential-differential style attack) [24], don't appear to better work on CRYPTON than the basic differential attack.

There are also several variants or generalizations of linear cryptanalysis. These include linear cryptanalysis using non-linear approximations [19], *generalized linear cryptanalysis* using I/O sums [7], and *partitioning cryptanalysis* [8], etc. We have not checked in detail the effectiveness of these attacks against CRYPTON. However, our observation on the diffusion property of π shows that any kind of I/O relations involving more than two bits in S-boxes should rapidly increase the number of active S-boxes involved in the overall I/O relations. So, we believe that there will be little chance of these attacks substantially improving the basic linear attack.

Finally, we note that there exists a specialized attack to SQUARE-like ciphers, the so-call *dedicated SQUARE attack* [6], which can also be applied to a reduced variant of CRYPTON (see [5]). However, this attack only uses the balancedness of XOR sum of intermediate round outputs for a set of different inputs, so its applicability is limited to at most a 6-round version of CRYPTON.

3.6 Key Schedule Cryptanalysis

Key schedule cryptanalysis is another important category of attacks on block ciphers. Typical weaknesses exploited in key schedule cryptanalysis include weak keys or semi-weak keys, equivalent keys, related keys and simple relations such as the complemetation property existing in DES (for details, see e.g. [13,14]). These weaknesses can be exploited to speed up an exhaustive key search or to mount related key attacks. Though most of these attacks on key schedules are not practical in normal use, they may be a serious flaw in certain circumstances (e.g., when a block cipher is used as a building block for hash functions).

The key schedule of CRYPTON is designed with the above known weaknesses in mind. First remember the two step generation of round keys in CRYPTON: First, a user key of 256 bits or less is transformed into 8 expanded keys via invertible nonlinear transformations. Then, the first 4 expanded keys are used to generate round keys in even rounds and the remaining 4 in odd rounds. In each round, the expanded keys are updated by a word rotation and bit or byte rotations and then xored with distinct constants to produce round keys.

The first step of the key schedule shows that no different user keys can produce the same expanded keys and that there is little possibility of simple relations between different user keys being preserved in expanded keys. Thus we believe that there are no equivalent keys or simple relations in the CRYPTON key schedule. It is also very unlikely that there exist related keys that can be used to mount related-key differential attacks or related-key slide attacks, since a nonlinearly transformed user key is applied 6 or 7 times throughout encryption, each time being updated by rotations and constant additions.

Weak keys or semi-weak keys, if any, are usually due to the symmetry in encryption and key scheduling processes. This symmetry can be destroyed most easily by using distinct round constants in the key schedule. In CRYPTON we used different rotation amounts and round constants for each round key. So, we also believe that no such keys exist in CRYPTON.

4 Implementation and Efficiency

The overall structure of CRYPTON allows a very high degree of parallelisms. This will result in high efficiency and flexibility in both software and hardware implementations.

The round transformation of CRYPTON can be efficiently implemented on a 32-bit microprocessor using table lookups, if we use 4 Kbytes of storage in addition. The idea is to precompute and store 4 tables of 256 words as follows:

$$SS_i[j] = \oplus_{k=0}^{3}(S_i[j] \wedge m_{i+k \bmod 4})^{\lll 8k} \text{ for } 0 \leq i \leq 3 \text{ and } 0 \leq j \leq 255.$$

We can then implement the odd round function $B = \rho_{oK}(A)$ by

$$B[j] = \oplus_{i=0}^{3} SS_{i+j \bmod 4}[a_{ij}] \oplus K[j] \text{ for } 0 \leq j \leq 3.$$

Similarly, the even round function can be implemented by $B = \rho_{eK}(A) = \rho_{oK}((A[1], A[0], A[3], A[2])^t)$.

We have implemented CRYPTON in C (with in-line assembly in the case of Pentium Pro) and measured its speed on 200 MHz Pentium Pro running Windows 95 (with 32 Mbytes of RAM) and on 167 MHz UltraSparc running Solaris 2.5. The result is shown in Table 5. Our optimized C code runs quite fast, giving an encryption rate of about 6.7 Mbytes/sec on Pentium Pro and about 4.4 Mbytes/sec on UltraSparc. The partial assembly code on Pentium Pro can encrypt/decrypt about 8.0 Mbytes per second, running about 20 % faster than the optimized C code. We expect that a fully optimized assembly implementation will run a little bit faster.

Language\Clocks	Key setup (enc/dec)	Encryption
In-line Asm (PP)	N/A	381
MSVC 5.0 (PP)	327 / 397	452
GNU C (US)	496 / 564	575

Table 5. Speed of CRYPTON on Pentium Pro and UltraSparc (for 128-bit keys)

The key setup time of CRYPTON is different for encryption and decryption. Decryption key setup requires a little more computation due to the need of transformation of expanded keys. Our encryption key schedule is very fast, taking much less time than one-block encryption (though the code for key scheduling was not fully optimized). As a result, CRYPTON will be very efficient for use as a building block for hash functions or in the case of encrypting/decrypting only a few blocks of data (e.g., MACs for entity authentication). Note that all the timings remain almost the same for different sizes of user keys.

CRYPTON can be efficiently implemented on other platforms as well. For smart card implementations, we can only store 256 bytes of the involution S-box S and compute each entry of S_i's using just one rotation. The RAM requirement is also very small, just 52 bytes in total (20 bytes for data variables and 32 bytes for a user key). So we can expect that CRYPTON will run quite fast on low-cost smart cards, since all computations can be efficiently implemented only using byte operations. Also, CRYPTON will be ideal to be implemented on DSPs which have multiple execution units due to its high parallelism.

optimized in	delay (nsec)	cycles	Mbits/sec	total (cell) area
Area	18.97	7	900	51527 (18323)
Time	10.24	7	1660	74021 (28180)

Table 6. Estimated speed of CRYPTON in gate array impl.(from Synopsys)

Hardware efficiency is one of design objectives of CRYPTON. To estimate the speed in hardware, we carried out some simulations with Synonsys using a commercial 0.35 micron gate array library. The result is shown in Table 6. This table shows that we can easily achieve a Giga bits/sec in hardware only using a small amount of chip area.

5 Conclusion

We described CRYPTON version 1.0, an enhanced version of our AES proposal, and analyzed its security and efficiency. CRYPTON was designed by considering efficiency in various implementation environments. Its symmetry in encryption and decryption greatly reduces the hardware complexity. The S-boxes and linear transformations are designed by considering efficient implementations in hardware logic as well. The key scheduling algorithm runs very fast and allows efficient implementations in hardware and under limited environments.

Our preliminary analysis shows that 12-round CRYPTON is far secure against most known attacks. At present the best attack on CRYPTON appears to be exhaustive key search. However, as usual, more extensive analysis should be done before practical applications of a newly introduced cipher, so we strongly encourage the reader to further investigate our new version of CRYPTON. We would greatly appreciate any reports on its analysis.

Acknowledgement

The author is very grateful to those people who helped him during the development of CRYPTON. Hyo Sun Hwang and Myung Hee Kang helped implementations in assembly and Java, and the hardware simulation was done by Eun Jong Hong. He would also like to thank the anonymous refrees for their constructive comments.

References

1. E.Biham, A.Biryukov and A.Shamir, Cryptanalysis of Skipjack reduced to 31 rounds, In *Advances in Cryptology-EUROCRYPT'99*, Springer-Verlag, 1999.

2. E.Biham, A.Biryukov and A.Shamir, Miss in the middle attacks on IDEA, Khufu, and Khafre, in *this proceedings*.
3. E. Biham and A. Shamir, Differential cryptanalysis of DES-like cryptosystems, *Journal of Cryptology*, v. 4, 1991, pp. 3-72.
4. J.Borst, Weak keys of CRYPTON, public comment submited to the NIST, 1998.
5. C.D'Halluin, G.Bijnens, V.Rijmen and B.Preenel, Attack on six rounds of CRYPTON, in *this proceedings*.
6. J.Daemen, L.Knudsen and V.Rijmen, The block cipher Square, In *Fast Software Encryption*, LNCS 1267, Springer-Verlag, 1997, pp.149-171.
7. C.Harpes, G.Kramer and J.Massey, A generalization of linear cryptanalysis and the applicability of Matsui's piling-up lemma, In *Advances in Cryptology-EUROCRYPT'95*, LNCS 921, Springer-Verlag, 1995, pp.24-38.
8. C.Harpes and J.Massey, Partitioning cryptanalysis, In *Fast Software Encryption*, LNCS 1267, Springer-Verlag, 1997, pp.13-27.
9. M.Hellman and S.Langford, Differential-linear cryptanalysis, In *Advances in Cryptology-CRYPTO'94*, LNCS 839, Springer-Verlag, 1994, pp.26-39.
10. H.M.Heys and S.E.Tavares, Substitution-permutation networks resistant to differential and linear cryptanalysis, *J. Cryptology*, 9(1), 1996, pp.1-19.
11. T.Jakobsen, Cryptanalysis of block ciphers with probabilistic non-linear relations of low-degree, In *Advances in Cryptology-CRYPTO'98*, LNCS 1462, Springer-Verlag, 1998, pp.212-222.
12. T.Jakobsen and L.R.Knudsen, The interpolation attack on block ciphers, In *Fast Software Encryption*, LNCS 1267, Springer-Verlag, 1997, pp.28-40.
13. J.Kelsey, B.Schneier and D.Wagner, Key-schedule cryptanalysis of IDEA, DES, GOST, SAFER, and triple-DES, In *Advances in Cryptology-CRYPTO'96*, LNCS 1109, Springer-Verlag, 1996, pp.237-252.
14. J.Kelsey, B.Schneier and D.Wagner, Related-key cryptanalysis of 3-WAY, Biham-DES, CAST, DES-X, NewDES, RC2, and TEA, In *Information and Communications Security*, LNCS 1334, Springer-Verlag, 1997, pp.233-246.
15. L.R.Knudsen, Truncated and higher order differentials, In *Fast Software Encryption*, LNCS 1008, Springer-Verlag, 1995, pp.196-211.
16. L.R.Knudsen and T.A.Berson, Truncated differentials of SAFER, In *Fast Software Encryption*, LNCS 1039, Springer-Verlag, 1996, pp.15-26.
17. B.S.Kaliski Jr. and M.J.B.Robshaw, Linear cryptanalysis using multiple linear approximations, In *Advances in Cryptology-CRYPTO'94*, LNCS 839, Springer-Verlag, 1994, pp.26-39.
18. B.S.Kaliski Jr. and M.J.B.Robshaw, Linear cryptanalysis using multiple linear approximations and FEAL, In *Fast Software Encryption*, LNCS 1008, Springer-Verlag, 1995, pp.249-264.
19. L.Knudsen and M.J.B.Robshaw, Non-linear approximations in linear cryptanalysis, In *Advances in Cryptology-EUROCRYPT'96*, LNCS 1070, Springer-Verlag, 1996, pp.252-267.
20. X.Lai, *On the design and security of block ciphers*, PhD thesis, ETH, Zurich, 1992.
21. X.Lai and J.L.Massey, Markov ciphers and differential cryptanalysis, In *Advances in Cryptology-EUROCRYPT'91*, LNCS 547, Springer-Verlag, 1991, pp.17-38.
22. C.H.Lim, CRYPTON: A new 128-bit block cipher, NIST AES Proposal, June 1998.
23. M.Matsui, Linear cryptanalysis method for DES cipher, In *Advances in Cryptology-EUROCRYPT'93*, LNCS 765, Springer-Verlag, 1994, pp.386-397.
24. D.Wagner, The boomerang attack, in *this proceedings*.

Attack on Six Rounds of CRYPTON

Carl D'Halluin, Gert Bijnens, Vincent Rijmen*, and Bart Preneel*

Katholieke Universiteit Leuven , ESAT-COSIC
K. Mercierlaan 94, B-3001 Heverlee, Belgium
carl.dhalluin@esat.kuleuven.ac.be
gert.bijnens@esat.kuleuven.ac.be
vincent.rijmen@esat.kuleuven.ac.be
bart.preneel@esat.kuleuven.ac.be

Abstract. In this paper we present an attack on a reduced round version of CRYPTON. The attack is based on the dedicated SQUARE attack. We explain why the attack also works on CRYPTON and prove that the entire 256-bit user key for 6 rounds of CRYPTON can be recovered with a complexity of 2^{56} encryptions, whereas for SQUARE 2^{72} encryptions are required to recover the 128-bit user key.

1 Introduction

The block cipher CRYPTON was recently proposed as a candidate algorithm for the AES [5]. In this paper we describe a chosen plaintext attack that works if the cipher is reduced to 6 rounds instead of the specified 12 rounds. Our attack is based on the dedicated SQUARE attack presented in [2], but because of the differences between SQUARE and CRYPTON, the attack has to be modified in several points.

Previous analysis of CRYPTON led to the discovery of a failure of the key scheduling, resulting in a number of weak keys [1,6]. Our attack works on a reduced version of CRYPTON for all keys. For a final optimisation of the attack, we exploit another feature of the key scheduling.

In Section 2 we give a short description of CRYPTON. We present the basic attack in Section 3. Section 4 discusses the recovery of the user key. Section 5 and Section 6 discuss the extension of the attack to five rounds, and Section 7 gives the six round attack. We conclude in Section 8.

2 Description of CRYPTON

The block cipher CRYPTON is based on SQUARE [2]. The plaintext data is ordered in 16 bytes, which are put in a square scheme, called the *state*. If A is the state at a certain moment, the different bytes of A are called $(A)_{ij}$ with i and j varying from 0 to 3 (see Figure 1). CRYPTON uses 6 elementary transformations.

---

* F.W.O. Postdoctoral Researcher, sponsored by the Fund for Scientific Research - Flanders (Belgium)

A_{03}	A_{02}	A_{01}	A_{00}
A_{13}	A_{12}	A_{11}	A_{10}
A_{23}	A_{22}	A_{21}	A_{20}
A_{33}	A_{32}	A_{31}	A_{30}

Fig. 1. Byte coordinates of the state

- $\sigma_{K_e^i}$ is a key addition (EXOR) with round key i. This operation is the same as the key addition in SQUARE.
- π_e and π_o are linear transformations that act on columns of the state. The π-transformations operate on two bits at a time, calculating a new value by exoring the old values of two bits in corresponding positions in three different bytes of the column. These operations are the replacement of the MDS-based θ in SQUARE. They can be implemented using four masks, denoted $M_0, \ldots M_3$.
- γ_e and γ_o are non-linear transformations that apply S-boxes to the different state bytes. They have the additional property that $\gamma_e = \gamma_o^{-1}$. These operations correspond to the single γ in SQUARE.
- τ is a simple transposition (upper row becomes rightmost column, lower row becomes leftmost column, ...). This operation is the same as the π of SQUARE. Note that $(D, C, B, A)^t$ means that A^t is the upper row and D^t is the lower row.

Throughout this text we use versions of CRYPTON with less rounds than the standard number of rounds which is 12. The standard version of CRYPTON is :

$$\text{Encrypt} = \phi_e \circ \rho_{eK_e^{12}} \circ \rho_{oK_e^{11}} \circ \cdots \circ \rho_{eK_e^2} \circ \rho_{oK_e^1} \circ \sigma_{K_e^0}$$

$$\text{with} \begin{cases} \phi_e = \tau \circ \pi_e \circ \tau \\ \rho_{eK} = \sigma_K \circ \tau \circ \pi_e \circ \gamma_e \\ \rho_{oK} = \sigma_K \circ \tau \circ \pi_o \circ \gamma_o \end{cases}$$

Since ϕ_e uses no key material, it is easily invertible by a cryptanalyst and therefore we do not consider it in the following text. For example a *five round version* of CRYPTON means in this text :

$$\text{Encrypt}_5 = \rho_{oK_e^5} \circ \rho_{eK_e^4} \circ \rho_{oK_e^3} \circ \rho_{eK_e^2} \circ \rho_{oK_e^1} \circ \sigma_{K_e^0}.$$

Unless stated otherwise the output state of round n is denoted R_n in this paper. R_0 represents the output after the initial key addition $\sigma_{K_e^0}$. PT represents the plaintext and CT represents the ciphertext. So $CT = \phi_e(R_{12})$.

3 Basic attack : 4 rounds of CRYPTON

In this section we will explain how the dedicated SQUARE attack [2] can be modified to attack CRYPTON. Due to the differences between both algorithms, the attack works in a slightly different way. The final 6-round attack allows to recover the entire 256-bit user key immediately, using less computer time than the equivalent attack on SQUARE, which only recovers a 128-bit key. This makes the attack much more significant on CRYPTON than on SQUARE.

First we explain the attack on 4 rounds of CRYPTON and the reason why it works. The attack on 4 rounds uses approximately 2^9 chosen plaintexts and their corresponding ciphertexts. We show a way to recover a 128-bit user key without using additional plaintexts. In the next Sections a 5-round and a 6-round attack on CRYPTON are described, which require significantly more chosen plaintexts.

Let a Λ-set be a set of 256 states that are all different in some of the (16) state bytes (the *active*) and all equal in the other state bytes (the *passive*). The 256 elements of the Λ-set are denoted Λ_a with a varying from 0 to 255. Let λ be the set of indices of the active bytes (indices varying from 0 to 3). We have:

$$\forall a, b \in \{0 \dots 255\} : \quad \begin{cases} (\Lambda_a)_{ij} \neq (\Lambda_b)_{ij} \text{ for } (i,j) \in \lambda \\ (\Lambda_a)_{ij} = (\Lambda_b)_{ij} \text{ for } (i,j) \notin \lambda. \end{cases}$$

We start with a Λ-set with a single active byte. From the definition it follows that this byte will take all 256 possible values {0x00, 0x01, ..., 0xff} over the different states in the Λ-set. As a consequence, the Λ-set is balanced, by which we mean:

$$\bigoplus_{a=0}^{255} (\Lambda_a)_{ij} = \text{0x00}, \qquad \forall i, j.$$

This is valid for the one active byte because $\bigoplus_{a=0}^{255} a = \text{0x00}$ and for the fifteen passive bytes because $\bigoplus_{a=0}^{255} b = \text{0x00}$ if b is a constant byte.

We now investigate the balancedness, the positions and the properties of the active bytes through the subsequent transformations. After each transformation we have a new set of active bytes, which is called the *state scheme*. If we say that the state scheme is balanced we mean that the transformation of the original Λ-set up to this point is still balanced. It is also important in the state scheme to know some properties of each byte e.g. this byte is a constant for each element of the Λ-set, or that byte takes every value of the set {0x00, 0x01, ..., 0xff} over the Λ-set (mathematically : $\bigcup_{a=0}^{255} (\Lambda_a)_{ij} = \{$0x00, 0x01, ..., 0xff$\}$).

Round 0 (initial key addition) The state scheme evolution through round 0 is displayed in Figure 2. We have a single active byte which takes 256 different values over the Λ-set (full black square in the figure). The 15 other bytes are passive and therefore they have a constant value over the Λ-set.

The initial key addition $\sigma_{K_e^0}$ does not change the balancedness of the state scheme because the EXOR-sum of 256 times the same key byte cancels out.

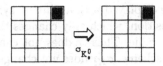

Fig. 2. State scheme through round 0

$\sigma_{K_e^0}$ cannot change the state scheme either because the EXOR-addition with a constant byte acts as a simple bijection in the set of all possible byte values {0x00, 0x01, ..., 0xff}. Hence, if we have 256 different byte values, the key addition will map them on 256 different byte values, and if we have 256 times the same byte value, the key addition will obviously map them on 256 times the same byte value.

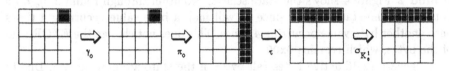

Fig. 3. State scheme through round 1

Round 1 γ_o does not change the state scheme nor the balancedness of the scheme since γ_o is bijective for each of the bytes. So 256 different byte values are mapped onto the same 256 different byte values. After π_o we have one active column. The other three columns are still passive. Now we investigate the properties of this active column. Therefore we have to take a closer look at the linear transformation π_o which acts separately on the four columns. Let A denote the input state of π_o and let B denote the output state. Now we can write π_o as

$$B = \pi_o(A)$$
$$\Updownarrow$$
$$(B)_{ij} = \bigoplus_{k=0}^{3} \left((A)_{kj} \wedge M_{(i+k) \bmod 4} \right),$$

where $\wedge$ is the binary AND-operator and M_i with $i = 0, 1, \ldots, 3$ is a masking word, leaving 6 bits of every byte unmasked. For example $M_0 = $ 0x3fcff3fc. In state A we have one active byte which takes 256 different values over the Λ-set. Now π_o acts on this Λ-set generating one active column, in which each of the four bytes contains 6 bits of the original active byte of state A. Hence each byte of the active column of state B must take 64 different values, each occurring exactly 4 times.

Taking the EXOR of 4 times the same byte results in 0x00; state $B = \pi_o(A)$ is still balanced. In Figure 3 the new active bytes, which take 64 different values each occurring 4 times, are displayed with a white + symbol in a black square. τ is a simple matrix transposition, which only changes the positions of the bytes, but does not change their value. Thus, τ does not change the balancedness or the properties of the state scheme. $\sigma_{K_e^1}$ does not change the balancedness or the properties either.

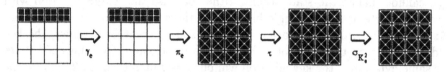

Fig. 4. State scheme through round 2

Round 2 Figure 4 shows the state scheme evolution through round 2. γ_e does not change the state scheme since γ_e will map a byte value occurring 4 times onto another byte value occurring 4 times. This does not change the EXOR-sum of the bytes, which remains 0x00.

π_e generates 16 active bytes (all bytes of the state are now active). Due to the specific structure of π_e (similar to that of π_o), each byte of the output state of π_e takes $n \leq 64$ different values. On a fixed position in the output state of π_e, every possible byte value (from 0x00 to 0xff) occurs either zero or a multiple of 4 times, due to π_e. On Figure 4 these bytes are shown as a white × symbol on a black square. This occurrence in multiples of 4 can be explained with the following example.

Suppose that we are working with nibbles [1]. We have a Λ-set consisting of 16 nibbles e.g. $\Lambda = \{1110, 1110, 1110, 1110, 1010, 1010, 1010, 1010, 1111, 1111, 1111, 1111, 0001, 0001, 0001, 0001\}$. We now have a similar situation as the real input Λ-set of π_e. Now we look at the effect of a binary nibble mask e.g. $M = 1110$ which leaves 3 of the 4 bits unmasked.

$1110 \wedge 1110 = 1110$	$1111 \wedge 1110 = 1110$
$1110 \wedge 1110 = 1110$	$1111 \wedge 1110 = 1110$
$1110 \wedge 1110 = 1110$	$1111 \wedge 1110 = 1110$
$1110 \wedge 1110 = 1110$	$1111 \wedge 1110 = 1110$
$1010 \wedge 1110 = 1010$	$0001 \wedge 1110 = 0000$
$1010 \wedge 1110 = 1010$	$0001 \wedge 1110 = 0000$
$1010 \wedge 1110 = 1010$	$0001 \wedge 1110 = 0000$
$1010 \wedge 1110 = 1010$	$0001 \wedge 1110 = 0000$

The table shows the effect of the bit masking. After the masking $\Lambda = \{1110, 1110, 1110, 1110, 1010, 1010, 1010, 1010, 1110, 1110, 1110, 1110, 0000, 0000, 0000, 0000\}$. Now the value 1110 occurs 8 times, the values 1010 and 0000 both

---

[1] nibble = four-bit quantity

occur 4 times, and the other possible nibble values do not occur at all. We see that the values in the resulting Λ-set occur in multiples of 4.

If we look at the real π_e then the only thing we do is masking (leaving unmasked 6 bits of every byte) and EXOR-additions. We can generalize our conclusion from above and say that on every byte position every byte value in the output state of π_e occurs in multiples of 4 over the Λ-set. This leaves the state balanced. τ and $\sigma_{K_e^2}$ do not change the state scheme or the balancedness for reasons mentioned before.

Fig. 5. State scheme through round 3

Round 3 γ_o does not change the state scheme properties or the balancedness since γ_o will map a byte value occurring a multiple of 4 times on another byte value occurring the same multiple of 4 times. This does not change the EXOR-sum of the bytes, which remains 0x00.

After π_o all bytes are still active but the different values no longer occur in multiples of four. This destroys our structure and limits the power of the whole attack. These active bytes are displayed in Figure 5 as grey squares. Nevertheless the scheme is still balanced because of the linearity of π_o. This can be proven as follows. Let A_a denote the balanced input state of π_o for the a-th element of the Λ-set, and let B_a denote the corresponding output state. Then we have the following:

$$B_a = \pi_o(A_a)$$

$$\Downarrow$$

$$\bigoplus_{a=0}^{255}((B_a)_{ij}) = \bigoplus_{a=0}^{255}\bigoplus_{k=0}^{3}\left(((A_a)_{kj}) \wedge M_{(i+k) \bmod 4}\right)$$

$$= \bigoplus_{k=0}^{3}\left(\underbrace{\bigoplus_{a=0}^{255}((A_a)_{kj})}_{=0x00} \wedge M_{(i+k) \bmod 4}\right)$$

$$= 0x00.$$

τ and $\sigma_{K_e^3}$ do not change the state scheme properties or the balancedness.

Round 4 The output of round 3 is balanced:

$$\bigoplus_{a=0}^{255}(R_3)_a = (0),$$

with (0) the all-zero state scheme $((0)_{ij} = \text{0x00}, \forall i, j)$. We drop the index a because the following formulae are valid for each element of the Λ-set. We have for the output of round 4:

$$R_4 = \rho_{eK_e^4}(R_3)$$
$$= \sigma_{K_e^4} \circ \tau \circ \pi_e \circ \gamma_e(R_3).$$

Taking the inverse of this formula and using the linearity of π_e and τ leads us to

$$R_3 = \gamma_o\left(\pi_e(\tau(R_4)) \oplus \pi_e(\tau(K_e^4))\right). \tag{1}$$

Since R_4 is known, we can determine $\pi_e(\tau(R_4))$ completely. Now we guess one of the 16 bytes of $\pi_e(\tau(K_e^4))$. Using (1) we can calculate R_3 for this byte position for all 256 members of our Λ-set. If the EXOR of all these values is zero then we have found a possible value for this key byte. We can do this independently for all 16 key bytes. Experiments show that only one or two values are possible for each key byte. If we do the same again starting with a different Λ-set, we can find the 128 bits of round key K_e^4 with overwhelming probability.

4 Calculation of the user key of 128 bits

In this section we show how to calculate the user key of 128 bits when we know one round key of 128 bits. In the previous section we have extracted round key K_e^4. The user key can now be calculated by taking into account the key expansion:

$$(V_e[3], V_e[2], V_e[1], V_e[0])^t = (\tau \circ \gamma_o \circ \sigma_P \circ \pi_o)((U[6], U[4], U[2], U[0])^t)$$
$$(V_e[7], V_e[6], V_e[5], V_e[4])^t = (\tau \circ \gamma_e \circ \sigma_Q \circ \pi_e)((U[7], U[5], U[3], U[1])^t)$$
$$T_0 = V_e[0] \oplus V_e[1] \oplus V_e[2] \oplus V_e[3]$$
$$T_1 = V_e[4] \oplus V_e[5] \oplus V_e[6] \oplus V_e[7]$$
$$E_e[i] = V_e[i] \oplus T_1 \text{ for } i = 0, 1, 2, 3$$
$$E_e[i] = V_e[i] \oplus T_0 \text{ for } i = 4, 5, 6, 7$$

with $U[i], i = 0, 1, \ldots, 7$ the user key and $E_e[i]$ the expanded keys. In [3] it is stated that if the user key is shorter than 256 bits it must be prepend by zero-words e.g. a 64-bit user key means $U[i] = \text{0x00000000}$ for $i > 1$.

We now try to calculate a 128-bit user key given K_e^4. Using appropriate shifts and constant additions we can easily find $E_e[0], E_e[1], E_e[2]$ and $E_e[3]$ given K_e^4

with the following formulae (see appendices in [3]):

$$K_e^4 = (K_e[19], K_e[18], K_e[17], K_e[16])^t$$
$$K_e[16] = E_e[0]^{\lll 8} \oplus RC_1$$
$$K_e[17] = E_e[1]^{\lll 24} \oplus RC_0$$
$$K_e[18] = E_e[2]^{\lll 16} \oplus RC_1$$
$$K_e[19] = E_e[3]^{\lll 8} \oplus RC_0.$$

Here $A^{\lll i}$ denotes the left-wise bit rotation of a 32-bit word A over i positions. The problem to be solved can be stated as follows : *Given $E_e[i]$ for $0 \leq i \leq 3$ calculate $U[i]$ for $0 \leq i \leq 3$ knowing that $U[j]$ for $4 \leq j \leq 7$ are all zero.* We are able to solve this problem with a byte-wise reconstruction of the unknown values T_0 and T_1.

Rightmost byte of T_1 (byte 0) First of all we have to guess byte 0 of T_1. This enables us to calculate byte 0 of $V_e[i]$ for $i = 0, 1, \ldots, 3$. Since

$$(V_e[3], V_e[2], V_e[1], V_e[0])^t = (\tau \circ \gamma_o \circ \sigma_P \circ \pi_o)((U[6], U[4], U[2], U[0])^t),$$

we find that

$$\sigma_P \circ \gamma_e \circ \tau (V_e[3], V_e[2], V_e[1], V_e[0])^t = \pi_o((U[6], U[4], U[2], U[0])^t).$$

We know the upper row of the left side of this expression. From the right side we know something about the structure of $\pi_o((U[6], U[4], U[2], U[0])^t)$ since $U[i] = $ 0x0 for $i = 4, 5, \ldots, 7$. This structure is:

2 + + 0	0 2 + +	+ 0 2 +	+ + 0 2
+ + 0 2	2 + + 0	0 2 + +	+ 0 2 +
+ 0 2 +	+ + 0 2	2 + + 0	0 2 + +
0 2 + +	+ 0 2 +	+ + 0 2	2 + + 0

The symbols in this scheme denote 2-bit quantities in the total state. The four symbols in the same row of a sub-group form together one byte of the state. E.g., 2 + + 0 in the top left corner denotes the leftmost byte of $U[0]^t$. A 0 or a 2 respectively indicate to copy the corresponding two bits of $U[0]$ or $U[2]$. A + indicates to write the EXOR of the corresponding two bits of $U[0]$ and $U[2]$. The scheme can be derived by taking into account the different masks used in the linear transformation π_o (see [3]).

Byte 1 of T_1 This byte can by found by checking the second row of $\pi_o((U[6], U[4], U[2], U[0])^t)$. The four 2-bit-positions in the scheme where we have a + symbol in the upper and the second row must contain the same 2-bit values. This results in approximately one possible value for byte 1 of T_1.

Byte 2 of T_1 This byte can be found by checking the third row of $\pi_o((U[6], U[4], U[2], U[0])^t)$. We can calculate in advance 12 2-bit-positions of the third row of the scheme since $s_1 \oplus s_2 = s_3$ with $s_1 s_2 s_3$ a random permutation of the symbols + 0 2. This also results in approximately one possible value for byte 2 of T_1.

Leftmost byte of T_1 (byte 3) Since we have the upper three rows of the scheme, we can calculate the lower row (using the same formula $s_1 \oplus s_2 = s_3$), and calculate back to the leftmost column of $(V_e[3], V_e[2], V_e[1], V_e[0])^t$. If we find four times the same value for the leftmost byte of T_1 by checking the $E_e[i]$ values, we have a possible user key. We do not expect that more than one valid user key can be found.

5 Addition of a fifth round at the end

In this section we add a fifth round in the end to the basic attack by guessing one column of round key K_e^5 at once. To recover K_e^4 we have to know only one of the 16 bytes of $\pi_e(\tau(R_4))$ at a time, so knowledge of one row of R_4 is sufficient. To add a fifth round to the attack we use the following formula:

$$R_5 = \sigma_{K_e^5} \circ \tau \circ \pi_o \circ \gamma_o(R_4)$$
$$\Downarrow$$
$$R_4 = \gamma_e \left(\pi_o(\tau(R_5)) \oplus \pi_o(\tau(K_e^5)) \right),$$

which is valid because of the linearity of π_o and τ.

If we guess a row of $\pi_o(\tau(K_e^5))$ we can calculate a single row of R_4 and a single column of $\pi_e(\tau(R_4))$. Since $R_3 = \gamma_o \left(\pi_e(\tau(R_4)) \oplus \pi_e(\tau(K_e^4)) \right)$ must be balanced, we can exclude approximately $\frac{255}{256}$ of our 2^{40} guessed key values (2^{32} for the row of $\pi_o(\tau(K_e^5))$ and 2^8 for the one byte of $\pi_e(\tau(K_e^4))$ gives 2^{40} guessed key values). This means that we have to repeat this procedure for at least 5 Λ-sets in order to find the round keys K_e^5 and K_e^4 from which we can calculate the entire 256-bit user key due to the simple key scheduling mechanism (see appendices in [3]).

6 Addition of a fifth round in the beginning

In this section we add a fifth round in the beginning to the basic attack. We try to generate Λ-sets with only one active byte (taking 256 different values) at the output of round 1. We start with a pool of 2^{32} plaintexts that differ only in the byte values of the first column. We assume a value for the 4 bytes of the first column of the first roundkey. This enables us to compose a few sets.

Let A be the desired output state of π_o of the first round and let PT be the plaintext state.

$$A = (\pi_o \circ \gamma_o \circ \sigma_{K_e^0})(PT)$$

$$\Updownarrow$$

$$PT = (\sigma_{K_e^0} \circ \gamma_e \circ \pi_o)(A)$$

$$= K_e^0 \oplus \gamma_e(\pi_o(A))$$

Since in $\gamma_e(\pi_o(A))$ only the first column is active, we can reuse the texts of our pool for every value of K_e^0. Given a Λ-set, we can recover the value of K_e^5 with our four round attack on rounds 2, 3, 4 and 5. We repeat the attack several times with different Λ-sets. If the values suggested for K_e^5 are inconsistent, we have made a wrong assumption for the column of K_e^0. With this method we can find K_e^0 and K_e^5, hence we can find the full 256 bits of the user key.

7 6-Round version of CRYPTON

The six round attack is a combination of the two previous extensions of the basic 4-round attack. Due to the specific generation of round key K_e^6 we can make an improvement of 2^{16} on the dedicated SQUARE attack, and recover the full 256 key bits.

We first guess 1 byte column of K_e^0 (2^{32} possibilities). For each guess we can generate some Λ-sets at the output of π_o of round 1 with the formula:

$$PT = \gamma_e(\pi_o(A)) \oplus K_e^0.$$

Addition of a round at the end requires the knowledge of a row of $\pi_e(\tau(K_e^6))$. If we know a column of K_e^0 then we also know 4 bytes of K_e^6:

$$K_e^0 = (K_e[3], K_e[2], K_e[1], K_e[0])^t$$
$$K_e[0] = E_e[0]$$
$$K_e[1] = E_e[1]$$
$$K_e[2] = E_e[2]$$
$$K_e[3] = E_e[3]$$
$$K_e^6 = (K_e[27], K_e[26], K_e[25], K_e[24])^t$$
$$K_e[24] = E_e[0]^{\lll 24} \oplus RC_1$$
$$K_e[25] = E_e[1]^{\lll 24} \oplus RC_{02}$$
$$K_e[26] = E_e[2]^{\lll 8} \oplus RC_1$$
$$K_e[27] = E_e[3]^{\lll 8} \oplus RC_{02}$$

If we want to know a row of $\pi_e(\tau(K_e^6))$ we have to know a column of K_e^6 and we have to guess only 16 bits instead of the full 32 bits as in the SQUARE attack if we choose the right columns of K_e^6.

This 6-round attack will recover K_e^0 and the equivalent K_e^6, but also K_e^5. From these values we can calculate $E_e[i]$ for $i = 0, 1, \ldots, 7$, hence we can calculate the entire 256-bit user key.

8   Conclusion

We have described attacks on several reduced round versions of the block cipher CRYPTON. Table 1 summarizes the requirements of the attacks. The 5-round (a) attack is described in section 5 and the 5-round (b) attack in section 6.

In its present form the described attack means no real threat to the full 12-round version of CRYPTON. However, after the discovery of weak keys [1, 6] of CRYPTON, this is the second time that the key scheduling of CRYPTON is brought into discredit.

Table 1. Requirements for the described attacks on CRYPTON.

Attack	# Plaintexts	Time	Memory
4-round	2^9	2^9	small
5-round (a)	2^{11}	2^{40}	small
5-round (b)	2^{32}	2^{40}	2^{32}
6-round	2^{32}	2^{56}	2^{32}

References

1. J. Borst, "Weak keys of Crypton," technical comment submitted to NIST.
2. J. Daemen, L. Knudsen and V. Rijmen, "The block cipher Square," *Fast Software Encryption, LNCS 1267*, E. Biham, Ed., Springer-Verlag, 1997, pp. 149–165.
3. Lim, "CRYPTON : A New 128-bit Block Cipher," available from [5].
4. Lim, "Specification and Analysis of Crypton Version 1.0," FSE '99, these proceedings.
5. NIST's AES home page, http://www.nist.gov/aes.
6. S. Vaudenay, "Weak keys in Crypton," announcement on NIST's electronic AES forum, cf. [5].

A   Attack on Six Rounds of CRYPTON version 1.0

In [4] a new version of CRYPTON is proposed, CRYPTON version 1.0. We explain briefly how to extend our results to version 1.0, which features two major changes.

1. The nonlinear transformations γ_o and γ_e use now two S-boxes instead of only one. This doesn't influence our attack
2. The key scheduling has been changed, both in the generation of the expanded keys and in the generation of the roundkeys from the expanded keys. This influences our attack, but we will see that the attack still applies.

A.1 Round key derivation in version 1.0

The relation between roundkey 0 and roundkey 6 is very important for the complexity of our attack. In the new version this relation is more complex and uses a new operation $A^{\lll_b i}$, which is defined as a left-wise bit rotation of each of the four bytes of the 32-bit word A. The new calculation of roundkey 0 and roundkey 6 is:

$$
\begin{array}{ll}
K_e[00] = E_e[0] & \oplus \; \text{0x09e35996} \\
K_e[01] = E_e[1] & \oplus \; \text{0xfc16ac63} \\
K_e[02] = E_e[2] & \oplus \; \text{0x17fd4788} \\
K_e[03] = E_e[3] & \oplus \; \text{0xc02a905f} \\
K_e[24] = (E_e[3]^{\lll_b 6})^{\lll 8} & \oplus \; \text{0xa345054a} \\
K_e[25] = (E_e[0]^{\lll_b 4})^{\lll 16} & \oplus \; \text{0x56b0f0bf} \\
K_e[26] = (E_e[1]^{\lll_b 4})^{\lll 24} & \oplus \; \text{0xbd5b1b54} \\
K_e[27] = (E_e[2]^{\lll_b 6})^{\lll 8} & \oplus \; \text{0x6a8ccc83}
\end{array}
$$

Notice that if we know one column of $(K_e[03], K_e[02], K_e[01], K_e[00])^t$ then we know 16 bytes of a certain column of $(K_e[27], K_e[26], K_e[25], K_e[24])^t$ because of the double occurrence of the $\cdot^{\lll 8}$ operator in the previous table. This is the reason why our six-round attack still works on version 1.0 with the gain of 2^{16} time.

B Calculation of the user key of 128 bits

B.1 Generation of the expanded key

We show in this section how we can calculate the 128-bit user key when we know one roundkey of 128 bits. In the specifications of CRYPTON version 1.0 [4] the new generation of the expanded keys is as follows.

Let $K = k_{u-1} \ldots k_1 k_0$ be a user key of u bytes ($u = 0, 1, \ldots, 32$). We assume that K is 256 bits long (by prepending by as many zeros as required).

1. Split the user key into U and V as: for $i = 0, 1, 2, 3$,

$$U[i] = k_{8i+6} k_{8i+4} k_{8i+2} k_{8i}, \qquad V[i] = k_{8i+7} k_{8i+5} k_{8i+3} k_{8i+1}.$$

2. Transform U and V using round transformations ρ_o and ρ_e, respectively, with all-zero round keys :

$$U' = \rho_o(U), \qquad V' = \rho_e(V).$$

3. Compute 8 expanded keys $E_e[i]$ for encryption as: for $i = 0, 1, 2, 3$,

$$E_e[i] = U'[i] \oplus T_1, \qquad E_e[i+4] = V'[i] \oplus T_0,$$

where $T_0 = \bigoplus_{i=0}^{3} U'[i]$ and $T_1 = \bigoplus_{i=0}^{3} V'[i]$.

Since we know that $U[i]$ and $V[i]$ are all-zero for $i = 2, 3$ we know the lower 2 rows of U and V. Since $U' = \tau \circ \pi_o \circ \gamma_o(U)$ we can calculate T_1, T_0 and the user key by a byte-wise reconstruction of T_1.

B.2 Reconstruction of the 128-bit user key

We have $\pi_o \circ \gamma_o(U) = \tau(U')$ with $U = (0x0, 0x0, U[1], U[0])^t$. Let $\gamma_o(U) = (b, a, 1', 0')^t$ with $b = 0x8d63b1b1$ and $a = 0xb18d63b1$. The a and b values can be calculated from the definition of γ_o and from the S-boxes [4]. Now we try to find the unknown values 0' and 1'.

If we guess byte 0 of T_1 (rightmost byte of T_1) it is possible to calculate the upper row of $\pi_o \circ \gamma_o(U)$. The structure of this state is:

0'	b	a	1'	1'	0'	b	a	a	1'	0'	b	b	a	1'	0'
b	a	1'	0'	0'	b	a	1'	1'	0'	b	a	a	1'	0'	b
a	1'	0'	b	b	a	1'	0'	0'	b	a	1'	1'	0'	b	a
1'	0'	b	a	a	1'	0'	b	b	a	1'	0'	0'	b	a	1'

The rows in this scheme are counted from top to bottom starting with row 0. The symbols in the scheme denote to copy the corresponding 2-bit values of the following 32-bit values:

$$\underline{0'} = (0' \oplus 1' \oplus a \oplus b) \oplus 0',$$
$$\underline{1'} = (0' \oplus 1' \oplus a \oplus b) \oplus 1',$$
$$\underline{a} = (0' \oplus 1' \oplus a \oplus b) \oplus a,$$
$$\underline{b} = (0' \oplus 1' \oplus a \oplus b) \oplus b.$$

Since we know the upper row of the scheme (due to our initial guess of byte 0 of T_1) we can calculate byte 1 of T_1 because we can calculate 4 times 2 bits of T_1 on the positions of the second row of the scheme where we find a $\underline{a}$ symbol (the symbols 1 in figure 6), because:

$$\underline{a} = (0' \oplus 1' \oplus a \oplus b) \oplus a$$
$$= (0' \oplus 1' \oplus a \oplus b) \oplus b \oplus b \oplus a$$
$$= \underline{b} \oplus (a \oplus b),$$

and we know $a \oplus b$. Now we can calculate row 1 of our scheme $\pi_o \circ \gamma_o(U)$ completely.

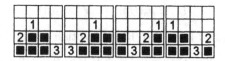

Fig. 6. 128-bit user key recovery

Next we calculate byte 2 of T_1 using the positions in row 2 where we find a $\underline{a}$ symbol (the symbols 2 in figure 6). We can check the correctness of byte 0 by checking 8 additional symbols in row 2 (the black squares in row 2 in figure 6) since we have the formulae:

$$\underline{a} \oplus \underline{1'} \oplus b = (0' \oplus 1' \oplus a \oplus b) \oplus a \oplus (0' \oplus 1' \oplus a \oplus b) \oplus 1' \oplus b$$
$$= (0' \oplus 1' \oplus a \oplus b) \oplus 0'$$
$$= \underline{0'}$$
$$\underline{1'} \oplus \underline{0'} \oplus a = \ldots$$
$$= \underline{b}.$$

and a and b are known in advance.

Finally we calculate byte 3 of T_1 using the formula $s_0 \oplus s_1 \oplus s_2 = s_3$ with $s_0 s_1 s_2 s_3$ a permutation of the symbols { $\underline{0'}$, $\underline{1'}$, $\underline{a}$, $\underline{b}$ }. If we obtain four times the same value for byte 3 (in each of the four columns), we have found T_1. If we obtain several different values for byte 3 of T_1 the initial assumption of byte 0 of T_1 was wrong and we have to continue guessing it.

If we have found a correct value for T_1 then we have found the state U' and U completely. So we can calculate $T_0 = \bigoplus_{i=0}^{3} U[i]$ so we have state V' and finally state V. $V[2]$ and $V[3]$ should both be 0x00000000.

On the Security of the 128-Bit Block Cipher DEAL

Stefan Lucks[*]

Theoretische Informatik
University of Mannheim, 68131 Mannheim A5, Germany
lucks@th.informatik.uni-mannheim.de

Abstract. DEAL is a DES-based block cipher proposed by Knudsen. The block size of DEAL is 128 bits, twice as much as the DES block size. The main result of the current paper is a certificational attack on DEAL-192, the DEAL variant with a 192-bit key. The attack allows a trade-off between the number of plaintext/ciphertext pairs and the time for the attacker's computations. Nevertheless, the DEAL design principle seems to be a useful way of doubling the block size of a given block cipher.

1 Introduction

The "data encryption standard" (DES) is the world's most well known symmetric cipher. Formally, the standard defines a 64-bit key, but 8 bits are defined as "parity bits" and only 56 bits are actually used as the encryption key, i.e., the DES key size is 56 bits. Brute-force attacks for recovering a key are feasible, today – and considered the only practical way of breaking DES. Thus, while the DES itself cannot be considered secure, it is still attractive to use it as a component for designing another cipher with an increased key size, such as triple DES. A concern both for DES and for triple DES is the block size of only 64 bits, which may lead to matching ciphertext attacks.

In [1], Knudsen proposes the r-round Feistel cipher DEAL with a block size of 128 bits. It uses DES in the round function and accepts three different key sizes, namely 128, 192, and 256 bits. For the first two sizes, the author recommends $r = 6$, for 256 bit keys, the number r of rounds should be 8. Depending on the key size, the three variants of DEAL are denoted DEAL-128, DEAL-192, and DEAL-256. DEAL is suggested as a candidate for the NIST AES standard.

This paper is organised as follows. In Section 2, a description of DEAL itself is given, Section 3 presents attacks on the six-round version of DEAL, and Section 4 deals with further concerns and conclusions.

---

[*] Supported by German Science Foundation (DFG) grant KR 1521/3-1.

2 A Description of DEAL

Next, we describe the block cipher DEAL and the key schedules for DEAL-128, DEAL-192, and DEAL-256.

2.1 The DEAL Core

A 128-bit plaintext is split up into two halves $(x_0, y_0) \in (\{0,1\}^{64})^2$. Two consecutive rounds j and $j + 1$ of DEAL take the 128-bit block $(x_{j-1}, y_{j-1}) \in (\{0,1\}^{64})^2$ and the two round keys R_j and R_{j+1} as the input to compute the output block $(x_{j+1}, y_{j+1}) \in (\{0,1\}^{64})^2$ by

$$x_j := x_{j-1}, \qquad\qquad y_j := y_{j-1} \oplus E_{R_j}(x_{j-1}),$$
$$x_{j+1} := x_j \oplus E_{R_{j+1}}(y_j), \quad \text{and} \quad y_{j+1} := y_j,$$

where $\oplus$ describes the bit-wise xor-operation for 64-bit strings and j is odd. By E, we denote the DES encryption function. Two rounds j and $j + 1$ are also described in Figure 1.

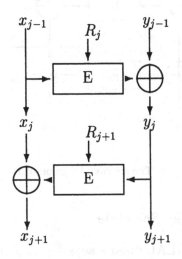

Fig. 1. Round j and $j + 1$ of DEAL, j odd

Thus, for DEAL-128 and DEAL-192 we need 6 round keys $R_1, \ldots R_6$, for DEAL 256 we need 8 round keys $R_1, \ldots R_8$. Internally, every round key is used as a DES key, ignoring the "parity bits" and hence consists of 56 bits. We need three "key scheduling" algorithms to generate the round keys from the given master key of 128, 192, or 256 bits.

See Figure 2 for a visual description of six rounds of DEAL.

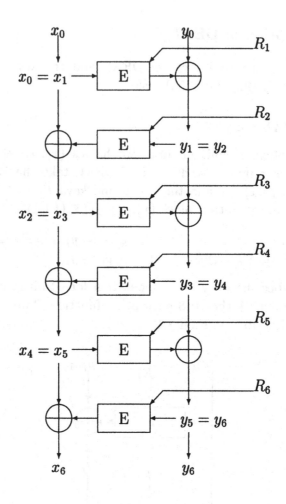

Fig. 2. The six-round version of DEAL

2.2 The DEAL Key Schedule

The key schedule of DEAL takes s keys $K_1, \ldots, K_s$ of 64 bits each ($s \in \{2, 3, 4\}$) and returns r round keys $R_1, \ldots, R_r$ of 56 bits each ($r \in \{6, 8\}$). The round keys are generated using DES encryption under a fixed DES-key R_* (which is $R_* = \texttt{0123456789abcdef}$ in hexadecimal notation). $\underline{1}$, $\ldots$, $\underline{4}$ are four different constant 64-bit strings, where none is $000\ldots0$. The DEAL-128 round keys are generated from K_1, K_2 as follows:

$$R_1 := E_{R_*}(K_1)$$
$$R_2 := E_{R_*}(K_2 \oplus R_1)$$
$$R_3 := E_{R_*}(K_1 \oplus R_2 \oplus \underline{1})$$

$$R_4 := E_{R_*}(K_2 \oplus R_3 \oplus \underline{2})$$
$$R_5 := E_{R_*}(K_1 \oplus R_4 \oplus \underline{3})$$
$$R_6 := E_{R_*}(K_2 \oplus R_5 \oplus \underline{4})$$

The DEAL-192 round keys are generated from K_1, K_2, and K_3 like this:

$$R_1 := E_{R_*}(K_1)$$
$$R_2 := E_{R_*}(K_2 \oplus R_1)$$
$$R_3 := E_{R_*}(K_3 \oplus R_2)$$
$$R_4 := E_{R_*}(K_1 \oplus R_3 \oplus \underline{1})$$
$$R_5 := E_{R_*}(K_2 \oplus R_4 \oplus \underline{2})$$
$$R_6 := E_{R_*}(K_3 \oplus R_5 \oplus \underline{3})$$

Given K_1, K_2, K_3, and K_4, the DEAL-256 round keys are:

$$R_1 := E_{R_*}(K_1)$$
$$R_2 := E_{R_*}(K_2 \oplus R_1)$$
$$R_3 := E_{R_*}(K_3 \oplus R_2)$$
$$R_4 := E_{R_*}(K_4 \oplus R_3)$$
$$R_5 := E_{R_*}(K_1 \oplus R_4 \oplus \underline{1})$$
$$R_6 := E_{R_*}(K_2 \oplus R_5 \oplus \underline{2})$$
$$R_7 := E_{R_*}(K_3 \oplus R_6 \oplus \underline{3})$$
$$R_8 := E_{R_*}(K_4 \oplus R_7 \oplus \underline{4})$$

The parity bits of the 64-bit values R_i are ignored when R_i is used as a DES-key (i.e., a DEAL round key), but relevant for computing R_{i+1}.

3 Attacking DEAL

Well known meet-in-the-middle techniques can be used to recover the DEAL round keys. This was stressed by Knudsen himself. The six-round version of DEAL is vulnerable to a meet-in-the-middle attack requiring roughly $(2^{56})^3 = 2^{168}$ encryptions. For the eight-round version, the attack needs roughly $(2^{56})^4 = 2^{224}$ encryptions.

Thus the theoretical key size of DEAL is approximately no more than 168 for the six-round version and 224 for the eight-round version. This bounds the theoretical key size of DEAL-192 (six rounds) and DEAL-256 (eight rounds). Due to their memory requirements, these meet-in-the-middle techniques are quite unrealistic, though trade-off techniques to save storage space at the cost of increased running time are known [3].

Note that finding a DEAL-n key by exhaustive key search (by "brute force") takes about $c * 2^n/2$ single DES encryptions with $c = 8$ for DEAL-192, $c = 9$ for DEAL-128, and $c = 11$ for DEAL-256. (One can reject most combinations of round keys *before* the last round. I.e., rejecting a combination of round keys takes about 5 DES encryptions for the six-round variants of DEAL and about 7 DES encryptions for the eight-round variant. In the case of DEAL-192, we need to generate the first two round keys at most every 2^{64} steps, while the round keys R_3, R_4, and R_5 are generated every step. This takes about 3 DES encryptions. The reasoning for DEAL-128 and DEAL-256 is similar.)

3.1 A Chosen Ciphertext Attack for the Six-Round Version

In addition to meet-in-the-middle attacks, Knudsen describes a chosen plaintext attack to recover the round keys of the six-round version of DEAL. His attack requires about 2^{121} DES-encryptions using roughly 2^{70} chosen plaintexts. This is significantly faster than the average number of DES-encryptions needed to break DEAL-128 by exhaustive key search (i.e., 2^{127} encryptions) and greatly faster than the number of DES-encryptions to break DEAL-192 (2^{191}). Due to the huge amount of chosen plaintexts, Knudsen claims that exhaustive key search nevertheless is less unrealistic than this attack.

We will use the same technique, but we are going backwards, i.e., our attack is a chosen ciphertext attack to gain information about the first round key R_1. Given the first 56-bit round key R_1, there are only 2^8 possible choices for the first sub-key K_1 of the master key. Knowing the last 56-bit round key instead of the first one, is somewhat less helpful for the attacker, due to the DEAL key schedule.

Recall the last five rounds of six-round DEAL. The round keys in use are $R_2, \ldots, R_6$, the input is the pair (x_1, y_1) of 64-bit strings (where $x_1 = x_0$ is the left half of the plaintext and y_1 is generated in the first round by $y_1 = y_0 \oplus E_{R_1}(x_1)$), and the output is the ciphertext (x_6, y_6). Consider two input/output pairs $((x_1, y_1), (x_6, y_6))$ and $((x_1', y_1'), (x_6', y_6'))$ with $y_1 = y_1'$, $y_6 = y_6'$, $x_1 \oplus x_1' = \alpha = x_6 \oplus x_6'$ and $\alpha \neq 0$.

First, we show that two such input/output pairs cannot both exist: Since $y_1 = y_1'$ and $y_6 = y_6'$, we have $x_3 \oplus x_3' = \alpha = x_5 \oplus x_5'$. On the other hand, $y_1 = y_2 = y_1' = y_2'$ and $x_1 \neq x_1'$, thus $y_3 = y_2 \oplus E_{R_3}(x_2) \neq y_3'$ and hence $E_{R_4}(y_3) \neq E_{R_4}(y_3')$. If $x_3 \oplus x_3' = \alpha$, then $x_5 \oplus x_5' = \alpha \oplus E_{R_4}(y_3) \oplus E_{R_4}(y_3') \neq \alpha$, in contradiction to the above.

Next, we exploit their non-existence to narrow down the number of possibilities for R_1 and hence K_1:

- Choose a fixed value $y_6 \in \{0,1\}^{64}$ and 2^{64} ciphertexts (s, y_6), where $s \in \{0,1\}^{64}$. Let $(x_0[s], y_0[s])$ denote the corresponding plaintexts. Then we expect to find about 2^{63} two-sets $\{s, t\} \subset \{0,1\}^{64}$ with $s \neq t$ and $x_0[s] \oplus x_0[t] = s \oplus t$.
- Check all possible 56-bit DES keys R, whether

$$y_0[s] \oplus E_R(x_0[s]) = y_0[t] \oplus E_R(x_0[t]).$$

As we have shown above, this is impossible if $R = R_1$. Hence, if "=" holds, we know $R \neq R_1$, which limits further key search. If $R \neq R_1$, the operation $E_R : \{0,1\}^{64}$ can be viewed as a random permutation, hence in this case "=" holds with a probability of 2^{-64}. Given 2^{63} such two-sets $\{s, t\}$, we expect to have reduced the possible choices for R_1 by 50%.

At first, we have 2^{56} choices for R_1, and the attack takes about $2^{63} * 2^{65} * 2 = 2^{120}$ DES-encryptions to reduce the number of choices for R_1 down to 2^{55}. Repeating the attack, we need another 2^{119} DES encryptions to reduce the number of choices down to 2^{54}, another 2^{118} DES encryptions to reduce it to 2^{53}, ..., hence we may pin down R_1 by doing no more than 2^{121} DES encryptions. This leaves open 2^8 choices for K_1.

Now, the complete master key can easily be recovered by exhaustive key search techniques. In the case of DEAL-128, we need $2^{64} * 2^8 = 2^{72}$ trials to find (K_1, K_2). For DEAL-192, we need $2^{64} * 2^{64} * 2^8 = 2^{136}$ trials to recover (K_1, K_2, K_3). Here though, exhaustive key search is not optimal. Since we have found the first round key of a six-round Feistel cipher, recovering the second round key requires a similar attack on a five-round Feistel cipher and hence is even simpler.

Theoretically, this attack is much better than exhaustive key search, and meet-in-the-middle. But due to the huge amount of chosen ciphertexts required, it is quite impractical.

3.2 A Dedicated Attack for DEAL-192

Next, we describe another chosen ciphertext attack. This attack takes more time than the previous one, but only needs $2^{32+\tau}$ chosen ciphertexts (with $0 < \tau \le 32$) instead of 2^{64}. E.g., for $\tau = 0.5$ the keyspace is reduced by about 50 %.

Recall the last four rounds of six-round DEAL, using the round keys R_3, R_4, R_5, and R_6. The input to the last four rounds is $(x_2, y_2) \in \{0,1\}^{64}$, the output is $(x_6, y_6) \in \{0,1\}^{64}$. Consider two input/output pairs $((x_2, y_2), (x_6, y_6))$ and $((x'_2, y'_2), (x'_6, y'_6))$ with $y_6 = y'_6$, $x_2 \oplus x'_2 = \alpha = x_6 \oplus x'_6$ and $\alpha \ne 0$. (The value $y_2 \oplus y'_2$ may be arbitrary.)

Two such input/output pairs cannot both exist: Since $x_6 \oplus x'_6 = \alpha$ and $y_6 = y'_6$, we have $x_5 \oplus x'_5 = \alpha = x_4 \oplus x'_4$, and hence $y_4 \oplus y'_4 \ne 0$. On the other hand, since $x_2 \oplus x'_2 = x_3 \oplus x'_3 = \alpha$, and $x_5 \oplus x'_5 = \alpha = x_4 \oplus x'_4$, we need $y_3 \oplus y'_3 = 0$. This is in contradiction to $y_4 = y_3$ and $y'_4 = y'_3$.

As above, we exploit the non-existence of such pairs for key recovery purposes:

- Choose a fixed value $y_6 = y'_6 \in \{0,1\}^{64}$ and $2^{32+\tau}$ different values $s \in \{0,1\}^{64}$, which gives $2^{32+\tau}$ different ciphertexts (s, y_6). Consider two such ciphertexts (x_6, y_6) and $(x'_6, y'_6))$ with $x_6 \ne x'_6$ and the corresponding plaintexts (x_0, y_0) and (x'_0, y'_0).
- For all possible 56-bit round keys R, compute $y_1 = y_0 \oplus E_R(x_0)$ and $y'_1 = y'_0 \oplus E_R(x'_0)$.
- For all possible 56-bit round keys S, compute $x_2 = x_1 \oplus E_S(y_1)$, and $x'_2 = x'_1 \oplus E_S(y'_1)$. If

$$x_2 \oplus x'_2 = x_6 \oplus x'_6,$$

then the key pair (R, S) can be discarded, i.e., $(R_1, R_2) \ne (R, S)$.

If (R, S) is the wrong key pair, we expect "=" to hold with a probability of 2^{-64}. Since we have $2^{32+\tau}$ chosen ciphertexts and thus $\binom{2^{32+\tau}}{2}$ $\approx 2^{2(32+\tau)}/2 \approx 2^{64} * 2^{2\tau-1}$ sets of exactly two ciphertexts, we expect the fraction of the candidates for (R_1, R_2) to be discarded to be roughly $1 - 2^{-2\tau}$, e.g. roughly 50 % for $\tau = 0.5$.

On a first look, the attack seems to require $2^{32+\tau} * 2^{56} * 2^{56} = 2^{144+\tau}$ single encryptions. Actually, if either of the round keys R and S is wrong, we expect to find values x_2, x'_2, x_6, and x'_6 with

$$x_2 \oplus x'_2 = x_6 \oplus x'_6,$$

after considering less than 2^{33} plaintext ciphertext pairs, on the average. No more encryption operations (or decryption operations) are needed to reject the pair (R, S) of round keys. Hence, the expected number of single encryptions is below $2^{33} * 2^{112} = 2^{145}$. Since $145 > 128$, this attack is not useful for DEAL-128.

On the other hand, the attack actually is useful for DEAL-192, the DEAL-variant with a key size of 192 bit. Note that the attack only narrows down the number of 192-bit keys from 2^{192} to about $2^{192-2\tau}$, i.e., on the average $8 * 2^{192-2\tau}/2$ additional single DES encryption are needed to find the correct key by brute force.

3.3 The Memory Requirements

For the attack described in Section 3.1, we need to store about 2^{64} plaintexts, each of 128 bit. This requires 2^{71} bits of memory – all other memory requirements are negligible, compared to this.

For the attack described in Section 3.2, the attacker apparently has to store all those about $2^{112-2\tau}$ 56-bit keys for the first two rounds, which are not discarded. The correct 56-bit key pair is not discarded, and can be found by further testing. Given a 56-bit key pair $(R, S) \in (\{0,1\}^{56})^2$, the "further testing" can be done by exhaustively searching $2^{8+8+64} = 2^{80}$ 64-bit key triples corresponding to (R, S) to find the correct one. If all 2^{80} key triples corresponding to the pair (R, S) are wrong, then (R, S) is wrong, too. Instead of storing the pairs (R, S) and later do the "further testing", one may test immediately and save the storage space.

What then dominates the storage space for the attack described in Section 3.2 is the necessity to store $2^{32+\tau}$ plaintexts, i.e., $2^{39+\tau}$ bits. The attack in Section 3.2 improves on the attack in Section 3.1 both with respect to storage space and to the number of chosen ciphertexts.

Table 1 shows the requirements for the attack in Section 3.2, depending on the parameter τ, i.e., the required number of chosen ciphertexts, the approximate number of single DES encryptions, and the approximate number of storage bits.

Table 1. Requirements for the attack from Section 3.2

parameter	chosen ciphertexts	single encryptions	memory
τ	$2^{32+\tau}$	$8 * 2^{191-2\tau} + 2^{145}$	$2^{39+\tau}$ bit
0.5	$2^{32.5}$	$8 * 2^{190}$	$2^{39.5}$ bit
1	2^{33}	$8 * 2^{189}$	2^{40} bit
8	2^{40}	$8 * 2^{175}$	2^{47} bit
16	2^{48}	$8 * 2^{159}$	2^{55} bit
24	2^{56}	$8 * 2^{143} + 2^{145}$	2^{63} bit

3.4 Chosen Plaintext Attacks

The chosen ciphertext attacks we described in Sections 3.1 and 3.2 target on the first round key R_1 or the first two round keys R_1 and R_2. In principle, these attacks do not depend on any key schedule but work well with DEAL-versions with independent round keys. For reasons of symmetry, they can also be run backwards as chosen plaintext attacks, then recovering the last round key or the last two round keys. In fact, the attack described in Section 3.1 can be viewed as the backward version of the chosen plaintext attack on DEAL with independent round keys, described by Knudsen [1]. (The attack in section 3.2 is new, though.)

The reason why we considered chosen ciphertext attacks instead of the possibly more natural chosen plaintext attacks, is the DEAL key schedule. It enables a more simple exploitation of knowing the first or the first two round keys, than knowing the last or the last two ones.

4 Final Remarks

4.1 The Effective Key Size

From a general point of view, the designer of a new cryptosystem should be pessimistic. I.e., when trying to evaluate the effective key size of a cipher, known standard techniques (such as meet in the middle) should be taken into consideration, even if they appear to be very unrealistic. This defines a safety margin, valuable if new and more practical attacks are found.

Thus, we consider the effective key size of DEAL-128 to be 121 bits (or less) and the effective key size of DEAL-256 to be no more than 224 bits. The effective key size of DEAL-192 is 121 bits (or less). In this sense, DEAL-192 does not improve on DEAL-128. If a variant of DEAL is needed faster than DEAL-256 but with an effective key-size of more than 121 bits, a seven-round version of DEAL would be appropriate.

4.2 The DEAL Key Schedule

The DEAL key-schedule is based on using slow but powerful encryption operations. On the other hand, the first round key R_1 does not depend on all (master-)sub-keys K_i (neither does R_2 depend on all sub-keys of DEAL-192 and DEAL-256, neither does R_3 depend on all sub-keys of DEAL-256). Once we have recovered R_1 (and/or R_2, R_3), recovering the complete master key is more easy than necessary. Under ideal circumstances, with randomly chosen keys $K_i \in \{0,1\}^{64}$, independently and according to the uniform probability distribution, this is a minor concern.

But Vaudenay [4] observed the following:

If the choice of the keys K_i is restricted, the attacks described in this paper can be improved. Think of the bytes of the keys K_i being restricted to a set of $c < 2^7$ printable characters. This indicates that there are only c^8 choices for K_i, and c^{24} choices for a DEAL-192 key. Since the number of choices for R_1 is reduced to c^8 instead of 2^{56} the attack in Section 3.1 becomes $2^{56}/c^8$ times faster. (Note that there is no speed-up for corresponding chosen plaintext attack described by Knudsen [1], since the number of choices for R_6 still is 2^{56}.) Similarly, the required number single encryptions for the attack in Section 3.2 is reduced to $8 * c^{24} * 2^{-2\tau} * 2^{-1} + 2^{33} * c^{16}$, instead of $8 * 2^{3*64} * 2^{-2\tau} * 2^{-1} + 2^{33} * 2^{2*56}$.

If we think of, say, $c = 64 = 2^6$, the effective key size of DEAL-192 is reduced to 144 bit. The attack in Section 3.1 would become 2^8 times faster. Depending on τ, the speed-up for the attack in Section 3.2 would be between 2^{16} and 2^{48}.

Also note that if a part of the key is compromised, then the security of DEAL depends on *which part* is compromised. E.g., if 64 bits of a DEAL-192 key are compromised, the remaining security should still be about the security of DEAL-128. Apparently, this is no problem if the 64 bits of K_3 are compromised. But if the attacker knows K_1, she effectively has to attack a five-round variant of DEAL with a 128-bit key, instead of something comparable to six-round DEAL-128.

Our concern regarding the key schedule could easily be fixed, requiring one additional encryption for DEAL-128, two for DEAL-192, and three for DEAL-256, applying the the same general design principle all DEAL key schedules are based on. For DEAL-128, we propose to use $R_2, \ldots,$ R_7 as the round keys (and hence throwing away R_1 after running the key schedule), where

$$R_7 := E_{R_*}(K_1 \oplus R_6 \oplus \underline{5}),$$

where $\underline{5}$ is a constant different from $000\ldots0$, $\underline{1}$, $\underline{2}$, $\underline{3}$, and $\underline{4}$. Similar modifications for DEAL-192 and DEAL-256 are obvious.

Note that the additional encryption operations require only between 1/6 and 3/8 of the time for the original key schedule, hence the slow-down for the above modification should be acceptable.

4.3 Conclusions and Open Problem

In spite of these concerns, DEAL is a simple but useful way of constructing a new block cipher based on another block cipher E, doubling the block size. There is no limitation to E=DES. One could as well view DEAL as a "mode of operation" of the underlying block cipher E, instead of a block cipher of its own right.

One may reasonably expect DEAL to be significantly more secure than its building block DES. It would be interesting to actually *prove* this, assuming the security of the underlying building block. This has been done before for cryptographic primitives based on other primitives, e.g. for the DES-based 64-bit block cipher DESX [2]. Such a result may seen as a justification of the construction's soundness, though the actual security of the construction also depends on the security of the underlying block cipher.

Acknowledgements

After discussing the DEAL security with me, Rüdiger Weis was perpetually nagging, waiting for the first version of this paper to be finished. I also thank Don Coppersmith for suggesting an improvement of the attack in Section 3.2 and Richard Outerbridge for discussing the key schedule. I appreciate the comments from the members of the program committee and their help in improving this presentation.

References

1. L. Knudsen: "DEAL – a 128-bit Block Cipher", February 21, 1998, revised May 15, 1998: http://www.ii.uib.no/~larsr/aes.html.
2. J. Kilian, P. Rogaway: "How to Protect DES Against Exhaustive Key Search", Neal Koblitz (ed.), Advances in Cryptology: Crypto '96, Springer LNCS 1109, 252–267, full version online:
   http://wwwcsif.cs.ucdavis.edu/~rogaway/papers/list.html.
3. P. van Oorschot, M. Wiener, "Improving Implementable Meet-in-the-Middle Attacks by Orders of Magnitude", Crypto '96 Springer LNCS 1109, 229–236.
4. S. Vaudenay, "On Comparing the Security of Block Ciphers", manuscript, 1998.

Cryptanalysis of a Reduced Version of the Block Cipher $E2$

Mitsuru Matsui and Toshio Tokita

Information Technology R&D Center
Mitsubishi Electric Corporation
5-1-1, Ofuna, Kamakura, Kanagawa, 247, Japan
matsui@iss.isl.melco.co.jp, tokita@iss.isl.melco.co.jp

Abstract. This paper deals with truncated differential cryptanalysis of the 128-bit block cipher $E2$, which is an AES candidate designed and submitted by NTT. Our analysis is based on byte characteristics, where a difference of two bytes is simply encoded into one bit information "0" (the same) or "1" (not the same). Since $E2$ is a strongly byte-oriented algorithm, this bytewise treatment of characteristics greatly simplifies a description of its probabilistic behavior and noticeably enables us an analysis independent of the structure of its (unique) lookup table. As a result, we show a non-trivial seven round byte characteristic, which leads to a possible attack of $E2$ reduced to eight rounds without IT and FT by a chosen plaintext scenario. We also show that by a minor modification of the byte order of output of the round function — which does not reduce the complexity of the algorithm nor violates its design criteria at all —, a non-trivial nine round byte characteristic can be established, which results in a possible attack of the modified $E2$ reduced to ten rounds without IT and FT, and reduced to nine rounds with IT and FT. Our analysis does not have a serious impact on the full $E2$, since it has twelve rounds with IT and FT; however, our results show that the security level of the modified version against differential cryptanalysis is lower than the designers' estimation.

1   Introduction

$E2$ [1] is a 128-bit block cipher designed by NTT, which is one of the fifteen candidates in the first round of the AES project. Its design criteria are conservative, adopting a Feistel network and a lookup table without shift and arithmetic operations (except multiplications in the initial transformation IT and the final transformation FT). Moreover $E2$ has a strongly byte-oriented structure; all operations used in the data randomization phase are byte table lookups and byte xor's except 32-bit multiplications in IT and FT, which successfully makes $E2$ a fast software cipher independent of target platforms, e.g. 8-bit microprocessors to 64-bit RISC computers.

This byte-oriented structure motivates us to cryptanalyze $E2$ by initially looking at relationship between the number/location of input byte changes and that of output byte changes. For instance, one byte change of input of the round function always results in five or six byte change of its output, which is a part of the design criteria of $E2$. However, when we change plural input bytes, say two bytes simultaneously, it is possible that only three output bytes are changed with the remaining five bytes unchanged.

Since the round function of $E2$ has eight input/output bytes, its bytewise change pattern can be represented by eight-bit information where a difference of two bytes is encoded into one bit information "0" (the same) or "1" (not the same). In this paper we call this change pattern "byte characteristic" or simply characteristic. Due to this simplification, it is not hard to create a complete 256×256 characteristic distribution table that exhausts all possibilities of input/output byte change patterns of the round function.

The next step of our analysis is to establish byte characteristics of the whole cipher and to find effective ones. Since the characteristics consist of sixteen bits, even a complete search for the best characteristic is possible in terms of computational complexity. We have reached an "iterative" byte characteristic of $E2$, which is non-trivial up to seven rounds. This leads to a possible attack of $E2$ reduced to eight rounds without IT and FT using 2^{100} chosen plaintext message blocks.

Also, we show that by a minor modification of the byte order of the output of the round function — which corresponds to change of BRL function [1] but does not reduce the complexity of the algorithm nor violates its design criteria at all —, a non-trivial nine round byte characteristic can be obtained, which results in a possible attack of the modified $E2$ reduced to ten rounds without IT and FT, and reduced to nine rounds with IT and FT using 2^{94} and 2^{91} chosen plaintext message blocks, respectively.

It should be pointed out that our analysis does not make use of the structure information of the lookup table; that is, our results hold for any (bijective) lookup table. However we will effectively use the fact that $E2$ has only one lookup table. This means that if $E2$ would have many different tables in its round function, our attack could be (sometimes) harder. We will state the reason of this phenomenon in a later section.

Our analysis does not have a serious impact on the full $E2$, since it has twelve rounds with IT and FT; however our results show that the security level of the modified version against differential cryptanalysis is lower than the designers' general estimation, which is applicable to both of the real and the modified $E2$.

2 Preliminaries

Figure 1 shows the entire structure of $E2$. Figures 2 to 4 shows its round function, initial transformation and final transformation, respectively. In these figures the broken lines show subkey information, where we do not treat its key scheduling part. The notations in these figures will be used throughout this paper. For the exact detail, see [1]. For readers' convenience, we give algebraic description of the variable d_i in the round function in terms of the intermediate values c_i as follows:

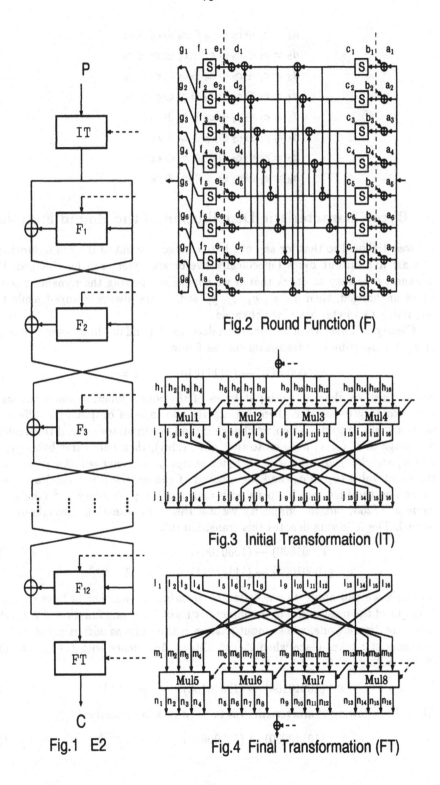

Fig.2 Round Function (F)

Fig.3 Initial Transformation (IT)

Fig.4 Final Transformation (FT)

Fig.1 E2

$$d_1 = c_2 \oplus c_3 \oplus c_4 \oplus c_5 \oplus c_6 \oplus c_7$$
$$d_2 = c_1 \oplus c_3 \oplus c_4 \oplus c_6 \oplus c_7 \oplus c_8$$
$$d_3 = c_1 \oplus c_2 \oplus c_4 \oplus c_5 \oplus c_7 \oplus c_8$$
$$d_4 = c_1 \oplus c_2 \oplus c_3 \oplus c_5 \oplus c_6 \oplus c_8$$
$$d_5 = c_1 \oplus c_2 \oplus c_4 \oplus c_5 \oplus c_6$$
$$d_6 = c_1 \oplus c_2 \oplus c_3 \oplus c_6 \oplus c_7$$
$$d_7 = c_2 \oplus c_3 \oplus c_4 \oplus c_7 \oplus c_8$$
$$d_8 = c_1 \oplus c_3 \oplus c_4 \oplus c_5 \oplus c_8$$

3 Byte Characteristic Distribution of the Round Function

$E2$ was designed so that for any one byte change of input of the round function, at least five output bytes (specifically five or six bytes) can be changed. For instance, it is easy to check that if we change a_1, leaving the remaining seven bytes unchanged, then g_1, g_2, g_3, g_4, g_5 and g_7 are always changed while the remaining two bytes are never changed.

Clearly this pattern of byte location does not depend on the amount of change of a_1. We describe this transition rule as follows:

$$(10000000) \rightarrow (11111010) \qquad p = 1. \tag{1}$$

Next, when we change two input bytes of the round function simultaneously, it is also easy to see that there are exactly two cases of output byte difference patterns. For example, when we change a_1 and a_5 simultaneously, if the amount of change of c_1 (Δc_1) is equal to that of c_5 (Δc_5), then only three bytes g_1, g_5 and g_8 are changed, otherwise all bytes except g_6 are changed. Assuming that the input value (a_1 to a_8) and the amount of change (Δa_1 and Δa_5) are given randomly, the first case happens with approximate probability 2^{-8} (the exact value is 1/255, but for simplicity we use this approximation throughout this paper). The following denotes this transition rule:

$$(10001000) \rightarrow (10001001) \qquad p = 2^{-8}, \tag{2}$$
$$(10001000) \rightarrow (11111011) \qquad p = 1 - 2^{-8}. \tag{3}$$

Similarly we can apply this notation to an arbitrary number of byte changes. Now one of the most useful byte characteristics of the round function of $E2$ is the following "cyclic" one, whose input pattern is the same as output pattern. This characteristic takes place when $\Delta c_1 = \Delta c_4 = \Delta c_6$, hence with the probability $(2^{-8})^2 = 2^{-16}$:

$$(10010100) \rightarrow (10010100) \qquad p = 2^{-16}. \tag{4}$$

Also, the following characteristic will be used in a later section:

$$(10110000) \rightarrow (10000010) \qquad p = 2^{-16}. \tag{5}$$

4 Byte Characteristic Distribution of $E2$

Using the cyclic characteristic shown in (4), we can obtain a seven round characteristic of $E2$ (without IT and FT) as shown in figure 5. Note that an xor operation outside the round function may cancel differences; that is $1 \oplus 1 = 0$ with probability $1/255$ and $1 \oplus 1 = 1$ with probability $254/255$. For simplicity again, we will regard these probabilities as 2^{-8} and 1, respectively. In figure 5, this cancellation happens three times (three bytes) at an xor operation after the sixth round function. As a result, the seven round characteristic holds with approximate probability $(2^{-16})^5 \times 2^{-24} = 2^{-104}$.

This means that when we change the first, fourth and sixth bytes of the plaintext block simultaneously without changing other bytes, then after the seventh round, the probability that the three bytes of the same location change and other bytes do not change becomes 2^{-104}. On the other hand, if the round function is a random function, the same change is expected to appear with probability $(2^{-8})^{13} = 2^{-104}$ again, since the number of unchanged bytes is thirteen. Therefore the expected number of "correct pairs" is the same as that of "wrong pairs".

Now remember that the correct pairs can be detected with probability 2^{-104} under the assumption that the amount of differences of the specified input bytes (Δa_1, Δa_4 and Δa_6 in this case) are given randomly. However if we are able to give plaintext pairs with non random differences in a chosen plaintext scenario, this probability may be greater. In fact when we generate input plaintext pairs such that the equation $\Delta a_1 = \Delta a_4 = \Delta a_6$ holds, then the transition probability of the second round function jumps to approximately 9.3×2^{-16}, not 2^{-16}, which is an experimental result. The reason of this increase is based on the fact that the following probability is significantly larger than 2^{-8} when $\Delta x = \Delta y$, while it is expected to be 2^{-8} in average when $\Delta x \neq \Delta y$.

$$P(\Delta x, \Delta y) \stackrel{def}{=} Prob_{x,y}\{S(x) \oplus S(x \oplus \Delta x) = S(y) \oplus S(y \oplus \Delta y)\}. \qquad (6)$$

The exact probability of $P(\Delta x, \Delta y)$ depends on the structure of the substitution table S, but it is easy to prove that for any S, $P(\Delta x, \Delta y)$ is larger than 2^{-8} when $\Delta x = \Delta y$. Also it should be pointed out that this phenomenon can be utilized in our analysis of $E2$ because $E2$ has only one substitution table in its round function. If the function S of the left hand side differs from that of the right hand side in the above definition, the distribution of $P(\Delta x, \Delta y)$ will be "flat", independent of Δx and Δy.

5 Possible Scenarios of an Attack of E2

5.1 $E2$ reduced to seven rounds without IT and FT

The discussions in the previous section show that for $E2$ reduced to seven rounds, when 2^{104} chosen plaintext pairs such that $\Delta P_1 = \Delta P_4 = \Delta P_6$ are given, the expected number of ciphertext pairs that have the difference pattern (10010100

00000000) is 9.3, where P_1, P_4 and P_6 denote the first, the fourth and the sixth byte of plaintext, respectively. Note that these plaintext pairs can be obtained using 2^{97} plaintexts message blocks (97=104-8+1); for instance, they are given as the direct product set of all possible 2^{64} patterns of the left half of plaintexts and arbitrarily chosen 2^{33} patterns of the right half.

On the other hand, for a random permutation with the same chosen plaintext pairs, the expected number of ciphertext pairs that have the difference pattern (10010100 00000000) is 1. This leads to the following scenario for distinguishing $E2$ reduced to seven rounds from a random permutation:

For a given cipher, if the number of ciphertext pairs that have the difference pattern (10010100 00000000) is equal to or greater than a pre-determined value t, regard it as $E2$ reduced to seven rounds, otherwise regard it as a random permutation.

To estimate an appropriate value for t, we need the following lemma, which can be easily proven:

Lemma 1. *When a trial where an event occurs with probability p is carried out n/p times, assuming p is sufficiently close to 0 and i is sufficiently smaller than n/p, the probability that the event occurs exactly i times is*

$$(e^{-n}n^i)/i!. \tag{7}$$

Using this lemma, we see that $t=4$ can be adopted in our case; for $E2$ reduced to seven rounds, the probability that the number of ciphertext pairs having the difference pattern (10010100 00000000) is equal to or greater than four is 98%, while for a random permutation, the probability is expected to be 2%.

5.2 $E2$ reduced to eight rounds without IT and FT

By applying again the seven round characteristic to the first seven rounds of $E2$ reduced to eight rounds without IT and FT, we can narrow down the possibilities of subkey of the final (the eighth) round using the following algorithm:

For each candidate for subkey of the final round, decrypt all ciphertext pairs by one round. Then if the number of pairs that have the difference pattern (10010100 00000000) after the seventh round is less than a pre-determined value t, discard the candidate as a wrong subkey.

Now let us use $2^{107} = 8 \times 2^{104}$ chosen plaintext pairs such that $\Delta P_1 = \Delta P_4 = \Delta P_6$. Then if the candidate is the correct subkey, the expected number of pairs that have the difference pattern (10010100 00000000) after the seventh round is $8 \times 9.3 = 74.4$; however if it is a wrong subkey, the number of pairs is expected to be 8. Note that these plaintext pairs can be obtained using 2^{100} plaintexts message blocks (100=107-8+1).

A direct calculation using lemma 1 shows that $t = 60$, for instance, can sufficiently narrow down the possibilities of subkey of the final round. Specifically, for the correct subkey, the probability that the number of pairs having the difference pattern (10010100 00000000) after the seventh round is equal to or greater than 60 is 96%, while for the wrong subkey, the probability is expected to be 2^{-103}.

The straightforward method for realizing the algorithm above requires complexity more than 2^{128}, but by discarding impossible pairs and introducing a counting method for the second layer subkey with 2^{64} counters, we can reduce the complexity to less than 2^{128}.

5.3 $E2$ with a modified round function

Our computer program has found that the seven round characteristic shown in figure 5 is the best one in the sense that it attains the maximal number of rounds with non-trivial probability. In this subsection, we try to find better characteristics by modifying the round function without violating its design criteria. Figure 7 is the modified round function we propose here. This modification — reordering output bytes of the round function, which is called BRL function — does not eliminate any original operations nor violates design criteria of $E2$.

This modified round function has the following "good" characteristics that correspond to equations (2) and (5) in the original round function, respectively:

$$(10001000) \rightarrow (10110000) \qquad p = 2^{-8}, \qquad (8)$$
$$(10110000) \rightarrow (10001000) \qquad p = 2^{-16}. \qquad (9)$$

Figure 6 shows a nine round characteristic which holds with probability $(2^{-8})^4 \times (2^{-16})^3 \times 2^{-24} = 2^{-104}$, while for a random round function the probability is expected to be $(2^{-8})^{14} = 2^{-112}$, which is significantly smaller. Therefore in a similar way to the previous subsection, we can extract subkey information of the final (the tenth) round of the modified $E2$ reduced to ten rounds without IT and FT.

The number of required plaintext pairs is 2^{109}, which can be generated from 2^{94} plaintext message blocks (94=109-16+1). Note that in this case we do not have to choose special plaintexts since the probability that correct pairs are detected is much larger than the probability that wrong pairs appear. An example of an appropriate value for t is 20; for the correct subkey of the final (the tenth) round, the probability that the number of pairs having the difference pattern (10001000 00000000) after the ninth round is equal to or greater than 20 is 99%, while for the wrong subkey, the probability is expected to be 2^{-121}.

Lastly let us consider the modified $E2$ reduced to nine rounds **with** IT and FT. In IT and FT, 32-bit multiplications with subkey are used. However, since this multiplication is modulo 2^{32}, upper 32-bit of the resultant 64-bit information is simply discarded. Hence this multiplication has the following trivial byte characteristic:

$$(1000) \rightarrow (1000) \qquad p = 1. \qquad (10)$$

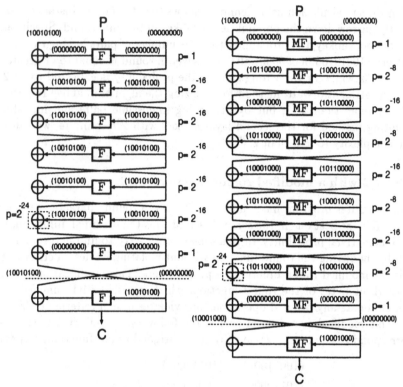

Fig.5 E2 reduced to eight rounds

Fig.6 Modified E2 reduced to
ten rounds

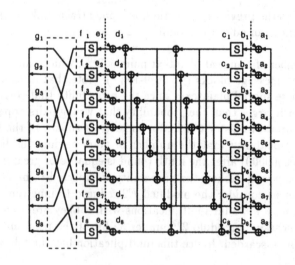

Fig.7 Modified Round Function (MF)

It follows from equation (10) that the characteristic shown in figure 6 can skip the IT and FT with probability 1. Therefore we have the following characteristic connecting a plaintext block and a ciphertext block direct:

$$(10001000\ 00000000) \rightarrow (10001000\ 00000000) \qquad p = 2^{-104}. \qquad (11)$$

This means that in a chosen plaintext scenario, we can distinguish the modified $E2$ reduced to nine rounds with IT and FT from a random permutation. Specifically, create 2^{106} plaintext pairs with the difference pattern (10001000 00000000) from 2^{91} plaintext message blocks (91=106-16+1) and encrypt them. Then if a ciphertext pair that has the difference pattern (10001000 00000000) is found, regard it as the modified $E2$ reduced to nine rounds with IT and FT, otherwise regard it as a random permutation ($t=1$). For $E2$ reduced to nine rounds with IT and FT, the probability that at least one ciphertext pair has the difference pattern (10001000 00000000) is 98%, while for a random permutation, the probability is expected to be only 2%.

6 Discussions and Conclusions

It is easily seen that the effectiveness of a byte characteristic can be evaluated by e = (hamming weight of the byte difference pattern of the ciphertext pair) $- log_2$ (the characteristic probability). If m exceeds 16, the characteristic is not applicable to our analysis.

We wrote a computer program for searching the best byte characteristic of the modified $E2$ for all possible ($8! = 40320$) choices of the BRL function. The following is the summary of the search:

maximal effective number of rounds of the best characteristic	effectiveness e	number of choices of the BRL function
7	16	27688
7	15	8760
7	14	976
9	15	2896

Table 1: The best characteristic and the number of choices of the BRL function [1]

The designers of $E2$ have conjectured that the best nine round (ordinary bitwise) characteristic probability of $E2$ is much smaller than $2^{-140.34}$; their evaluation methodology does not depend on a choice of BRL function [1].

Our analysis shows that for most cases (maximal effective number of rounds = 7), including the real $E2$, this estimation works well. However for the remaining 2896 cases, we can explicitly show a nine round bitwise differential (not characteristic) whose probability is bigger than 2^{-120}, which is significantly larger than the designers' estimation. This indicates that in a byte-oriented algorithm, we should be careful of existence of detectable differentials with high probability.

---

[1] After the publication of an earlier version of this paper, Shiho Moriai [5] showed a better attack of the real $E2$ based on another seven-round byte characteristic, whose effectiveness is 15; we confirmed that this is the real best byte characteristic of $E2$.

References

1. NTT-Nippon Telegraph and Telephone Corporation: E2 : Efficient Encryption algorithm. http://info.isl.ntt.co.jp/e2
2. Biham,E.,Shamir,A.: Differential Cryptanalysis of the Data Encryption Standard. Springer Verlag (1993)
3. Knudsen,L.R,Berson,T.A.: Truncated Differentials of SAFER. Third International Workshop of Fast Software Encryption, Lecture Notes in Computer Science 1039, Springer-Verlag(1996).
4. Lai,X.,Massey,J.L.,Murphy,S.: Markov Ciphers and Differential Cryptanalysis. Advances in Cryptology -Eurocrypt'91, Lecture Notes in Computer Science 547, Springer-Verlag(1991).
5. Moriai,S.: A talk at rump session in sixth international workshop of Fast Software Encryption (1999).

On the Decorrelated Fast Cipher (DFC) and Its Theory

Lars R. Knudsen and Vincent Rijmen *

Department of Informatics, University of Bergen, N-5020 Bergen

Abstract. In the first part of this paper the decorrelation theory of Vaudenay is analysed. It is shown that the theory behind the proposed constructions does not guarantee security against state-of-the-art differential attacks. In the second part of this paper the proposed Decorrelated Fast Cipher (DFC), a candidate for the Advanced Encryption Standard, is analysed. It is argued that the cipher does not obtain provable security against a differential attack. Also, an attack on DFC reduced to 6 rounds is given.

1 Introduction

In [6,7] a new theory for the construction of secret-key block ciphers is given. The notion of decorrelation to the order d is defined. Let C be a block cipher with block size m and C^* be a randomly chosen permutation in the same message space. If C has a d-wise decorrelation equal to that of C^*, then an attacker who knows at most $d-1$ pairs of plaintexts and ciphertexts cannot distinguish between C and C^*. So, the cipher C is "secure if we use it only $d-1$ times" [7]. It is further noted that a d-wise decorrelated cipher for $d = 2$ is secure against both a basic linear and a basic differential attack. For the latter, this basic attack is as follows. A priori, two values a and b are fixed. Pick two plaintexts of difference a and get the corresponding ciphertexts. Repeat a number of times. The attack is successful if and only if at least one ciphertext pair with difference b can be found in a number of tries that is significantly less than 2^m. Let $P(a,b) = \Pr(C(X \oplus a) = C(X) \oplus b)$ denote the probability of the differential with plaintext difference a and ciphertext difference b, where the probability is taken over all plaintexts X. To measure the security of the constructions against the basic differential attack the probabilities of the differentials are averaged over all keys, denoted $E(P(a,b))$. It is then argued that if $E(P(a,b))$ can be upper bounded sufficiently low for all values of a and b, e.g., $E(P(a,b)) \approx 2^{-m}$, then the differential attack will not succeed.

Also, in [7] two families of ciphers are proposed both with the above proofs of security against the basic attacks.

---

* F.W.O. postdoctoral researcher, sponsored by the Fund for Scientific Research, Flanders (Belgium).

The Families of Ciphers

COCONUT: This is a family of ciphers parameterised by $(p(x), m)$, where m is the block size and $p(x)$ is an irreducible polynomial of degree m in $GF(2)[x]$. A COCONUT cipher is a product cipher $C_3 \circ C_2 \circ C_1$, where C_1 and C_3 are "any (possibly weak) ciphers" [7], and C_2 is defined

$$C_2(y) = Ay + B \bmod p(x),$$

where A, B and y are polynomials of degree at most $m - 1$ in $GF(2)[x]$. The polynomials A and B are secret and act as round keys. Since the COCONUT family has "perfect decorrelation" to the order two it is claimed that the ciphers are secure against the linear and differential attacks.

PEANUT: This is a family of Feistel ciphers parameterised by (m, r, d, p), where m is the block size (in bits), r is the number of rounds, d is the order of the (partial) decorrelation, and p a prime greater than $2^{m/2}$. The round function F takes a text string and d subkeys each of length $m/2$,

$$F(x) = g((k_1 \cdot x^{d-1} + k_2 \cdot x^{d-2} + \ldots + k_{d-1} \cdot x + k_d \bmod p) \bmod 2^{m/2}),$$

where g is any permutation on $m/2$ bits. The DFC is a member of this family (cf. Section 3).

The PEANUT family does not have perfect decorrelation like the COCONUT family. This is due to both the use of the Feistel structure and to the round functions, which are not perfect decorrelated. The multiplications mod p and mod $2^{m/2}$ were chosen since they allow for more efficient implementations in software as compared to multiplication in $GF(2^n)$. The price to pay is that this leads to only partial decorrelated functions. However for sufficiently large values of r it is shown that the ciphers are secure against the linear and differential attacks [7].

In the first part of the paper it is shown that the above constructions based on the decorrelation theory do not necessarily result in ciphers secure against state-of-the-art differential attacks. Example ciphers from both families are shown to be weak. In the second part of this paper we analyse the Decorrelated Fast Cipher (DFC), which was submitted as a candidate for the Advanced Encryption Standard (AES). DFC is an 8-round Feistel cipher and member of the PEANUT family. It is shown that for any fixed key, there exist very high probability differentials for the round function. Also, a differential attack is given on DFC reduced to 6 rounds.

2 Analysis of the Constructions

In this section it will be shown that the constructions in the previous section will not resist differential attacks, thereby indicating a weakness of the decorrelation theory [7].

When analyzing the resistance of a cipher against differential attacks, one often computes the probabilities of differentials over all plaintexts and all keys [4]. (Also, one distinguishes between characteristics and differentials; we use the latter name for both concepts.) For one particular class of iterated ciphers, the Markov ciphers, the probabilities of r-round differentials can be computed as the product of the probabilities of the involved r one-round differentials under the assumption of independent round keys. Moreover, the probabilities are taken only over all possible round keys. However, in an attack the encrypted texts are typically encrypted under a fixed, but secret, key. To deal with this, one assumes that the *hypothesis of stochastic equivalence* holds.

Hypothesis 1 (Hypothesis of stochastic equivalence [4]) *For virtually all high-probability differentials it holds for a substantial fraction of the keys that the probability of the differential for the used key is approximately equal to the average probability of the differential, when averaged over all keys.*

The main reason for the criticism of the constructions based on the decorrelation theory, is that this hypothesis does not hold for the case of the decorrelation modules $k_1 x + k_2$ in $\mathrm{GF}(2^m)$ nor for multiplication modulo p modulo $2^{m/2}$ for prime p.

It is shown in the following that the distributions of differences through the "decorrelation modules", $k_1 x + k_2$, are very key-dependent. When considering multiplication in the field $\mathrm{GF}(2^m)$ with exclusive-or as the difference operation, for any given input difference $a \neq 0$ and output difference b, the probability of the differential $P(a, b)$ (notation from previous section) for a fixed key, is either 0 or 1. To see this, let x and $x + a$ be two inputs to the module. The difference in the outputs then is, $k_1 x + k_2 + k_1(x + a) + k_2 = ak_1$. So, although $E(P(a, b))$ (the average probability taken over all values of the key) can be upper bounded sufficiently low, in an attack one fixed key is used, and differentials of probability 0 and 1 can be found and exploited.

Note that the proof of security against the basic differential attack of the introduction is not affected by these observations. Assume that $P(a, b) \approx 2^{-m}$ for an m-bit block cipher (notation as in the introduction). If the attacker is restricted to choose the values in the differentials before analysing the received ciphertexts the proof of security holds. However, this is not a realistic restriction in our opinion. If for every fixed key there are high probability differentials, an attacker will be able to detect this in an attack and exploit it.

Consider the COCONUT family. In [7] it is shown that C will be secure against the basic differential attack independently of the choices of the ciphers C_1 and C_3. First note that COCONUT versions where $C_1 = C_3 = \mathrm{id}$ (the identity function) have high probability differentials for any fixed key. Also, such ciphers are easily broken using two known plaintexts. One simply solves two equations in two unknowns and retrieves A and B. (This is also noted in [7].) However, we argue based on the above discussion that if a COCONUT cipher is secure against a (state-of-the-art) differential attack for a fixed key then it is because at least one or both of C_1 and C_3 contribute to this security.

In [8] Wagner cryptanalyses COCONUT'98, a member of the COCONUT family. The attack is a differential attack, which exploits that high probability differentials exist for both C_1 and C_3.

Consider next a variant of the PEANUT family of ciphers for $d = 2$, which use multiplication in $GF(2^{m/2})$ in the round function and let g be any affine mapping in $GF(2^{m/2})$. The reason goes along the same lines as the reasoning of the claim for COCONUT. All differentials through the decorrelation modules have probabilities either 0 or 1, and the same holds for differentials through the round function, since g is affine. Consequently, since this holds for all round functions, there are differentials of probability 0 and 1 for the whole cipher.

Consider now the PEANUT family. The multiplications mod p mod $2^{m/2}$ were chosen since they allow for more efficient implementations in software as compared to multiplication in $GF(2^m)$. Consider constructions for $d = 2$ with multiplication defined in $GF(p)$, for prime $p > 2^{m/2}$, where the Feistel round function is

$$F(x) = g((k_1 \cdot x + k_2 \bmod p) \bmod 2^{m/2})$$

for any permutation g. Let first g be the identity function and let $p = 2^{m/2} + t$, where t is small. Let the difference between two $m/2$-bit texts, x_1 and x_2, be defined as $d(x_1, x_2) = x_1 - x_2 \bmod p$ (subtraction modulo p). In the following it is examined how such a difference distributes through F. First, note that for randomly chosen y, where $0 \leq y < p$, it holds that $(y \bmod p) \bmod 2^{m/2} = y \bmod p$ with probability $p_1 = 2^{m/2}/(2^{m/2} + t) \approx 1$. So,

$$d(F(x_1), F(x_2)) = d(k_1 \cdot x_1 + k_2 \bmod p, k_1 \cdot x_2 + k_2 \bmod p)$$

with probability at least $(p_1)^2$. But since the multiplication modulo p is linear with respect to the defined difference, one gets that

$$d(F(x_1), F(x_2)) = k_1(x_1 - x_2) \bmod p$$

with probability at least $(p_1)^2$. The halves in the Feistel cipher are combined using the exclusive-or operation, however it is also noted in [7, Th. 9] that the proof of security for the construction remains valid if the group operation is replaced by any other group operation. Assume therefore that the halves are combined using addition modulo $2^{m/2}$. Let w_1 and w_2 be the two $m/2$-bit halves from a previous round which are combined with the outputs $F(x_1)$ and $F(x_2)$ of the current round. Assume $d(w_1, w_2) = \beta$. Then with probability $1/2$, $w_1 + F(x_1) \bmod 2^{m/2} = w_1 + F(x_1)$ in Z, thus if $d(F(x_1), F(x_2)) = \alpha$, then

$$d(F(x_1) + w_1 \bmod 2^{m/2}, F(x_2) + w_2 \bmod 2^{m/2}) = \alpha + \beta$$

with probability $1/4$.

To sum up, differences modulo p in the round functions of PEANUT distribute non-uniformly. For any fixed round key, a given difference in the inputs to F results in differences in the outputs of F with very high probabilities. Above it was assumed that g was the identity function. The point which is made here is that if members of the PEANUT family are secure against differential attacks, then it is because g resists the differential attacks, and not because of the decorrelation module by themselves. In the next section a particular member of the PEANUT family is analysed, where the function g is not the identity function.

Note that the high probability differentials described in this section are key-dependent and therefore unknown to an attacker. However, the fact that the key is fixed in an attack means, that the high probability differentials will occur. This can be exploited in a standard attack, e.g., if the attacker guesses the first-round key and/or the last-round key, the keys which produce high probability differentials for the reduced cipher will be good candidates for the correct value of the key(s). Furthermore, also differentials with probability significantly below 2^{-m} can be used in a differential attack. This is illustrated by the attack we present in Section 5.

3 The Decorrelated Fast Cipher

The Decorrelated Fast Cipher (DFC) [2] has been submitted as a candidate for the AES encryption standard [5]. DFC is a member of the PEANUT family, described above. In the following a more precise definition of the DFC is given. For a complete description of DFC the reader is referred to [2].

3.1 General Structure

DFC is a block cipher with the classical Feistel structure. It uses 8 rounds to transform a 128-bit plaintext block into a 128-bit ciphertext block, under the influence of a key that can have a length up to 256 bits. The user key is expanded to 8 128-bit round keys K_i. Every round key is split into two 64-bit halves, denoted A_i and B_i. In every round, the round function uses the right half of the text input and the two 64-bit round key halves to produce a 64-bit output. This output is exored with the left half of the text input. Subsequently, both halves are swapped, except in the last round.

3.2 The Round Function

Let X denote the 64-bit text input. First a modular multiplication is performed, followed by an additional reduction.

$$Z = \left(A_i \cdot X + B_i \bmod (2^{64} + 13)\right) \bmod 2^{64} \qquad (1)$$

Subsequently, the 'confusion permutation' is applied to Z: the value is split into two 32-bit halves, denoted Z_l and Z_r. Z_l is exored with a constant KC. Z_r is exored with a table entry that is determined by the 6 least significant bits of the original Z_l. Both halves are swapped, and the result is added with a 64-bit constant KD.

$$Y = ((Z_r \oplus RT[Z_l \bmod 64]) \ll 32) + (Z_l \oplus KC) + KD \bmod 2^{64}$$

The result Y is the output of the round function.

3.3 The Key Scheduling

The key scheduling first pads the user key with a constant string until a 256-bit string K is obtained. Subsequently, K is divided into two 128-bit parts K_1 and K_2. The keys K_1 and K_2 define each an invertible transformation, denoted $E_1()$ and $E_2()$ respectively. Let RK_O denote a string of 128 zero bits. Then the round keys of DFC are defined as follows.

$$RK_i = E_1(RK_{i-1}) \text{ if } i \text{ is odd} \tag{2}$$

$$RK_i = E_2(RK_{i-1}) \text{ if } i \text{ is even} \tag{3}$$

4 The Distribution of Differences in DFC

First note that since DFC is a member of the PEANUT family, versions of DFC which use only the decorrelation modules in the round function have very high probability differentials. However, the round function of DFC is more than that. To measure the distribution of differences through the round function of DFC we first consider a simplified version. First change all exors to additions modulo 2^{64} and remove the nonlinear S-box RT. This version is hereafter called DFC'. The swapping of the 32-bit halves inside the F-function is retained. Note that the proof of security for DFC' is the same as for DFC. Consider one round of DFC'. Define the difference of two 64-bit texts as the subtraction modulo p. The following test was implemented. Randomly choose a difference (α_L, α_R), where both α's are 64 bits, in the inputs to one round. Randomly choose a pair w_1, w_2 of texts with difference α_L in the left halves. Randomly choose a pair of round keys. For n random choices of x_1 compute the differences of the outputs y_1 and y_2 of the function F for inputs x_1 and $x_2 = (x_1 - \alpha_R) \bmod p$. Compute and store the differences of $y_1 + w_1 \bmod 2^{64}$ and $y_2 + w_2 \bmod 2^{64}$. Since modulo 2^{64} operations used to combine the halves in DFC' are not completely compatible with modulo $p = 2^{64} + 13$ operations, differentials are examined for the addition of the Feistel cipher halves in addition to the round function F.

It is infeasible to do tests for all 2^{64} inputs, but as we will see, this is not necessary in order to determine the distribution of the differences. In 10 tests with $n = 10,000$ input pairs, the number of possible differences in the outputs and the probabilities of the highest one-round differential were recorded. The 10,000 pairs of inputs lead to only an average of 13.6 possible output differences. The average probability of the best one-round differential was 3/8. In similar tests with 1,000,000 pairs, the average number of possible output differences was 14.0 still with an average probability of 3/8. Thus it can be expected that the corresponding numbers for all possible inputs are close to these estimates. Note also, these tests were performed for one randomly chosen input difference, thus, by considering many (all) possible input differences higher probability differentials can be expected.

Thus, despite the fact that the round function is almost perfectly decorrelated, very high probability differentials exist for any fixed key.

Table 1. Results of the experiments on simplified versions of DFC. Probabilities of best differentials for a randomly chosen input difference in 10 tests with randomly chosen keys. (*) Average in 10 tests of best differential for 100 randomly chosen input differences.

	max. probability	# output diff.
DFC'	3/8	14
DFC"	1/128	808
DFC" (*)	0.37	370

Consider next a version of DFC where all exors are replaced by additions modulo 2^{64}, but where RT is unchanged, hereafter called DFC". Note that the proof of security for DFC" is the same as for DFC.

In 10 tests similar to the above with $n = 10,000$ input pairs, the number of possible differences in the outputs was an average of 715 and the probabilities of the highest one-round differential were 1/100 on the average. In similar tests with 1,000,000 pairs, the average number of possible output differences was 808 with an average probability of 1/128. This is no surprise, since when the 6 bits input to RT in a differential are different, the outputs of the round will look random in one half. Since these 6 bits are equal with probability 1/64, these results are in correspondence with the test results on DFC'. Moreover, for a fixed key there are input differences such that the 6 bits input to RT are equal in more than the average case, and the probability of the differential will be higher. To test this phenomenon, we implemented some further tests. In 10 tests a randomly chosen key was used. In each tests for each of 100 randomly chosen input differences, 100,000 input pairs were generated and the output differences recorded. The probabilities of the best such differentials for the 10 keys ranged from 1/22 to 3/5 with an average of 0.37 and 370 possible output differences. Table 1 summarizes the results of the experiments.

Since the only difference between the round functions of DFC" and DFC is the use of three additions mod 2^{64} instead of three exors, it has been clearly demonstrated that if DFC for a fixed key is secure against differential attacks it is because of the use of mixed group operations and not because of the decorrelation modules.

Estimating the uniformity of differences and computing the probabilities of differentials are much harder for real DFC. To get an indication of such results, a version of DFC with 32-bit blocks was implemented, hereafter denoted DFC_{32}. The round function takes as input a 16-bit block, uses multiplication modulo the prime $p = 2^{16} + 3$ followed by a reduction modulo 2^{16}. The RT-table has 16 entries (the size of the table is chosen as the size of the inputs (in bits) to the round function, in the spirit of DFC) with randomly chosen values, and the constants KC and KD were chosen at random.

In 100 tests, the number of possible differences in the outputs and the probabilities of the highest one-round differential were recorded for one randomly chosen input difference and for all 2^{16} inputs.

Table 2. Results of the experiments on a scaled-down version of DFC. Probabilities of best differentials for a randomly chosen input difference in 100 tests with randomly chosen keys. (*) Average in 100 tests of best differential for 100 randomly chosen input differences.

	max. probability	# output diff.
DFC$_{32}$	1/397	6700
DFC$_{32}$ (*)	1/91	1750

The 2^{16} pairs of inputs lead to an average of 6700 possible output differences. The average probability of the best one-round differential was 1/397 (and 1/21 in the best case). By considering 100 input differences for every chosen key, the number of possible output differences dropped to 1750, and the average best probability increased to 1/91 (and 1/18 in the best case).

Table 2 summarizes the results of the experiments.

It can be argued that the RT-table chosen in this scaled-down version of DFC is too big relatively to DFC. Repeating the last test above, this time with a 2-bit RT-table, the number of possible output differences dropped to 1051, and the average best probability increased to 1/49 (and 1/7 in the best case).

Based on the tests conducted here, it is hard to estimate the exact effect for the proposed DFC (without any modifications). However, the tests strongly indicate that the round function of DFC distributes differences modulo p in a very non-uniform way, and that high probability differentials exist.

Summarizing, it was demonstrated that if the DFC is secure against the differential attacks it will be because of the elements that are independent of the proof of security. Also, it was clearly indicated that high probability differentials will exist for DFC for any fixed key.

5   A Differential Attack

The high probability differentials of the previous section might lead to a straight-forward differential attack on DFC. However, the large block size of DFC makes it hard to perform such tests. It is left as an open problem for the time being.

In the following we present an attack on DFC when reduced to six of the proposed eight rounds. The attack does not depend directly on the findings in the previous version, but these are incorporated in a possible improvement described later. The attack uses a differential with S/N-ratio < 1. As explained in [1] and [3], this type of differentials can be used in a similar way as 'ordinary' differentials with S/N-ratio > 1 to mount a differential attack. Before the attack is explained, we mention a property of the DFC key schedule that is useful in the attack.

5.1   A Key Scheduling Weakness

The first round key is defined as $RK_1 = E_1(RK_0)$. The string RK_0 is constant and the transformation $E_1()$ depends on one half of the key bits. The consequence is that the entropy of the first round key is at most one half of the entropy of the user key, e.g., for a 128-bit user key, the first round key has only an entropy of 64 bits. This property makes it easier for an attacker to bypass the first round by guessing the key.

5.2 The F-function Is Almost Bijective

The F-function of DFC is almost bijective. The only non-invertible part of the F-function is the reduction modulo 2^{64} after the modular multiplication in (1). Let x_1, x_2 be two different inputs and let $y_i = A \cdot x_i + B$, where A and B are the secret keys. The inputs x_1, x_2 will be mapped to the same output if and only if

$$(y_1 \bmod (2^{64} + 13)) \bmod 2^{64} = (y_2 \bmod (2^{64} + 13)) \bmod 2^{64}.$$

If $x_1 \neq x_2$, the equality can only hold if either $y_1 \bmod (2^{64} + 13) \in \{0, 1, \ldots, 12\}$ and $y_2 = y_1 + 2^{64}$, or $y_1 \bmod (2^{64} + 13) \in \{2^{64}, 2^{64} + 1, \ldots, 2^{64} + 12\}$ and $y_2 = y_1 - 2^{64}$. For fixed values of A and B, there can be at most 26 tuples (x_1, x_2) with $0 \leq x_1, x_2 < 2^{64}$, that result in equal output values.

It follows that for any key $K = (A, B)$

$$\sum_{\alpha \neq 0} P(\alpha \to 0 | K) \leq 26 \cdot 2^{-64}.$$

Because for every value of α, $P(\alpha \to 0 | K)$ is a multiple of 2^{-64}, there are for every round key value K at most 26 α's such that the probability is larger than zero.

5.3 A 5-Round Differential with Low Probability

Consider the 5-round differential with both input difference and output difference equal to $(\alpha, 0)$, where α is an arbitrary value, different from zero. (We use the bitwise exor as difference operation.) In this section we will try to give an upper bound for the probability of this differential. In order for our attack to work, this upper bound should be significantly smaller than 2^{-64}.

On Figure 1 it is easy to see that a pair that follows the differential, will have a difference of $(0, \alpha)$ at the input of the second round, and $(\alpha, 0)$ at the output of the fourth round. In the second round, the input difference to the F-function will lead to a certain output difference, denoted β. Similarly, reasoning backwards, it follows that in the fourth round, the difference at the input of the F-function equals α. The output difference is denoted γ. It follows that the third round will have input difference (α, β) and output difference (γ, α). This requires that $\beta \equiv \gamma$ and that the output difference of the F-function in the third round is zero and the input difference β.

Note that the differential does not specify any particular value of β. The probability of the differential is thus given by the sum over all β-values of the probabilities of the characteristics.

$$P_{\text{dif}} = \sum_{\beta} P_{\text{char}(\beta)}$$

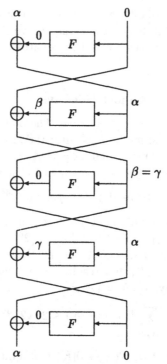

Fig. 1. A 5-round differential with very low probability.

We will approximate the probabilities of the characteristics by the product of the probabilities of the composing one-round characteristics. This may in fact cause inaccuracies, but it is a common assumption. The exact probability of the differential is not very important for our attack, and the experimental results confirm our analysis. We feel that a more exact calculation of the probability would needlessly complicate the analysis.

As already explained in Section 2 and Section 4, the probability of a one round characteristic depends heavily on the value of the round key.

$$P_{\text{dif}} \approx \sum_{\beta} P(\alpha \to \beta \mid K = K_2)P(\beta \to 0 \mid K = K_3)P(\alpha \to \beta \mid K = K_4) \quad (4)$$

When calculating the probability of a characteristic, a distinction is made between the cases $\beta = 0$ and $\beta \neq 0$. If $\beta = 0$

$$P_{\text{char}(\beta=0)} = P(\alpha \to 0 \mid K = K_2)P(\alpha \to 0 \mid K = K_4)$$

Under the assumption of independent rounds, it follows from Section 5.2 that $P_{\text{char}(\beta=0)} \leq (26/2^{64})^2 < 2^{-118}$.
If $\beta \neq 0$

$$P_{\text{char}(\beta)} = P(\alpha \to \beta \mid K = K_2)P(\beta \to 0 \mid K = K_3)P(\alpha \to \beta \mid K = K_4).$$

It follows from Section 5.2 that for every value of K_3 there are at most 26 β-values such that the probability is larger than zero. Also, from Section 4 it follows that for every value of the round key, there are (α, β) tuples such that $P(\alpha \to \beta)$ is relatively "high". Let us denote this probability by p_1. For most other values of (α, β), the probability is much lower than p_1, possibly zero. We denote this probability by p_2. The values of (α, β) which correspond to high and low probabilities depend on the value of the round keys. The worst scenario for the attack would be that the round key values are selected such that there are values of α and β with high $P(\alpha \to \beta)$ in both the second and the fourth round, and where also $P(\beta \to 0)$ is nonzero in the third round. The attack uses many different α values, therefore it can be expected that some of the α values will give a high $P(\alpha \to \beta)$ in the second or the fourth round, where β has nonzero $P(\beta \to 0)$ in the third round. However, it can be argued that for almost all keys it is highly unlikely that there will exist an α such that $P(\alpha \to \beta)$ is high in the second and the fourth round for a suitable β. For almost all keys, the probability of the differential will be at most $26 \cdot 2^{-64} \cdot p_1 \cdot p_2$ for all values of α. It is confirmed by the experiments performed, that this probability is sufficiently low for the attack to work.

5.4 The Actual Attack

The attack on 6 rounds works in almost the same way as the attack on 6-round DEAL [3]. The main differences are the following:

1. The probability of the 5-round differential is not 0, but very low.
2. The attack uses chosen ciphertexts instead of chosen plaintexts. This reason for this is that if the user key length is less than 256 bits, the first-round key of DFC has a lower entropy than the last-round key. It is therefore easier to recover.

The attack starts as follows. Choose 2^{64} ciphertexts with a fixed right half and a variable left half, say $C_i = (X_i, R)$. Obtain the corresponding plaintexts, say $P_i = (Y_i, Z_i)$. Compute $X_i \oplus Z_i$ and find matches $X_i \oplus Z_i = X_j \oplus Z_j$. About 2^{63} matches can be expected. Let $\alpha = X_i \oplus X_j = Z_i \oplus Z_j$. Guess a value for the first-round key. For all the matching pairs, encrypt the plaintexts one round. If the difference after the first round is $(\alpha, 0)$, the guessed key value is wrong with high probability. For the correct value of the first-round key, in some rare cases the probability of getting right pairs might be relatively high, but as explained earlier in by far the most cases this ratio is very low. Assuming that a wrong key produces uniformly distributed output differences, the difference $(\alpha, 0)$ will occur with probability 2^{-64} for each analysed pair. Thus, $2^{-64} \cdot 2^{63} = 0.5$ good pairs can be expected. Discarding all the key guesses that produce a good pair will eliminate about half of the wrong key values. Repeating this attack 64 times eliminates almost all the wrong key values. The attack requires about $64 \cdot 2^{64} = 2^{70}$ chosen ciphertexts and $(2^{64} + 2^{63} + \ldots + 2 + 1) \cdot 2^{64} \approx 2^{129}$ evaluations of the round function, which is roughly equivalent to 2^{126} encryptions.

Table 3. Experimental results for DFC$_{32}$, reduced to 6 rounds. All results are averages over 10 tests. For every structure, 2^{16} ciphertexts with a fixed right half are decrypted. The last column lists the average number of surviving wrong key guesses after all the runs. (The attack starts with 2^{16} possible values for the key.)

# structures	# wrong keys remaining
16	22.4
17	14.3
18	8.1
19	4.3
20	2.1
21	1.2

Table 4. Adjusted chosen text requirements and work load of the attack on 6 rounds of DFC.

key length	# chosen texts	work load
128	2^{71}	2^{127}
192	$1.5 \cdot 2^{71}$	2^{158}
256	2^{72}	2^{190}

5.5 Implementation

We implemented this attack on DFC$_{32}$, a reduced version of DFC that operates on blocks of 32 bits. All constants and tables were reduced accordingly and the prime $2^{16} + 3$ was chosen for the modular multiplication. Because of the key scheduling weakness (cf. Section 5.1), the first-round key of DFC$_{32}$ has 16 bits entropy. The results of the previous section predict that 16 structures of 2^{16} texts should allow to determine uniquely the 16-bit key. The results of 10 tests are given in Table 3.

After repeating the basic attack sufficiently many times only a few candidates are left for the secret key. The correct value of the secret key never resulted in the 5-round differential as described above, which justifies the approximations made in Section 5.3. The experiments suggest that in practice a little more chosen plaintexts are required then predicted by the theory, because we get less good pairs than expected for the wrong key guesses. The net result is that every structure eliminates only 39% of the remaining key candidates, instead of the expected 50%. We therefore have to adjust our estimates for the plaintext requirements and the work load of our attack on 6 rounds of DFC. Increasing the plaintext requirements and the work load with a factor two is more than sufficient. The results are given in Table 4, together with the estimates for attacks on DFC with other key lengths. The estimates for the work load use one encryption as the unit operation. The estimate for 256 bit keys is pessimistic, because in that case it is easy to speed up significantly the round function evaluations since the modular multiplication does not have to be repeated for every new key guess.

5.6 A Possible Improvement

In this section a possible improvement of the attack is outlined which may reduce the complexity. The attack uses the observations in Section 4.

Consider again the 5-round differential of the previous section, but allow now the nonzero half of the difference in the last round to be different from the nonzero half of the difference in the first round. The differential starts with a difference $(\alpha, 0)$. After the first round, the difference is $(0, \alpha)$. In the second round, the inputs to F with difference α leads to an output difference β. At the output of the 5th round, a difference $(\delta, 0)$ is required. In the fourth round the inputs to F with difference δ leads to an output difference γ. It follows that $\beta \equiv \gamma$. The attack works as follows. Choose a structure of ciphertexts with equal right halves. For all values of the first-round key(s) K_1, find the plaintext pairs which yield equal inputs to F in the second round. For each such pair, one knows the input differences to F in the second and fourth rounds, and that the two output differences of F in the two rounds are equal. Since the number of output differences of F are limited for any given difference in the inputs, cf. Section 4, this gives an attacker information about the relation between one half of each of the keys K_2 and K_4. Note that the distribution of differences through F depends mostly on one half of the round keys. Repeat this procedure a number of times for each value of the first-round key. The value of the first-round key which gives rise to a frequent relation between the keys K_2 and K_4 is expected to be the correct value. It remains an open problem to what extent this variant of the attack will reduce the complexity of the previous attack.

6 Conclusions

We showed that the constructions of ciphers in the COCONUT and PEANUT families are weak against differential attacks. The main observation is that for a fixed key (which is the scenario of an attack) high probability differentials can be found. We analysed one particular member of the PEANUT-family: the DFC. It was shown that variants of DFC with only small modifications and with the same proof of security as the original, are vulnerable to a differential attack. For the proposed DFC it was indicated that differentials with high probabilities exist for the round function. Also, an attack, not directly related to these findings, on the proposed DFC reduced to six of eight rounds was given. Although the attack requires a large running time it is believed that the outlined possible improvement will be faster.

The results in this paper do not contradict the theory of decorrelation [7]. More specifically, and in accordance with [7], ciphers which are d-wise decorrelated are provably secure against the following attacks.

1. Any chosen plaintext attack using at most $d - 1$ plaintexts.
2. If $d \geq 2$, the basic differential attack, where an attacker is restricted to choose the values in the differentials before the attack.
3. If $d \geq 2$, the basic linear attack.

The point we make is that restricting the attacker to such basic attacks does not lead to a strong proof of security. More specifically, we showed how some more advanced differential techniques can be used to attack decorrelated ciphers in general and reduced versions of DFC in particular. Although the decorrelation theory may be a valuable contribution to cryptographic research, it does not guarantee resistance against state-of-the-art differential attacks.

Acknowledgments

The authors thank Serge Vaudenay and the anonymous referees of the programme committee for helpful comments.

References

1. J. Borst, L.R. Knudsen, V. Rijmen, "Two attacks on reduced IDEA," *Advances in Cryptology, Proceedings Eurocrypt '97, LNCS 1233*, W. Fumy, Ed., Springer-Verlag, 1997, pp. 1-13.
2. H. Gilbert, M. Girault, P. Hoogvorst, F. Noilhan, T. Pornin, G. Poupard, J, Stern, S. Vaudenay, "Decorrelated fast cipher: an AES candidate," *Technical report*, available from http://www/ens.fr/~vaudenay/dfc.html. Submitted as an AES candidate. See also http://www.nist.gov/aes/.
3. L.R. Knudsen. DEAL - a 128-bit block cipher. Technical Report 151, Department of Informatics,University of Bergen, Norway, February 1998. Submitted as an AES candidate. See also http://www.nist.gov/aes/.
4. X. Lai, J.L. Massey, and S. Murphy. Markov ciphers and differential cryptanalysis. In D.W. Davies, editor, *Advances in Cryptology - EUROCRYPT'91, LNCS 547*, pages 17-38. Springer Verlag, 1992.
5. NIST's AES homepage, http://www.nist.gov/aes.
6. S. Vaudenay, "Feistel ciphers with L_2-decorrelation," *Preproceedings of SAC'98*, August '98, Kingston (Canada).
7. S. Vaudenay. "Provable Security for Block Ciphers by Decorrelation," In *STACS'98, Paris, France, LNCS 1373*, Springer-Verlag, 1998, pp. 249-275.
8. D. Wagner. The boomerang attack. In these proceedings.

Scramble All, Encrypt Small

Markus Jakobsson *   Julien P. Stern **   Moti Yung * * *

Abstract. In this paper, we propose a new design tool for "block encryption", allowing the en/decryption of arbitrarily long messages, but performing en/decryption on only a single block (e.g., 128 bit block), where the rest of the message is only processed by a good scrambling function (e.g., one based on an ideal hash function). The design can be a component in constructing various schemes where the above properties gives an advantage. A quite natural use of our scheme is for *remotely keyed encryption*. We actually solve an open problem (at least in the relaxed ideal hash model and where hosts are allowed to add randomness and integrity checks, thus giving a length increasing function); namely, we show the existence of a secure remotely keyed encryption scheme which performs only *one* interaction with the smart-card device.

1 Introduction

We provide a basic design allowing encryption and decryption to be performed by combining a high quality scrambling technique with a strong encryption/decryption mechanism. In particular the method applies to cooperation between an untrusted (potentially exposed) but computationally potent device and a trusted (highly secure) but computationally weak device. The method achieves an appropriate balance of computation and trust by employing a scrambling mechanism, which is modeled as an ideal length preserving one-way function which can be built from a regular ideal (random oracle like) hash function.

While following the usual Feistel structure for block cipher design, we show that most of the work can be done by the (publicly known and invertible) scrambling, requiring only a small portion to be performed by encryption. This situation allows a design which can be useful when the encryption is more expensive than the scrambling, or when it is otherwise limited. This is the case when the encryption is done by a small device (e.g. a smart card) which is slower than a general host's software (which has more computational power, but is less secure -- thus encryption keys must never be exposed to the host). We call the design "scramble all, encrypt small."

A most natural application of our protocol is for "remotely keyed encryption", which we motivate below. Yet, our protocol is of independent interest

---

* Information Sciences Research Center, Bell Labs, Murray Hill, New Jersey 07974
www.bell-labs.com/user/markusj

** UCL Crypto Group, Batiment Maxwell, 3 Place du levant, B-1348 Louvain-la-Neuve, Belgium (stern@dice.ucl.ac.be), and Laboratoire de Recherche en Informatique, Université de Paris-Sud, Batiment 490, F-91405 Orsay Cedex, France (stern@lri.fr).

*** CertCo Inc. New York. (moti@cs.columbia.edu, moti@certco.com).

and can be used in other settings, for example to speed up certain encryption processes. In particular, our construction nicely applies in the context of traitor tracing [CFN94, Pfi96, NP98]. In traitor tracing, the data is encrypted with a random key, which is itself encrypted so that only users with legitimate keys can decrypt it (so the keys can be traced). Instead of encrypting the data with a random key, we can simply scramble it and encrypt a single block in the same way the random key is encrypted.

The need for remotely keyed encryption was nicely motivated by Blaze. Let us recall the motivation. Today's relatively open environment of hosts (e.g., Internet or Intranet servers) leads to a rather paradoxical situation in terms of security architecture: The hosts which are the gateways to the outside world (or internal users) are frequently required to perform cryptographic tasks, simply because they often use encryption to communicate at a low level, and as such, are the most vulnerable to various attacks (or even to exposure by simple implementation flaws). Given a cryptographic application or service, what is often neglected is its embedding environment and the implementation. It is argued that given that general software and the operating system running the software may be susceptible to viruses, Trojan horses, and other related attacks, there is a substantial risk of attackers momentarily gaining control of networked computers and the information stored by these. Therefore, secret keys should not be kept or used in this environment whenever possible. On the other hand, smart cards and other computational platforms with reduced risks of attacks often have a very limited computational ability and low storage capabilities. Consequently, it is desirable to divide the computation between an untrusted but powerful device (which we will call the slave) and a trusted but weak device (the master).

This problem, which in its encryption incarnation is known as *remotely keyed encryption schemes* (RKES) was proposed in [Bla96] with no model or proof and with certain subtle problems. Several solutions have already been suggested to solve this problem [Bla96, Luc97, BFN98]. If we momentarily disregard the security issues, the common aspect of these three schemes is that they ask a smartcard to generate a "temporary" key, which depends on the message, and which is used to encrypt the largest part of the message. This generates a "binding" between the message and the device via the encryption. They later ask to hide this key. A formal model and secure solution for this (based on pseudorandom functions) was given in [BFN98]; their solution requires two accesses to the smartcard per operation.

While our system provides the same functionality, the use of the "scramble all, encrypt small" notion is different: in our scheme, the host does *not* perform any encryption. It simply scrambles the message in a publicly available (and invertible) way (after adding randomness and integrity check), and then deprives an adversary of the ability to invert the scrambling by letting the smartcard encrypt just a small part of the scrambled message. Also, in our scheme, there is a *single* access to the trusted smart card which performs a *single* decryption/encryption operation before replying. This is implied by the fact that the host does not use a temporary key for encryption and does not encrypt at all, but rather the host employs scrambling of high quality. In some sense the earlier constructions can be viewed as an unbalanced Feistel (Luby-Rackoff type) encryption. Namely, pseudorandom permutation based on pseudorandom functions, where the pseudorandom functions are on the smart card. This seems to require two applications of the pseudorandom function. This implies (only intuitively) the need for two calls to the card. Thus, to get the result with "a single call" to the smart card we rely on the ideal (random oracle) hash model. It is an open question whether this stronger assumption model is necessary for achieving the "single call" result.

Since the host does not use encryption, the method gives a way to encrypt arbitrarily long messages (with strong notion of security), while encrypting only one block (of size, say 128/ 256 bits). We also allow the host to add randomness to the encryption (this can be viewed as an added random IV) so we can formalize our mechanism and security w.r.t. an overall randomized encryptions (which eases the difficulty of pseudorandom ones as in the earlier works). The host also adds an integrity check to prevent message modifications and other attacks.

We validate our design by giving a proof of security assuming the scrambling is an ideal hash and the small encryption is an ideal block cipher (random permutation).

From an engineering perspective, the *Bear* and *Lion* designs [AB96] have taught how to encrypt an arbitrary long block given fast stream ciphers. This is suitable for applications with large messages. While we have the same applications in mind, we teach how to minimize the encryption mechanism to a small block of size 128 bits, say. This minimization may be due to configuration and performance constraints. Thus, our design where only small portions are encrypted (rather than the entire large block which here is only scrambled without a key) may be called "*Cub*" as opposed to "Bear" and "Lion". Note that we do not claim that there is a universal performance advantage of Cub over the earlier designs which applies to all working environments. On the contrary, we understand very well that stream cipher encryption may be fast comparing to a good scrambling mechanisms. What is more interesting is the minimization of encryption itself and the confinement of the entire cryptographic operation.

Finally, we remark that since the design deals with the constraints of having a slow encryption whose use is minimized, it may fit well when the encryption employed is obviously much slower than available good scrambling techniques based on cryptographic hash functions. If the available encryption is based on public-key, the relative performance resembles the gap of "remotely keyed encryption".

Remark on presentation: While we present a general two-process method, its implementation as a "remotely keyed" mechanism is the prime example and will serve as the working example (since it is concrete and it further adds environmental constraints).

Outline: Section 2 discuss previous work on the subject. Section 3 introduces our model, and section 4 presents the basic tools we will use. Section 5 explains our new solution. Validation of the design via a security proof is given in section 6 and experimental results are outlined in section 7. Finally section 8 presents open problems and concludes the work.

2 Related Work

There are many issues in block cipher design (for extensive review see the appropriate sections in [Sch96, MOV97]). Feistel introduced the fundamental notion of rounds where a one-way function of half the "current message" is exor-ed into the other half. Provable constructions based on one-way functions that act globally on half the block (analogous to "large s-boxes") were first investigated by Luby and Rackoff [LR88]; their functions were based, in fact, on pseudorandom functions. Many other investigations followed which included simplifications of the analysis and the proof of security and variations/ simplifications of the round functions (see [Mau92, Luc96, NR97]).

In particular, employing stream-ciphers for fast block message encryption in the style of Luby Rackoff was presented in [AB96]. Their design like the one in this work is suitable for block cipher operations for large blocks, which may be typical in software oriented mechanisms. Adding public scrambling via hashing prior to encryption was considered in the past. A prime example is the scrambling using ideal hash and pseudorandom generator in [BR94]. Another example is in a work (coauthored by the third author) [IBM-pa.]. However, none of these works put forth the notion of global scrambling combined with local (small block) encryption as a possible provable design. Related work which we have learned about recently, is in [MPR97, MPRZ98]. They do suggest a design where scrambling via hashing is done prior to partial encryption as in our case, but they do not give a security validation proof. They suggested their design to standardization committees, and our validation proof may support their effort. Their work does not have the context or the consideration for remotely keyed encryption; rather they suggest it in the context of public-key encryption. The goal of the current work is to suggest minimized encryption which is validated and can be used systematically whenever needed, possible or useful. We characterize scenarios (alternatives) in working environments where we get performance advantage.

Blaze's remotely key encryption protocol [Bla96] was based on the idea of letting the host send the card one block which depends on the whole message. This block would be encrypted with the smart card secret key, and would also serve as a "seed" for the creation of a "temporary" secret key, that will be used by the host in order to encrypt the rest of the message. However, as Lucks [Luc97] pointed out, Blaze's scheme had problems in that in allowed an adversary to forge a new valid plaintext/ciphertext pair after several interactions with the card. Lucks suggested an alternative model and protocol, which in turn, was attacked by Blaze, Feigenbaum and Naor [BFN98] who further demonstrated the subtleties of this problem. They showed that the encryption key used for the largest part of the message is deterministically derived from the two first blocks of the message, hence an adversary who takes control of the host will be able to decrypt a large set of messages with only one query. They derived a careful formal model and a scheme based on pseudorandom functions. Very recently, Lucks [Luc99] further extended their security model and suggested a faster scheme. In contrast, we will allow randomized encryption and we will rely on ideal (random oracle) hash functions.

Our work makes sure that missing a small piece of the scrambled data (via encryption) while keeping the rest available makes it hard to recover the message. This bears some relationship to Rivest's notion of All-Or-Nothing encryption [Riv97]. Informally, given a symmetric cipher, a mode of encryption is defined to be *strongly non-separable* when it encrypts s blocks of plaintext into t blocks of ciphertext ($t \geq s$) which are such that an attacker cannot get any information on the plaintext without decrypting *all* the ciphertext blocks. In order to obtain strongly non-separable encryption, Rivest suggests to perform an "all-or-nothing" transform on the plaintext, followed by a regular encryption of the result. There is an obvious parallel between our scrambling step and the all-or-nothing transform. As a matter of fact, our scrambling step possesses a slightly more general property than the strong non-separability. It has the property that no information can be gained on the pre-image of a scrambling as soon as *any* k-bits are missing (in the design we fix which k bits to hide). The two preprocessing steps are interchangeable: Rivest's all-or-nothing transform could be followed by a single encryption, and our scrambling yields an all-or-nothing encryption mode. However, the motivations of the two notions are very different. Our goal is to design a scheme which minimizes encryption with a given key, while Rivest's goal is to make brute-force decryption more difficult to an adversary. As a final note, we should point out that our techniques is much more efficient than the one proposed in [Riv97], notably because we do not use encryption during the preprocessing step.

3 Model and Definitions

We will present a two-stage model: scrambling and encryption. As noted above, the presentation follows the remotely keyed encryption model.

3.1 Model

Our scheme involves two connected devices: a computationally potent device, let us call this device the *slave* device, and a computationally weak device, which we denote the *master* device.

We assume a limited and low bandwidth communication channel between the master and the slave. We trust the master device to follow the protocols and to be tamper resistant. We only trust the slave device to *be able to* perform the operations it is asked to. On the other hand, we do not trust it for being intrusion resistant: we assume that an adversary may take full control of it for some time period. During this preliminary period the adversary may in particular obtain any information that the slave has and also interact with the master in any way he likes.

We would like to construct schemes that allow the slave device to perform encryption (and decryption) on large messages at high speed, with the help of private information owned by the master device. In the full generality, we may consider that the master can own keys corresponding to any kind of encryption (symmetric, public-key, probabilistic or non-probabilistic), and that the encryption obtained at the end of the protocol can be of any of the previous types. However, for public-key we may employ the master only for decryption, and with symmetric encryption the type of queries and attacks is larger (since "encryption queries" are meaningful). We consider as our example model of choice a master which employs an ideal cipher (e.g., a (pseudo)-random permutation), and a slave which performs sampling of a randomized IV, and scrambling via a public ideal (random oracle) hash.

The requirements on the schemes are as follow:

Balanced computation. The slave should perform the largest possible part of the computation, the master should perform the lowest. Their respective parts of the computation can be proportional to their computing rate (thus we balance the time spent by each component). Other choices of resource balancing are possible– e.g., limit the slow component to a "constant usage" and vary the fast component as a function of the message size.

Low communications. The number of interactions between the slave and the master should be low, and each of these interactions should need only a small amount of communication. Ideally, there should be only one interaction per protocol.

Security. Intuitively and informally, we require that after having taken control of the slave and making a number of queries (bounded by some polynomial) to the master, and then losing the control of the slave, an adversary will not have any advantage in distinguishing subsequent plaintext/ciphertext pairs from random pairs. Variations on the security requirements are possible: e.g., the adversary may choose the plaintext for which a distinguishing challenge is required. Other challenges than distinguishability are possible as well. Here, we will consider two attacks. (Though the above talks about "polynomial time" and "advantages" in general terms, we will actually compute actual probabilities of successful attacks).

Of course, the interaction and the encryption blocks are still large enough in the size of the security parameter. Namely, the security of the protocol is assured sub-exponentially in the size of that block (e.g., 128 or 256 bit size).

3.2 Definitions

Configuration A *probabilistic remotely key encryption scheme* (PRKES), consists of two protocols, one for encryption, the other for decryption, both executed on two communicating devices. These devices are (1) a probabilistic machine (machine with a truly random generator) called a "master" and (2) a machine called a "slave". (The slave can also be probabilistic in some designs. In fact, herein we model the slave as an ideal cipher, namely a random permutation). Given an input to the slave, it interacts with the master and produces an output. The input includes an indicator for performing either encryption or decryption, possibly a size parameter, and the argument (resp. cleartext or ciphertext).

Background for attacks Let us review attacks on the protocol.

The polynomial-time attacker A (we will use concrete assumptions regarding the "polynomial-time power") has a **challenge** phase, and one or more **probing** (tampering) phases. Typically the probing enables the adversary to activate the device up to some bound (some polynomial in the key length). The probing is a preliminary step prior to the challenge (or a prior step followed by additional probing with certain restriction after the challenge has been issued).

In the *challenge phase*, a certain goal is required from A:

Distinguishability challenge: A is presented with a challenge pair c_1, c_2, which is either a plaintext/ciphertext pair or a random pair from the same distribution. (Below we specify one such distribution).

Valid pair creation challenge: Another possible type of challenge, yielding another attack, is to ask A to exhibit one plaintext/ciphertext pair more than the number of probes he performed.

The *probing phase*. As noted above it can come before the challenge but also some limited part of it can be allowed to occur after the challenge.

We consider two probing phases regarding PRKES:

System probing: The attacker gets input-output access to the slave but not to its memory. Namely, he uses the slave as an oracle.

Master probing: The attacker gets full access to the memory of the slave. He can use the slave to interact with the master (input-output access) on queries of its own using the master as an oracle.

Attacks and security against them Let us next describe the entire attack. We consider two types of attack, which differs only by the challenge phase, described below.

An *adaptive chosen-message chosen-ciphertext attack with distinguishability challenge* includes:

– first phase: A performs "master probing". We assume that it performs up to p_1 pre-challenge probes. We also assume that the slave is *reset* (to a random state) after the intrusion, that is before the second phase. (This insures that no state information on the slave is known after the probing).

- second phase (distinguishability challenge): *A presents a plaintext* (or plaintexts) *pl* and gets a challenge pair (plaintext, value) whose plaintext part is *pl* and the value part is either a ciphertext of the plaintext or a random value, each case chosen with probability $1/2$.

- third phase: *A* performs "system probing" where he can ask any oracle query (including further encryptions of the challenge plaintext) *BUT* is not allowed to perform a *decryption* query on the ciphertext of the challenge pair. We allow up to p_2 such post-challenge probes.

Security: We say that a PRKES is *secure* against a distinguishability attack if for a plaintext of its choice, *A* cannot distinguish a valid {plaintext/ciphertext} pair from a {plaintext/random-text} pair with probability asymptotically better than $1/2$ (for the same chosen plaintext).

An *adaptive chosen-message chosen-ciphertext attack with valid pair creation challenge* includes:

- first phase: *A* performs "master probing". We assume that it performs up to p_1 pre-challenge probes. We also assume that the slave is *reset* (to a random state) after the intrusion, that is before the second phase. (This insures that no state information on the slave is known after the probing).

- second phase (valid pair creation challenge): *A* is challenged to exhibit $p_1 + 1$ valid plaintext/ciphertext pairs.

Security: We say that a PRKES is *secure* against a valid pair creation attack if *A* is able to answer the challenge only with an asymptotically small probability (to be computed concretely).

Remark: It should be noted here that our definition is different from the basic definition in [BFN98]. Here the definition follows the one in (adaptive) chosen ciphertext security (See [NY90, RS92, DDN91, BDPR98]). This is due to a difference in the model. In [BFN98], length preserving encryption was considered. As a consequence, their encryption model was deterministic, and thus, their definition required the introduction of an *arbiter* to filter the choice of *A* in the second phase (whereas in our case, internal randomization may allow oracle style probing on the challenge). In a recent extended version of their paper [BFN99], a formal model and treatment of length increasing functions was given as well; it formalized an indistinguishability attack. Our indistinguishability attack is of a similar nature.

4 Basic Tools

Ideal hash function We assume the existence of an ideal hash function (a function whose behavior is indistinguishable from a random oracle, see [BR93]). In numerous practical constructions, the validation or indication of the security of the design was based on such an assumption; we use the assumption in the same manner here. In practice, the ideal hash function may be replaced by a strong hash (such as one based on SHA-1). Then from this hash function, we show how to construct, in a very simple manner, an *ideal length-preserving* one-way function H which – apart from the fact that its output has the same length as its input – has the same properties as an ideal hash function.

Let h be an ideal hash function and l be the size of the hash produced by this function. Let x be a message of size n. We assume, for ease of explanation, that l divides n.

We define H_i as $H_i(x) = h(t||i||h(x))$ (where $||$ denotes the concatenation and t is a tag designated specifically for this usage of the hash function, and which can include a specific number and the length of x).

Then, we can define $H(x)$ as being the concatenation of the $H_i(x)$ so that the size of $H(x)$ matches the size of x:

$$H(x) = H_0||H_1||\ldots||H_{n/(l-1)}$$

If l does not divide n, we simply concatenate with the first bits of an extra $H_{1+(n/(k-1))}$, as to ensure that the sizes match.

It is easy to argue that since each sub-block of H depends on the whole message, that if h is ideal in the random oracle model, H is ideal as well. (In short, this is so since any weakness (say, a bias from randomness or predictability) with H can translate to a weakness on one of the blocks and thus to a weakness with h). We comment that if (unlike the construction above) each block of H is not global (sensitive to all bits) there may be problems. These problems arise either from the definition of ideal hash function and also certain concrete problems as pointed out at in [And95].

While the above construction allows us to build a pseudo-random stream of the same size of the message without relying on other assumptions than ideal-ness of the hash function, we can, for efficiency reasons, replace the above quadratic construction by faster ones. A single regular hashing of the message can be used as a seed for a pseudo-random number generator, which can be, for instance, the PRNG suggested in [AB96]. We can also employ the Panama cipher [DC98] (which combines hashing and stream cipher).

Encryption function We now discuss the properties that we require for the encryption function used by the master (smartcard). We require the encryption to be at least pseudorandom (a pseudorandom permutation or function). This assures "strong security" in the sense that no partial information is revealed about the input given the output (and vice versa). It protects as in semantic security except for the "block repeat problem" where the encryption of the same block is deterministic. If we add a random IV we get rid of this "issue" as well.

Denote by k_{in} the input size of the cipher, and by k_{out} its output size. For symmetric ciphers, without IV we have $k_{in} = k_{out}$. Indeed this may be a pseudorandom function (such as encrypting a block in an EBC or CBC mode; or we may allow adding IV increasing the input size). $k_{in} = k$ is our security parameter (namely we will achieve security while allowing polynomial probes in its size) and we assume that the encryption above is invertible with probability $1/(2^{(k\delta)})$ for some constant δ (to an adversary which gets to see a concrete given bound of cleartext ciphertext pairs). When validating our design we will assume the encryption to be an ideal cipher, namely a random permutation (so that the probability of inverting above can be easily related to the number of cleartext ciphertext pairs available to a concrete attacker).

5 The Scheme

Let n be an integer, which represents the size of a message to be encrypted, and let $M \in \{0,1\}^n$ be this message. Also let k be a security parameter. We will denote by x the secret key held by the card, and by $E(\cdot)$ and $D(\cdot)$ the encryption and decryption functions used by the card. Finally, we will denote by H a length preserving hash function, as defined in the previous section.

We first present the encryption scheme:

Encryption

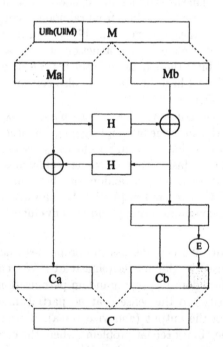

Fig. 1. The Encryption Algorithm

The encryption protocol is sketched in figure 1 and precisely goes as follows:

Slave computation Let M be the plaintext to be encrypted. The slave first chooses an uniformly chosen random number U of size polynomial in the security parameter (say k_{in} bits without loss of generality) and pads M on the left with $R = U\|h(M,U)$.

Then, if the resulting string is of odd size, an additional padding of one random bit is performed (this can be dealt with by the definition of the hash function h). Remark: we assume the length of the input is known and fixed, otherwise a byte with the actual length of the randomness can be appended as well; this also enables dealing with encryption of small messages.

Then, the resulting string $(\tilde{M})$ is split in two equal size parts, M_a, M_b ($\tilde{M} = (M_a\|M_b)$), and the slave computes:

$$C_b = M_b \oplus H(M_a)$$
$$C_a = M_a \oplus H(C_b)$$

Master computation The slave extracts the k_{in} last bits of C_b (say S) and asks the master to encrypt it. The master computes the encryption T of S ($T = E(S)$) and sends it back. This ciphertext is k_{out} bits long.

Final slave operation The slave finally erases the k_{in} last bits of C_b and replaces them by T.

Decryption

The decryption protocol is as follows:

Master computation Let C be the ciphertext to be decrypted. C is split into two equal parts (assuming the master's encryption is non-expanding), C_a, C_b ($Y = (C_a\|C_b)$). The slave extracts the k_{out} last bits of C_b (say T) and asks the master to decrypt this string. The master computes a decryption S of T ($S = D(T)$) and sends it back.

Slave computation The host replaces the k_{out} last bits of C_b by S to obtain $\tilde{C}_b$ ($k_{in} = k_{out}$, if not we simply adapt the lengths and the halving of the intermediate ciphertext). The slave computes:

$$M_a = C_a \oplus H(\tilde{C}_b)$$
$$M_b = \tilde{C}_b \oplus H(M_a)$$

The slave finally recovers the initial random IV at the beginning of M_a and recovers M from the two parts. He checks whether the random IV part is correct (that is if the random IV is of the form $U\|h(M,U)$), and if so returns the message M, else it outputs "error".

6 Security

We will next sketch the proof showing that our scheme is secure against an adaptive chosen-message chosen-ciphertext attack. This will validate the design as secure as long as the scrambling function is ideal (i.e., polynomially indistinguishable from a random oracle or intuitively not easily distinguishable from a large random table) and the master's encryption is not easily distinguishable from an ideal encryption. (Based on the ideal hash and encryption we can calculate the attack success by calculating probability of certain detection event performed by the attacker, such as the detection of a valid ciphertext in the challenge).

We will analyze both attacks (challenges): valid pair creation and indistinguishability.

Let us first analyze the master probing phase (which is performed in both attacks). The attacker has taken control over the slave and can query the master without any filtering, both for encryption and decryption. Hence, at the end of the master probing phase, he has potentially gathered a list of p_1 plaintext/ciphertext pairs for the master's inner encryption.

6.1 Against the valid pair creation attack

Informally, the core of the proof is to show that it will be possible to get information on only one valid plaintext/ciphertext pair for the global encryption out of a valid plaintext/ciphertext pair for the master encryption, (except with negligible probability).

With this type of challenge, there is no additional slave probing phase, as we can assume that everything potentially done during the slave probing phase can be done during the master probing phase.

Assume that the attacker $\mathcal{A}$, after performing p_1 queries to the master, is able to produce $p_1 + 1$ valid plaintext/ciphertext pairs for the whole encryption.

Call S the part to be given as input to the master (that is, with the notations of section 5, the k_{in} last bits of $H(R||M_1) \oplus M_2$). Then, we have two cases: either for all $p_1 + 1$ pairs, S is different, or it is the same for at least two of them.

In the first case, $\mathcal{A}$ can be straightforwardly adapted to build an attacker which breaks the master encryption, as it exhibits p_1+1 valid encryption/decryption pairs for the master after only p_1 queries. We assumed the master's encryption can only be inverted with probability $2^{-k_{in}\delta}$ for some small constant δ, hence in the first case, the attacker can fulfill the challenge only with probability $2^{-k_{in}\delta}$ (in the ideal cipher case this probability is easily derived from the number of encryption probes).

In the second case, if two master's inputs are the same, it means that $\mathcal{A}$ was able to find two distinct pairs (U, M), (U', M') such that the two values $H(U||h(M,U)||M_1) \oplus M_2$ and $H(U'||h(M',U')||M_1') \oplus M_2'$ match on their k_{in} last bits.

Let us analyze the probability that such a collision occurs. The above can be rewritten:

$$H(U\|h(M,U)\|M_1) \oplus H(U'\|h(M',U')\|M_1') = M_2 \oplus M_2'$$

In order to be able to find such a relation, the hash function H has to be evaluated on its inputs (because of the random oracle model). This means that M_2 and M_2' have to be fixed prior to the evaluation of the left part. So, M_2 and M_2' being fixed, A was in fact able to find two couples (U, M_1) and (U', M_1') such that $H(U\|h(M,U)\|M_1) \oplus H(U'\|h(M',U')\|M_1')$ match on their k_{in} last bits with a given constant.

Now, we consider two sub-cases, whether $h(M,U)$ and $h(M',U')$ are equal or not. If they are not equal, the attack performed in simply a birthday attack on a part of the hash function H, whose probability of success (based on the assumption on H) is $2^{-\frac{k_{in}}{2}}$. If they are equal (which can only happen if M_2 and M_2' match on their k_{in} last bits), then A was able to find a collision on the hash function, (which occurs only with probability $2^{-k_{in}\gamma}$ for some constant γ given the access limitation of the adversary).

Finally, (under concrete limited access of the adversary to the hash, and encryption boxes, formalized as bound on the success probability), will be able to answer the challenge with probability bounded by:

$$2^{-k_{in}\delta} + 2^{-k_{in}/2} + 2^{-k_{in}\gamma}$$

This is a negligible and controllable concrete probability of successful attack.

6.2 Against the distinguishability attack

Note that, for the distinguishability attack, the attacker can always guess the challenge and due to the challenge being random it has probability $1/2$ of being correct. The only other way for the attacker is to probe and perform encryptions and decryptions and match them against the challenge.

In this type of attack, A first performs p_1 master probes. Then, in the second phase, the attacker has lost control of the slave. He is presented a challenge pair (of which he can choose the plaintext which we call the target plaintext.) His goal is to guess with probability substantially larger than $1/2$ whether the challenge pair represents a valid encryption pair (i.e. whether the ciphertext is a correct encryption of the plaintext).

We first consider the security without the third slave probing phase. We will show afterwards that this phase does not help the attacker.

Again, we have two cases: either the k_{out} last bits of the ciphertext match a ciphertext from the master ciphertext list or not. In the first case (which happen with probability $p_1 2^{-k_{out}}$), A will be able to decrypt and to answer the challenge.

In the second case, in order to be able to answer correctly to the challenge, he as to be able to find out whether the following relations hold:

$$\begin{cases} C_b \oplus M_b = H(M_a) \\ C_a \oplus M_a = H(C_b) \end{cases}$$

However, he has no information about the k_{in} last bits of C_b (but with probability $2^{-k_{in}\delta}$, if he successfully inverts the master's encryption), and he has no information on the k_{in} first bits of M_a (because the slave was reset after the intrusion, and thus he cannot predict the value or the random number chosen by the slave).

So, in order to be able to check with some advantage if the above relations hold, the attacker has to guess the value of H on M_a (to validate the first eq. based on partial availability of C_b) or the value of H on C_b (to validate via the second eq.). This can be done with probability $2^{-k_{in}}$ for each (since only if the right string is guessed it is validated via the random oracle hash).

Hence, with only the initial master probing phase, the probability that $\mathcal{A}$ can correctly answer the challenge is $1/2 + 2^{-k_{in}\delta} + p_1 2^{-k_{out}} + 2^{-k_{in}+1}$.

Now, let us analyze what the attacker can do after the last slave probing phase.

Recall, that $\mathcal{A}$ is allowed to perform p_2 slave probes. He is allowed to query the encryption of any message, and the decryption of any message but the ciphertext challenge.

Of course, we assume that the ciphertext challenge has not already been decrypted, that is the k_{out} last bits of the challenge do not appear in any of the p_1 pairs previously obtained.

If he queries for encryption on a different plaintext than the challenge plaintext, he will not get any information (at best, he will obtain a ciphertext which he can decrypt (with the help of the p_1 pairs previously obtained), and will be able to retrieve the random IV of the slave).

If he queries for encryption on the target plaintext, then he will obtain information on the challenge only if he actually obtains the target ciphertext (which happens if the random IV (which is totally under the control of the slave now) is the same as in the challenge, which happens with probability $2^{-k_{in}}$.

If he queries for decryption, the best he can try is to query for a decryption of a ciphertext which matches the challenge on its k_{out} last bits. In this case, he will be able to find the decryption of the master's encryption on these bits if he can guess the random IV of the slave, that is, again, with probability $2^{-k_{in}}$.

Finally, the probability that he can answer the challenge is:

$$1/2 + 2^{-k_{in}\delta} + p_1 2^{-k_{out}} + 2^{-k_{in}+1} + p_2 2^{-k_{in}}$$

This is, again, a controllable probability (due to the actual limitations of the adversary) that can be made as close to $1/2$ as we want as we allow probing, by proper choice of k_{in}, k_{out}.

7 Experimental Results

We now briefly comments on the efficiency of our scheme within the suggested context of hardware assisted encryption. We implemented it on a personal computer (a PentiumPro(tm) 200). We chose our security parameters (k_{in} and k_{out}) to be 128 bits long. Times for the scrambling part are summarized in the table below.

length (bits)	1024	2048	4096	8192	16384	32768	65536
time (ms)	0.6	1.0	1.8	3.6	7.1	14.2	28.3

These speeds are not at first very impressive, but they have to be compared to a case where the master device (typically a smartcard) performs all the computation alone. Taking the DES as an example, implementations on smartcards theoretically range from 5 ms to 20 ms per block, but are often in the vicinity of 40 ms in order to prevent differential fault analysis [Nac]. Taking 40 ms for two DES blocks as an optimistic average value, we summarize the encryption speed of a smartcard based DES for messages of the same size as above.

length (bits)	1024	2048	4096	8192	65536
time (ms)	320	640	1280	2560	20480

Assuming that the encryption is pipelined, and choosing to encrypt $98304 = 3.2^{16}$ bits blocks (which makes the master and the slave computation workload about equal), we can encrypt with our scheme at a rate of about 2460 kbits/s, which has to be compared to the 3.2 kbits/s rate of the smartcard alone. We comment that in the context of public-key encryption, assuming that a smartcard can perform an 1024 bit RSA encryption in about one second, our design allows the encryption in one second of a 300 kilobyte message with the smart card's public-key.

8 Conclusion

We have presented the notion of "scramble all, encrypt small." We showed how it fits within the "remotely keyed encryption." The principle demonstrated by the notion can be employed elsewhere as a sub-structure, for example if the scrambling is not "ideal" we may iterate the basic overall encryption many times (adding randomness only at the first iteration, or avoiding adding randomness). Also, we may first perform more "Feistel scrambling" rounds. These types of variations and extensions and their impact on security (and its proof) under different assumptions about the scrambling component are interesting open questions. Variations on attacks, challenges and notions of security are also of interest.

9 Acknowledgments

We would like to thank Mike Matyas and Ron Rivest for pointing out related work and for discussions. We also thank Ross Anderson, Joan Daemen, Antoine

Joux, and the anonymous referees on the program committee for their valuable remarks which improved the presentation of the paper.

References

[AB96] Ross Anderson and Eli Biham. Two practical and provably secure block ciphers: BEAR and LION. In Dieter Gollman, editor, *Fast Software Encryption: Third International Workshop*, number 1039 in LNCS, pages 113–120, Cambridge, UK, 1996. Springer-Verlag.

[AB96] W. Aiello and S. Rajagopalan and R. Vankatesan. High Speed Pseudorandom Number Generation With Small Memory. These proceedings.

[And95] Ross Anderson. The classification of hash functions. In *Codes and Ciphers - Cryptography and Coding IV*, pages 83–93, 1995.

[BDPR98] Mihir Bellare and Anand Desai and David Pointcheval and Philip Rogaway. Relations among notions of security for public-key encryption schemes. In Hugo Krawczyk, editor, *Advances in Cryptology—Crypto '98* Number 1462 in Lectures Notes in Computer Science, pages 26–45. Springer-Verlag, 1998.

[BR93] Mihir Bellare and Philip Rogaway. Random oracles are practical: a paradigm for designing efficient protocols. In *1-st ACM Conference on Computer and Communication Security* Nov. 3–5, 1993, pages 62–73. ACM Press.

[BR94] Mihir Bellare and Philip Rogaway. Optimal Asymmetric Encryption. In Alfredo De Santis, editor, *Advances in Cryptology—EUROCRYPT 94*, number 950 in LNCS, pages 92–111. Springer-Verlag, 1994.

[Bla96] Matt Blaze. High-bandwidth encryption with low-bandwidth smartcards. In Dieter Gollman, editor, *Fast Software Encryption: Third International Workshop*, number 1039 in Lecture Notes in Computer Science, pages 33–40, Cambridge, UK, 1996. Springer-Verlag.

[BFN98] Matt Blaze, Joan Feigenbaum, and Moni Naor. A formal treatment of remotely keyed encryption. In Kaisa Nyberg, editor, *Advances in Cryptology—EUROCRYPT 98*, number 1403 in LNCS, pages 251–265. Springer-Verlag, 1998.

[BFN99] Matt Blaze, Joan Feigenbaum, and Moni Naor. A formal treatment of remotely keyed encryption. Full version of Eurocrypt 98.

[CFN94] Benny Chor, Amos Fiat, and Moni Naor. Tracing traitors. In Yvo G. Desmedt, editor, *Proc. CRYPTO '95*, pages 257–270. Springer, 1994. Lecture Notes in Computer Science No. 839.

[DC98] J. Daeman and C.S.K.Clapp. Fast hashing and stream encryption with PANAMA. In Serge Vaudenay, editor, *Fast Software Encryption: Fifth International Workshop*, number 1372 in Lecture Notes in Computer Science, pages 60–74, 1998. Springer-Verlag.

[DDN91] Danny Dolev, Cynthia Dwork, and Moni Naor. Non-malleable cryptography (extended abstract). In *Proc. of the Twenty Third Annual ACM Symposium on Theory of Computing*, pages 542–552, 6–8 May 1991.

[IBM-pa.] USA patents: 5,796,830 and 5,815,573 to Johnson et al.

[LR88]   Michael Luby and Charles Rackoff. How to construct pseudorandom permutations and pseudorandom functions. *SIAM J. Computing*, 17(2):373–386, April 1988.

[Luc96] Stefan Lucks. Faster Luby-Rackoff Ciphers. In Dieter Gollman, editor, *Fast Software Encryption: Third International Workshop*, number 1039 in Lecture Notes in Computer Science, pages 189–203, 1996. Springer-Verlag.

[Luc97] Stefan Lucks. On the security of remotely keyed encryption. In Eli Biham, editor, *Fast Software Encryption: 4th International Workshop*, number 1267 in LNCS, pages 219–229, 1997. Springer-Verlag.

[Luc99] Stefan Lucks. Accelerated Remotely Keyed Encryption. These proceedings.

[MPR97] Stephen M. Matyas, Mohammad Peyravian, and Allen Roginsky. Encryption of Long Blocks Using a Short-Block Encryption Procedure. IBM Technical Report, TR 29.2236, Research Triangle Park, North Carolina, March 1997.

[MPRZ98] Stephen M. Matyas, Mohammad Peyravian, Allen Roginsky and Nev Zunic. Reversible Data Mixing Procedure for efficient public-key encryption. *Computer and Security* V. 17 N. 3, pages 265–272, 1998.

[Mau92] Ueli Maurer. A simplified and generalized treatment of Luby-Rackoff pseudorandom permutation generators. In R. Rueppel, editor, *EUROCRYPT 92*, number in LNCS, pages 239–255. Springer-Verlag, 1993.

[MOV97] Alfred J. Menezes, Paul C. van Oorschot and Scott A. Vanstone. Handbook of Applied Cryptography, 1997. CRC Press LLC.

[Nac]   David Naccache. Personal communication.

[NP98]   Moni Naor and Benny Pinkas. Threshold Traitor Tracing. In Hugo Krawczyk, editor, *Proc. CRYPTO 98*, number 1462 in LNCS, pages 502–517. Springer-Verlag, 1998.

[NR97]   Moni Naor and Omer Reingold. On the construction of pseudo-random permutations: Luby-Rackoff revisited. In *Proc. 29-th STOC* ACM Press, May 4–6 1997, El-Paso, Texas, pages 189–199.

[NY90]   Moni Naor and Moti Yung. Public-key cryptosystems provably secure against chosen ciphertext attack. In *Proc. 22-th STOC*, pages 427–437, 1990. ACM.

[Pfi96] Birgit Pfitzmann. Trials of traced traitors. In Ross Anderson, editor, *Information Hiding*, volume 1174 of *Lecture Notes in Computer Science*, pages 49–64, Springer-Verlag, 1996.

[RS92]   C. Rackoff and D.R. Simon. Non-interactive zero-knowledge proof of knowledge and chosen ciphertext attack. In J. Feigenbaum, editor, *Proc. CRYPTO 91*, number 576 in LNCS, pages 433–444. Springer-Verlag, 1992.

[Riv97] Ronald L. Rivest. All-or-Nothing Encryption and the Package Transform. In Eli Biham, editor, *Fast Software Encryption: 4th International Workshop*, number 1267 in LNCS, pages 210–218, 1997. Springer-Verlag.

[Sch96] Bruce Schneier. *Applied Cryptography: protocols, algorithms, and source code in C*, John Wiley and Sons Inc., 2-d ed., 1996.

Accelerated Remotely Keyed Encryption

Stefan Lucks*

Theoretische Informatik
University of Mannheim, 68131 Mannheim A5, Germany
lucks@th.informatik.uni-mannheim.de

Abstract. Remotely keyed encryption schemes (RKESs) support fast encryption and decryption using low-bandwidth devices, such as secure smartcards. The long-lived secret keys never leave the smartcard, but most of the encryption is done on a fast untrusted device, such as the smartcard's host.

This paper describes an new scheme, the length-preserving "accelerated remotely keyed" (ARK) encryption scheme and, in a formal model, provides a proof of security. For the sake of practical usability, our model avoids asymptotics.

Blaze, Feigenbaum, and Naor gave a general definition for secure RKESs [3]. Compared to their length-preserving scheme, the ARK scheme is more efficient but satisfies the same security requirements.

1 Introduction

A *remotely keyed encryption scheme* (RKES) distributes the computational burden for a block cipher with large blocks between two parties, a *host* and a *card*. We think of the host being a computer under the risk of being taken over by an adversary, while the card can be a (hopefully tamper-resistant) smartcard, used to protect the secret key. We do not consider attacks to break the tamper-resistance of the smartcards itself. The host knows plaintext and ciphertext, but only the card is trusted with the key.

An RKES consists of two protocols, one for *encryption* and one for *decryption*. Given a β-bit input, either to encrypt or to decrypt, such a protocol runs like this: The host sends a *challenge value* to the card, depending on the input, and the card replies a *response value*, depending on both the challenge value and the key. This exchange of values can be iterated. During one run of a protocol, every challenge value may depend on the input and the previously given response values, and the response values may depend on the key and the previous challenge values. (In this paper, we disregard probabilistic RKESs, where challenge and/or response values also may depend on random coin flips.)

---

* Supported by German Science Foundation (DFG) grant KR 1521/3-1.

1.1 History

The notion of *remotely keyed encryption* is due to Blaze [2]. Lucks [5] pointed out some weaknesses of Blaze's scheme and gave formal requirements for the security of RKESs:

(i) *Forgery security:* If the adversary has controlled the host for $q-1$ interactions, she cannot produce q plaintext/ciphertext pairs.
(ii) *Inversion security:* An adversary with (legitimate) access to encryption must not be able do decrypt and vice versa.
(iii) *Pseudorandomness:* The encryption function should behave randomly, for someone neither having access to the card, nor knowing the secret key.

While Requirements (i) and (ii) restrict the abilities of an adversary with access to the smartcard, Requirement (iii) is only valid for *outsider adversaries*, having no access to the card. If an adversary could compute forgeries or run inversion attacks, she could easily distinguish the encryption function from a random one.

1.2 Pseudorandomness – Towards a Better Definition

It is theoretically desirable that a cryptographic primitive always appears to behave randomly for everyone without access to the key. So why not require pseudorandomness with respect to insider adversaries?

In any RKES, the amount of communication between the host and the card should be smaller than the input length, otherwise the card could just do the complete encryption on its own. Since (at least) a part of the input is not handled by the smartcard, and, for the same reasons, (at least) a part of the output is generated by the host, an insider adversary can easily decide that the output generated by herself is not random.

Recently, Blaze, Feigenbaum, and Naor [3] found a better formalism to define the pseudorandomness of RKESs. Their idea is based on the adversary gaining direct access to the card for a certain amount of time, making q_h interactions with the card. For the adversary having lost direct access to the card, the encryption function should behave randomly. An attack is divided into two phases:

1. During the *host phase* (h-phase), the adversary is an insider, sends challenge values to the card and learns the card's response values. She may run through the en- and the decryption protocol and may also deviate from the protocol (note though, that the card always interprets the "next value" it reads as the next challenge value, until the current protocol is finished).
   At the end of the h-phase, the adversary loses direct access to the card, i.e., is no longer an insider.
2. In the *distinguishing phase* (d-phase), the adversary chooses texts and asks for their en- or decryptions. The answers to these queries are either chosen randomly, or by honestly en- or decrypting according to the RKES.
   The adversary's task is to distinguish between the random case and honest encryption.

Consider an adversary having encrypted the plaintext P^* and learned the corresponding ciphertext C^* during the h-phase. If she could ask for the encryption of P^* or the decryption of C^* during the d-phase, her task would be quite easy. In the d-phase, we thus need to "filter" texts that appeared in the h-phase before. But since the adversary may deviate from the protocol, it is not easy to formally define which texts are to be filtered out. The authors of [3] require an arbiter algorithm B to sort out up to q_h texts. This algorithm need not actually be implemented, it simply needs to exist. (The formal definition below looks quite complicated. Readers with few interest in formalisms should keep in mind that the arbiter B treats the special case that in the d-phase the adversary A asks for values already known from the h-phase. As will become clear below, the arbiter B for our scheme does exist and actually is quite simple.)

Throughout this paper, "random" always means "according to the uniform probability distribution". By $x \oplus y$ we denote the bit-wise XOR of x and y.

After that much discussion, we give the formal definitions (which are not much different from the ones in [3]).

1.3 Definitions

A (length-preserving) RKES is a pair of protocols, one for en- and one for decryption, to be executed by a host and a card. The length of a ciphertext is the same as that of the corresponding plaintext.

Let B be an algorithm, the "arbiter algorithm", which is initialized with a transcript of the communication between host and card during the h-phase.

During the *host phase* (h-phase), A may play the role of the host and execute both the card's protocols up to q_h times, together. A may send challenge values to the card not generated according to the protocol and does learn the corresponding response values.

During the *distinguishing phase* (d-phase), A chooses up to q_d texts T as queries and asks for the corresponding en- or decryptions.

W.l.o.g., we prohibit A to ask equivalent queries, i.e., to ask twice for the encryption of T, to ask twice for the decryption of T, or to ask once for the encryption of a T and some time before or after this for the decryption of the corresponding ciphertext. (Encrypting under a length-preserving RKES is a permutation, hence A doesn't learn anything new from asking equivalent queries.)

Before the d-phase starts, a switch S is randomly set either to 0 or to 1. If the arbiter B acts, A's query is answered according to the RKES; B can act on most q_h queries.

Consider the queries B does not act on. The answers are generated depending on S. Consider A asking for the en- or decryption of a text $T \in \{0,1\}^\beta$ with $\beta > a$. If $S = 0$, the response is evaluated according to the RKES. If $S = 1$, the response is a random value in $\{0,1\}^\beta$.

At the end of the d-phase, A's task is to guess S. A's advantage adv_A is

$$\mathrm{adv}_A = \big| \, \mathrm{prob}[\text{``}A \text{ outputs } 1\text{''} \mid S = 1] - \mathrm{prob}[\text{``}A \text{ outputs } 1\text{''} \mid S = 0] \, \big|$$

By q_h, we denote the number of interactions between the adversary A and the card during the h-phase, by q_d we denote the number of queries A asks during the d-phase; $q := q_h + q_d$ denotes the total query number.

A RKES is (t, q, e)-secure, if there exists an arbiter algorithm B such that any t-time adversary A with a total query number of at most q has an advantage of at most e.

1.4 Building Blocks and Security Assumptions

In this section, we describe the building blocks we use for our scheme. As will be proven below, our scheme is secure if its building blocks are secure. Note that definitions of standard cryptographic and complexity theoretic terms are left out here; they can be found e.g. in [4].

By a and b with $b \geq a$, we denote the blocksizes of our building blocks (while our scheme itself is able to encrypt blocks which may grow arbitrarily large). **Note that a and b are important security parameters!** We may use, say, a 64-bit block cipher such as triple DES as pseudorandom permutation, but this has significant consequences for the security of our scheme, even if the adversary cannot break triple DES.

Our **building blocks** are
- an a-bit blockcipher E (i.e., a family of pseudorandom permutations E_K over $\{0,1\}^a$),
- a family of pseudorandom functions $F_K\{0,1\}^b \longrightarrow \{0,1\}^a$ (F may be a b-bit blockcipher, if $a < b$ we ignore the last $b - a$ bits of the output),
- a hash function $H : \{0,1\}^* \longrightarrow \{0,1\}^b$, and
- a length-preserving stream cipher $S : \{0,1\}^* \longrightarrow \{0,1\}^*$, depending on an a-bit key. In practice, S may be an additive stream cipher, i.e., a pseudorandom bit generator where each bit of the output is XOR-ed with the plaintext (or ciphertext, if we think of S^{-1}). Just as well, S may be designed from the block cipher E, using a standard chaining mode such as CBC.

For the analysis, we assume our building blocks (such as block ciphers) to behave like their ideal counterparts (such as random permutations). This "ideal world" view allows us to define the resistance of our scheme against adversaries with unbound running time:

A RKES is (q, e)-secure, if any adversary A with a query-complexity of at most q has an advantage of at most e.

Consider our RKES being (q, e)-secure in the ideal world, but not $(t, q, e+\epsilon)$-secure in the real world. If either t is large enough to be infeasible or $\epsilon \geq 0$ is small enough to be negligible, the notion "(q, e)-secure" can still approximatively describe the scheme's true security. Otherwise, we have found an attack on (at least) one of the underlying building blocks. Being (q, e)-secure for reasonable values of q and e implies that the construction itself is sound.

This is a standard argument for many cryptographic schemes, being composed from other cryptographic schemes and "provably secure".

Our **security assumptions** are
1. E_K is a random permutation over $\{0,1\}^a$, and for $K \neq K'$ the permutations E_K and $E_{K'}$ are independent.
2. $F_K\{0,1\}^b \longrightarrow \{0,1\}^a$, is a random function, i.e., a table of 2^b random values in $\{0,1\}^a$. Similarly to above, two random functions depending on independently chosen keys are assumed to be independent.
3. H is collision resistant, i.e., the adversary does not know and is unable to find a pair $(V, V') \in \{0,1\}^*$ with $V \neq V'$ and $H(V) \neq H(V')$ if $V \neq V'$.
4. S_K is a length-preserving stream cipher, depending on a key $K \in \{0,1\}^a$. I.e., for every number n, every plaintext $T \in \{0,1\}^n$, every set of keys $L = \{K_1, \ldots, K_r\} \subseteq \{0,1\}^a$ and every key $K \in \{0,1\}^a$, $K \notin L$, the value $S_K(T) \in \{0,1\}^n$ is a random value, independent of T, $S_{K_1}(T), \ldots$, $S_{K_n}(T)$. Similarly, the value $S^{-1}(T)$ is a random value, independent of $S_{K_1}^{-1}(T), \ldots, S_{K_n}^{-1}(T)$.

We do not specify the key sizes of E and F. We implicitly assume the security level of E and F (and thus their key size) to be long enough that breaking either of them is infeasible.

In the world of complexity theoretical cryptography, the usage of asymptotics is quite common. While this may simplify the analysis, it often makes the results less useful in practice. From a proof of security, the implementor of a cryptographic scheme may conclude the scheme to be secure if the security parameters are chosen large enough – but such a result provides little help to find out how large is "large enough". (Often, the implementor can find this out by very diligently reading and understanding the proof, though.)

This paper avoids asymptotics. If we call an amount of time to be "infeasible", we are talking about a *fixed amount of computational time*. What actually is considered infeasible depends on the implementors/users of the scheme and their threat model. Similarly, we use the word "negligible".

2 The ARK Encryption Scheme

Using the above building blocks, we describe the accelerated remotely keyed (ARK) encryption scheme. For the description, we use two random permutations E_1, E_2 over $\{0,1\}^a$ and two random functions $F_1, F_2 : \{0,1\}^b \longrightarrow \{0,1\}^a$. In practice, these components are realized pseudorandomly, depending on four different keys.

The encryption function takes any β-bit plaintexts, encrypts it, and outputs a β-bit ciphertext. The blocksize β can take any value $\beta \geq a$.

We represent the plaintext by (P, Q) with $P \in \{0,1\}^a$ and $Q \in \{0,1\}^{\beta-a}$; similarly we represent the ciphertext by (C, D) with $C \in \{0,1\}^a$ and $D \in \{0,1\}^{\beta-a}$. For the protocol description, we also consider intermediate values $X, Z \in \{0,1\}^b$ and $Y \in \{0,1\}^a$. The encryption protocol works as follows:

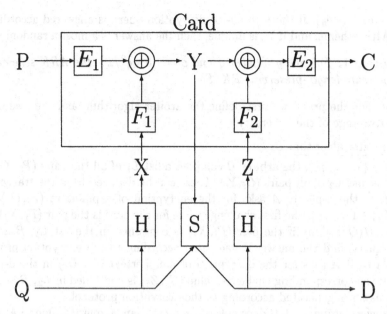

Fig. 1. The ARK encryption protocol.

1. Given the plaintext (P, Q), the host sends P and $X := H(Q)$ to the card.
2. The card responds with $Y := E_1(P) \oplus F_1(X)$.
3. The host computes $D := S_Y(Q)$.
4. The host sends $Z := H(D)$ to the card.
5. The card responds with $C := E_2(Y \oplus F_2(Z))$.

Decrypting (C, D) is done like this:

1. The host sends C and $Z = H(D)$ to the card.
2. The card responds with $Y = E_2^{-1}(C) \oplus F_2(Z)$.
3. The host computes $Q = S_Y(D)$.
4. The host sends $X = H(Q)$ to the card.
5. The card responds with $P = E_1^{-1}(Y \oplus F_1(X))$.

Note that by first encrypting any plaintext (P, Q) under any key and then decrypting the result the ciphertext under the same key, one gets (P, Q) again.

3 The Security of the ARK Scheme

By P_i, X_i, Y_i, Z_i, and C_i we denote the the challenge and response values of the i-th protocol execution, which may be either a en- or a decryption protocol. The protocol can either be executed in the h-phase, indicated by $i \in \{1, \ldots, q_h\}$, or in the d-phase, indicated by $i \in \{q_h + 1, \ldots, q\}$. A value Y_i is "unique", if $Y_i \notin \{Y_1, \ldots, Y_{i-1}, Y_{i+1}, \ldots, Y_q\}$. The ARK schemes security greatly depends on the values Y_k in the d-phase being unique, except when B acts ("in the d-phase" indicates $k > q_h$). If the k-th en- or decryption query is answered according to the ARK scheme, and if Y_k is unique, then the answer is almost a random value.

Theorem 1. *For every number q and $e = 1.5 * q^2/2^a$, the ARK scheme is a (q, e)-secure length-preserving RKES.*

Proof. For the proof, we first define the arbiter algorithm, and then we bound the advantage of the adversary.

The arbiter algorithm B:

For $i \in \{1, \ldots, q_h\}$, the arbiter B compiles a list L_1 of all the pairs (P_i, X_i) and another list L_2 of all pairs (C_i, Y_i). These can be deduced from the transcript.

If, in the d-phase, A asks for the encryption of a plaintext (P_j, Q_j) with $j \in \{q_h + 1, \ldots, q\}$, the first challenge value for the card is the pair (P_j, X_j) with $X_j = H(Q_j)$. Only if the pair (P_j, X_j) is contained in the list L_1, B acts on that query, and the answer is generated according to the encryption protocol. Similarly, if A asks for the decryption of a ciphertext (C_j, D_j) in the d-phase, and if the corresponding challenge value (C_j, Z_j) is contained in L_2, B acts and the answer is generated according to the decryption protocol.

Now we argue, that B does not act on more than q_h queries. Due to Assumption 3, i.e., due to the collision resistance of H, the adversary A does not know more than one value Q with $H(Q) = X_i$. For the same reason, A does not know more than one value D with $H(D) = Z_i$. Hence for every $i \in \{1, \ldots, q_h\}$, A can ask no more than one plaintext (P_j, Q_j) to be encrypted during the d-phase, where the corresponding pair (P_j, X_j) would be found in the list L_1. Similarly, we argue for decryption queries. Finally, consider a plaintext $T = (P_j, Q_j)$ and the corresponding ciphertext $T' = (C_j, D_j)$. Asking for the encryption of T is equivalent to asking for the decryption of T', and we only regard non-equivalent queries. We observe: $((P_j, H(Q_j))$ is in the list $L_1) \Leftrightarrow ((C_j, H(D_j))$ is in $L_2)$.

The advantage of A:

In short, the remainder of the proof is as follows:

> Both for $S = 0$ and $S = 1$, we define what it means for the the k-th query ($k \in \{q_h + 1 \ldots, q\}$) to be "BAD$_k$". We define sets U_k and show that if query k is not BAD$_k$, the response is a uniformly distributed random value in U_k. Further, we evaluate the probability that the k-th query is BAD$_k$. We write BAD* if any query k in the d-phase is BAD$_k$. If not BAD*, then all the answers to A are randomly chosen according to a probability distribution induced by the sets U_k, and thus do not depend on S. This allows us to bound the advantage of A:
>
> $$\text{adv}_A \leq \text{prob}[\text{BAD}^*|S = 0] + \text{prob}[\text{BAD}^*|S = 1].$$

Let $k > q_h$ and A be asking for the encryption of a plaintext $(P_k, Q_k) \in \{0,1\}^a \times \{0,1\}^{\beta-a}$.

We assume $(P_k, X_k) \notin \{(P_1, X_1), \ldots, (P_{k-1}, X_{k-1})\}$. If $j \in \{1, \ldots, q_h\}$ and $(P_j, X_j) = (P_k, X_k)$, then B acts and the answer to this query does not depend on S. If $j \in \{q_h + 1 \ldots, k-1\}$, then $(P_j, Q_j) \neq (P_k, Q_k)$, because the j-th and the k-th query are not equivalent. If $(P_j, Q_j) \neq (P_k, Q_k)$, then $(P_j, X_j) = (P_k, X_k)$ would indicate a collision $Q_j \neq Q_k$ for H, something we assume A can't find.

Depending on previous protocol executions and responses, we define the set $U_k \subseteq \{0,1\}^a \times \{0,1\}^{\beta-a}$ of ciphertexts:

$$U_k := \left(\{0,1\}^a - \{C_1, \ldots, C_{k-1}\}\right) \times \left(\{0,1\}^{\beta-a}\right).$$

For $S = 1$, the ciphertext (C_k, D_k) is a uniformly distributed random value in $\{0,1\}^a \times \{0,1\}^{\beta-a}$. We define $\text{BAD}_k :\Leftrightarrow C_k \in \{C_1, \ldots, C_{k-1}\}$. Obviously, if not BAD_k, then (C_k, D_k) is a uniformly distributed random value in U_k. Further:

$$\text{prob}[\text{BAD}_k | S = 1] \leq \frac{k-1}{2^a}.$$

Now, we concentrate on $S = 0$. Here, we define

$$\text{BAD}_k :\Leftrightarrow \left(Y_k \in \{Y_1, \ldots, Y_{k-1}\} \text{ or } C_k \in \{C_1, \ldots, C_{k-1}\}\right)$$

Obviously, if not BAD_k, then $(C_k, D_k) \in U_k$. Also, if not BAD_k, then Y_k is not in $\{Y_1, \ldots, Y_{k-1}\}$, and then $S_{Y_k}(Q)$ is a uniformly distributed random value in $\{0,1\}^{\beta-a}$. Further, if $Z_j = Z_k$, then due to $Y_j \neq Y_k$, we have $C_j \neq C_k$. Apart from this restriction, C_k is a uniformly distributed random value in $\{0,1\}^a$, and especially: if not BAD_k, the ciphertext (C_k, D_k) is uniformly distributed in U_k.

If $X_j \neq X_k$, then $F_1(X_j)$ and $F_1(X_k)$ are two independent random values in $\{0,1\}^b$, and so are Y_j and Y_k. If $(P_k, X_k) \notin \{(P_1, X_1), \ldots, (P_{k-1}, X_{k-1})\}$ for every $j \in \{1, \ldots, k-1\}$, we have $P_j \neq P_k$ if $X_j = X_k$. In this case $Y_j \neq Y_k$. Hence $\text{prob}[Y_j = Y_k] \leq 2^{-a}$. Similarly, we get $\text{prob}[C_j = C_k | Y_j \neq Y_k] \leq 2^{-a}$. This gives

$$\text{prob}[\text{BAD}_k | S = 0] \leq 2 \frac{k-1}{2^a}.$$

Thus:

$$\text{prob}[\text{BAD}^* | S = 1] \leq \sum_{k=q_h+1}^{q} \text{prob}[\text{BAD}_k | S = 1] \leq \frac{1}{2} \frac{q^2}{2^a},$$

and

$$\text{prob}[\text{BAD}^* | S = 0] \leq \sum_{k=q_h+1}^{q} \text{prob}[\text{BAD}_k | S = 0] \leq \frac{q^2}{2^a}.$$

Due to the symmetric construction of the ARK encryption protocol, the same argument applies if A, as the k-th query, asks for the decryption of the ciphertext (C_k, D_k) instead of asking for an encryption. Hence, the advantage of A is

$$\text{adv}_A \leq \frac{3}{2} * \frac{q^2}{2^a}.$$

$\square$

4 The BFN Scheme [3]

In [3], the Blaze, Feigenbaum, and Naor describe a length-preserving RKES which we shortly refer to as the "BFN-scheme". As the ARK scheme is claimed to be *accelerated*, we need to compare the BFN scheme and the ARK scheme. Similarly to the ARK scheme, we represent the plaintext by (P, Q) with $P \in \{0,1\}^a$ and $Q \in \{0,1\}^{\beta-a}$, and the ciphertext by (C, D) with $C \in \{0,1\}^a$ and $D \in \{0,1\}^{\beta-a}$. Further, we consider $X, Z \in \{0,1\}^b$ and $I, J, Y \in \{0,1\}^a$. (Note that [3] only considers $b = a$.)

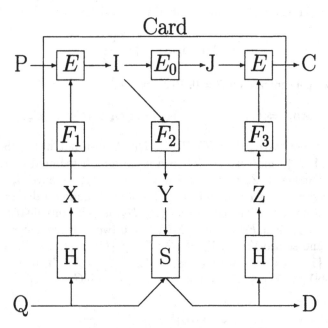

Fig. 2. The BFN encryption protocol [3].

As building blocks, we need one random permutation E_0 over $\{0,1\}^a$, three random functions $F_1, F_2 : \{0,1\}^b \to \{0,1\}^a$, $F_3 : \{0,1\}^a \to \{0,1\}^a$, and a block cipher E (i.e., a family of random permutations) E_K over $\{0,1\}^a$, depending on a key $K \in \{0,1\}^b$). The encryption protocol works as follows:

1. Given the plaintext (P, Q), the host sends P and $X := H(Q)$ to the card.
2. The card computes $X^* := F_1(X)$, and uses X^* as the key for E.
3. The card computes $I := E_{X^*}(P)$.
4. The card computes $J := E_0(I)$.
5. The card responds $Y := F_2(I)$ to the host.
6. The host computes $D := S_Y(C)$.
7. The host sends $Z := H(D)$ to the card.
8. The card computes $Z^* := F_3(Z)$, and uses Z^* as the key for E.

9. The card responds $C := E_{Z^*}(Y)$ to the host.

Decrypting (C, D) is done the obvious way.

Obviously, the ARK and the BFN scheme work quite similarly:

1. The cryptographic calculations on the side of the host are exactly the same for both protocols.
2. The communication between the host and the card is exactly the same for both protocols.
3. Inside the card, the ARK scheme needs four evaluations of cryptographic functions such as E_i and F_j. (Also, it needs two bit-wise XOR operations.) In contrast to this, the BFN scheme needs six evaluations of cryptographic functions.
4. Also inside the card, the ARK scheme allows the keys for the cryptographic functions to be chosen once and for all. On the other hand, the BFN scheme requires two evaluations of the block cipher E, where the keys are dynamically chosen, depending on some of the challenge values.

The third point indicates that, when implementing both schemes using the same building blocks, the BFN scheme's smartcard operations should take 50 % more time than the ARK scheme's smartcard operations. Due to the last point, things actually can be much worse for the BFN scheme. This greatly depends on the choice of the block cipher E and the key set-up time of E.

5 Final Remarks

5.1 The Importance of the Building Blocks

It should be stressed that our proof of security is with respect to any attack an adversary can come up with. Often, proofs of security in cryptography only deal with specific attacks, such as differential or linear cryptanalysis.

On the other hand, for practically using the ARK scheme, one has to instantiate the generic building blocks we are using. Our proof of security is only applicable, if all building blocks are secure, i.e., satisfy the security assumptions specified in this paper.

Hence, ARK scheme implementors have the freedom of choice to select their building blocks – and take the responsibility for the building blocks to be secure. If the building blocks are secure, the scheme is secure, too.

5.2 Inversion Security

This paper's reasoning is based on the security definition of Blaze, Feigenbaum and Naor [3], which seems to be more suitable than the one of Lucks [5]. It requires RKESs to be pseudorandom with respect to ex-insiders. Consider the RKES Σ being pseudorandom with respect to ex-insiders.

Clearly, Σ is pseudorandom with respect to outsiders, too. Also, Σ is forgery secure. Otherwise, the adversary could execute the protocol $q - 1$ times in the h-phase to predict q plaintext/ciphertext pairs. In the d-phase, the adversary could ask for the encryptions of these q plaintexts, and compare the results with her own predictions. (Note that the arbiter B can act on at most $q - 1$ plaintexts.)

But what about inversion security? Obviously, this property is quite desirable for some applications. Consider the RKES Σ^*, a simple modification of Σ. Both the en- and the decryption protocol of Σ^* start with an additional challenge value $\beta \in \{0, 1\}$. The encryption protocol of Σ^* goes like this:

1. The host sends β to the card.
2. If $\beta = 0$, both parties follow the encryption protocol of Σ.
   Else, both parties follow the decryption protocol of Σ.

Similarly, we may define the decryption protocol of Σ^*. Note that we did change the protocol, but the en- and decryption functions remain the same. Since the additional challenge value just allows the adversary another way to execute the decryption protocol, the security of Σ^* and Σ is the same:

Theorem 2. Σ is (q, e)-secure $\iff$ Σ^* is (q, e)-secure.

On the other hand, Σ^* clearly is inversion insecure. If, e.g., we only allow the adversary to execute the encryption protocol of Σ^*, via $\beta = 1$ she can decrypt any ciphertext, because she can still run the decryption protocol of Σ.

Hence, inversion security is a property of its own right, not covered by the above notion of "(q, e)-security".

5.3 Implementing the ARK Scheme

For actually implementing the ARK scheme, one needs to instantiate the building blocks with cryptographic functions. In this context, the role of the blocksizes a and b are important. Note that the parameter b is simply ignored in the proof of security. But we require the hash function $H : \{0, 1\}^* \to \{0, 1\}^b$ to be collision resistant. Thus, it must be infeasible to do close to $\sqrt{2^b}$ *offline calculations*. On the other hand, due to Theorem 1 the ARK scheme's construction is sound if the total query number $q \ll \sqrt{2^a}$. This restricts the number of *online calculations* for the adversary.

The difference between offline calculations (using any hardware the adversary has money for) and online calculations on smartcards allows the implementor to chose $b > a$. The current author recommends $b \geq 160$ and $a \geq 128$.

The hash function H can be a dedicated hash function such as SHA-1 or RIPEMD-160. The block cipher E needs to be a 128-bit block cipher, such as the (soon to be chosen) DES-successor AES. In this case, the pseudorandom functions F_K must map a 160-bit input to a 128-bit output. One can realize these functions as message authentication codes (MACs), e.g. as CBC-MACs based on E. Such MACs are provably secure [1].

Finally, for the encryption function S we have a couple of choices. S may either be a dedicated stream cipher, such as RC4, or a block cipher in a standard chaining mode, such as CBC or OFB. If one is using a block cipher, using the same one as inside the smartcard is reasonable.

Sometimes, a given application allows the security architect to drastically restrict the number of en- and decryptions during the lifetime of a key. If this number is well below 2^{32}, we may even use a 64-bit block cipher for E, e.g. triple DES. In this case, we need to observe two things:

1. The number of en- or decryptions should never exceed a previously defined bound $q^* \ll 2^{32}$, say $q^* = 2^{24}$. The card should be provided with a counter, to ensure the card to stop working after q^* protocol executions.
2. The encryption function S is defined to take an a-bit value as the key. Knowing one plaintext-part Q_j and the corresponding ciphertext part $C_j = S_{Y_j}(Q_j)$, the a-bit key Y_j can be found by brute force, on the average in 2^{a-1} steps. For $a = 64$, one should modify the ARK scheme and choose another key-dependent function to stretch the 64-bit value Y to get a larger key. E.g., think of using the block cipher E under a new key K_3, and send the 128-bit value $(Y_j, E_{K_3}(Y_j))$ to the card. This allows a key size for S of up to 128 bits. During the h-phase, the adversary learns q_h pairs of known plaintext Y_j and ciphertext $E_{K_3}(Y_j)$. This is no problem, since we anyway assume E to behave pseudorandomly.

References

1. M. Bellare, J. Kilian, P. Rogaway, "The Security of Cipher Block Chaining", in *Crypto 94*, Springer LNCS 839, 341–358.
2. M. Blaze, "High-Bandwidth Encryption with Low-Bandwidth Smartcards", in *Fast Software Encryption 1996* (ed. D. Gollmann), Springer LNCS 1039, 33–40.
3. M. Blaze, J. Feigenbaum, M. Naor, "A Formal Treatment of Remotely Keyed Encryption". in *Eurocrypt '98*, Springer LNCS.
4. M. Luby, *"Pseudorandomness and Cryptographic Applications"*, Princeton University Press, Princeton, 1996.
5. S. Lucks, "On the Security of Remotely Keyed Encryption", in *Fast Software Encryption 1997* (ed. E. Biham), Springer LNCS 1267, 219–229.

Miss in the Middle Attacks on IDEA and Khufu

Eli Biham* Alex Biryukov** Adi Shamir***

Abstract. In a recent paper we developed a new cryptanalytic technique based on *impossible differentials*, and used it to attack the Skipjack encryption algorithm reduced from 32 to 31 rounds. In this paper we describe the application of this technique to the block ciphers IDEA and Khufu. In both cases the new attacks cover more rounds than the best currently known attacks. This demonstrates the power of the new cryptanalytic technique, shows that it is applicable to a larger class of cryptosystems, and develops new technical tools for applying it in new situations.

1 Introduction

In [5, 17] a new cryptanalytic technique based on impossible differentials was proposed, and its application to Skipjack [28] and DEAL [17] was described. In this paper we apply this technique to the IDEA and Khufu cryptosystems. Our new attacks are much more efficient and cover more rounds than the best previously known attacks on these ciphers.

The main idea behind these new attacks is a bit counter-intuitive. Unlike traditional differential and linear cryptanalysis which predict and detect statistical events of highest possible probability, our new approach is to search for events that never happen. Such impossible events are then used to distinguish the cipher from a random permutation, or to perform key elimination (a candidate key is obviously wrong if it leads to an impossible event).

The fact that impossible events can be useful in cryptanalysis is an old idea (for example, some of the attacks on Enigma were based on the observation that letters can not be encrypted to themselves). However, these attacks tended to be highly specific, and there was no systematic analysis in the literature of how to identify an impossible behavior in a block cipher and how to exploit it in order to derive the key. In this paper we continue to develop these attacks including the general technique called *miss in the middle* to construct impossible events and a general *sieving attack* which uses such events in order to cryptanalyze the block-cipher. We demonstrate these techniques in the particular cases of the IDEA and Khufu block ciphers. The main idea is to find two events with

* Computer Science Department, Technion – Israel Institute of Technology, Haifa 32000, Israel, biham@cs.technion.ac.il, http://www.cs.technion.ac.il/~biham/.
** Applied Mathematics Department, Technion – Israel Institute of Technology, Haifa 32000, Israel.
*** Department of Applied Mathematics and Computer Science, Weizmann Institute of Science, Rehovot 76100, Israel, shamir@wisdom.weizmann.ac.il.

Year [Author]	Rounds	Type	Chosen Plaintexts	Time of Analysis
1993 [23]	2	differential	2^{10}	2^{42}
1993 [23]	2.5	differential	2^{10}	2^{106}
1993 [10]	2.5	differential	2^{10}	2^{32}
1997 [9]	3	differential-linear	2^{29}	2^{44}
1997 [9]	3.5	truncated-differential	2^{56}	2^{67}
1998 This paper	3.5*	impossible-differential	$2^{38.5}$	2^{53}
	4**	impossible-differential	2^{37}	2^{70}
	4.5***	impossible-differential	2^{64}	2^{112}

* From the second to the middle of the fifth round.
** From the second to the end of the fifth round.
*** From the middle of the first to the end of the fifth round.

Table 1. Summary of our attacks on IDEA with reduced number of rounds compared to the best previous results

probability one, whose conditions cannot be met together. In this case their combination is the impossible event that we are looking for. Once the existence of impossible events in a cipher is proved, it can be used directly as a distinguisher from a random permutation. Furthermore, we can find the keys of a cipher by analyzing the rounds surrounding the impossible event, and guessing the subkeys of these rounds. All the keys that lead to impossibility are obviously wrong. The impossible event in this case plays the role of a *sieve*, methodically rejecting the wrong key guesses and leaving the correct key. We stress that the miss in the middle technique is only one possible way to construct impossible events and the sieving technique is only one possible way to exploit them.

In order to get a sense of the attack, consider a cipher $E(\cdot)$ with n-bit blocks, a set of input differences $\mathcal{P}$ of cardinality 2^p and a corresponding set of output differences $\mathcal{Q}$ of cardinality 2^q. Suppose that no difference from $\mathcal{P}$ can cause an output difference from $\mathcal{Q}$. We ask how many chosen texts should be requested in order to distinguish $E(\cdot)$ from a random permutation? In general about 2^{n-q} pairs with differences from $\mathcal{P}$ are required. This number can be reduced by using structures (a standard technique for saving chosen plaintexts in differential attacks, see [6]). In the optimal case we can use structures of 2^p texts which contain about 2^{2p-1} pairs with differences from $\mathcal{P}$. In this case $2^{n-q}/2^{2p-1}$ structures are required, and the number of chosen texts used by this distinguishing attack is about $2^{n-p-q+1}$ (assuming that $2p < n - q + 1$). Thus, the higher is $p + q$ the better is the distinguisher based on the impossible event.

This paper is organized as follows: In Section 2 we propose attacks on IDEA [20]. We develop the best known attack on IDEA reduced to 3.5 rounds and the first attacks on 4 and 4.5 rounds, as described in Table 1. In Section 3 we show that this technique can also be applied to Khufu [24]. Section 4 concludes the paper with a discussion of provable security of ciphers against differential attacks, and describes several impossible differentials of DES, FEAL, and CAST-256.

2 Cryptanalysis of IDEA

The International Data Encryption Algorithm (IDEA) is a 64-bit, 8.5-round non-Feistel block cipher with 128-bit keys, proposed by Lai and Massey in 1991 [20]. It is a modified version of a previous design by the same authors [19], with added strength against differential attacks [6].

Although almost a decade has passed since its introduction, IDEA resisted intensive cryptanalytic efforts [23, 10, 11, 13, 16, 9, 14]. Progress in cryptanalyzing round-reduced variants was very slow, starting with an attack on a two round variant of IDEA in 1993 [23] by Meier and leading to the currently best attack on 3.5 rounds published in 1997 [9] by Borst et. al. In [18, page 79] IDEA reduced to four rounds was claimed to be secure against differential attacks. Table 1 summarizes the history of attacks on IDEA and our new results described in this paper (all attacks in this table are chosen plaintext attacks). In addition to these attacks two relatively large easily detectable classes of weak keys were found: In [11] 2^{51} weak keys out of the 2^{128} keys were found to be detectable with 16 chosen plaintexts and 2^{17} steps using differential membership tests, and in [14] 2^{65} weak keys were found to be detectable given 20 chosen plaintexts with a negligible complexity under differential-linear membership tests. Still the chance of choosing a weak key at random is about 2^{-63} which is extremely low. Related key attacks [7] on 3.5 rounds [16] and on 4 rounds [14] of IDEA were developed but these are mainly of theoretical interest. Due to its strength against cryptanalytic attacks, and due to its inclusion in several popular cryptographic packages (such as PGP and SSH) IDEA became one of the best known and most widely used ciphers.

Before we describe the attacks we introduce our notation. IDEA is an 8.5-round cipher using two different half-round operations: key mixing (which we denote by T) and M-mixing denoted by $M = s \circ MA$, where MA denotes a multiplication-addition structure and s denotes a swap of two middle words.[4] Both MA and s are involutions. T divides the 64-bit block into four 16-bit words and mixes the key with the data using multiplication modulo $2^{16} + 1$ (denoted by $\odot$) with $0 \equiv 2^{16}$ on words one and four, and using addition modulo 2^{16} (denoted by $\boxplus$) on words two and three. The full 8.5-round IDEA can be written as

$$IDEA = T \circ s \circ (s \circ MA \circ T)^8 = T \circ s \circ (M \circ T)^8.$$

We denote the input to the key mixing step T in round i by X^i, and its output (the input to M) by Y^i. The rounds are numbered from one and the plaintext is thus denoted by X^1. We later consider variants of IDEA with a reduced number of rounds which start with M instead of T. In these variants the plaintext is denoted by Y^1 (and the output of M is then X^2). See Figure 1 for a picture of one round of IDEA.

---

[4] As usual the composition of transformations is applied from right to left, i.e., MA is applied first, and the swap s is applied to the result.

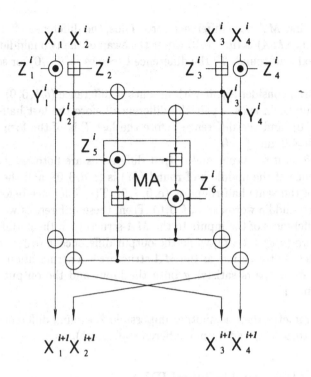

Fig. 1. One round of IDEA

In the rest of this section we describe a 2.5-round impossible differential of IDEA (in terms of XOR differences), and chosen plaintext attacks on IDEA reduced to 4 and 4.5 rounds using this impossible differential, which are faster than exhaustive search. We also describe a similar attack on 3.5-rounds of IDEA, which is more than 2^{14} times faster than the best previously known attack [9] and which uses 2^{17} times less chosen plaintexts. One interesting feature of these attacks is that they are independent of many of the design details of IDEA: They work for any choice of the MA permutation, and for any order of the $\odot$ and $\boxplus$ operations in the key-mixing T. In addition they depend only marginally on the choice of the key-scheduling of IDEA.

2.1 A 2.5-round Impossible Differential of IDEA

Our main observation is that IDEA has a 2.5-round differential with probability zero. Consider the 2.5 rounds $M \circ T \circ M \circ T \circ M$. Then the input difference $(a, 0, a, 0)$ (where 0 and $a \neq 0$ are 16-bit words) cannot cause the output difference $(b, b, 0, 0)$ after 2.5 rounds for any $b \neq 0$. To prove this claim, we make the following observations:

1. Consider a pair with an input difference $(a, 0, a, 0)$ for $a \neq 0$. In such a pair, the inputs to the first MA-structure have difference zero, and the outputs

of the first MA have difference zero. Thus, the difference after the first half-round $(s \circ MA)$ is $(a, a, 0, 0)$ (after the swap of the two middle words). After the next half-round (T) the difference becomes $(c, d, 0, 0)$ for some $c \neq 0$ and $d \neq 0$.

2. Similarly, consider a pair with an output difference $(b, b, 0, 0)$ for $b \neq 0$ after 2.5 rounds. In such a pair the difference before the last half-round (M) is $(b, 0, b, 0)$, and the difference before the last T is of the form $(e, 0, f, 0)$ for some $e \neq 0$ and $f \neq 0$.

3. Therefore, if the input and output differences are both as above, the input difference of the middle half-round (M) is $(c, d, 0, 0)$, and the output difference of the same half-round is $(e, 0, f, 0)$. The difference before the swap of the two middle words is $(e, f, 0, 0)$. From these differences we conclude that the differences of the inputs to the MA-structure in the middle half-round is non-zero $(c, d) = (e, f)$, while the output difference is $(c \oplus e, d \oplus f) = (0, 0)$. This is a contradiction, as the MA-structure is a permutation. Consequently, there are no pairs satisfying both the input and the output differences simultaneously.

Due to symmetry there is another impossible 2.5-round differential, with input difference $(0, a, 0, a)$ and output difference $(0, 0, b, b)$.

2.2 An Attack on 3.5-Round IDEA

Consider the first 3.5 rounds of IDEA $T \circ (M \circ T)^3$. We denote the plaintext by X^1 and the ciphertext by Y^4. The attack is based on the 2.5-round impossible differential with two additional T half-rounds at the beginning and end, and consists of the following steps:

1. Choose a structure of 2^{32} plaintexts X^1 with identical X_2^1, identical X_4^1, and all possibilities of X_1^1 and X_3^1.

2. Collect about 2^{31} pairs from the structure whose ciphertext differences satisfy $Y_3^{4'} = 0$ and $Y_4^{4'} = 0$.

3. For each such pair
   (a) Try all the 2^{32} possible subkeys of the first T half-round that affect X_1^1 and X_3^1, and partially encrypt X_1^1 and X_3^1 into Y_1^1 and Y_3^1 in each of the two plaintexts of the pair. Collect about 2^{16} possible 32-bit subkeys satisfying $Y_1^{1'} = Y_3^{1'}$. This step can be done efficiently with 2^{16} time and memory complexity.
   (b) Try all the 2^{32} possible subkeys of the last T half-round that affect X_1^4 and X_2^4, and partially decrypt Y_1^4 and Y_2^4 into X_1^4 and X_2^4 in each of the two ciphertexts of the pair. Collect about 2^{16} possible 32-bit subkeys satisfying $X_1^{4'} = X_2^{4'}$. This step can be done efficiently with 2^{16} time and memory complexity.
   (c) Make a list of all the 2^{32} 64-bit subkeys combining the previous two steps. These subkeys cannot be the real value of the key, as if they do, there is a pair satisfying the differences of the impossible differential.

4. Repeat this analysis for each one of the 2^{31} pairs obtained in each structure and use a total of about 90 structures. Each pair defines a list of about 2^{32} incorrect keys. Compute the union of the lists of impossible 64-bit subkeys they suggest. It is expected that after about 90 structures, the number of remaining wrong key values is: $2^{64} \cdot (1 - 2^{-32})^{2^{31} \cdot 90} \approx 2^{64} \cdot e^{-45} \approx 0.5$ and thus the correct key can be identified as the only remaining value.

5. Complete the secret key by analyzing the second differential $(0, a, 0, a)$. Similar analysis will give 46 new key bits (16 bits out of 64 are in common with the bits that we already found, and two bits 17 and 18 are common between the 1st and 4th rounds of this differential). Finally guess the 18 bits that are still not found to complete the 128-bit secret key.

This attack requires about $2^{38.5}$ chosen plaintexts and about 2^{53} steps of analysis.

A naive approach here (which works for any key schedule) requires 2^{64} steps and 2^{64} memory. A memory-efficient implementation requires only 2^{48} memory. In the particular case of rounds 2–4 of the key schedule of IDEA the subkeys of the 2nd and the 4th rounds have 11 key bits in common. Using this observation the attack requires only 2^{53} steps and 2^{37} memory.

2.3 An Attack on a 4-Round IDEA

The attack is also applicable to IDEA reduced to 4 rounds: $(M \circ T)^4$, from second to the fifth round (inclusive). We denote the plaintext by X^2 and the ciphertext by X^6. Depending on the starting round and on the differential being used $((a, 0, a, 0)$ or $(0, a, 0, a))$, there is a varying amount of overlap between the subkey bits. In the case of our choice (from second to the fifth round, with the first differential), we will work with subkeys:

$$Z_1^2[97 \ldots 112], Z_3^2[26 \ldots 41], Z_1^5[76 \ldots 91], Z_2^5[92 \ldots 107], Z_5^5[12 \ldots 27], Z_6^5[28 \ldots 43],$$

these have 69 distinct key bits out of $6 \cdot 16 = 96$. The attack guesses the two subkeys Z_5^5, Z_6^5 of the last MA structure, and for each guess performs the previous attack on 3.5 round IDEA. More precisely,

1. For each guess of Z_5^5, Z_6^5:
   (a) Decrypt the last half round of all the structures, using the guessed subkeys.
   (b) For each structure find all pairs with zero differences in the third and fourth words, leaving about 2^{31} pairs per structure.
   (c) For each pair:
      i. Notice that at this point we already know Z_3^2 due to the subkey overlap. Thus, we calculate the difference of the third words:
      $$(Z_3^2 \boxplus X_3^2) \oplus (Z_3^2 \boxplus X_3^{2*}),$$
      and find the key Z_1^2, which produces the same difference in the first words:
      $$(Z_1^2 \odot X_1^2) \oplus (Z_1^2 \odot X_1^{2*}).$$
      On average only one Z_1^2 is suggested per pair.

ii. Similarly find the pairs of keys Z_1^5 and Z_2^5 which cause equal differences at the 5th round. Since Z_1^2 and Z_2^5 share eleven key bits, we are left with about 2^5 choices of subkey pairs, and thus with about 2^5 choices of newly found 37 subkey bits. These choices are impossible.

(d) We need about 50 structures to filter out all the wrong keys (this is because we fix many key bits at the outer-most loop):

$$2^{37} \cdot \left(1 - \frac{2^5}{2^{37}}\right)^{2^{31} \cdot 50} \approx 2^{37} \cdot e^{-37} \approx 2^{-16}$$

2. After analyzing all the structures only a few possible subkey values remain. These values are verified using auxiliary techniques.

This attack requires about $50 \cdot 2^{32} \approx 2^{38}$ chosen plaintexts packed into structures as in the previous section. The total complexity of this attack consists of about $2^{32} \cdot 2^{38}$ half-round decryption (MA) steps which are equivalent to about 2^{67} 4-round encryptions plus about $2^{32} \cdot 2^{37} \cdot 2^5 \approx 2^{74}$ simple steps. When these steps are performed efficiently, they are equivalent to about 2^{70} 4-round encryption steps, and thus the total time complexity is about 2^{70} encryptions.

2.4 An Attack on a 4.5-Round IDEA

In this section we describe our strongest attack which can be applied to the 4.5 rounds of IDEA described by: $M \circ (T \circ M)^4$ which start after the first T half-round. We denote the plaintext by Y^1 and the ciphertext by X^6. In addition to the 64 key bits considered in the previous section we now need to find the subkeys of the two additional M half-rounds. We observe however, that only 16 of these key bits are new, and the other 48 bits are either shared with the set we found in the previous section, or are shared between the first and the last half-rounds. Therefore, it suffices to guess 80 key bits in order to verify whether the impossible differential occurs. These key bits are 12–43, 65–112, covering the subkeys:

$$Z_5^1[65 \ldots 80], Z_6^1[81 \ldots 96], Z_1^2[97 \ldots 112], Z_3^2[26 \ldots 41],$$

$$Z_1^5[76 \ldots 91], Z_2^5[92 \ldots 107], Z_5^5[12 \ldots 27], Z_6^5[28 \ldots 43].$$

The attack consists of the following steps:

1. Get the ciphertexts of all the 2^{64} possible plaintexts.
2. Define a structure to be the set of all 2^{32} encryptions in which X_2^2 and X_4^2 are fixed to some arbitrary values, and X_1^2 and X_3^2 range over all the possible values. Unlike the previous attacks, these structures are based on the intermediate values rather than on the plaintexts.
3. Try all the 2^{80} possible values of the 80 bits of the subkeys. For each such subkey
   (a) Prepare a structure, and use the trial key to partially decrypt it by one half-round with the keys Z_5^1 and Z_6^1 to get the 2^{32} plaintexts.

(b) For each plaintext find the corresponding ciphertext and partially decrypt the last two half-rounds by the trial subkeys $(Z_5^5, Z_6^5$ and $Z_1^5, Z_2^5)$. Partially encrypt all pairs in the structure with the subkeys Z_1^2 and Z_3^2.

(c) Check whether there is some pair in the structure which satisfies the 64-bit condition $Y_1^{2'} = Y_3^{2'}$, $X_1^{5'} = X_2^{5'}$, $Y_3^{5'} = 0$, and $Y_4^{5'} = 0$.

(d) If there is such an impossible pair, the trial 80-bit value of the subkeys cannot be the right value.

(e) If there is no such pair in the structure, try again with another structure.

(f) If no pairs are found after trying 100 structures, the trial 80-bit value is the real value of the 80 bits of the key.

4. Assuming that an unique 80 bit value survives the previous steps, the remaining 48 bits of the key can be found by exhaustive search.

This attack requires 2^{64} plaintexts, and finds the key within 2^{112} steps using about 2^{32} memory. This is about 2^{16} times faster than exhaustive search. See Table 1 for a summary of our attacks on IDEA compared to the best previous attacks.

3 Attacks on Khufu

Khufu and Khafre are two 64-bit block 512-bit key ciphers designed by Merkle [24] with a fast software implementation in mind. Khufu is faster than Khafre due to a smaller number of rounds but has a much slower key-setup. The strength of Khufu is based on key-dependent 8x32-bit S-boxes. These are unknown to an attacker and thus defy analysis based on specific properties of the S-boxes. The only additional way in which the key is used is at the beginning and at the end of the cipher, where 64-bit subkeys are XORed to the plaintext and to the ciphertext. The cipher is a Feistel cipher, so the input to a round is split into two 32-bit halves L and R. Each round consists of the following simple steps:

1. Use the least significant byte of L as an input to the S-box: $S[LSB(L)]$.
2. XOR the output of the S-box with R: $R = R \oplus S[LSB(L)]$.
3. Rotate L by several bytes according to the rotation schedule.
4. Swap L and R.

The S-box is changed every eight rounds in order to avoid attacks based on guessing a single S-box entry. The rotation schedule of Khufu for every eight rounds is: $2, 2, 1, 1, 2, 2, 3, 3$ (byte rotations to the right). Since our attack works equally well for any rotation schedule which uses all four bytes of each word every eight consecutive rounds, we simplify the description of the attack by assuming that all the rotations are by a single byte to the left. A description of this simplified version of Khufu can be found in Figure 2. Khafre differs from Khufu only in two aspects: its S-boxes are known, and it XORs additional 64-bit subkeys to the data every eight rounds. The best currently known attack on Khafre is by Biham and Shamir [6], which requires about 1500 chosen plaintexts for attacking 16 rounds, and about 2^{53} chosen plaintexts for attacking 24 rounds. The

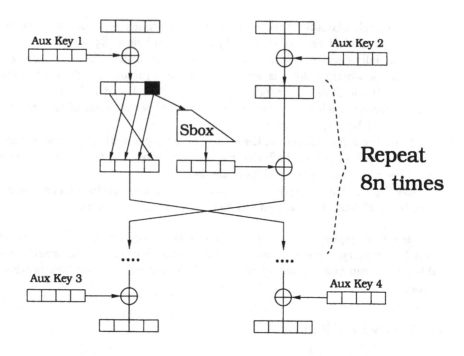

Fig. 2. Description of Khufu and Khafre

best attack on Khufu is by Gilbert and Chauvaud [12]. It attacks the 16-round Khufu, and requires about 2^{43} chosen plaintexts and 2^{43} operations (preliminary information on the secret key can be derived with about 2^{31} chosen plaintexts in 2^{31} steps). It is believed that Khufu is stronger than Khafre, since Khufu has secret key-dependent S-boxes, which prohibit attacks based on analysis of specific S-boxes.

Interestingly the approach described in this section is not very sensitive to the differences between these two ciphers, and works well for both of them since it is independent of the concrete choice of the S-boxes and (surprisingly) does not assume their knowledge by an attacker.

3.1 Impossible Differentials of Khufu and Khafre

In this section we describe long impossible differentials for Khufu and Khafre. The impossibilities stem mainly from the fact that the avalanche effect of the difference can be postponed by eight rounds. This leads to many eight round differentials with probability one, whose concatenation is contradictory. Due to the byte-oriented structure, these differentials come in sets of 256 or larger, and allow tight packing into structures. We study mainly the differentials with an eight byte input difference 000000+0, where '0' denotes a byte with zero

Rounds	Input	Output
14	000000+0 $\not\to$ *00**00*
15	000000+0 $\not\to$ 000**00*
16	000000+0 $\not\to$ 000*000*
17	000000+0 $\not\to$ 0000000*

Table 2. Impossible Differentials of Khufu and Khafre

difference, and '+' denotes a byte with arbitrary non-zero difference; '*' is later used to denote a byte with any (zero or non-zero) difference. However, two byte and three byte input differences are possible as long as $p + q$ remains constant (see the relevant discussion in the Introduction). Notice that a XOR of two different S-box entries necessarily looks like ++++, since the S-boxes are built from four permutations. Let us study one of these differentials in some more detail. To simplify presentation, we assume that Khufu and Khafre are implemented without swaps, and that the S boxes are used alternatingly in the left half and the right half.

The differential we describe below spans 16 rounds of Khufu and Khafre. It covers a set of 256 input differences for which a set of 2^{16} output differences is impossible.

1. Consider a pair of inputs with difference 000000+0. After eight rounds this difference is always of the form ++++00+0.
2. Similarly consider a pair with the output difference 000*000* after the 16th round. This output difference can only be derived from a difference 00*000*0 at the output of the 10th round, as the differing S bytes do not affect any S box between these rounds.
3. Therefore, the output difference of the S box in round 9 has the form 00+0⊕000*=00+*.
4. However, the input difference of the S box in round 9 must be non-zero, and due to the design of the S boxes, the output differences must have the form ++++, which contradicts the form 00+*.

This impossible differential is described in Figure 3. The above representation ensures that we write intermediate differences in the same order as in the figure. A 17-round impossible differential 000000+0$\not\to$0000000* is reached by adding one round to this 16-round impossible differential, while canceling the difference in the left half of the ciphertexts. The impossible differentials of this kind are summarized in Table 2.

3.2 The New Attacks

The best known attack against Khufu can attack up to 16 rounds and the best known attack against Khafre can attack up to 24 rounds. Using the impossible differential described above, we can attack Khufu and Khafre with up to 18

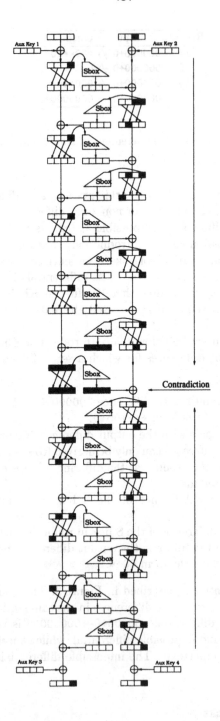

Fig. 3. The 16-Round Impossible Differential of Khufu and Khafre (simplified by equal rotations in all rounds). In this figure white squares represent zero differences, gray squares represent the zero differences which are also input bytes to the S boxes, and black squares represent bytes of type + or *

rounds. Consequently, the new 18-round attack is only interesting in the case of Khufu. For the sake of simplicity, we describe only a less-complicated attack on Khufu with 16 rounds which requires 2^{46} complexity.

This attack uses the 15-round impossible differential $000000+0\not\to000**00*$. Since the S-boxes are unknown, we can always assume that the bytes of the last subkey can be arbitrarily set to zero, yielding an equivalent (but modified) description of the corresponding S-boxes (and using a modified first subkey).

1. Encrypt structures of 256 plaintexts differing only in the 7th byte (we count the bytes of the block from left to right).
2. Check all the 2^{15} pairs contained in the structure and retain only those ciphertext differences of the form $+++*00+*$ (i.e., discard all the non-zero differences in the fifth and sixth bytes and all the zero differences in the second and third bytes of the ciphertexts). On average about half a pair remains for each structure.
3. Denote the inputs to the S-box used in the last round in a particular pair by i and j. Denote the ciphertext difference by $C' = C'_1, C'_2, \ldots, C'_8$. For each remaining pair the following constraint on the three first bytes of $S[i] \oplus S[j]$ cannot be satisfied:
$$(S[i] \oplus S[j])_{1,2,3} = C'_{1,2,3}$$

About two structures (2^9 chosen plaintexts) suffice to find the first such constraint. About 2^{37} constraints are required in order to actually derive the full description of three of the four output bytes of an S-box. Thus, this attack requires about 2^{46} chosen plaintexts. The rest of the S box information can be derived by auxiliary techniques.

It is interesting to note that these attacks are particularly sensitive to redundancy in the plaintexts. If the distribution of the plaintexts is not uniform, then in some cases we can efficiently convert these chosen message attacks into known-plaintext and even ciphertext-only attacks, as described in [8].

4 Concluding Remarks

Since the introduction of differential cryptanalysis in 1990 various approaches to the design of ciphers with provable security against this attack were suggested (see for example [2, 27, 22]). One way of proving a cipher to be secure against differential attack is to show an upper bound on the probability of the best differential. For example in [27] for a Feistel cipher with a bijective F function the probability of a three-round (or longer) differential was proved to be smaller than $2p^2$, where p is the highest probability for a non-trivial one-round differential.[5] This result makes it possible to construct Feistel ciphers with few rounds which are provably resistant against conventional differential cryptanalysis (for example, four rounds with best differential probability $\leq 2^{61}$). Examples of such ciphers are $\mathcal{KN}$ [27][6] and MISTY [21].

---

[5] A better bound of p^2 was proved later by Aoki and Ohta.

[6] Recently broken by high-order differential techniques [29, 15].

Notice however that any four and five round Feistel cipher has lots of impossible differentials, which are independent of the exact properties of the round function. For example, if the round function is bijective then for any value of $a \neq 0$, we have an impossible five-round differential $(a, 0) \not\to (a, 0)$, since it causes a zero output difference at the third round, but the round function is bijective and the input difference of this round is non-zero (this was already observed in [17] in the case of DEAL).

Using the properties of the round function one can usually extend the impossible differentials to cover even more rounds of a cipher. In the case of DES we can devise 7-round impossible differentials which hold for any choice of the S boxes, i.e., they still hold even if the S boxes are replaced by arbitrary (possibly unknown or key dependent) choices, and even if their order becomes key dependent (for example as in [4]), or the S boxes change from round to round. Let Θ be the (XOR) linear subspace spanned by the elements of $\{00400000_x, 00200000_x, 00000002_x\}$, and let $\mu \in \Theta$ and $\eta \in \Theta \oplus \xi$, where $\xi = 00000004_x$. Then, the differentials $(\mu, 0) \not\to (\eta, 0)$ and $(\eta, 0) \not\to (\mu, 0)$ are impossible for any such choice of μ and η. Consider the plaintext difference $(\mu, 0)$ and the ciphertext difference $(\eta, 0)$. The input and output differences of the F function in the first round are zero. The input difference of the F function in the second round is μ, and thus only one S box is active in this round. The output difference of this S box may activate up to six S boxes in the next round, not including S3 and S8. As the active bit in ξ enters S8, this input bit of the fourth round is not affected by neither μ nor by the output difference of the third round. Similarly, this bit is affected by the ciphertext difference, as it is active in η, and it cannot be canceled by the output difference of the fifth round, due to the same reasons that it cannot be affected by the output difference of the third round. Therefore, this bit is both 0 and 1 in the input of the fourth round, which is a contradiction.

FEAL [25, 26] has three 3-round characteristics with probability one. Using two such characteristics, with additional three rounds in between results in the following impossible differential (where a subscript x denotes a hexadecimal number):

$$(02000000_x, 8080000_x) \not\to (02000000_x, 8080000_x).$$

In this case the characteristics with probability one ensure that the data after round three and before round seven have the same difference: $(02000000_x, 8080000_x)$. Therefore, the output difference of the F-function in round five is zero, and thus the input difference of F in this round is zero as well (since F in FEAL is bijective). The input difference of F in round four is 02000000_x and the output difference must be 80800000_x which is impossible in the F function of FEAL (for example bit 19 of the output always differs for the specified input difference).

CAST-256 [1] has 20-round impossible differential (17 forward rounds and 3 backward rounds, or vice versa) with inputs and outputs which differ only by one word.

Another general belief is that large expanding S-boxes (n bits of input, m

bits of output, $n \ll m$) offer increased security against differential attacks. In particular 8x32 bit S-boxes are very popular, and can be found in Khufu, Khafre, CAST, Blowfish, Twofish and other ciphers. However, the difference distribution tables of such S-boxes contain very few possible entries – at most 2^{15}, and all the other $2^{32}-2^{15}$ pairs of input/output differences are impossible. This facilitates the construction of impossible differentials and can thus make such schemes more vulnerable to the new type of attacks described in this paper.[7]

References

1. C. M. Adams, *The CAST-256 Encryption Algorithm*, AES submission, available at http://www.entrust.com/resources/pdf/cast-256.pdf.
2. C. M. Adams, S. E. Tavares, *Designing S-boxes for Ciphers Resistant to Differential Cryptanalysis*, Proceedings of the 3rd symposium on State and Progress of Research in Cryptography, pp. 181–190, 1993.
3. I. Ben-Aroya, E. Biham, *Differential Cryptanalysis of Lucifer*, Journal of Cryptology, Vol. 9, No. 1, pp. 21–34, 1996.
4. E. Biham, A. Biryukov, *How to Strengthen DES Using Existing Hardware*, Lecture Notes in Computer Science 917, Advances in Cryptology - Proceedings of ASIACRYPT'94, pp. 398–412, Springer Verlag, 1995.
5. E. Biham, A. Biryukov, A. Shamir, *Cryptanalysis of Skipjack Reduced to 31 Rounds Using Impossible Differentials*, Lecture Notes in Computer Science, Advances in Cryptology – Proceedings of EUROCRYPT'99, Springer-Verlag, 1999.
6. E. Biham, A. Shamir, *Differential Cryptanalysis of the Data Encryption Standard*, Springer-Verlag, 1993.
7. E. Biham, *New Types of Cryptanalytic Attacks Using Related Keys*, J. of Cryptology, Vol. 7, pp. 229–246, 1994.
8. A. Biryukov, E. Kushilevitz, *From Differential Cryptanalysis to Ciphertext-Only Attacks*, Lecture Notes in Computer Science 1462, Advances in Cryptology – Proceedings of CRYPTO'98, pp. 72–88, Springer-Verlag, 1998.
9. J. Borst, L. R. Knudsen, V. Rijmen, *Two Attacks on Reduced IDEA (extended abstract)*, Lecture Notes in Computer Science 1223, Advances in Cryptology – Proceedings of EUROCRYPT'97, pp. 1–13, Springer-Verlag, 1997.
10. J. Daemen, R. Govaerts, J. Vandewalle, *Cryptanalysis of 2,5 Rounds of IDEA (extended abstract)*, Technical Report ESAT-COSIC Technical Report 93/1, Department of Electrical Engineering, Katholieke Universiteit Leuven, March 1993.
11. J. Daemen, R. Govaerts, J. Vandewalle, *Weak Keys of IDEA*, Lecture Notes in Computer Science 773, Advances in Cryptology – Proceedings of CRYPTO'93, pp. 224–231, Springer-Verlag, 1994.
12. H. Gilbert, P. Chauvaud, *A chosen plaintext attack of the 16-round Khufu cryptosystem*, Lecture Notes in Computer Science 839, Advances in Cryptology – Proceedings of CRYPTO'94, pp. 359–368, Springer-Verlag, 1994.
13. P. Hawkes, L. O'Connor, *On Applying Linear Cryptanalysis to IDEA*, Lecture Notes in Computer Science 1163, Advances in Cryptology – Proceedings of ASIACRYPT'96, pp. 105–115, Springer-Verlag, 1996.

---

[7] This also facilitated the conventional type of differential attacks on Khafre described in [6].

14. P. Hawkes, *Differential-Linear Weak Key Classes of IDEA*, Lecture Notes in Computer Science 1403, Advances in Cryptology – Proceedings of EUROCRYPT'98, pp. 112–126, Springer-Verlag, 1998.

15. T. Jakobsen, *Cryptanalysis of Block ciphers with probabilistic Non-linear relations of Low Degree*, Lecture Notes in Computer Science 1462, Advances in Cryptology – Proceedings of CRYPTO'98, pp. 212–222, Springer-Verlag 1998.

16. J. Kelsey, B. Schneier, D. Wagner, *Key-Schedule Cryptanalysis of IDEA, G-DES, GOST, SAFER, and Triple-DES*, Lecture Notes in Computer Science 1109, Advances in Cryptology – Proceedings of CRYPTO'96, pp. 237–251, Springer-Verlag, 1996.

17. L. R. Knudsen, *DEAL - A 128-bit Block Cipher*, AES submission, available at http://www.ii.uib.no/~larsr/papers/deal.ps, 1998.

18. X. Lai, *On the Design and Security of Block Ciphers*, Ph.D. thesis, Swiss Federal Institute of Technology, Zurich 1992.

19. X. Lai, J. L. Massey, *A Proposal for a New Block Encryption Standard*, Lecture Notes in Computer Science 473, Advances in Cryptology – Proceedings of EURO-CRYPT'90, pp. 389–404, Springer-Verlag, 1991.

20. X. Lai, J. L. Massey, S. Murphy, *Markov Ciphers and Differential Cryptanalysis*, Lecture Notes in Computer Science 547, Advances in Cryptology – Proceedings of EUROCRYPT'91, pp. 17–38, Springer-Verlag, 1992.

21. M. Matsui, *New Block Encryption Algorithm MISTY*, Lecture Notes in Computer Science 1267, Fast Software Encryption - 4th International Workshop (FSE'97), pp. 54–68, Springer-Verlag, 1997.

22. M. Matsui, *New Structure of Block Ciphers with Provable Security Against Differential and Linear Cryptanalysis*, Lecture Notes in Computer Science 1039, Fast Software Encryption - 3rd International Workshop (FSE'96), pp. 205–218, Springer Verlag, 1996,

23. W. Meier, *On the Security of the IDEA Block Cipher*, Lecture Notes in Computer Science 765, Advances in Cryptology – Proceedings of EUROCRYPT'93, pp. 371–385, Springer-Verlag, 1994.

24. R. C. Merkle, *Fast Software Encryption Functions*, Lecture Notes in Computer Science 537, Advances in Cryptology – Proceedings of CRYPTO'90, pp. 476–501, Springer-Verlag, 1990.

25. S. Miyaguchi, A. Shiraishi, A. Shimizu, *Fast Data Encryption Algorithm FEAL-8*, Review of Electrical Communications Laboratories, Vol. 36, No. 4, pp. 433–437, 1988.

26. S. Miyaguchi, *FEAL-N specifications*, NTT, 1989.

27. K. Nyberg and L. R. Knudsen, *Provable Security Against a Differential Attack*, Journal of Cryptology, Vol. 8, No. 1, pp. 27–37, 1995.

28. *Skipjack and KEA Algorithm Specifications*, Version 2.0, 1998. Available at the National Institute of Standards and Technology's web-page, http://csrc.nist.gov/encryption/skipjack-kea.htm.

29. T. Shimoyama, S. Moriai, T. Kaneko, *Improving the High Order Differential Attack and Cryptanalysis of the KN Cipher*, Lecture Notes in Computer Science 1396, Proceedings of the First International Workshop on Information Security (ISW'97) (Japan), pp. 32–42, Springer-Verlag 1997.

Mod n Cryptanalysis, with Applications Against RC5P and M6

John Kelsey*, Bruce Schneier**, and David Wagner***

Abstract. We introduce "mod n cryptanalysis," a form of partitioning attack that is effective against ciphers which rely on modular addition and bit rotations for their security. We demonstrate this attack with a mod 3 attack against RC5P, an RC5 variant that uses addition instead of XOR. We also show mod 5 and mod 257 attacks against some versions of a family of ciphers used in the FireWire standard. We expect mod n cryptanalysis to be applicable to many other ciphers, and that the general attack is extensible to other values of n.

1 Introduction

Nearly all modern statistical attacks on product ciphers work by learning some way to distinguish the output of all but the last rounds from a random permutation. In a linear attack, there is a slight correlation between the plaintext and the last-round input; in a differential attack, the relationship between a pair of inputs to the last round isn't quite random. Partitioning attacks, higher-order differential attacks, differential-linear attacks, and related-key attacks all fit into this pattern.

Mod n cryptanalysis is another attack along these lines. We show that, in some cases, the value of the last-round input modulo n is correlated to the value of the plaintext modulo n. In this case, the attacker can use this correlation to collect information about the last-round subkey. Ciphers that sufficiently attenuate statistics based on other statistical effects (linear approximations, differential characteristics, etc.) are not necessarily safe from correlations modulo n.

1.1 The Rest of This Paper

The rest of this paper is organized as follows. First, in Section 2 we introduce mod 3 cryptanalysis and develop the tools we need to attack RC5P. Next, in Section 3 we develop the attack on RC5P and show how it can be applied in a reasonably efficient way to break RC5P variants with quite a few rounds. Section 4 analyzes M6, a family of ciphers proposed for digital content protection.

* Counterpane Systems; 101 E Minnehaha Parkway, Minneapolis, MN 55419, USA; kelsey@counterpane.com.
** Counterpane Systems; schneier@counterpane.com.
*** University of California Berkeley, Soda Hall, Berkeley, CA 94720, USA; daw@cs.berkeley.edu.

Finally, in Section 5 we discuss what we've discovered so far, consider some generalizations to our techniques, and point out a number of interesting open questions whose answers we hope will be the subject of future research.

Also, in Appendix A we demonstrate why our definition of bias is the right one and recall some important facts about the χ^2 test.

2 Tools for Mod 3 Cryptanalysis

In mod 3 cryptanalysis, we trace knowledge of the mod 3 value of some part of a cipher's block through successive rounds of the cipher, leaving ourselves with some information about the input to the last round or two that lets us distinguish it from a randomly-selected block. The attack is conceptually very similar to Matsui's linear cryptanalysis [Mat94,Bih95,KR94,KR95,KR96], though it is properly included in the class of partitioning attacks [HKM95,HM97] developed by Harpes and Massey. We also draw somewhat from Vaudenay's statistical cryptanalysis [Vau96].

In this paper, we will use the shorthand term "mod 3 value" to stand for the value we get when we take some selected 32-bit part of a block, and reduce it modulo 3. A mod 3 value may thus be only 0, 1, or 2. In a randomly-selected 32-bit block, we would expect 0, 1, and 2 to occur as mod 3 values with almost identical likelihood. (If we automatically discarded any block with the value $2^{32}-1$, we would have perfectly equal probabilities.) As a block cipher's successive rounds operate on its block, the block should become harder and harder to distinguish from a randomly-selected block, without knowledge of the cipher's round keys. Mod 3 cryptanalysis works when the block's mod 3 value is still not too hard to distinguish from that of a random block, very late into the cipher. (In the same sense, linear cryptanalysis works when the parity of some subset of the block's bits is still not too hard to distinguish from that of a random block, very late into the cipher.)

2.1 Approximating Rotations

The insight that first led us to consider mod 3 cryptanalysis at all involved the behavior of the mod 3 value of some 32-bit word, X, before and after being rotated by one bit. When we consider X as a 32-bit integer, and $X \lll 1$ as X rotated left by one bit, we can rewrite the effects of the rotation in terms of integer arithmetic:

$$X \lll 1 = \begin{cases} 2X, & \text{if } X < 2^{31} \\ 2X + 1 - 2^{32}, & \text{if } X \geq 2^{31} \end{cases}$$

The first thing to notice is that $2^{32} \equiv 1 \bmod 3$. Thus, $X \lll 1 \equiv 2X \bmod 3$, because $2X + 1 - 2^{32} \equiv 2X \bmod 3$.

From this, we can derive the effect of any larger number of rotations. For instance,

$$X \lll 2 \equiv (X \lll 1) \lll 1 \equiv 2 \times 2 \times X \equiv X \bmod 3$$

In general, we have

$$X \lll n \equiv 2^n X \equiv 2^{n \bmod 2} X \bmod 3$$

so rotating by any odd number of bits multiplies the mod 3 value by 2, while multiplying by any odd number of bits leaves the mod 3 value unchanged. This means that when we know the number of bits a 32-bit block was rotated, and what its input mod 3 value was, we also know what its output mod 3 value was.

Next let us consider the case where we know the input mod 3 value, but not the rotation amount. We do *not* lose all knowledge of the output mod 3 value. Indeed, some traces of X leak, because we know

$$X \lll n \bmod 3 = \begin{cases} 2X \bmod 3, & \text{if } n \text{ odd} \\ X \bmod 3, & \text{if } n \text{ even} \end{cases}$$

Note that in the case of $X \bmod 3 = 0$, we have $X \lll n \equiv 0 \bmod 3$, regardless of n. Thus $\Pr[X \lll n \equiv X \bmod 3] = 4/6$ when X is uniformly distributed, and we have some incomplete knowledge on $X \lll n$.

We can express the propagation of partial information using the notation of probability vectors. Let the probability vector p_X represent the distribution of X, so that the j-th component of p_X is $\Pr[X = j]$. Then, for example, if $Y = X \lll 1$ and $p_X = [0, 1/2, 1/2]$, we find that $p_Y = [0, 1/2, 1/2]$. As another example, a uniformly-distributed random variable U is represented by the probability vector $p_U = [1/3, 1/3, 1/3]$.

It is also tempting to think of operations such as $\lll$ in terms of their transition matrix M (where $M_{i,j} = \Pr[f(X) = j | X = i]$). However, as will be discussed below, there are subtle pitfalls with such an approach.

In some cases it is also useful to view rotations as a multiplication modulo $2^{32} - 1$. The key observation is that we have the relation

$$x \lll j \equiv 2^j x \bmod (2^{32} - 1)$$

for rotations left by j bits. Reducing both sides modulo 3, we obtain $x \lll j \equiv 2^j x \bmod 3$. (This is valid because 3 divides $2^{32} - 1$.) This is another way to derive the mod 3 approximation of rotations given above.

We can also see that we get a good mod p approximation $x \lll j \equiv 2^j x \bmod p$ for bit-rotations whenever p divides $2^{32} - 1$. Section 5 explores this direction in more detail.

2.2 Approximating Addition Modulo 2^{32}

A similar analysis works for addition mod 2^{32}. Consider a simple description of mod 2^{32} addition in terms of integer addition:

$$X + Y \bmod 2^{32} = \begin{cases} X + Y, & \text{if there was no carry out} \\ X + Y - 2^{32}, & \text{if there was a carry out} \end{cases}$$

Since $2^{32} \equiv 1$ modulo 3, this can be rewritten as

$$(X + Y \bmod 2^{32}) \bmod 3 = \begin{cases} X + Y \bmod 3, & \text{if there was no carry out} \\ X + Y - 1 \bmod 3, & \text{if there was a carry out} \end{cases}$$

Sometimes, we know the distribution of the carry. For example, we might know that the high-order four bits of Y are all ones, and so know that the carry-out probability is around 0.98. We can then rewrite this approximation as:

$$X + Y \bmod 2^{32} \bmod 3 = \begin{cases} X + Y \bmod 3, & \text{with prob. } 0.02 \\ X + Y - 1 \bmod 3, & \text{with prob. } 0.98 \end{cases}$$

2.3 Biases and the l_2 Norm

As we discussed above, the probability vector $p_U = (1/3, 1/3, 1/3)$ is approximately what we would expect from a random 32-bit block. It would be nice to have some measure of distance from the uniform distribution. In this paper, we use the l_2 norm[1] as our measure of bias. The bias of a probability vector p_X is defined using this distance measure as

$$\|p_X - p_U\|^2 = \sum_j (p_X[j] - p_U[j])^2.$$

Intuitively, the larger the bias, the fewer samples of a block described by p_X are necessary to distinguish those blocks from a random sequence of blocks. Appendix A motivates and formalizes this measure of bias: we find that $O(1/\|p_X - p_U\|^2)$ samples suffice to distinguish the distribution p_X from uniform and that the χ^2 test may be used to implement the distinguisher.

3 Mod 3 Cryptanalysis of RC5P

RC5 is a conceptually simple block cipher designed by Ron Rivest [Riv95] and analyzed in [KY95,KM96,Sel98,BK98,KY98]. The cipher gets its strength from data-dependent rotations, a construct also used in Madryga [Mad84], Akelarre [AGMP96], RC6 [RRS+98,CRRY98], and Mars [BCD+98]. Presently, 16 rounds (each RC5 round consists of two Feistel rounds) of RC5 is considered to be secure. RC5P is an RC5 variant described in [KY98] and conjectured to be as secure as RC5. It is identical to RC5, except that the XORs in RC5 are replaced with additions modulo 2^{32} in RC5P.

In this section, we discuss a mod 3 attack on RC5P. We have implemented simplified versions of the attack on RC5P with up to seven full rounds (fourteen half rounds), but without input or output whitening. (This attack took about three hours on a 133 MHz Pentium.) We conjecture that this attack might be extended to as many as nineteen or twenty rounds for at least the most susceptible keys.

The RC5P round function is as follows:

---

[1] Also called the Euclidian Squared Distance in [HM97].

$$L := L + R$$
$$L := L \lll R$$
$$L := L + sk_{2i}$$
$$R := R + L$$
$$R := R \lll L$$
$$R := R + sk_{2i+1}$$

3.1 Modeling the RC5P Round Function

We initially tried to predict the bias of multiple RC5P rounds using several mathematical tools (transition matrices, matrix norms, second-largest eigenvalues, etc.). However, we found that precise analytical methods were surprisingly difficult to develop for RC5P, because of a lack of independence between rounds: in technical terms, RC5P is not a Markov cipher with respect to mod 3 approximations. As a result, multiplying the biases or transition matrices of each individual round gives incorrect answers.

For these reasons, we abandoned our pursuit of precise mathematical models and turned to empirical measurements. Let (P_L, P_R) and (C_L, C_R) represent the plaintext and ciphertext after encrypting by R rounds. For convenience, we choose plaintexts so that $(P_L \bmod 3, P_R \bmod 3)$ is fixed: in practice, each of the nine possibilities give about the same test results. Then we empirically compute the probability distribution of $(C_L \bmod 3, C_R \bmod 3)$ and measure its bias using the χ^2 test. More precisely, we count the number of texts needed for the χ^2 score to exceed a certain threshold. Since $(C_L \bmod 3, C_R \bmod 3)$ has 9 possible outcomes, we use a chi-square test with 8 degrees of freedom. To give some baseline figures, a threshold of $\chi^2_{2^{-16},8} = 37$ has a probability of about 2^{-16} of occurring in a random sequence of inputs, while a test value of $\chi^2_{2^{-32},8} = 62$ has a probability of about 2^{-32} of occurring in a random sequence of inputs.

We used this technique to estimate the number of texts needed to distinguish R rounds of RC5P, for $1 \leq R \leq 8$. For each choice of R, we ran 50 trials of the previous test and computed the average number of texts needed as well as a 90% confidence interval. Our measurements are presented in Figure 1; note that the y axis is scaled logarithmically.

3.2 Mounting the Attack

Overview of the Attack Here, we discuss a chosen-plaintext chi-square attack on RC5P without pre- or post-whitening. The attack can clearly be applied with the whitening, or with only known plaintexts; in each case, we require more texts and more processing. In the final version of this paper, we will specify attacks on more versions of the cipher, as well as having more complete experimental data.

We make use of the mod 3 values of the two 32-bit halves of the RC5P block to select one of nine partitions into which to put the block. Given a sequence of N RC5P blocks, we can count how many fall into each of the nine partitions, and

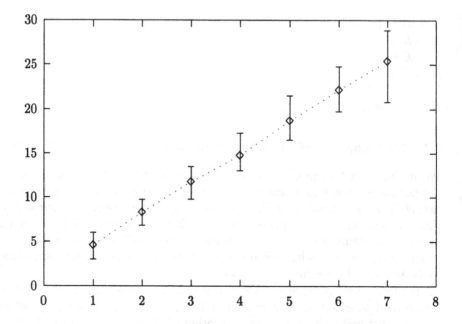

Fig. 1. Number of known texts needed to distinguish R rounds of RC5P from random.

use this count to compute a chi-square score, as discussed above. Informally, the chi-square score allows us to distinguish between a uniformly random selection of these partitions, as we would expect from the output of a random permutation, and a biased selection of these partitions, as we would expect from a cipher with a good mod 3 approximation available.

The attack works as follows:

1. Request the encryptions of N chosen plaintexts, where N is chosen according to the criteria given below.
2. For each resulting ciphertext, try all 48 possible combinations of mod 3 value and high-order four bits for the last half-round's subkey. Use this guess to predict the mod 3 values of both 32-bit halves of the block before the last half round, and keep count of these values for each guess.
3. Use these counts to calculate a chi-square score with eight degrees of freedom, based on splitting the block into nine possible categories based on the two mod 3 values.
4. Select the partial guess with the highest chi-square score as the most likely guess.
5. Assuming the above guess is correct, begin the process again, this time guessing the next six bits of subkey. Continue this process, guessing six bits of subkey at a time, until the last four bits of subkey are remaining. Guess those four bits and test the guesses in the same way.
6. The result is a guess which is likely to be correct of the last half-round's subkey. Using this value, we can peel the last half-round off all the ciphertexts,

and use the resulting values to mount the attack again on a version of the cipher with one fewer half-rounds.

Choosing the Plaintexts We choose the plaintexts to try to maximize the bias in the selection of a partition after N rounds. In practice, this means attempting to bypass most of the effects of the first full round of RC5P. We thus choose P_L, P_R such that:

1. The high-order eight bits of P_L and P_R are all zeros.
2. The low-order five bits of P_L and P_R are all zeros.
3. $P_L \bmod 3 \equiv P_R \bmod 3 \equiv 0$.

To understand why this makes sense, we must consider the first round of RC5P without the whitening in some detail. Recall that the operations are:

1. $L := L + R$
2. $L := L \lll R$
3. $L := L + sk_0$
4. $R := R + L$
5. $R := R \lll L$
6. $R := R + sk_1$

When the high-order eight bits of both P_L and P_R are zeros, the high-order seven bits of L after step one must be zeros, and there is no chance of a carry in that addition. Recall that when there is not a carry in mod 2^{32} addition, the mod 3 values of the addends can be added together mod 3 to get the correct mod 3 value for the sum. Because the low five bits of R are zeros, there is no rotation in step two. Thus, in step three, we know that the high-order seven bits of L are zeros before the addition. Unless the high-order seven bits of sk_0 are all ones, there will never be a carry in that addition, either. *Thus, L will, for 127/128 possible keys, have the same mod 3 value for all inputs chosen as we have described.*

The high-order seven bits of L after the third step are no longer known, but will be closely related for all the texts. There will be only two possible values for these high seven bits, depending on whether there was a carry into them in step three's addition.

The high order eight bits of R going into the addition in the fourth step are zeros; thus only if all eight high-order bits of L are ones will there ever be a carry in this addition. For nearly all values of sk_0, it will thus not be possible for there to be a carry in this addition, either.

The low-order five bits of L after the addition in step three will be constant. Thus, the rotation in step five will be by a constant amount. Rotation by a constant amount of a constant mod 3 value will yield a constant mod 3 value. Thus the mod 3 value of R will be constant for nearly all keys after step five. In step six, there is an addition with sk_1. After this step, it will be possible for R to have one of two mod 3 values. Depending on the high-order few bits of sk_1,

R may be nearly balanced between these two values, or may be strongly biased towards one or the other of them.

The result of the way we choose the plaintexts is thus, for nearly all keys, to bypass nearly the first full round of RC5P for the sake of our mod 3 approximation. Instead of the possibility of being in all nine different partitions after the first round, for most keys the texts can only be in one of two partitions after the first round.

Making the Initial Guess Having collected N ciphertexts, corresponding to the N chosen plaintexts, we now make an initial guess of the high-order four bits and mod 3 value of the final half-round's subkey, which we will refer to as sk_f. There are 48 possible values for this guess; we try each guess against all N ciphertexts.

Each guess suggests a value of the right half of the block before the final half-round was applied. Consider the decryption of the final half-round:

1. $R := R - sk_f$
2. $R := R \ggg L$
3. $R := R - L$

In the first step, we must determine, based on the known value of R and the guessed parts of sk_f, what the result of the subtraction will be. This is dependent upon the mod 3 value of sk_f, and also its high-order four bits. In the second step, we must use the known rotation amount from L to determine what the resulting R value will be. The resulting mod 3 value of R is determined only by the low-order bit of L. However, the total rotation amount determines which bits of R from the first step will end up in the high-order bits. Finally, in the third step, we must use the known L value, along with what is known about the R value input, to determine the result of this final subtraction. For most ciphertexts, we know only the mod 3 value of R going into this operation. However, for some rotation amounts in step two, we also know the likely values for the high-order few bits of R going into the third step.

We can model this by noting that there are many different subkey words sk_{guess} which share the same high-order four bits and mod 3 value as a given guess to be tested. We can choose a reasonable representative from the set of these, and get a fair approximation to its behavior. We thus derive sk_{model} by setting its high-order four bits to the value required by the guess, setting the rest of the bits to alternate between zero and one bits, and then incrementing the result as necessary to get the guessed mod 3 value. We then carry out a trial decryption with this partial key guess, get a resulting pair of mod 3 values, and keep count of how many of each value results from the trial decryption.

To distinguish between the right and wrong partial values for sk_f, we use those counts to compute chi-square scores, and choose the highest chi-square score as the most likely value. For sufficiently large values of N, we have seen experimentally that this is very likely to select the right partial value for sk_f.

Weak Key Rounds	Average Key Rounds	Texts	Work
11	8	2^{29}	5×2^{35}
13	10	2^{37}	5×2^{43}
15	12	2^{45}	5×2^{51}
17	14	2^{53}	5×2^{59}
19	16	2^{61}	5×2^{67}

Table 1. Estimates of Difficulty of Attacking RC5P With Many Rounds.

Continuing the Guess Assuming the previous guess was correct, we can extend this guess. We guess the next four or six bits of sk_f, updating sk_{model} appropriately. The new sk_{model} is very little improved at determining whether there will be a borrow in the subtraction of the first step, but for some rotation amounts in the second step, it has a strong impact on determining whether there will be a borrow in the subtraction in the third step. For each guess, we again keep count of the mod 3 values of the two halves after it is applied, and we again select the guess with the largest chi-square value.

Continuing the Attack After the full sk_f value is known, we peel off the last half-round, and apply the attack anew to the resulting cipher.

3.3 Resources Required for the Full Attack

According to our preliminary experiments, the full attack has an acceptably high probability of success using N texts, where N is the number of texts necessary to get a chi-square value high enough that in practice, it simply could not have occurred by chance.

Our experimental data suggest that each additional round requires roughly sixteen times as many texts to get about the same χ^2 score on average, and that there are especially vulnerable keys for which we can expect to get sufficiently high χ^2 scores even with an extra two to three rounds, with the same N.

The work required for the attack is approximately $5 \times 2^6 \times N$. Table 1 shows our predictions for the approximate workfactor and number of texts needed to break RC5P.

3.4 Results and Implications

There are several practical implications of our results:

1. RC5P, the RC5 variant with XORs changed to mod 2^{32} additions, is much less secure than was previously believed [KY98]. We suggest a minimum of 22 rounds for reasonable security when used with a 128-bit key.

2. Other ciphers which use rotations and additions, but no multiplications or XORs, are likely to also be vulnerable. In particular, all elements other than additions and rotations in such ciphers should be carefully reviewed to see whether they have good mod 3 approximations. In some cases modular multiplication may also be vulnerable, depending upon the modulus: for instance, $f(x) = a \cdot x \bmod (2^{32} + 5)$ is vulnerable to mod 3 cryptanalysis, since $2^{32} + 5 = 3^3 \times 47 \times 3384529$.

3. Multiplication mod 2^{32} as done in RC6, and XORing as done in both RC6 and RC5, are both very difficult to approximate mod 3. Hence, these operations generally make ciphers resistant to the attack. However, the specific cipher designs need to be reviewed to verify that they are used in a way that actually helps defeat the attack. RC5 and RC6 seem to be resistant to this attack, as does Mars. But see our analysis of M6 in Section 4 for an example of a cipher that uses rotations, additions, and XORs yet still succumbs to mod n attacks.

4. Placing the multiplication or XORing only at the beginning and end of the cipher is probably not effective in making the cipher resistant to mod 3 cryptanalysis, since there are often clever analytical tricks to bypass these operations.

Mixing operations from different algebraic groups was the guiding principle behind several ciphers—IDEA [LMM91], Twofish [SKW+98], etc.—and that still seems like a good idea.

3.5 RC6

Note that our mod 3 attack suggests a new design principle for RC6-like ciphers. If the f function $x \mapsto x \times (2x + 1) \bmod 2^{32}$ in RC6 had instead been defined as $x \mapsto x \times (2x + 1) \bmod m$ for some other value of m, powerful mod n attacks might be possible.

For instance, if 3 divides m, then we have a probability-1 approximation for the f function. In this case, the RC6 variant obtained by replacing the XORs with additions (and also using the modulus m instead of 2^{32} in the definition of f) could be broken by mod 3 cryptanalysis. For example, with the IDEA-like modulus $m = 2^{32} - 1$, RC6 would be in serious trouble if we replace the XORs by additions.

This suggests the design principle that $\gcd(m, 2^{32} - 1) = 1$. (The mysterious number $2^{32} - 1$ comes from the formulation of rotations as multiplication by powers of two modulo $2^{32} - 1$; see Section 2.1.)

4 M6

M6 is a family of ciphers proposed for use in the IEEE1394 FireWire standard, a peripherals bus for personal computers [FW1,FW2].[2] M6 is used for encrypting

---

[2] M6 is based on work done in [THN91]. Note that no full description of M6 is publicly available, due to export considerations [Kaz99]. However, a general description of the

copyrighted and other protected content between the computer and the peripheral.

For convenience, we briefly describe an example of a M6 cipher here (specifically, the example given in [FW2], an earlier draft of the standard). See also Figure 2 for a pictorial illustration.

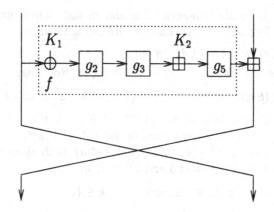

Fig. 2. One round of a M6 block cipher

The cipher uses a 10-round Feistel structure. The f function is defined by

$$g_1(x) = x \oplus K_1 \qquad\qquad g_2(y) = (y \lll 2) + y + 1 \bmod 2^{32}$$
$$g_3(z) = (z \lll 8) + z \bmod 2^{32} \qquad g_4(a) = a + K_2 \bmod 2^{32}$$
$$g_5(b) = (b \lll 14) + b \bmod 2^{32} \qquad f(x) = (g_5 \circ g_4 \circ g_3 \circ g_2 \circ g_1)(x).$$

The round function F updates a 64-bit block (x, y) according to

$$F((x,y)) = (y + f(x) \bmod 2^{32}, x).$$

M6 typically uses 40 bit keys (although the algorithm also allows for keys up to 64 bits long), and the key schedule is very simple. Let K_1 be the high 32 bits of the key, and W be the lower 32 bits of the key (so that K_1 and W share 24 bits in common). Set $K_2 = K_1 + W \bmod 2^{32}$. Then K_1, K_2 are the output of the key schedule.

The standard also suggests that other variations on the basic construction above can be created by changing the order of the g functions, by swapping additions for XORs (or vice versa), and/or by changing the rotation amounts. Each round may use a different variation of the basic scheme. As a result, we get a family of ciphers, which we will call the M6 ciphers.

For concreteness, we focus on the example cipher given above. However, we note that the same techniques also apply to many other ciphers in the M6 family:

---

family of ciphers from which M6 is drawn from can be found in [Hit97]. Our techniqes are applicable to most ciphers in this family.

as long as the last g function is of the form $b \mapsto (b \lll \alpha) + b + \beta \bmod 2^{32}$ and the output of the f function is combined with the block by addition, we will be able to apply mod n techniques. Thus, a large fraction of the M6 ciphers can be broken by mod n attacks.

4.1 A mod 5 Attack

We note that f is highly non-surjective, and in fact admits excellent mod 5 approximations. In particular, we have the following theorem.

Theorem 1. $f(x) \bmod 5 \in \{0, 4\}$ *for all* x.

Proof: It suffices to show that $g_5(b) \bmod 5 \in \{0, 4\}$. Note that

$$g_5(b) = (b \lll 14) + b - 2^{32}k \equiv (2^{14} + 1)b - 2^{32}k \bmod 2^{32} - 1$$

using the relation $b \lll 14 \equiv 2^{14}b \bmod 2^{32} - 1$ from Section 2.1. It is not hard to see that $k \in \{0, 1\}$ (just observe that $(b \lll 14) + b < 2^{33}$).

Note that 5 divides $2^{32} - 1$, so we may reduce both sides of the relation modulo 5. Since $2^{14} + 1 \equiv 0 \bmod 5$ and $2^{32} \equiv 1 \bmod 5$, we get

$$g_5(b) \equiv -k \bmod 5, \qquad k \in \{0, 1\}.$$

This proves our desired result. $\qquad\qquad\square$

We next analyze the round function F using Theorem 1. The Feistel function is combined via addition mod 2^{32}, which makes things easy. Let $(y', x) = F((x, y))$, so that $y' - y = f(x) \bmod 2^{32}$. Rewriting the latter equation to eliminate the "mod" gives:

$$y' - y = f(x) + 2^{32}k, \qquad k \in \{-1, 0\}.$$

Reducing both sides modulo five, we get:

$$y' - y \bmod 5 \in \{0, 3, 4\}.$$

It is not hard to see that $f(x) \bmod 5$ is uniformly distributed on $\{0, 4\}$ and k is uniformly distributed on $\{-1, 0\}$, so we see that $y' - y \bmod 5 = f(x) + k \bmod 5$ takes on the values $0, 3, 4$ with probabilities $1/4, 1/4, 1/2$.

This can now be applied to the whole cipher. Let P_L be the left half of the plaintext and C_L the left half of the ciphertext. We see that $C_L - P_L$ is the sum of five independent random variables whose value modulo five has the distribution $(1/4, 0, 0, 1/4, 1/2)$. Thus the distribution of $C_L - P_L \bmod 5$ is the five-fold convolution of $(1/4, 0, 0, 1/4, 1/2)$, or approximately:

$$p_{C_L - P_L \bmod 5} = (0.248, 0.215, 0.161, 0.161, 0.215).$$

The same holds for the right halves.

So a significant amount of information is leaked from the plaintext through to the ciphertext. For instance, $C_L \bmod 5$ has a nearly $1/4$ chance of being equal to $P_L \bmod 5$, which is significantly greater than the $1/5$ chance one would expect from a strong cipher. The bias of the difference is about 0.00577, which indicates that with a hundred or so known texts we could easily distinguish the cipher from random.

4.2 Attacks mod 257 and 1285

In fact, the cipher is even worse the analysis above might indicate. The Feistel f function also admits excellent mod 257 approximations. These approximations are easy to use in a key-recovery attack, because they disclose the value of K_2 mod 257.

When we combine the mod 257 and mod 5 attacks, we get an attack mod $1285 = 5 \times 257$ which is even better than either one alone. (This observation is due to Lars Knudsen [Knu99].)

Theorem 2. $f(x) - 965 \cdot K_2 \bmod 1285 \in \{0, 319, 320, 639, 640, 1284\}$ *for all* x.

Proof: Using a similar argument to that found in the proof of Theorem 1, we find that $g_3(z) \equiv 257z - i \bmod (2^{32} - 1)$, where $i \in \{0, 1\}$ represents a carry bit. Also, we have

$$f(x) = g_5(g_3(z) + K_2) \equiv (2^{14} + 1)(257z - i + K_2 - j) - k \bmod (2^{32} - 1)$$

where $j, k \in \{0, 1\}$ are the carry bits in the computation of g_4 and g_5. Reducing both sides modulo $1285 = 5 \times 257$, we find

$$f(x) \equiv 965(K_2 - i - j) - k \bmod 1285, \qquad i, j, k \in \{0, 1\}.$$

Here we have used the identities $2^{32} - 1 \equiv 0 \bmod 1285$, $2^{14} + 1 \equiv 0 \bmod 5$, and $2^{14} + 1 \equiv 965 \bmod 1285$. The theorem follows. $\qquad\square$

Moreover, our simulations show that the distribution of $f(x) - 965K_2 \bmod 1285$ is highly non-uniform. Repeating the analysis given for our mod 5 attack, we find that the distribution of $X_L = C_L - P_L - 5 \cdot 965 \cdot K_2 \bmod 1285$ has bias 0.0556, so a few dozen known texts should be enough to distinguish the cipher from random using a mod 1285 attack.

In fact, the distribution of X_L has only 59 non-zero entries (with most of the probability density concentrated on only a fraction of them), so given one known text we can immediately eliminate all but 59 possibilities for $K_2 \bmod 1285$ just by looking at the left half of the plaintext and ciphertext. The expected number of guesses needed to find $K_2 \bmod 1285$ from X_L is easily calculated to be about 9. Then we can recover the remainder of the key with a search over the 2^{30} possibilities for K given the guess at $K_2 \bmod 1285$. In other words, given one known text we can find the key with expected 2^{33} offline trial encryptions; this is already 16 times faster than exhaustive search.

If more known texts are available, we can do even better. Each text gives us one observation at X_L. If we also look at the right halves of each text, we can double the number of available observations. With several dozen known texts, we expect to be able to recover $K_2 \bmod 1285$ with relatively good accuracy. Therefore, when a few dozen known texts are available, we can find the 40-bit key with expected 2^{29} offline trial encryptions. This demonstrates that the level of security afforded by the example M6 cipher is extremely low, even for a 40-bit cipher.

Powerful ciphertext-only attacks may also be mounted if we use just the mod 257 attack on its own. Divide the left half of the plaintext into bytes as $P_L = (w, x, y, z)$. We find that $P_L \equiv z - y + x - w \bmod 257$, so if the bytes of the plaintext are biased $P_L \bmod 257$ will be too. When the plaintext is ASCII-encoded text, we expect very significant biases to remain after encryption, and in this case the value of $K_2 \bmod 257$ will leak after a sufficient number of cipher-texts. (For instance, when the plaintext is composed only of the letters 'a'–'z', we have $81 \leq (P_L \bmod 257) \leq 181$.)

M6 could be easily strengthened against mod n attacks with a small change: simply always use XOR instead of addition when combining the output of the f function with the block. (It is worth pointing out that no mere change in rotation amounts can secure M6 against mod n attacks.) With such a defense, some attacks might still be possible given a very large pool of known texts, but since the cipher was only designed for a 40-bit keylength, the results might be good enough for practical purposes.

4.3 MX

We also note that our analysis techniques can be applied to MX [ATFS98], another cipher with an internal structure similar to that of the example M6 cipher described above. The primary difference is that MX allows for secret round-dependent rotation and addition constants inside the round function. For instance, MX's version of g_5 is defined as $g_5(x) = (x \lll s_3) + x - \gamma \bmod 2^{32}$ where s_3, γ are fixed round constants (not dependent on the secret key). It is not hard to see that g_5 has a good mod n approximation no matter the value of s_3, α, and therefore the MX round function will always be sufficiently biased to allow for excellent mod n attacks.

5 Generalizations, Conclusions, and Open Questions

In this paper, we have discussed a new cryptanalytic attack that is extremely powerful against ciphers based only upon addition and rotation. We have also demonstrated an apparent weakness in RC5P, and given a successful attack against a substantial fraction of the M6 family of ciphers.

This shows that the strength of RC5 relies heavily on the mixture of XORs and additions—differential cryptanalysis breaks the variant with only XORs [BK98], and we have shown that mod 3 cryptanalysis is a very powerful attack against the variant with only additions. We conclude that the mixing of additions and XORs in RC5 is not just a nice touch: it is absolutely essential to the security of the cipher.

Note that we can also consider mod p attacks, for any prime p dividing $2^{32} - 1$. The prime factorization of $2^{32} - 1$ is $3 \times 5 \times 17 \times 257 \times 65537$, so there is no shortage of potential candidates for p.

One of the potential problems with using values of $p > 3$ is that a rotation can now involve a multiplication by any value in the set $S_p = \{2^j \bmod p : j = $

$0, 1, \ldots\}$. Fortunately (for the attacker), when $p = 2^k + 1$ divides $2^{32} - 1$ we have the nice property that $|S_p| = 2k$ (since $2^k = -1 \bmod p$ and $2^{2k} = 1 \bmod p$), so generalized mod p attacks might be even more successful against RC5P than our mod 3 attack was.

Of course, we can also consider mod n attacks where n is not necessarily prime. When n is composite, a mod n attack is the rough equivalent of mod p cryptanalysis with multiple approximations. If the prime factorization of n is $p_1 \times \cdots \times p_m$, then by the Chinese remainder theorem all mod n attacks may be decomposed into m attacks modulo each p_j.

A number of open questions remain, which we hope to see investigated in the near future. Among them:

1. Other moduli than 3, 5, and 257 might have some advantages in this kind of attack. Section 5 contains some early work in this direction, but more is needed.
2. Other ciphers that might be vulnerable to mod p attacks. As a rule, ciphers that use only addition and rotation are likely to be vulnerable, as are ciphers that use addition and some nonlinear operations (such as S-boxes) which have a good mod p approximation.
3. We have made a number of observations in this paper based on experiments; we would like to find improved mathematical models to explain these observations, and solidify our predictions about events we can't verify experimentally.
4. We suspect that a variant of differential cryptanalysis can be defined for some ciphers, using differences mod n instead of mod 2^{32}. Much of the same mathematical apparatus can be used for this class of attack as for our attack.
5. Data-dependent rotations are handled poorly by the standard analytic techniques available to us (namely, linear attacks and differential attacks with XOR or mod 2^{32}-based differences). We are interested in other properties that can be used in differential- or linear-like attacks, but which will survive rotation (and particularly data-dependent rotation) better than fixed XOR differences.

6 Acknowledgements

We are very grateful to Doug Whiting for useful discussion early in our development of mod n attacks, and to Niels Ferguson for his helpful comments. Thanks also to Lars Knudsen for describing the mod 1285 attack on M6, and for pointing out an error in an early version of Theorem 2.

References

[ATFS98] M. Aikawa, K. Takaragi, S. Furuya, M. Sasamoto, "A lightweight Encryption Method Suitable for Copyright Protection," *IEEE Trans. on Consumer Electronics*, vol.44, n.3, pp.902–910, 1998.

[AGMP96] G. Álvarez, D. De la Guia, F. Montoya, and A. Peinado, "Akelarre: A New Block Cipher Algorithm," *Workshop on Selected Areas in Cryptography (SAC '96) Workshop Record*, Queens University, 1996, pp. 1–14.

[BCD+98] C. Burwick, D. Coppersmith, E. D'Avignon, R. Gennaro, S. Halevi, C. Jutla, S.M. Matyas, L. O'Connor, M. Peyravian, D. Safford, and N. Zunic, "MARS — A Candidate Cipher for AES," NIST AES Proposal, Jun 98.

[Bih95] E. Biham, "On Matsui's Linear Cryptanalysis," *Advances in Cryptology — EUROCRYPT '94 Proceedings*, Springer-Verlag, 1995, pp. 398–412.

[BK98] A. Biryukov and E. Kushilevitz, "Improved Cryptanalysis of RC5," *Advances in Cryptology — EUROCRYPT '98 Proceedings*, Springer-Verlag, 1998, pp. 85–99.

[CRRY98] S. Contini, R. Rivest. M. Robshaw, and Y.L. Yin, "The Security of the RC6 Block Cipher," Version 1.0, RSA Laboratories, 20 Aug 1998.

[FW1] *Content Protection for Digital Transmission System*, 5C compromise proposal version 0.91, 17-Feb-1998, Hitachi, Intel, Matsushita, Sony, and Toshiba.

[FW2] *Response for Data Protection System for Digital Transmission of Copy Protected Information*, Version 0.99, pp. 8–12, Hitachi, Matsushita, and Sony.

[HKM95] C. Harpes, G. Kramer, and J. Massey, "A Generalization of Linear Cryptanalysis and the Applicability of Matsui's Piling-up Lemma," *Advances in Cryptology — EUROCRYPT '95 Proceedings*, Springer-Verlag, 1995, pp. 24–38.

[HM97] C. Harpes and J. Massey, "Partitioning Cryptanalysis," *Fast Software Encryption, 4th International Workshop Proceedings*, Springer-Verlag, 1997, pp. 13–27.

[Hit97] Hitachi, "Symmetric key encipherment method 'M6' for IEEE 1394 bus encryption/authentication," Submission 1997-4-25, Proposal for IEEE 1394, Copy Prorection Technical Working Group, 1997.

[Kaz99] T. Kazuo, personal communication, 19 Mar 1999.

[KM96] L.R. Knudsen and W. Meier, "Improved Differential Attacks on RC5," *Advances in Cryptology — CRYPTO '96*, Springer-Verlag, 1996, pp. 216–228.

[Knu99] L. Knudsen, personal communication, 6 Apr 1999.

[KR94] B. Kaliski Jr., and M. Robshaw, "Linear Cryptanalysis Using Multiple Approximations," *Advances in Cryptology — CRYPTO '94 Proceedings*, Springer-Verlag, 1994, pp. 26–39.

[KR95] B. Kaliski Jr., and M. Robshaw, "Linear Cryptanalysis Using Multiple Approximations and FEAL," *Fast Software Encryption, Second International Workshop Proceedings*, Springer-Verlag, 1995, pp. 249–264.

[KR96] L. Knudsen and M. Robshaw, "Non-Linear Approximations in Linear Cryptanalysis," *Advances in Cryptology — EUCROCRYPT '96*, Springer-Verlag, 1996, pp. 224–236.

[KY95] B. Kaliski and Y.L. Yin, "On Differential and Linear Cryptanalysis of the RC5 Encryption Algorithm," *Advanced in Cryptology — CRYPTO '95*, Springer-Verlag, 1995, pp. 171–184.

[KY98] B. Kaliski and Y.L. Yin, "On the Security of the RC5 Encryption Algorithm," RSA Laboratories Technical Report TR-602, Version 1.0, Sep 98.

[LMM91] X. Lai, J. Massey, and S. Murphy, "Markov Ciphers and Differential Cryptanalysis," *Advances in Cryptology — CRYPTO '91 Proceedings*, Springer-Verlag, 1991, pp. 17–38.

[Mad84] W.E. Madryga, "A High Performance Encryption Algorithm," *Computer Security: A Global Challenge*, Elsevier Science Publishers, 1984, pp. 557–570.

[Mat94] M. Matsui, "Linear Cryptanalysis Method for DES Cipher," *Advances in Cryptology — EUROCRYPT '93 Proceedings*, Springer-Verlag, 1994, pp. 386–397.

[Riv95] R.L. Rivest, "The RC5 Encryption Algorithm," *Fast Software Encryption, 2nd International Workshop Proceedings*, Springer-Verlag, 1995, pp. 86–96.

[RRS+98] R. Rivest, M. Robshaw, R. Sidney, and Y.L. Yin, "The RC6 Block Cipher," NIST AES Proposal, Jun 98.

[Sel98] A.A. Selcuk, "New Results in Linear Cryptanalysis of RC5," *Fast Software Encryption, 5th International Workshop*, Springer-Verlag, 1998, pp. 1–16.

[SKW+98] B. Schneier, J. Kelsey, D. Whiting, D. Wagner, C. Hall, and N. Ferguson, "Twofish: A 128-Bit Block Cipher," NIST AES Proposal, 15 June 1998.

[THN91] K. Takaragi, K. Hashimoto, and T. Nakamura, "On Differential Cryptanalysis," *IEICE Transactions*, vol E-74, n. 8, Aug 1991, pp. 2153-2158.

[Vau96] S. Vaudenay, "An Experiment on DES Statistical Cryptanalysis," *3rd ACM Conference on Computer and Communications Security*, ACM Press, 1996, pp. 139–147.

A   The χ^2 Test

In this section we study how to distinguish a source with distribution p_X from a source with the uniform distribution p_U. The optimal algorithm is the χ^2 test, and we briefly recall its definition, as well as several standard results, here.

The χ^2 test allows one to test the hypothesis that the source has distribution p_U. Suppose we have n (independent) observations, and let n_i denote the number of times the source took on the value i. Treating each n_i as a random variable (subject to the constraint that $\sum n_i = n$), the χ^2 statistic is defined as:

$$\chi^2(n_1,\ldots,n_k) = \sum_i \frac{(n_i - \mathbf{E}_U n_i)^2}{\mathbf{E}_U n_i}.$$

Here $\mathbf{E}_U n_i$ denotes the expected value of n_i under the assumption that the source has distribution p_U. It is not hard to see that $\mathbf{E}_U n_i = n/k$, so the χ^2 statistic is just $k/n \sum_i (n_i - n/k)^2$. In the χ^2 test, we compare the observed χ^2 statistic to $\chi^2_{a,k-1}$ (the threshold for the χ^2 test with $k-1$ degrees of freedom and with significance level a).

We can easily compute the expected value of the χ_2 statistic.

Theorem 3. $\mathbf{E}_X \chi^2(n_1,\ldots,n_k) = nk\|p_X - p_U\|^2 + k - k\|p_X\|^2.$

Corollary 1. $\mathbf{E}_U \chi^2 = k - 1.$

We can see that if $n = c/\|p_X - p_U\|^2$, then $\mathbf{E}_X \chi^2 = ck + k - k\|p_X\|^2$. Since we will usually be interested in the case where $p_X \approx p_U$, we find $\mathbf{E}_X \chi^2 \approx (c+1)k-1$. Thus $\mathbf{E}_X \chi^2$ differs from $\mathbf{E}_U \chi^2$ by a significant amount when $c = \Omega(1)$.

In summary, we can conclude that $n = \Theta(1/\|p_X - p_U\|^2)$ observations suffice to distinguish a source with distribution p_X from a source with distribution p_U. This shows that our definition of the bias of p_X as $\|p_X - p_U\|^2$ was well-chosen.

The Boomerang Attack

David Wagner

U.C. Berkeley

`daw@cs.berkeley.edu`

Abstract. This paper describes a new differential-style attack, which we call the boomerang attack. This attack has several interesting applications. First, we disprove the oft-repeated claim that eliminating all high-probability differentials for the whole cipher is sufficient to guarantee security against differential attacks. Second, we show how to break COCONUT98, a cipher designed using decorrelation techniques to ensure provable security against differential attacks, with an advanced differential-style attack that needs just 2^{16} adaptively chosen texts. Also, to illustrate the power of boomerang techniques, we give new attacks on Khufu-16, FEAL-6, and 16 rounds of CAST-256.

1 Introduction

One of the most powerful cryptanalytic techniques known in the open literature is differential cryptanalysis [BS93]. Differential analysis has been used to break many published ciphers. It is understandable, then, that block cipher designers are typically quite anxious to ensure security against differential style attacks.

The usual design procedure goes something like this. The algorithm designer obtains somehow an upper bound p on the probability of any differential characteristic for the cipher. Then the designer invokes an oft-repeated "folk theorem" to justify that any successful differential attack will require at least $1/p$ texts to break the cipher, which is supposed to allow us to conclude that the cipher is safe from differential attacks.

Unfortunately, this folk theorem is wrong. We exhibit an attack—which we call the boomerang attack—that can allow an adversary to beat the $1/p$ bound in some cases[1]. In particular, if the best characteristic for half of the rounds of the cipher has probability q, then the boomerang attack can be used in a successful attack needing $O(q^{-4})$ chosen texts. In some cases, we may have $q^{-4} \ll p^{-1}$, in which case the boomerang attack allows one to beat the folk theorem's bound. Also, boomerang attacks sometimes allow for a more extensive use of structures than is available in conventional differential attacks, which makes boomerang techniques more effective than the preceding discussion might suggest.

---

[1] Note that Biham *et al.*'s impossible differentials [BBS98,BBS99] also disprove the folk theorem. They show that if one can find a differential of sufficiently *low* probability, the cipher can be broken. However, the boomerang attack in fact lets us make an sharper statement: even if no differential for the whole cipher has probability that is too high or too low, the cipher might still be vulnerable to differential-style attacks.

| Cipher | (Rounds) | Our Attack | |
		Data Complexity	Time Complexity
COCONUT98	(8)	2^{16} CP	2^{38}
Khufu	(16)	2^{18} CP	2^{18}
CAST-256	(16)	$2^{49.3}$ KP	$2^{49.3}$
FEAL	(6)	4 CP	-

KP — known-plaintext, CP — adaptive chosen-plaintext/ciphertext.

Table 1. Summary of our attacks.

We give a surprisingly sharp example of this possibility in Sections 3–5 below, where we show how to break COCONUT98 [V98] with just 2^{16} chosen texts and 2^{38} work, despite a proof that the best characteristic for the whole cipher must have probability $p \approx 2^{-64}$. Our attack makes crucial use of a characteristic for half of the cipher with probability $q \approx 2^{-4}$. This shows that the folk theorem can fail spectacularly, even for real-world ciphers.

We also extend the boomerang attack to use techniques from truncated differential analysis (see Section 6). As a result, we are able to analyze ciphers which admit good truncated differentials. In Section 7 we show how to break 16 rounds of Khufu with 2^{18} adaptive chosen plaintexts and ciphertexts and very little work. We also consider CAST-256 in Section 9, where we show how to break 16 rounds with $2^{49.3}$ known texts[2]. Section 9 also briefly sketches the inside-out attack, a dual to the boomerang attack. Finally, Section 10 discusses some related work, and Section 11 concludes the paper. See Table 1 for our table of results.

2 The boomerang attack: A generic view

The boomerang attack is a differential attack that attempts to generate a quartet structure at an intermediate value halfway through the cipher.

The attack considers four plaintexts P, P', Q, Q', along with their respective ciphertexts C, C', D, D'; we will defer describing how these are generated until later. Let $E(\cdot)$ represent the encryption operation, and decompose the cipher into $E = E_1 \circ E_0$, where E_0 represents the first half of the cipher and E_1 represents the last half. We will use a differential characteristic, call it $\Delta \to \Delta^*$, for E_0, as well as a characteristic $\nabla \to \nabla^*$ for E_1^{-1}.

We want to cover the pair P, P' with the characteristic for E_0, and to cover the pairs P, Q and P', Q' with the characteristic for E_1^{-1}. Then (we claim) the pair Q, Q' is perfectly set up to use the characteristic $\Delta^* \to \Delta$ for E_0^{-1}.

[2] See also Appendix B, where we show that CAST-256 would be much weaker if the round ordering was reversed: in particular, boomerang attacks would be able to break 24 rounds of this variant with $2^{48.5}$ chosen texts. Please note that this 24-round boomerang attack does not apply to the real CAST-256 AES proposal.

Let's examine why this is so. Consider the intermediate value after half of the rounds. When the previous three characteristics hold, we have

$$E_0(Q) \oplus E_0(Q') = E_0(P) \oplus E_0(P') \oplus E_0(P) \oplus E_0(Q) \oplus E_0(P') \oplus E_0(Q')$$
$$= E_0(P) \oplus E_0(P') \oplus E_1^{-1}(C) \oplus E_1^{-1}(D) \oplus E_1^{-1}(C') \oplus E_1^{-1}(D')$$
$$= \Delta^* \oplus \nabla^* \oplus \nabla^* = \Delta^*,$$

Note that this is exactly the condition required to start the characteristic $\Delta^* \to \Delta$ for the inverse of the first half of the cipher. When this characteristic also holds, we will have the same difference in the plaintexts Q, Q' as found in the original plaintexts P, P'. This is why we call it the boomerang attack: when you send it properly, it always comes back to you.

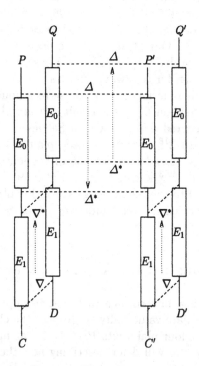

Fig. 1. A schematic of the basic boomerang attack.

We define a right quartet as one where all four characteristics hold simultaneously. The only remaining issue is how to choose the texts so they have the right differences. We suggest generating $P' = P \oplus \Delta$, and getting the encryptions C, C' of P, P' with two chosen-plaintext queries. Then we generate D, D' as $D = C \oplus \nabla$ and $D' = C' \oplus \nabla$. Finally we decrypt D, D' to obtain the plaintexts Q, Q' with two adaptive chosen-ciphertext queries. See Figure 1 for a pictorial depiction of the basic boomerang attack.

In the remainder of the paper, we consider several concrete attacks using the boomerang attack.

3   The COCONUT98 algorithm

The COCONUT98 cipher [V98] may be of special interest to some readers because of its reliance on the recently-developed theory of decorrelation techniques for block cipher design [V97,V98,V98b,GG+98]. Using decorrelation techniques, [V98] proves that the full COCONUT98 cipher admits no good differential characteristics. Despite this fact, we observe that there are differential characteristics of very high probability for half of the cipher, and we make extensive use of these characteristics in our attack. This suggests that the decorrelation design technique may fail to provide security against advanced differential attacks in some cases if extra care is not taken. This is not to suggest that the decorrelation approach is fundamentally flawed—indeed, decorrelation theory seems like a very useful tool for the cipher designer—but rather that the theoretical results must be interpreted with caution.

We briefly recount the description of the COCONUT98 algorithm. CO-CONUT98 uses a 256-bit key $K = (K_1, \ldots, K_8)$. The key schedule generates eight round subkeys $k_1, \ldots, k_8$ as

i	1	2	3	4
k_i	K_1	$K_1 \oplus K_3$	$K_1 \oplus K_3 \oplus K_4$	$K_1 \oplus K_4$

i	5	6	7	8
k_i	K_2	$K_2 \oplus K_3$	$K_2 \oplus K_3 \oplus K_4$	$K_2 \oplus K_4$

The last four key words are used to build a decorrelation module

$$M(xy) = (xy \oplus K_5 K_6) \times K_7 K_8 \bmod \mathrm{GF}(2^{64})$$

where concatenation of symbols (e.g. xy) represents the concatenation of their values as bitstrings.

Next, we build a Feistel network as follows. Let

$$\phi(x) = x + 256 \cdot S(x \bmod 256) \bmod 2^{32}$$
$$F_i((x,y)) = (y, x \oplus \phi(ROL_{11}(\phi(y \oplus k_i)) + c \bmod 2^{32}))$$
$$\Psi_i = F_{4i+4} \circ F_{4i+3} \circ F_{4i+2} \circ F_{4i+1}$$

where $ROL_{11}(\cdot)$ represents a left rotation by 11 bits, c is a public 32-bit constant, and $S : \mathbf{Z}_2^8 \to \mathbf{Z}_2^{24}$ is a fixed S-box.

With this notation, COCONUT98 is defined as $\Psi_1 \circ M \circ \Psi_0$. In other words, COCONUT98 consists of four Feistel rounds with subkeys $k_1, \ldots, k_4$, followed by an evaluation of the decorrelation module M, and finally four more Feistel rounds with subkeys $k_5, \ldots, k_8$.

4 Differential characteristics for COCONUT98

This section discusses the differential characteristics of COCONUT98. In the following discussion, let $e_j = 2^j$ be the 32-bit XOR difference with just the j-th bit flipped. (Subscripts are taken modulo 32, for convenience in modeling the $ROL(\cdot, 11)$ operation.)

We note that the Feistel rounds of COCONUT98 admit very good differential characteristics. The main observation is that $e_j \rightarrow e_{j+11}$ by the Feistel function with probability 1/2 when $j \in J = \{8, 9, \ldots, 19, 20, 29, 30, 31\}$.[3] Similarly, $e_j \oplus e_k \rightarrow e_{j+11} \oplus e_{k+11}$ with probability 1/4 when $j, k \in J$ $(j \neq k)$.

Using this idea, we can build many good characteristics for four rounds of COCONUT98. For example, the characteristic

$$(e_{19}, e_{18} \oplus e_8) \rightarrow (e_{18} \oplus e_8, e_{29}) \rightarrow (e_{29}, e_{18}) \rightarrow (e_{18}, 0) \rightarrow (0, e_{18})$$

for Ψ has probability $0.83 \cdot 2^{-4} \approx 2^{-4.3}$. Of course, by symmetry we also get corresponding backwards characteristics for decryption through four Feistel rounds.

This suggests that we ought to try to find some way to take advantage of these high-probability characteristics for the half-cipher in our analysis. However, the task is not so easy as it might first look. If we try to mount a traditional differential attack on the whole cipher, the decorrelation module M will immediately cause serious difficulties. When the key words K_7, K_8 are unknown, it is very difficult to push any differential characteristic through M. More precisely, every differential $\delta \rightarrow \delta^*$ for M with $\delta, \delta^* \neq 0$ has average probability $1/(2^{64} - 1)$, where the probability is averaged over all possible key values. In short, the decorrelation module prevents us from pushing a differential characteristic past M.

This is where the boomerang attack comes in handy: the boomerang quartet property allows us to control the effect of the decorrelation module in the middle.

The crucial idea which lets the attack work is that M is affine, and thus for any fixed key there are excellent characteristics $\nabla^* \rightarrow M^{-1}(\nabla^*)$ of probability 1 for M^{-1}. Take $E_0 = \Psi_0$ and $E_1 = \Psi_1 \circ M$. Then if $\nabla \rightarrow \nabla^*$ is a good characteristic for Ψ_1^{-1} we will obtain a good characteristic $\nabla \rightarrow M^{-1}(\nabla^*)$ for E_1^{-1}. It does not matter that $M^{-1}(\nabla)$ is unknown to the attacker; the crucial property is that it depends only on the key (and not on the values of the ciphertexts).

Let us estimate the success probability for this technique. We need two characteristics for Ψ_0, and two for Ψ_1^{-1}, to hold. Thus, a simple estimate at the probability p of success is

$$p \geq \Pr[\Delta \rightarrow \Delta^* \text{ by } \Psi_0]^2 \, \Pr[\nabla \rightarrow \nabla^* \text{ by } \Psi_1^{-1}]^2$$

---

[3] At first glance, it might appear that the probability is 1/8, because there are three additions in the F function and thus three carry bits to control. However, the three carries are not independent, and in fact we can handle three carries as easily as one by noting that $x \mapsto (x + a \bmod 2^{32}) + b \bmod 2^{32}$ (two carries) is equivalent to $x \mapsto x + c \bmod 2^{32}$ (one carry) where $c = a + b$.

The rotate does not destroy this property, so long as we avoid the most significant bits, which explains our choice of J. Empirically, the probabilities are $0.47, 0.44, 0.38$ for $j = 18, 19, 20$ and $0.47, 0.44$ for $j = 29, 30$. For other values of j, the probability is very close to 1/2.

where $\Delta, \Delta^*, \nabla, \nabla^*$ may be chosen arbitrarily by the attacker to maximize p.

It turns out that this estimate can be refined a bit. We note that the same attack works even if we do not predict the exact value of ∇^* ahead of time, but instead merely require that the difference after decrypting by Ψ_1 is the same in the two pairs P, Q and P', Q'. A similar observation also holds for Δ^*. Therefore, we may sum over all values for Δ^*, ∇^*, to obtain

$$p \approx \sum_{\Delta^*} \Pr[\Delta \to \Delta^* \text{ by } \Psi_0]^2 \cdot \sum_{\nabla^*} \Pr[\nabla \to \nabla^* \text{ by } \Psi_1^{-1}]^2.$$

For COCONUT98, this can be used to significantly increase the probability of attack. Empirically, we find that $\Delta = \nabla = (e_{10}, e_{31})$ provides $p \approx 0.023 \cdot 0.023 \approx 1/1900$.

5 The basic boomerang attack on COCONUT98

Next we show how to use the quartet property established above to mount a practical attack on COCONUT98. We use a 1-R attack, so the criterion for success is that $Q \oplus Q' = (?, e_{31})$ where ? represents an arbitrary word. This improves the success probability p by a factor of two, to $1/950$.

It is immediately clear from this discussion that COCONUT98 can be easily distinguished from an ideal cipher with at most about $950 \cdot 4 = 3800$ adaptive chosen plaintext/ciphertext queries. However, we aim for more: a key-recovery attack.

The key-recovery attack proceeds along relatively standard lines. In about $16 \cdot 950$ trials requiring $16 \cdot 950 \cdot 4$ adaptive chosen plaintext/ciphertext queries, we generate about 16 useful quartets. Note that the signal-to-noise is extremely high, so we should be able to filter out all wrong quartets very effectively.

First, we recover K_1. We guess K_1, and peel off the first round. We use the fact that if P, P', Q, Q' form a quartet with the property above, then the XOR difference after one round of encryption must be $(e_{31}, 0)$ for both the P, P' pair and the Q, Q' pair. This condition holds for $1/2$ of the wrong key values. Therefore each quartet gives one bit of information on K_1 from the P, P' pair and another bit of information from the Q, Q' pair. With 16 useful quartets, we expect K_1 to be identified uniquely.

Next, we recover $K_2 \oplus K_4$ by decrypting up one round and examining the XOR difference in the C, D pair and in the C', D' pair. The details are very similar to those used to learn K_1.

This allows us to peel off the first and last rounds of the cipher. Then we repeat the attack on the reduced cipher. For instance, we can use about $8 \cdot 144 \cdot 4$ more adaptive chosen plaintext/ciphertext queries to generate about 8 useful quartets for the reduced cipher if we use the same settings for Δ, ∇, since then the success probability p increases to about $1/144$. Using these 8 useful quartets for the reduced cipher we learn K_3; and we repeat the attack iteratively until the entire key is known.

In all, the complexity of the attack is about $16 \cdot 950 \cdot 4 + 8 \cdot 144 \cdot 4 + \ldots \approx 2^{16}$ adaptive chosen plaintext/ciphertext queries. The attack requires $8 \cdot 2 \cdot 32 \cdot 2^{32} = 2^{41}$ offline computations of the F function, which is work comparable to that required for 2^{38} trial encryptions. The attack can also be converted to a known-plaintext attack, but then the complexity increases dramatically to 2^{52} texts.

The best conventional attack on COCONUT98 we could find was a meet-in-the-middle attack that exploits a weakness in the key schedule. However, the meet-in-the-middle attack requires approximately 2^{96} trial encryptions, so our chosen-text boomerang attack compares very favorably to it. See Appendix A for more details on the meet-in-the-middle attack.

Fixing the cipher would require careful changes to its internal design. One possible approach would be to replace the four-round Feistel network Ψ by a transformation with much more strength against differential cryptanalysis (say, 16 rounds instead of 4). Another possible approach is to use a decorrelation module in each round; this seems likely to prevent boomerang-style attacks, and is in fact the approach proposed in the DFC AES submission [GG+98]. (Using just a decorrelation module before the first round and after the last round is not enough—differential-style attacks are still possible.)

It is clear that the mere use of decorrelation techniques is not enough to guarantee security against differential-style attacks. At the same time, although it does not provide the conjectured 2^{64} security level, COCONUT98's decorrelation module does seem to improve the cipher's security. Without a decorrelation module, COCONUT98 would be vulnerable to conventional differential attacks requiring on the order of 2^8 chosen texts, so in this case the decorrelation module seems to have approximately squared the security level of the base cipher.

6 Extensions to truncated differential analysis

So far we have confined the discussion to conventional differential characteristics, but it seems natural to wonder whether boomerang attacks can also be made to work using truncated differentials. The answer is yes, but there are some difficulties.

The pitfall with extensions to truncated differentials is that

$$\Pr[\Delta \to \Delta^* \text{ by } F] = \Pr[\Delta^* \to \Delta \text{ by } F^{-1}]$$

always holds for conventional differential characteristics, but can fail to hold for truncated characteristics. Note that our analysis in earlier sections assumed that if $\Delta \to \Delta^*$ by the first half of the cipher, then $\Delta^* \to \Delta$ holds with the same probability for the inverse of the first half of the cipher. For truncated differentials, this assumption in general is not correct.

A more accurate formula for the success probability p of a boomerang attack with truncated differentials is

$$p \approx \sum_{w \oplus x \oplus y \oplus z = 0} \Pr[\Delta \to w \text{ by } E_0] \times \Pr[\nabla \to x \text{ by } E_1^{-1}] \times$$

$$\Pr[\nabla \to y \text{ by } E_1^{-1}] \times \Pr[z \to \Delta \text{ by } E_0^{-1}].$$

This formula is rather unwieldy, but fortunately it can often be simplified substantially to

$$p \approx \Pr[\Delta \to \Delta^*] \times \Pr[\nabla \to \nabla^*]^2 \times \Pr[\Delta^* \to \Delta] \times$$
$$\Pr[w \oplus x \oplus y \in \Delta^* \mid w \in \Delta^*, x, y \in \nabla^*].$$

If the truncated differentials Δ^*, ∇^* are linear (i.e. closed under $\oplus$), as is usually the case, the last term in the formula above is easily computed.

7 Khufu

We describe a boomerang attack that breaks 16 rounds of Khufu [Mer90] with 2^{18} adaptively chosen plaintext/ciphertext queries and a comparable workfactor. This is an improvement over the best previous result, a differential attack on Khufu-16 needing 2^{31}–2^{43} chosen texts (depending on whether one wants a distinguishing or key-recovery attack) [GC94].

In our boomerang attack, we exploit that there are excellent truncated differentials available for both halves of the cipher. For the first half of the cipher, we use

$$\Delta = (0, 0, 0, a, b, c, d, e) \to (0, 0, 0, a, 0, 0, 0, 0) = \Delta^*,$$

which holds with probability 2^{-32} in the forward direction and probability 1 in the reverse direction. We will hold a fixed throughout the attack. For the inverse of the last half of the cipher, we use $\nabla = (0, 0, 0, a, 0, 0, 0, 0) \to (0, 0, 0, a, f, g, h, i) = \nabla^*$, which holds with probability 1. Also, due to a careful choice of ∇^*, Δ^*, we have $\Pr[w \oplus x \oplus y \in \Delta^* \mid w \in \Delta^*, x, y \in \nabla^*] = 1$. Thus 2^{-32} of the quartets chosen according to these differences will form right quartets.

One can use structures to reduce the number of texts needed. Choose a pool of 2^{16} plaintexts (L, R_i) with L held fixed and R_i varying. Also, form another pool of 2^{16} plaintexts as (L', R'_j) where $L' = L \oplus (0, 0, 0, a)$ and R'_j varies. For each ciphertext C obtained by encrypting one of these 2^{17} plaintexts, we decrypt $D = C \oplus \nabla$ to get the plaintext Q. We look for Q, Q' with a difference of $(0, 0, 0, a)$ in the left half of the block; such a pair probably indicates a right quartet. This choice of structures is expected to provide about one right quartet, although one wrong quartet will probably also survive the initial filtering phase.

Once we have a (suggested) right quartet formed by (L, R_i) and (L', R'_j), we can use it to obtain more right quartets at little cost. We form another 2^{10} quartets by choosing $P = (L \oplus (\alpha, \beta, 0, 0), R_i)$, $P' = (L' \oplus (\alpha, \beta, 0, 0), R'_j)$ where α, β take on 2^{10} possible values; C, C', D, D', Q, Q' are generated from P, P' as before. Now each such quartet is guaranteed to be a right quartet (if $(L, R_i), (L', R'_j)$ formed a right quartet) because we have successfully bypassed the first round. Thus, any wrong quartets which survived the earlier filtering phase are easily eliminated. Furthermore, given 2^{10} right quartets we expect to be able to form 2^{10} equations of the form $S_1(x) \oplus S_1(y) = z$ for known values of x, y, z, and this should be sufficient to recover S_1 up to a XOR by a 32-bit constant. Then the 8-round reduced cipher can be broken trivially.

In total, this attack on Khufu-16 requires $2^{18} + 4 \times 2^{10} \approx 2^{18}$ adaptively chosen texts. The workfactor is minimal.

8 FEAL

One can also apply boomerang techniques to FEAL. There are 3-round differential characteristics with probability one [BS93], so we immediately obtain an efficient boomerang attack that distinguishes FEAL-6 from a random permutation with only four adaptive chosen plaintext/ciphertext queries. (This elegant observation is due to Eli Biham [Bih99].)

9 Inside-out attacks

In this section, we sketch a description of the "inside-out attack," which may be viewed as a dual to the boomerang attack. The difference is that the boomerang attack works from the outside in while the inside-out attack works from the inside out.

In the inside-out attack, we search for pairs of texts which contain a desired difference Δ at the intermediate value after half the rounds. We hope that the differential $\Delta \to \Delta'$ for E_1 and the differential $\Delta \to \Delta^*$ for E_0^{-1} both hold. In this case, we will have recognizable differences Δ^* and Δ' in the plaintexts and ciphertexts of the pair. If we accumulate enough pairs with the difference Δ halfway through the cipher, we should be able to find at least one right pair where both differentials hold.

To illustrate these ideas in action, we analyze 16 rounds of CAST-256. CAST-256 [Ada98] is a generalized Feistel block cipher, whose simplicity makes it a nice test-bed to explore the properties of generalized Feistel round structures.

We briefly recall the definition of CAST-256 here. The 128-bit block is divided into four 32-bit words, and a Feistel function $F : \mathbf{Z}_2^{32} \to \mathbf{Z}_2^{32}$ is used to update the block. There are two types of rounds, which we shall call "A rounds" and "B rounds" in a choice of terminology inspired by Skipjack. An A round encrypts the input block (w, x, y, z) to $(z, w, x, y \oplus F(z))$, and a B round encrypts to $(x, y, z \oplus F(w), w)$. Note that $A \approx B^{-1}$; by this we mean that the structure of the inverse of a B round is the same as the structure of an A round, not that they are true functional inverses. With this terminology, the CAST-256 cipher structure is defined as $B^{24} \circ A^{24}$, i.e. 24 A rounds followed by 24 B rounds.

The CAST-256 structure admits many nice truncated differentials. In our boomerang attack, we will use $\Delta = (0, 0, 0, a) \to (0, b, c, a) = \Delta'$, which holds with probability 1 for 8 B rounds, and $\Delta = (0, 0, 0, a) \to (0, d, e, a)$, which holds with probability 1 for decrypting though 8 A rounds.

The signal-to-noise ratio of the inside-out attack will be reasonably good, because right pairs can be recognized by a 96-bit filtering condition.

To implement the attack, we collect $2^{49.3}$ known texts encrypted under 16 rounds of CAST-256. By the birthday paradox, we expect to see three right pairs among those texts, which can be readily recognized. (We also expect to get three wrong pairs, but they should be eliminated in the next phase.) Then we search over the last round subkey. Each guess at the 37 key bits entering the last round suggests 2^5 possible values for the 37 key bits entering the next-to-last round; the three right pairs allow us to uniquely recognize the correct values for the last two round subkeys. The first two round subkeys can be recovered by analogous techniques. Finally, the attack may be repeated on the reduced-round cipher.

To sum up, we see how to break 16 rounds of CAST-256 with an inside-out attack that needs just $2^{49.3}$ known texts and very little work. This attack is independent of the definition of F function or key schedule, and depends only on the round structure.

There are two implications of our analysis. First, it indicates that CAST-256 reduced to 16 rounds would not be adequately secure. Since CAST-256 with 48 rounds is 2–2.5 times slower on high-end CPUs than the fastest AES candidates [SK+98], this suggests that CAST-256's security-to-performance ratio may not be as high as some other contenders. On the other hand, security clearly must take precedence over performance, and here our analysis provides some support for the CAST-256 design. We have seen that CAST-256's round ordering is ideally-suited to resist boomerang attacks (see Appendix B), and due to the sheer number of rounds, it seems very hard to extend our inside-out attack to the full cipher.

10 Related work

The boomerang attack is closely related to many other ideas that have previously occurred in the literature. As a result, there are many different ways to think about the boomerang attack. In this section, we will try to survey the possibilities.

The boomerang attack is related to the differential-linear attack of [HL94]. In a differential-linear attack, one covers E_0 with a truncated differential $\Delta \to \Delta^*$, covers E_1^{-1} with a linear approximation $\Gamma \to \Gamma^*$, and finally covers E_1 with a second approximation $\Gamma^* \to \Gamma$; there is also the additional requirement that $\Gamma^* \cdot x$ be constant for all $x \in \Delta^*$. From this perspective, one could think of the boomerang attack as a "differential-differential" attack (if the reader will indulge a slight abuse of terminology).

A similar observation is that the boomerang attack is closely related to higher-order differential techniques [Lai94,Knu95]. As noted in Section 6, the pairs P, Q, P', Q' don't actually need to follow $\nabla \to \nabla^*$: it is sufficient that $E_1^{-1}(P) \oplus E_1^{-1}(P') \oplus E_1^{-1}(Q) \oplus E_1^{-1}(Q') = 0$, and this may be viewed (in a very approximate sense) as a higher-order differential of order two. In this way, the boomerang attack can be considered as an intermediate step between conventional differential and higher-order differential attacks.

Another precursor of the boomerang attack is the "double-swiping" attack [KSW97], a differential related-key attack on NewDES-1996 that can, in retrospect, be viewed as a boomerang-style attack (with minor adjustments to take advantages of related-key queries, as allowed in [KSW97]'s extended threat model).

One of the interesting features of the boomerang attack is that it is apparently very well-suited to the analysis of ciphers that use asymmetric round functions[4]. Asymmetric round functions can be classified into one of two types: the A round, which has better diffusion in the forward direction than in the reverse direction, and the B round, which has better diffusion in the reverse direction. We note that when the first half of the cipher is built of B-type rounds and the last half is built of A-type rounds, boomerang attacks seem to be especially dangerous because they allow one to probe from both endpoints at the same time.

This supplies some intuition for how the boomerang attack works. It would not be unreasonable to think of the boomerang attack as a differential meet-in-the-middle attack that uses differentials to work from the outside in; the interesting bit is what happens where the differentials "meet" in the middle of the cipher.

One disadvantage of the boomerang attack is that it inherently requires the ability to perform both adaptive chosen-plaintext and adaptive chosen-ciphertext queries at once, a rare requirement to find in a practical attack. We are aware of only two other attacks with this property: (1) the adaptive chosen-plaintext/ciphertext attack on the 3-round Luby-Rackoff cipher, which is also used to good effect in some of Knudsen's work [Knu98] on Luby-Rackoff ciphers with more rounds, and (2) Biham *et. al*'s yo-yo game [BB+98], which is closely related to their more-famous miss-in-the-middle attack [BBS98,BBS99].

The relation between the boomerang attack and the miss-in-the-middle attack is a close and interesting one. It seems that the boomerang attack is little more than a chosen-plaintext/ciphertext version of the miss-in-the-middle attack. In particular, if $\Pr[\Delta \to \Delta^*] = \Pr[\nabla \to \nabla^*] = 1$ and $\Delta^* \cap \nabla^* = \emptyset$, then the same pair of differentials can be used to obtain either a miss-in-the-middle attack (using the impossible differential $\Delta \to \nabla$) or a boomerang attack.

This paper showed that in some special cases the boomerang attack can improve on the miss-in-the-middle attack, if adaptive chosen plaintext/ciphertext queries are available. However, this seems to be the exception rather than the rule. For several ciphers—including Skipjack and CAST-256—miss-in-the-middle attacks penetrate through more rounds than boomerang attacks [BBS98,BBS99]. Though a thorough comparison of the two types of attacks continues to elude us, we hope that this work will stimulate further research into the interaction between these two attacks.

11 Conclusions

We have described a new way to use differential-style techniques for cryptanalysis of block ciphers. Our attacks can break some ciphers that are immune to ordinary differential cryptanalysis, and can provide a powerful new way to analyze ciphers

---

[4] See Appendix B for a concrete example of this.

with asymmetrical round structures. To protect against these attacks, cipher designers should ensure that there are no good differentials for the first or last half of their cipher.

12 Acknowledgements

We are grateful to a number of readers whose comments have improved the paper substantially: Serge Vaudenay offered a number of helpful comments on an early version of this paper and allowed us to use his nice one-line summary of the attack; Eli Biham suggested looking at reduced-round versions of FEAL, and pointed out the relevance of the 3-round characteristics of probability 1; Carlisle Adams, Alex Biryukov, and the anonymous reviewers gave helpful feedback on the exposition; and finally, we would like to thank all those patient readers who suggested including Figure 1 in this paper.

References

[Ada98] C. Adams, "The CAST-256 Encryption Algorithm," NIST AES Proposal, Jun 98.

[Ada99] C. Adams, personal communication, Feb 1999.

[BBS98] E. Biham, A. Biryukov, A. Shamir. "Cryptanalysis of Skipjack Reduced to 31 Rounds using Impossible Differentials," *EUROCRYPT'99*, to appear.

[BBS99] E. Biham, A. Biryukov, A. Shamir. "Miss in the Middle Attacks on IDEA, Khufu, and Khafre," this volume.

[BB+98] E. Biham, A. Biryukov, O. Dunkelmann, E. Richardson, A. Shamir, "Initial Observations on the Skipjack Encryption Algorithm," *SAC'98*, Springer-Verlag, 1998.

[Bih99] E. Biham, personal communication, Mar 1999.

[BS93] E. Biham, A. Shamir, *Differential Cryptanalysis of the Data Encryption Standard*, Springer-Verlag, 1993.

[BC+98] C. Burwick, D. Coppersmith, E. D'Avignon, R. Gennaro, S. Halevi, C. Jutla, S.M. Matyas, L. O'Connor, M. Peyravian, D. Safford, and N. Zunic, "MARS — A Candidate Cipher for AES," NIST AES Proposal, Jun 98.

[GG+98] H. Gilbert, M. Girault, P. Hoogvorst, F. Noilhan, T. Pornin, G. Poupard, J. Stern, S. Vaudenay, "Decorrelated Fast Cipher: an AES Candidate," NIST AES Proposal, Jun 98.

[GC94] H. Gilbert and P. Chauvaud, "A chosen plaintext attack of the 16-round Khufu cryptosystem," *CRYPTO'94*, LNCS 839, Springer-Verlag, 1994.

[GLC98] D. Georgoudis, D. Lerous, and B.S. Chaves, "The 'Frog' Encryption Algorithm," NIST AES Proposal, Jun 98.

[HL94] M. Hellman and S. Langford., "Differential–linear cryptanalysis," *CRYPTO'94*, LNCS 839, Springer-Verlag, 1994.

[KSW97] J. Kelsey, B. Schneier, D. Wagner, "Related-Key Cryptanalysis of 3-WAY, Biham-DES, CAST, DES-X, NewDES, RC2, and TEA," *ICICS'97*, Springer-Verlag, 1997.

[Knu95] L.R. Knudsen, "Truncated and Higher Order Differentials," *Fast Software Encryption, 2nd International Workshop Proceedings*, Springer-Verlag, 1995.

[Knu98] L. Knudsen, "DEAL—A 128-bit Block Cipher," NIST AES Proposal, Jun 98.

[Lai94] X. Lai, "Higher Order Derivations and Differential Cryptanalysis," *Communications and Cryptography: Two Sides of One Tapestry*, Kluwer Academic Publishers, 1994, pp. 227–233.

[Mer90] R. C. Merkle, "Fast Software Encryption Functions", *CRYPTO'90*, Springer-Verlag, 1990.

[NW97] R. Needham and D. Wheeler, "TEA Extensions," unpublished manuscript, Mar 1997.

[NSA98] NSA, "Skipjack and KEA algorithm specifications," May 1998. Available from http://csrc.ncsl.nist.gov/encryption/skipjack-1.pdf.

[Saa98] M.-J. Saarinen, "Cryptanalysis of Block Tea," unpublished manuscript, 20 Oct 1998.

[SK+98] B. Schneier, J. Kelsey, D. Whiting, D. Wagner, C. Hall, N. Ferguson, "Performance Comparison of the AES Submissions," *Second AES Conference*, 1999.

[V97] S. Vaudenay, "A cheap paradigm for block cipher strengthening," LIENS tech report 97-3, 1997.

[V98] S. Vaudenay, "Provable Security for Block Ciphers by Decorrelation," *STACS'98*, Springer-Verlag LNCS 1373, 1998.

[V98b] S. Vaudenay, "Feistel Ciphers with L_2-Decorrelation," *SAC'98*, Springer-Verlag, 1998.

[Yuv97] G. Yuval, "Reinventing the Travois: Encryption/ MAC in 30 ROM Bytes," *FSE'97*, LNCS 1267, 1997.

A Meet-in-the-middle attack on COCONUT98

The very simple key schedule used in COCONUT98 exposes it to meet-in-the-middle attacks. The problem is that there are only 96 bits of entropy in the first four round subkeys, and a similar property holds for the last four round subkeys. Therefore, with just four known texts and about 2^{96} offline work, one can break COCONUT98 using standard meet-in-the-middle techniques[5]. The workfactor of this attack is disappointingly low for a cipher with a 256-bit key.

When the key is chosen non-uniformly, e.g. from a passphrase, this attack can be even more deadly. If we assume a key entropy of 4 bits/byte (probably a gross overestimate for most passphrases), the workfactor of the meet-in-the-middle attack can be reduced to approximately 2^{48} trial encryptions. This is much faster than exhaustive keysearch.

B A CAST-256 variant

In this section, we consider a simple CAST-256 variant obtained by exchanging the order of the A rounds and the B rounds. (In other words, the variant cipher

---

[5] Specifically: Obtain four known text pairs P_j, C_j for $j = 1, 2, 3, 4$. Guess K_3, K_4. For each possibility for K_1, store $(\Psi_0(P_0) - \Psi_0(P_1))/(\Psi_0(P_2) - \Psi_0(P_3)), K_1$ in a lookup table keyed on the first component. Finally, for each possibility for K_2, we compute $(\Psi_1^{-1}(C_0) - \Psi_1^{-1}(C_1))/(\Psi_1^{-1}(C_2) - \Psi_1^{-1}(C_3))$ and look for a match in the lookup table.

uses the B rounds first.) The primary contribution is that such a variant can be readily analyzed using boomerang attacks.

Please note that this attack *does not* apply to CAST-256 (only to a variant with a different round structure)[6]. Since the designers of CAST-256 already knew of the need to apply the A rounds first [Ada99], we feel that the variant does injustice to the spirit of the CAST-256 design. We focus on CAST-256 primarily because it makes such a simple, clean platform for analysis of novel round structures. We believe our attack on this CAST-256 variant gives new insights into the properties of various ciphers with generalized Feistel round structures [NSA98,BC+98,GLC98,Yuv97,NW97,Saa98], so we hope the analysis is of independent interest.

The sheer number of rounds makes it hard to mount good attacks on the full 48-round CAST-256. In this section, we show that boomerang attacks with complexity $2^{48.5}$–2^{65} are possible on 24–25 rounds of the variant cipher. These attacks do not appear to extend to the original CAST-256 round ordering, so we believe this provides some additional justification that CAST-256 is using the right round ordering.

A SIMPLE ATTACK ON 24 ROUNDS. We use the truncated differential $\Delta = (0, 0, 0, a) \to (b, c, d, a) = \Delta^*$ for the 12 B rounds (where a may take on any non-zero value, and b, c, d are arbitrary). For the inverse of the last half of the cipher, we use a similar truncated differential: namely, $\nabla = (0, 0, 0, e) \to (f, g, h, e) = \nabla^*$.

Using the machinery developed in Section 6, the computation of the success probability is straightforward. Both of these truncated differentials have probability 1, and $\Delta^* \to \Delta$ has probability 2^{-96}. Finally, we note that

$$\Pr[w \oplus x \oplus y \in \Delta^* \mid w \in \Delta^*, x, y \in \nabla^*] = \Pr[a \oplus e \oplus e' \neq 0] = 1 - 2^{-32},$$

so the overall success probability is $p \approx 2^{-96}$.

We start the attack by choosing 2^{32} plaintexts P_i where the first three words are held fixed and the last takes on all 2^{32} possibilities, and we obtain the corresponding ciphertexts C_i. For each such ciphertext C_i, we generate $2^{16.5}$ new ciphertexts $D_{i,j}$ by varying the final word. Then we decrypt each $D_{i,j}$ to obtain the corresponding plaintext $Q_{i,j}$. This gives us 2^{63} choices for P, P' from the pool of plaintexts P_i and another 2^{33} choices for D, D' from the $D_{i,j}$. In all, there will be 2^{96} possible quartets to choose from. About $p \approx 2^{-96}$ of them will form right quartets, so we expect to see one right quartet. The excellent filtering available (we can filter on all 128 bits of $Q \oplus Q'$) allows us to eliminate all the wrong quartets with high probability.

This immediately gives a way to distinguish the 24-round CAST-256 variant from a ideal cipher with $2^{48.5}$ adaptively chosen texts and a low workfactor.

A KEY-RECOVERY ATTACK ON 25 ROUNDS. The same ideas can also be used to develop key recovery attacks. For instance, we can break the 25-round variant obtained by prepending one more B round at the beginning with 2^{65} chosen

---

[6] See also Section 9, which analyzes 16 rounds of the real CAST-256 cipher (without any re-ordering of the rounds).

texts and a similar amount of work. Due to lack of space, we give only a very brief sketch of the attack: we bypass the first round with structures, and then in the analysis phase we guess the first-round subkey, peel off the first round, and check for the existence of right quartets.

DISCUSSION. It is worth comparing our results to what is attainable with conventional truncated differential cryptanalysis. In the case of this CAST-256 variant, boomerang attacks seem to compare favorably for up to 24 rounds, due to the asymmetric round structure, but for more than 25 rounds conventional techniques are at least as good as the boomerang.

The astute reader will have noticed that our truncated differentials $\Delta \rightarrow \Delta^*$ (for the 12 B rounds) and $\nabla^* \rightarrow \nabla$ (for the 12 A rounds) can be readily concatenated to obtain a truncated differential $\Delta = (0,0,0,a) \rightarrow (0,0,0,a) = \nabla$ of probability 2^{-96} for the entire cipher. The resulting 24-round differential will have probability 2^{-96}, and can be used in a conventional truncated differential attack that distinguishes the 24-round CAST-256 variant from a ideal cipher with 2^{65} (non-adaptive) chosen plaintexts. Note that you can also get a miss-in-the-middle attack on the 24-round variant with the same techniques, since $(0,0,0,a) \rightarrow (0,0,0,a')$ is an impossible differential when $a \neq a'$. This gives an attack that uses 2^{65} chosen plaintexts and not much work.

Thus, our 24-round boomerang attack ($2^{48.5}$ adaptive chosen-plaintext and chosen-ciphertext queries) seems better than the conventional truncated differential attack (2^{65} chosen plaintexts) or the miss-in-the-middle attack (2^{65} chosen plaintexts), but it loses its advantage at 25 rounds.

One reason why the boomerang attack succeeds against the CAST-256 variant is that CAST-256 rounds exhibit a definite asymmetry. In both Skipjack and CAST-256, the A rounds have weaker diffusion in the reverse direction than in the forward direction, while the B rounds are stronger in the reverse direction. Thus, the combination of A and B rounds makes conventional differential attacks harder than usual: whether we attack the cipher or the inverse cipher, we will have to push a differential through 12 "strong rounds". In contrast, the boomerang attack allows us to follow the path of least resistance in both directions, because we cover the B rounds with a differential running in the forward direction and cover the A rounds with a differential running in the reverse direction. This makes the boomerang attack especially well-suited to the analysis of a cascade of B rounds followed by A rounds.

By the same line of reasoning, boomerang techniques would be especially weak at analyzing the real CAST-256 cipher, where the A rounds precede the B rounds. A boomerang attack on CAST-256 would be attacking the cipher at all of its strongest points, and thus boomerang techniques would be a particularly poor tool for analyzing the real CAST-256 round structure.

Towards Making Luby-Rackoff Ciphers Optimal and Practical

Sarvar Patel[1], Zulfikar Ramzan[2*], and Ganapathy S. Sundaram[1]

[1] Bell Labs, Lucent Technologies,
67 Whippany Road,
Whippany, NJ 07981,
{sarvar, ganeshs}@bell-labs.com

[2] 'Laboratory for Computer Science,
Massachusetts Institute of Technology,
Cambridge MA 02139,
zulfikar@theory.lcs.mit.edu

Abstract. We provide new constructions for Luby-Rackoff block ciphers which are efficient in terms of computations and key material used. Next, we show that we can make some security guarantees for Luby-Rackoff block ciphers under much weaker and more practical assumptions about the underlying function; namely, that the underlying function is a secure Message Authentication Code. Finally, we provide a SHA-1 based example block cipher called Sha-zam.

1 Introduction

The design of block ciphers whose security provably relies on a hard underlying primitive has been a popular area of contemporary cryptographic research. The path breaking paper of Luby and Rackoff [7] described the construction of pseudorandom permutation generators from pseudorandom function generators, which enabled the formalism of the notion of a block cipher. This theoretical breakthrough has stimulated a lot of research and ciphers based on this principle are often termed *Luby-Rackoff Ciphers*. Recall that block ciphers are private-key cryptosystems with the property that the length of the plaintext and ciphertext blocks are the same. Pseudorandom permutations can then be interpreted as block ciphers that are secure against adaptive chosen plaintext and ciphertext attacks. These permutations are closely related to the concept of pseudorandom functions which was defined by Goldreich, Goldwasser and Micali (GGM) [5]. These are functions which are "indistinguishable" from random functions in polynomial time. The GGM construction relied on the notion of pseudorandom bit generators, i.e., bit generators whose output cannot be distinguished from a sequence of random bits by any efficient method.

---

* Work done while this author was at Lucent Technologies

The core of a Luby-Rackoff cipher is a Feistel network. The use of Feistel networks for cipher design is not new, in fact it is one of the central design principles of DES. The original construction of Luby and Rackoff consists of four Feistel permutations, each of which requires the evaluation of a pseudorandom function. The proofs of security that were provided were subsequently simplified by Maurer [9] where he provided a rather generalized treatment based on information theoretic (as opposed to complexity theoretic) ideas. In what follows we review some of the more popular results in this field.

We start with the problem of producing a $2n$ bit pseudorandom permutation from n bit pseudorandom functions. Luby and Rackoff used the method of Feistel Networks. Clearly, from an information theoretic point of view, one would need at least two rounds of n bit pseudorandom functions (whose entropy is n bits) since the entropy of the permutations required is $2n$ bits. Now we check if two rounds are enough. Here Luby and Rackoff showed that if only two rounds were used and if an attacker chose two different inputs with the same "right half of n bits" then he can easily distinguish the outputs from a truly random permutation. Hence they suggested the use of at least three rounds, which is secure against chosen plaintext attacks. As it turned out, three rounds was not resistant to adaptive chosen ciphertext attacks, and in fact they showed that four rounds was sufficient to guarantee resistance to adaptive chosen plaintext and ciphertext attacks. The proof involved choosing four different pseudorandom functions in the four rounds.

Following this work, and the paper of Maurer [9], Lucks further generalized the proofs to include *unbalanced Feistel networks*. The main contribution of his work is the notion of a *difference concentrator* which is a non-cryptographic primitive that replaces the pseudorandom function in the first round but yet offers the same security. Parallel to this, a lot of research has concentrated on obtaining variants of Luby-Rackoff constructions where the number of different pseudorandom functions used in the four rounds is minimized. For example, see [12], [16]. This minimization is motivated by the fact that pseudorandom functions are computationally intensive to create and hence any reduction in the number of different functions used directly leads to a more efficient construction. Following these works, Naor and Reingold [10], established a very efficient generalization, where they formalized Lucks' treatment by using strongly universal hash functions. In [10], they achieve an improvement in the computational complexity by using only two applications of pseudorandom functions on n bits to compute the value of a $2n$ bit pseudorandom permutation. The central idea is to sandwich the two rounds of Feistel networks involving the pseudorandom functions between two pairwise independent $2n$ bit permutations. In other words, let f be a pseudorandom function on n bits and let h_1, h_2 be two pairwise independent $2n$ bit permutations (for example $h_i(x) = a_i x + b_i \bmod p$, where a_i, b_i are uniformly distributed). Then Naor and Reingold proved that h_1 followed by two Feistel rounds using f followed by h_2 is a $2n$ bit pseudorandom permutation. They generalized this construction by relaxing the pairwise independence condition on the exterior permutation rounds but changed the interior rounds to include two different pseudorandom functions. This piece of work represents the state of the art in efficiency related to Luby-Rackoff ciphers.

Another line of research has focused on how to enhance the security of Luby-Rackoff ciphers. Patarin [12] has shown that a Luby-Rackoff permutation can be distinguished from a random permutation using $O(2^{\frac{n}{2}})$ queries. In a related work, [1] showed how to obtain pseudorandom functions on $2n$ bits from pseudorandom functions on n bits using Benes networks. More recently, Patarin [13] has shown that six rounds of the Luby-Rackoff construction (instead of four) results in a pseudorandom permutation which cannot be distinguished from a random permutation with advantage better than $O(\frac{m^3}{2^{2n}})$, where m is the number of queries.

In this paper we show some new constructions of more practical Luby-Rackoff block ciphers from the standpoint of efficiency of computations. In addition, we provide security guarantees for Luby-Rackoff ciphers under weaker and more practical assumptions about the underlying primitive. We start with the Naor-Reingold construction but in a more general context of Abelian groups (as opposed to n bit vectors) and introduce new improvements in efficiency. With the same pseudorandom function in rounds 2 and 3, our universal hash functions in the 1st and 4th rounds operate only on half the data as opposed to the entire data thereby improving on the Naor-Reingold construction. Note that the round functions involve the group operation for encryption, and the difference operation for decryption as opposed to the usual XOR operation for both encryption and decryption.

We employ a novel construct called a *Bi-symmetric $\epsilon - \Delta$-Universal Hash Function*. We also give an example of such a Bi-symmetric $\epsilon - \Delta$-universal hash function that can be implemented much more efficiently than standard universal hash function constructions. Another interesting variation in the proof of security is that we show that even if the underlying function is only a secure Message Authentication Code (as opposed to the much stronger pseudorandom function) no adversary can easily invert Luby-Rackoff block ciphers. Finally, we provide a SHA-1 based example block cipher.

This paper is organized as follows: Section 2 includes the preliminaries, followed by the main results in section 3. Here we define the notion of a *Bi-symmetric $\epsilon - \Delta$* universal hash function, and provide an example. This concept is central to our proof of the main theorem. The security of Luby-Rackoff ciphers using a secure MAC is discussed in section 4. A SHA-1 based example cipher is included in section 5. In section 6 we discuss issues related to the optimality of Luby-Rackoff ciphers.

2 Preliminaries

Let H be a family of functions going from a domain D to a range G, where G is an Abelian Group with '+' and '-' as the addition and subtraction operators respectively. Let ϵ be a constant such that $1/|G| \leq \epsilon \leq 1$. The probabilities denoted below are all taken over the choice of $h \in H$.

Definition 1. *H is a Δ−universal−family of hash functions if for all $x, y \in D$ with $x \neq y$, and all $a \in G$, $Pr[h(x) - h(y) = a] \leq 1/|G|$. H is called ϵ − almost − Δ − universal if $Pr[h(x) - h(y) = a] \leq \epsilon$. An example is the linear hash $h(x) = ax \bmod p$ with $a \neq 0$.*

Definition 2. *H is a strongly universal family of hash functions if for all $x, y \in D$ with $x \neq y$ and all $a, b \in G$, $Pr[h(x) = a, h(y) = b] \leq 1/|G|^2$. H is ϵ−almost− strongly − universal family of hash functions if $Pr[h(x) = a, h(y) = b] \leq \epsilon/|G|$. An example is the linear congruential hash $h(x) = ax + b \bmod p$ with $a \neq 0$.*

Definition 3 (Basic Feistel Permutation). *Let f be a mapping from G to G. We denote by $\overline{f}$ the permutation on $G \times G$ defined as $\overline{f}(x) = (x_R, (x_L + f(x_R))$ where $x = (x_L, x_R)$, and $x_L, x_R \in G$.*

Definition 4 (Feistel Network). *Let $f_1, \ldots, f_s$ be mappings from G to G, then we denote by $\Psi(f_1, \ldots, f_s)$ the permutation on $G \times G$ defined as*

$$\Psi(f_1, \ldots, f_s) = \overline{f_s} \circ \ldots \circ \overline{f_1} \tag{1}$$

Theorem 1 (Luby-Rackoff). *The permutation on $G \times G$ defined by*

$$\Psi(f_1, f_2, f_3, f_4) \tag{2}$$

where the f_i are keyed pseudorandom functions is a secure block cipher in the sense that it cannot be distinguished from a random permutation by a polynomially bounded adversary who mounts an adaptive chosen plaintext/ciphertext attack.

3 Improving Luby-Rackoff Ciphers

In this section we provide a construction and proof of a more optimized version of a Luby-Rackoff cipher. Our construction is more practical than the one given by Naor and Reingold in [10] – which is currently the state of the art in Luby-Rackoff style block ciphers. Here is the main theorem proven in [10]:

Theorem 2 (Naor-Reingold). *Let f_1, f_2 be keyed pseudorandom functions. Let h_1, h_2 be strongly universal hash functions which as permutations on $G \times G$. Then, the permutation on $G \times G$ defined by*

$$h_2 \circ \Psi(f_1, f_2) \circ h_1 \tag{3}$$

is a secure block cipher in the sense that it cannot be distinguished from a random permutation by a polynomially bounded adversary who mounts an adaptive chosen plaintext/ciphertext attack.

The Naor-Reingold construction was a major breakthrough in the design of Luby-Rackoff ciphers since they were able to completely remove two calls of the expensive pseudorandom functions, and in some sense replace them with much more efficient non-cryptographic strongly universal hash functions.

Naor and Reingold mentioned two possible optimizations to their original construction and proved them to be secure block ciphers. The first is to use the same PRF in rounds two and three, thus saving key material: $h_2 \circ \Psi(f, f) \circ h_1$. The other possible optimization is to use the construction $\Psi(h_1, f_1, f_2, h_2)$ where the h_i are $\epsilon - \Delta$-universal hash functions which now operate on only *half* the data, as opposed to the entire $2n$ bit data. This construction saves running time and key material. Unfortunately, trying to realize both optimizations simultaneously $(\Psi(h_1, f, f, h_2))$, leads to an attack. [1] In particular, suppose that the $\epsilon - \Delta$-universal hash function we use is the linear hash $(h_a(x) = ax)$ over the field $GF(2^n)$. First we encrypt $(0,0)$ which results in the left half of the ciphertext being $V = f(f(h_1(0))) + h_1(0)$. Then we decrypt $(0,0)$ also resulting in the right half of the plaintext being $R = f(f(h_2(0))) + h_2(0)$. When $h_a(x) = ax$, then $h_1(0) = 0 = h_2(0)$. Thus V=R clearly allowing us to distinguish the cipher from a random permutation. Groups where addition and subtraction are different may not be susceptible to this attack.

This raises the question of whether or not one can use the same PRF's in rounds two and three and have an *efficient* non-cryptographic function operating on only half the bits in rounds 1 and 4. In this paper, we give a construction which answers this question in the affirmative.

We employ a novel construct called a *Bi-symmetric $\epsilon - \Delta$-Universal Hash Function* instead of the standard universal hash functions given in [10]. We also give an example of such a Bi-symmetric-Δ-universal hash function that can be implemented much more efficiently on many platforms than standard universal hash function constructions. Using these *Bi-symmetric $\epsilon - \Delta$-Universal Hash Functions* in rounds one and four, and the same PRF in rounds 2 and 3, we can get a secure and efficient Luby-Rackoff style cipher.

These hash functions, as defined below, possess two properties: the first one is the usual $\epsilon - \Delta$-universal property. The second property is different, and enables us to prevent the aforementioned attack.

Definition 5. *Let G be an Abelian Group and let '$-$' and '$+$' denote the subtraction and addition operations with respect to this group. Then H is a family of Bi-symmetric $\epsilon - \Delta$-universal Hash Functions if for all x, y with $x \neq y$, and all δ, $\Pr_{h \in H}[h(x) - h(y) = \delta] \leq \epsilon$ and for all x', y' and for all δ $\Pr_{h_1, h_2 \in H}[h_1(x') + h_2(y') = \delta] \leq \epsilon$.*

Typically we want ϵ to be extremely small – around $O(1/2^n)$ for inputs and outputs of size n bits.

Theorem 3. *Let h_1, h_2 be Bi-symmetric $\epsilon - \Delta$-universal hash functions, and let f be a random function. The block cipher defined by a four round Feistel network $\Psi(h_1, f, f, h_2)$ cannot be distinguished from a random permutation with probability better than $O(m^2 \cdot \epsilon)$ where m is the number of queries made by the*

---

[1] Daniel Bleichenbacher, personal communication

adversary (who may have unlimited power), and all the operations are performed in an Abelian group G.

Maurer [9] presented a very simple proof of security of the original Luby-Rackoff construction. Naor-Reingold [10] gave a more formal structure for proving adaptive security of Luby-Rackoff ciphers. Fortunately, the conditions that need to be satisfied for the security of the block cipher as presented by a Maurer type treatment are the same as the conditions resulting from the more formal treatment of Naor-Reingold. Hence the proof we present follows the simpler presentation of [9], but only proves security in the non-adaptive case. We can, however, easily prove adaptive security by following the treatment in [10].

Proof. Suppose we make m plaintext/ciphertext queries to a black box which can encrypt/decrypt. Moreover, we make these queries in a non-adaptive fashion; e.g. we make them all at once. Based on the responses of the black box, we must determine whether the black box contains a truly random permutation or a permutation of the form $\Psi(h_1, f, f, h_2)$.

Now, suppose we have a $2n$ bit plaintext message M_i where we denote the leftmost n bits as L_i and the rightmost n bits as R_i. The following equations describe the process by which this plaintext is encrypted by the Feistel network we consider:

$$S_i = L_i + h_1(R_i) \tag{4}$$
$$T_i = R_i + f(S_i) \tag{5}$$
$$V_i = S_i + f(T_i) \tag{6}$$
$$W_i = T_i + h_2(V_i) \tag{7}$$

where $+$ is the addition operation in the group G. Here (V, W) is the encrypted output of the plaintext (L, R). Similarly we can describe the decryption process where the "inputs" are (V, W) and the "outputs" are (L, R). Suppose that following transcript describes the responses of the encryption/decryption black box:

$$\langle (L_1, R_1), (V_1, W_1) \rangle, \ldots, \langle (L_m, R_m), (V_m, W_m) \rangle \tag{8}$$

We can assume without loss of generality that these queries are all distinct because making the same query twice doesn't help you. That is for all $1 \leq i < j \leq m$ $(L_i, R_i) \neq (L_j, R_j)$ and $(V_i, W_i) \neq (V_j, W_j)$. Now, let $\mathcal{E}_S$ denote the event that the elements in the set $S = \{S_1, \ldots, S_m\}$ are all different, and let $\mathcal{E}_T$ denote the event that the elements in the set $\mathcal{T} = \{T_1, \ldots, T_m\}$ are all different (where S_i and T_i are defined as above). Finally, let $\mathcal{E}_{ST}$ denote the event that the sets S and $\mathcal{T}$ are disjoint. Now, we consider what each event entails. First let's examine the case that the query made was an encryption query; i.e. the input was (L_i, R_i) and the output was (V_i, W_i) . If $\mathcal{E}_T$ occurs, then all the V_i's will be random because $V_i = S_i + f(T_i)$ and since the T_i's are distinct and f is a random function, it follows that $S_i + f(T_i)$ is random. Similarly, if both $\mathcal{E}_S$ and $\mathcal{E}_{ST}$ occur, then W_i will be random. This happens because $W_i = T_i + h_2(V_i) = R_i + f(S_i) + h_2(V_i)$

and $f(S_i)$ is random because f is a random function, and the S_i's are distinct and different from all the T_j's.

Now we look at the case for decryption queries. The inputs in this case are (V_i, W_i) and the outputs are (L_i, R_i). Following the same lines of reasoning as above, we want the "outputs" (L_i, R_i) to be random. This happens if the inputs to the random functions in rounds 2 and 3 are distinct. Therefore, the conditions we need are specified by the events $\mathcal{E}_S$, $\mathcal{E}_T$ and $\mathcal{E}_{ST}$.

Now, if $\mathcal{E}_T$, $\mathcal{E}_S$, and $\mathcal{E}_{ST}$ all occur, then the adversary cannot distinguish our Feistel permutation from a random permutation, except with negligible probability less than $m^2/2^{2n}$ [10]. All that remains is to derive a bound on the probability that at least one of these events does not occur. Let $\mathcal{E}_S^C$, $\mathcal{E}_T^C$, $\mathcal{E}_{ST}^C$ denote the complements of these events. We proceed to derive our bounds:

$$Pr[\mathcal{E}_S^C \text{ or } \mathcal{E}_T^C] \leq \Sigma_{1 \leq i < j \leq m} \Pr[T_i = T_j] + \Sigma_{1 \leq i < j \leq m} \Pr[S_i = S_j] \tag{9}$$

$$\leq \Sigma_{1 \leq i < j \leq m} \Pr[W_i - h_2(V_i) = W_j - h_2(V_j)] \tag{10}$$

$$+ \Sigma_{1 \leq i < j \leq m} \Pr[L_i + h_1(R_i) = L_j + h_1(R_j)] \tag{11}$$

$$\leq \Sigma_{1 \leq i < j \leq m} \Pr[h_2(V_i) - h_2(V_j) = W_i - W_j] \tag{12}$$

$$+ \Sigma_{1 \leq i < j \leq m} \Pr[h_1(R_i) - h_1(R_j) = L_j - L_i] \tag{13}$$

$$\leq m(m-1)/2 \cdot (\epsilon + \epsilon) \tag{14}$$

where the last inequality follows from the previous one by the following argument: if $V_i = V_j$ (similarly $R_i = R_j$) then it follows that $W_i \neq W_j$ (similarly $L_j \neq L_i$) by distinctness of queries; hence the event occurs with probability 0 in this case. If $V_i \neq V_j$ (similarly $R_i \neq R_j$), then the bound follows by the Bi-symmetric $\epsilon - \Delta$-universality property of the h_i.

Moreover, the above analysis holds regardless of whether the S_i or T_i were generated by the process of an encryption query or a decryption query. All that remains is to bound the probability that $\mathcal{E}_{ST}$ does not occur:

$$\Pr[\mathcal{E}_{ST}^C] \leq \Sigma_{1 \leq i \leq j \leq m} \Pr[S_i = T_j] \tag{15}$$

$$\leq \Sigma_{1 \leq i \leq j \leq m} \Pr[L_i + h_1(R_i) = W_j - h_2(V_j)] \tag{16}$$

$$\leq \Sigma_{1 \leq i \leq j \leq m} \Pr[h_1(R_i) + h_2(V_j) = W_j - L_i] \tag{17}$$

$$\leq m^2 \cdot \epsilon \tag{18}$$

where the last inequality follows from the previous one by the Bi-symmetric $\epsilon - \Delta$-universality property of H. Finally, we can apply a union bound to get:

$$\Pr[\mathcal{E}_S^C \text{ or } \mathcal{E}_T^C \text{ or } \mathcal{E}_{ST}^C] \leq 2m^2 \cdot \epsilon \tag{19}$$

This concludes the proof. $\square$

3.1   An Example Bi-symmetric $\epsilon - \Delta$-universal hash function

Definition 6. *Let p be a prime. Define the square hash family of functions from Z_p to Z_p as:*

$$h_x(m) \equiv (m + x)^2 \bmod p \tag{20}$$

Theorem 4. *The square hash family of functions is $\Delta - universal$.*

Proof: For all $m \neq n \in Z_p$, and $\delta \in Z_p$: $\Pr_x[h_x(m) - h_x(n) = \delta] = \Pr_x[(m + x)^2 - (n + x)^2 = \delta] = \Pr_x[m^2 - n^2 + 2(m - n)x = \delta] = 1/p$, where the last inequality follows since for any given $m \neq n \in Z_p$ and $\delta \in Z_p$ there is a unique x which satisfies the equation $m^2 - n^2 + 2(m - n)x = \delta$. $\qquad\square$

Theorem 5. *The square hash is a Bi-symmetric $\epsilon - \Delta$-universal family of hash functions.*

Proof: We have already proved the first property and need to prove the property that for all m, n and for all δ $\Pr_{x,y \in H}[h_x(m) + h_y(n) = \delta] \leq \epsilon$. $\Pr_{x,y}[(m + x)^2 + (n + y)^2 = \delta \bmod p] = \Pr_{x,y}[x^2 + 2xm + m^2 + n^2 + y^2 + 2ny - \delta = 0 \bmod p]$ There are at most 2 solutions for x for a given key y, so altogether there are at most 2^{n+1} solutions out of 2^{2n} possible keys x, y. So $\Pr_{x \in H}[h_x(m) + h_x(n) = \delta] = \frac{2}{2^n} = \frac{1}{2^{n-1}}$. If we count the number of solutions by further reducing this modulo 2^n, then ϵ increases by a small factor. $\qquad\square$

We remark that the function $h_x(m) \equiv (m + x)^2 \bmod p \bmod 2^n$ is also a Bi-symmetric $\epsilon - \Delta$-universal family of hash functions for a slightly larger value of ϵ. This function is more useful for implementation purposes since we often work over addition modulo 2^n (e.g. bit strings of length n). The Square Hash family requires much less computation time on many platforms than the traditional linear hash. The speedup occurs because squaring an n-bit number requires roughly half the number of basic word multiplications than actually multiplying two n-bit numbers. Thus square hash requires fewer operations and instructions to implement. More details can be found in [14].

4 Proving Security Under MAC Assumption

We give an alternate proof of security of our construction. This proof utilizes a weaker, but perhaps more practical, assumption, and makes a weaker claim on security of our block cipher. In particular, we show that if the underlying function f in our Feistel Network works as a secure *Message Authentication Code (MAC)*, then it is infeasible for an adversary to come up with a random plaintext/ciphertext pair after mounting an adaptive chosen plaintext/ciphertext attack. Some earlier work on the relationship between unpredictability (MACs) and indistinguishability was studied in [11]. We now define the relevant notions and then prove our claim.

The goal of message authentication codes is for one party to efficiently transmit a message to another party in a way that enables the receiving party to determine whether or not the message he receives has been tampered with. The setting involves two parties, Alice and Bob, who have agreed on a pre-specified secret key x. There are two algorithms used: a signing algorithm S_x and a verification algorithm V_x. If Alice wants to send a message M to Bob then she first computes a message authentication code, or MAC, $\mu = S_x(M)$. She sends (M, μ) to Bob, and upon receiving the pair, Bob computes $V_x(M, \mu)$ which returns 1 if the MAC is valid, or returns 0 otherwise. Without knowledge of the secret key x, it should be next to impossible for an adversary to construct a message and corresponding MAC that the verification algorithm will be accept as valid.

The formal security requirement for a Message Authentication Code was defined by Bellare, Canetti and Krawczyk [3]. In particular, we say that an adversary forges a MAC if, when given oracle access to (S_x, V_x), where x is kept secret, the adversary can come up with a valid pair (M^*, μ^*) such that $V_x(M^*, \mu^*) = 1$ but the message M^* was never made an input to the oracle for S_x. Here is a formal definition of an alternate, but equivalent formulation:

Definition 7. *We say that a function f_k is an (ϵ, q)-secure Message Authentication Code (MAC), if the probability that an adversary can successfully perform the following experiment is bounded by ϵ:*

1. *(Adversary is given black box access to f_k) The adversary makes q possibly adaptively chosen queries to a black box for f_k – that is the adversary comes up with a message m_1 gets to see $f_k(m_1)$, and from this information comes up with a query m_2, gets to see $f_k(m_2)$, and so on until making a query m_q, and getting to see $f(m_q)$.*
2. *The adversary comes up with a pair $(m, f_k(m))$ where m is different from any message queried in the first part. That is, $m \neq m_i$ for $1 \leq i \leq q$.*

Message Authentication has been a well studied problem, and there are a number of schemes which are widely believed to be secure. We show that we can use any of these schemes as the underlying function f in our block cipher and still get a fairly secure encryption scheme.

We now explain what it means for a cryptosystem to be *randomly-secure* against adaptive chosen message/ciphertext attacks. The definition has a similar flavor to the above definition for MACs.

Definition 8. *We say that a secret key encryption algorithm E_k is (ϵ, q)-randomly-secure against adaptive chosen plaintext/ciphertext attacks if no adversary can successfully perform the following experiment with probability better than ϵ:*

1. *(The adversary is given black box access to E_k) The adversary makes q possibly adaptively chosen plaintext/ciphertext queries to a black box for E_k; for example, the adversary comes up with a message m_1 gets to see $E_k(m_1)$, and from this information comes up with a query m_2, gets to see $E_k(m_2)$, and so on until making a query m_q and getting to see $E_k(m_q)$.*
2. *For a given randomly chosen message (or ciphertext) the adversary comes up with the corresponding ciphertext (or plaintext). This message (ciphertext) is different from any message (ciphertext) queried in the first part.*

We remark that there are alternate, and more stringent, definitions of security for symmetric key encryption schemes.

Theorem 6. *Let f be a $(\epsilon_1, 2q)$-secure MAC, and let h_1, h_2 be ϵ_2-Δ-universal hash functions. Then, $\Psi(h_1, f, f, h_2)$ is $(\epsilon_1 + q^2 \epsilon_2^2, q)$-randomly-secure under adaptive chosen plaintext/ciphertext attacks.*

Proof. The overall idea is to show that given any adversary A' who can break the encryption scheme (given black box access to the encryption and decryption mechanisms), we can construct an adversary A who can break the underlying MAC f (given black box access to the MAC function f). A will work as follows. First, A picks two hash functions h_1 and h_2 at random from a family of ϵ_2-Δ-universal hash functions. Then A proceeds simulating A'. At some point A' is going to make a query which could be in either of two forms: "Please give me the encryption of a message m" or "Please give me the decryption of a ciphertext c." In either case, A must answer this query for A' in a legitimate fashion. A can do this easily by making two calls to the black box for f and simulating the encryption or decryption algorithms. For example, if the ith query is an encryption query on a message $M_i = (L_i, R_i)$, then A computes values S_i, T_i, V_i, W_i according to equations 4, 5, 6, and 7.

We see that A calls the black box for f whenever it computes T_i and V_i. Decryption queries are handled in a similar fashion. Now, after A' finishes making q queries, (which results in A having made $2q$ queries) it will output a ciphertext (V, W) and the corresponding plaintext (L, R) – if the plaintext is different from plaintexts given during all the encryption queries made by A', and the ciphertext differs from the ones given during the decryption queries made by A', then A' has successfully broken the encryption scheme. Now, we translate this break of the encryption into something that breaks the underlying MAC f with high probability. So, we now may have derived two potential (Message, Tag) pairs. A computes:

$$S = L + h_1(R) \tag{21}$$
$$T = W - h_2(V) \tag{22}$$
$$Tag(S) = T - R \tag{23}$$
$$Tag(T) = V - S \tag{24}$$

If you work out the equations, it's easy to see that $Tag(S) = f(S)$ and $Tag(T) = f(T)$. Therefore, $(S, Tag(S)$ and $(T, Tag(T))$ are valid Message/Tag pairs. It appears as if we are done, but there is still one technicality remaining. Recall that when we defined the notion of a secure MAC, we require that the message output by the adversary must differ from the messages that the adversary gave to the black box during the query phase. We must now bound the probability that $S = S_i$ for some i $(1 \leq i \leq q)$.

$$Pr[\exists i \; 1 \leq i \leq q \text{ such that } S = S_i] \tag{25}$$
$$= Pr[\exists i \text{ such that } L + h_1(R) = L_i + h_1(R_i)] \tag{26}$$
$$\leq \Sigma_{i=1}^{q} Pr[L + h_1(R) = L_i + h_1(R_i)] \tag{27}$$
$$\leq q\epsilon_2 \tag{28}$$

The last equation follows from the previous because h_1 is an ϵ_2-Δ-universal hash function. Similarly, one can show that

$$Pr[\exists i\ 1 \leq i \leq q \text{ such that } T = T_i] \leq q\epsilon_2 \tag{29}$$

Since the hash functions h_1 and h_2 were chosen independently at random, it follows that likelihood that both $S = S_i$ and $T = T_i$ is at most $(q\epsilon_2)^2$.

What remains is to find a lower bound for the success probability of A'. We can do this by first deriving a lower bound for the success probability of A. A is successful whenever both of two conditions happen:

Condition 1 A' outputs a message and a valid ciphertext for that message. (i.e. A' is successful.)

Condition 2 At least one of the S, T that are generated do not coincide with something that was queried before; i.e. you can use the message and ciphertext to generate a valid message/tag pair where the message was not part of a previous query.

An easier way to proceed is to derive an upper bound for the probability that A fails, and subtract that number from 1. Suppose that the probability of condition 1 being met is at least ϵ_3 – then $Pr[\text{Condition 1 doesn't happen}] \leq (1 - \epsilon_3)$. Now, we know that condition 2 fails to occur with probability at most $(q\epsilon_2)^2$. Therefore, by a union bound, $Pr[A \text{ is unsuccessful}] \leq 1 - \epsilon_3 + (q\epsilon_2)^2$. Therefore, $Pr[A \text{ is successful}] \geq \epsilon_3 - (q\epsilon_2)^2$. Now, by assumption we have that $Pr[A \text{ is successful}] \leq \epsilon_1$. Therefore, it follows that $\epsilon_3 \leq \epsilon_1 + q^2\epsilon_2^2$ – which is a bound on success probability of A'. We have thus shown that we break the cipher with probability at most $\epsilon_1 + q^2\epsilon_2^2$ after making q queries. And this concludes the proof. $\square$

5 An Example Block Cipher: Sha-zam

In this section we discuss the design of *Sha-zam*, a block cipher based on constructions and theorems proved earlier. We use SHA-1 as the underlying primitive instead of a family of pseudorandom functions. Replacing pseudorandom functions by cryptographic functions (with desired properties) is not new. Biham and Anderson [2], propose the use of SHA-1 in conjunction with stream ciphers to design block ciphers. Also, Lucks used MD5 with an unbalanced Feistel network and Guttman's construction uses SHA-1 but different from the Luby Rackoff construction. In our design we do not use any stream ciphers. Instead we rely entirely on the improved versions of the Luby Rackoff construction and use SHA-1 as our underlying primitive. Recall that in section 4 we showed that Luby-Rackoff ciphers are secure if the underlying primitive is a secure MAC. Here security is with respect to some form of invertibility. From a practical standpoint the use of SHA-1 is justified. For example, the internet RFC HMAC-SHA-1 [4] assumes that forging a tag using SHA-1 as the underlying MAC is hard.

In addition to SHA-1 we use the Square Hash function (SQH) which we have introduced earlier. This cipher is driven by a *key scheduling generator* whose security is also related to SHA-1. Hence we get efficient re-use of code. Based on our results in earlier sections, under the assumption SHA-1 is pseudorandom we have that Sha-zam is a block cipher secure against adaptive chosen plaintexts and ciphertext attacks. Under the weaker assumption that SHA-1 is a secure MAC we show that no adversary can invert Sha-zam.

If C is an n-bit string, we denote by $prefix_k(C)$ the $n - k$ bit prefix of C (i.e. the first $n - k$ bits of C). We denote by $SHA(IV, x)$ the 160 bit output produced by SHA-1 on a 512 bit user specified input x and the standard IV. Our block cipher, which we call Sha-zam, takes as input a 320 bit block M and outputs a 320 bit ciphertext C. We denote $M = (L, R)$ where L is the left 160 bits of M and R is the right 160 bits of M. Also, we prefer to keep IV secret. In our construction we use three keys k_1, k_2, k_3.

Encryption with Sha-zam

Input: Plaintext Stored in L, R – each of which is 160 bits
Private Key: $k = (k_1, k_2, k_3)$ where:
k_1, k_3 are 160 bits each, and k_2 is 352 bits.
If IV not secret: then use the standard 160 bit IV.

Output: Ciphertext stored in V,W – each of which is 160 bits

Procedure: $S = L + SQH_{k1}(R) \bmod 2^{160}$
$T = R + SHA(IV, S, k_2) \bmod 2^{160}$
$V = S + SHA(IV, T, k_2) \bmod 2^{160}$
$W = T + SQH_{k_3}(V) \bmod 2^{160}$

Decryption with Sha-zam

Input: Ciphertext Stored in V,W – each of which is 160 bits
Private Key: $k = (k_1, k_2, k_3)$ where:
k_1, k_3 are 160 bits each, and k_2 is 352 bits.
If IV note secret: then use the standard 160 bit IV.

Output: Plaintext stored in L,R

Procedure: $T = W - SQH_{k_3}(V) \bmod 2^{160}$
$S = V - SHA(IV, T, k_2) \bmod 2^{160}$
$R = T - SHA(IV, S, k_2) \bmod 2^{160}$
$L = S - SQH_{k_1}(R) \bmod 2^{160}$

Our block cipher can be implemented efficiently. Specifically, it can encrypt messages in roughly the same time as it would take DES to accomplish this same task.

We describe a practical and secure pseudo-random generator, which we use for key scheduling. The security is based on SHA-1. If we run our generator using a randomly selected key as an input seed, we can securely generate the necessary bits needed for the secret key of our block cipher. We make use of a 512 bit prespecified global constant C. We almost never use the entire constant C but often take some specified prefix of it depending on the length of the key we're working with. We now describe our generator. Given a seed s we generate pseudorandom bits as follows:

Description of Generator
Input: seed s

1. Let $s_0 = s$
2. For $i = 1$ to m do
      Let $s_i = SHA(IV, prefix(C), s_{i-1})$
3. Output: $\langle h(s_1), \ldots, h(s_m) \rangle$

In step 3 above, h refers to a hash function chosen from a universal class. For example, the linear congruential hash function is any finite field is a very good candidate. The proof of security of this key scheduling generator will be presented elsewhere, [15].

6 A Discussion on Optimality

Since the invention of Luby-Rackoff ciphers, considerable progress has been made with respect to making the construction more efficient. Specifically, as noted in the introduction, most of the focus has been in "reducing" the number of invocations of a random function and the amount of key material used. Following the work of Lucks [8], Naor-Reingold have produced extremely efficient constructions with the help of hash functions and just two calls to a random function. In the present work, we have described a further generalization by using a different class of hash functions operating on only half the size of the input, in addition to a reduction in the key material. Is the end of progress in sight? We now discuss what it might mean for a Luby-Rackoff cipher to be optimal. We present various parameters of interest, and discuss how our proposal fits within this discussion.

1. Minimal number of rounds: Luby-Rackoff in their original paper showed that two rounds are not enough and 3 rounds are needed for plaintext security. Furthermore in order to resist adaptive attacks four rounds are needed. Our construction also consists of 4 rounds.
2. Maximal Security: Patarin [12] showed that the 4 round Luby-Rackoff construction can be distinguished from a random permutation with probability $O(\frac{m^2}{2^n})$ with m queries. We meet this bound as stated in Theorem 1. We can reduce the distinguishing probability by increasing the number of rounds, but this would violate the previous critirea.

3. Minimal Rounds of PRFs: Since the output of the block cipher is $2n$ bits long, it would seem that two n bit PRFs are necessary to insure cryptographic security. We also use only two PRFs in rounds two and three. For rounds one and four we use non-cryptographic called Bi-symmetric $\epsilon - \Delta$-universal functions, which add to the efficiency significantly.

4. Reusing the same PRF: It has been the goal of many papers to reduce the number of different PRFs that are used, ultimately hoping to use just one PRF. We achieve this goal by just using one PRF in rounds two and three.

5. Minimal Data Size Operated on by Non-cryptographic function: Our Bi-symmetric $\epsilon - \Delta$-universal hash function in rounds one and four operate on n bits of the data. If we operated on any smaller part of the data then we would open ourselves to collisions that can be detected with lower number of queries, thus increasing the distinguishing probability and decreasing security.

6. Reusing Hash Functions: It might be tempting to use the same universal hash function in rounds 1 and 4 to save key material. However, using the same hash h in both rounds, in groups where $g = -g$ for all $g \in G$, unfortunately leads to an attack which we now describe.

   Consider the group of n bit vectors with respect to the usual XOR operation. When we encrypt $(0,0)$, the left half of the resulting ciphertext is $V = f(f(h(0))) + h(0)$. Then we decrypt $(0,0)$ also, thus resulting in $R = f(f(h(0))) + h(0)$. Since V and R are equal, we immediately distinguish the block cipher from a random permutation.

   In our construction we may be able to use the same h. This seems plausible due to the fact our network operates with Abelian groups whose operations are not symmetric (i.e. $+$ and $-$ are different), where we may be able to exploit the use of specialized hash functions with the property $Pr_{h \in H}[h(x) + h(y) = \delta] \leq \epsilon$ for all x, y, and δ. When working in the cyclic group of integers modulo 2^n, we note that the Square hash function satisfies this specialized property. In particular, even if the above property does not suffice, other properties of square hash might aid in proving our claim. We leave this for further study.

7 Conclusion

In this paper we have described some novel improvements to Luby-Rackoff ciphers. We introduce the concept of a Bi-symmetric $\epsilon - \Delta$ universal hash function and provide an example of such a class. This concept when applied to the Naor Reingold construction of a Luby-Rackoff cipher improves the efficiency. In addition we show that under the weaker and more practical assumption of secure MAC we show that Luby Rackoff ciphers are hard to invert. We discuss the design of a new cipher based on these improvements - Sha-zam, whose security is related to SHA-1.

Acknowledgments

We would like to thank Daniel Bleichenbacher and Peter Winkler for useful comments on earlier versions of this paper. We would also like to thank Omer Reingold for very helpful comments.

References

[1]   W. Aiello, R. Venkatesan, Foiling birthday attacks in length-doubling transformations, *Advances in Cryptology - EUROCRYPT '96*, LNCS 1070, 307–320, 1996.

[2]   R. Anderson, E. Biham, Two practical and provably secure block ciphers, BEAR and LION, *Fast Software Encryption*, LNCS 1039, 113–120, 1996.

[3]   M. Bellare, R. Canetti, H. Krawczyk, Keying hash functions for message authentication, *Advances in Cryptology*, LNCS 1109, 1996.

[4]   M. Bellare, R. Canetti, H. Krawczyk. HMAC: Keyed-Hashing for Message Authentication, *Internet RFC*, 2104, February 1997.

[5]   O. Goldreich, S. Goldwasser, and A. Micali, How to construct random functions?, *Journal of ACM*, 33: 792–807, 1986.

[6]   P. Gutmann, documentation to SFS release 1.20 - SFS7.DOC, URL:http:/www.cs.auckland.ac.nz/pgut01/sfs.html, 1995.

[7]   M. Luby, and C. Rackoff, How to construct pseudorandom permutations from pseudorandom functions, *SIAM Journal of Computing*, 17: #2, 373–386, 1988.

[8]   S. Lucks, Faster Luby-Rackoff ciphers, *Proc. Fast Software Encryption*, LNCS, 1039, 189–203, 1996.

[9]   U. Maurer, A simplified and generalized treatment of Luby-Rackoff pseudorandom permutation generators, *Advances in Cryptology - EUROCRYPT '92*, LNCS 658, 239–255, 1992.

[10]   M. Naor, O. Reingold, On the construction of pseudo-random permutations: Luby-Rackoff revisited, *J. of Cryptology*, vol. 12, 29–66, 1999. Preliminary version in: *Proc. 29th Annual ACM STOC*, 189–199, 1997.

[11]   M. Naor, O. Reingold, From unpredictability to indistinguishability: A simple construction of pseudo-random functions from MACs, *Advances in Cryptology - CRYPTO '98*, LNCS, 267–282, 1998.

[12]   J. Patarin, New results on pseudorandom permutation generators based on the DES scheme, *Advances in Cryptology - CRYPTO '91*, LNCS, 301–312, 1991.

[13]   J. Patarin, Improved security bounds for pseudorandom permutations, *4th ACM Conference on Computer and Communications Security*, 142–150, 1997.

[14]   S. Patel, Z. Ramzan, Square hash: Fast message authentication via optimized universal hash functions, *preprint*.

[15]   S. Patel, Z. Ramzan, G. S. Sundaram, On constructing pseudorandom generators based on cryptographic hash functions, *In preparation*.

[16]   J. Pieprzyk, How to construct pseudorandom permutations from single pseudorandom functions, *Advances in Cryptology - EUROCRYPT '90*, LNCS 473, 140–150, 1991.

[17]   U. S. Department of Commerce/ N. I. S. T, *Secure Hash Algorithm*, FIPS 180, April 1995.

A New Characterization of Almost Bent Functions

Anne Canteaut[1], Pascale Charpin[1], and Hans Dobbertin[2]

[1] INRIA - projet CODES
BP 105, 78153 Le Chesnay, France
Anne.Canteaut,Pascale.Charpin@inria.fr
[2] German Information Security Agency
P.O.Box 20 03 63, 53133 Bonn, Germany
dobbertin@skom.rhein.de

Abstract. We study the functions from $\mathbf{F}_2^m$ into $\mathbf{F}_2^m$ for odd m which oppose an optimal resistance to linear cryptanalysis. These functions are called almost bent. It is known that almost bent functions are also almost perfect nonlinear, *i.e.* they also ensure an optimal resistance to differential cryptanalysis but the converse is not true. We here give a necessary and sufficient condition for an almost perfect nonlinear function to be almost bent. This notably enables us to exhibit some infinite families of power functions which are not almost bent.

1 Introduction

This paper is devoted to the study of the functions f from $\mathbf{F}_2^m$ into $\mathbf{F}_2^m$ which achieve the highest possible nonlinearity. This means that any non-zero linear combination of the Boolean components of f is as far as possible from the set of Boolean affine functions with m variables. When m is odd, the highest possible value for the nonlinearity of a function over $\mathbf{F}_{2^m}$ is known and the functions achieving this bound are called almost bent. These functions play a major role in cryptography; in particular their use in the S-boxes of a Feistel cipher ensure the best resistance to linear cryptanalysis. It was recently proved [5] that the nonlinearity of a function from $\mathbf{F}_2^m$ into $\mathbf{F}_2^m$ corresponds to the minimum distance of the dual of a linear code $\mathcal{C}_f$ of length $(2^m - 1)$. In particular when f is a power function, $f : x \mapsto x^s$, this code $\mathcal{C}_f$ is the cyclic code $\mathcal{C}_{1,s}$ of length $(2^m - 1)$ whose zeros are α and α^s (α denotes a primitive element of $\mathbf{F}_{2^m}$). It was also established [6] that if a function over $\mathbf{F}_2^m$ for odd m ensures the best resistance to linear cryptanalysis, it also ensures the best resistance to differential cryptanalysis. For the associated code $\mathcal{C}_f$, this means that if its dual (or orthogonal) code, denoted by $\mathcal{C}_f^\perp$, has the highest possible minimum distance, then $\mathcal{C}_f$ has minimum distance at least 5. But the reciprocal does not hold. Using Pless power moment identities [22] and some ideas due to Kasami [13], we make this condition necessary and sufficient by adding a requirement on the divisibility of the weights of $\mathcal{C}_f^\perp$. Since the divisibility of the weights of the cyclic code $\mathcal{C}_{1,s}^\perp$ is completely determined by McEliece's theorem [17], the determination of the values of s such that the power function $x \mapsto x^s$ is almost bent on $\mathbf{F}_{2^m}$ is now reduced to a combinatorial problem. This notably yields a very fast algorithm for checking if a power function over $\mathbf{F}_{2^m}$ is almost bent, even for large values of m. McEliece's theorem can also be used for proving that $\mathcal{C}_{1,s}^{\perp}$ contains a codeword whose weight does not have the appropriate divisibility. We are then able to prove that, for some infinite families of values of s the power function $x \mapsto x^s$ is not almost bent on $\mathbf{F}_{2^m}$.

The next section recalls the link between the weight distribution of the duals of cyclic codes with two zeros and the nonlinearity of a function from $\mathbf{F}_{2^m}$ into $\mathbf{F}_{2^m}$. In Section 3 we develop a new theoretical tool for studying the weight distribution of some linear codes, which generalizes some ideas due to Kasami. Combined with McEliece's theorem, this method provides a new characterization of almost bent power mappings. Section 4 then focuses on power functions $x \mapsto x^s$ over $\mathbf{F}_{2^m}$ for odd m when the exponent s can be written as $s = 2^{\frac{m-1}{2}} + 2^i - 1$. This set of exponents contains the values which appear in both Welch's and Niho's almost bent functions. We here prove that for most values of i, $x \mapsto x^{2^{\frac{m-1}{2}} + 2^i - 1}$ is not almost bent on $\mathbf{F}_{2^m}$. In Section 5 we finally give a very simple necessary condition on the exponents s providing almost bent power functions on $\mathbf{F}_{2^m}$ when m is not a prime; in this case we are able to eliminate most values of s. We also prove that the conjectured almost perfect nonlinear function $x \mapsto x^s$ with $s = 2^{4g} + 2^{3g} + 2^{2g} + 2^g - 1$ over $\mathbf{F}_{2^{5g}}$ is not almost bent.

2 Almost bent functions and cyclic codes with two zeros

2.1 Almost perfect nonlinear and almost bent functions

Let f be a function from $\mathbf{F}_2^m$ into $\mathbf{F}_2^m$. For any $(a, b) \in \mathbf{F}_2^m \times \mathbf{F}_2^m$, we define

$$\delta_f(a, b) = \#\{x \in \mathbf{F}_2^m, \, f(x + a) + f(x) = b\}$$
$$\lambda_f(a, b) = |\#\{x \in \mathbf{F}_2^m, \, a \cdot x + b \cdot f(x) = 0\} - 2^{m-1}|$$

where $\cdot$ is the usual dot product on $\mathbf{F}_2^m$. These values are of great importance in cryptography especially for measuring the security of an iterated block cipher using f as a round permutation [6]. A differential attack [2] against such a cipher exploits the existence of a pair (a, b) with $a \neq 0$ such that $\delta_f(a, b)$ is high. Similarly a linear attack [16] is successful if there is a pair (a, b) with $b \neq 0$ such that $\lambda_f(a, b)$ is high. The function f can then be used as a round function of an iterated cipher only if both

$$\delta_f = \max_{a \neq 0} \max_b \delta_f(a, b) \quad \text{and} \quad \lambda_f = \max_a \max_{b \neq 0} \lambda_f(a, b)$$

are small. Moreover if f defines the S-boxes of a Feistel cipher, the values of δ_f and λ_f completely determine the complexity of differential and linear cryptanalysis [21, 20].

Proposition 1. *[21] For any function $f : \mathbf{F}_2^m \to \mathbf{F}_2^m$,*

$$\delta_f \geq 2 .$$

In case of equality f is called almost perfect nonlinear *(APN).*

Proposition 2. *[24, 6] For any function* $f : \mathbf{F}_2^m \to \mathbf{F}_2^m$,

$$\lambda_f \geq 2^{\frac{m-1}{2}} .$$

In case of equality f is called almost bent (AB).

Note that this minimum value for λ_f can only be achieved if m is odd. For even m, some functions with $\lambda_f = 2^{\frac{m}{2}}$ are known and it is conjectured that this value is the minimum [23, p. 603].

From now on the vector space $\mathbf{F}_2^m$ is identified with the finite field $\mathbf{F}_{2^m}$. The function f can then be expressed as a unique polynomial of $\mathbf{F}_{2^m}[X]$ of degree at most $(2^m - 1)$. Note that the values of δ_f and λ_f are invariant under both right and left compositions by a linear permutation of $\mathbf{F}_{2^m}$. Similarly, if f is a permutation, $\delta_f = \delta_{f^{-1}}$ and $\lambda_f = \lambda_{f^{-1}}$. We can then assume that $f(0) = 0$ without loss of generality.

Both APN and AB properties can also be expressed in terms of error-correcting codes. We use standard notation of the algebraic coding theory (see [15]). The (Hamming) weight of any vector $x \in \mathbf{F}_2^n$ is denoted by $wt(x)$. Any linear subspace of $\mathbf{F}_2^n$ is called a binary linear code of length n and dimension k and is denoted by $[n, k]$. Any $[n, k]$-linear code $\mathcal{C}$ is associated with its dual $[n, n - k]$-code, denoted by $\mathcal{C}^\perp$:

$$\mathcal{C}^\perp = \{x \in \mathbf{F}_2^n, \ x \cdot c = 0 \ \forall c \in \mathcal{C}\} .$$

Any $r \times n$ binary matrix H defines an $[n, n - r]$-binary linear code $\mathcal{C}$:

$$\mathcal{C} = \{c \in \mathbf{F}_2^n, \ cH^T = 0\}$$

where H^T is the transposed matrix of H. We then say that H is a parity-check matrix of $\mathcal{C}$. The proofs of the following results are developed by Carlet, Charpin and Zinoviev in [5]:

Theorem 1. *Let f be a function from $\mathbf{F}_{2^m}$ into $\mathbf{F}_{2^m}$ with $f(0) = 0$. Let $\mathcal{C}_f$ be the linear binary code of length $2^m - 1$ defined by the $2m \times (2^m - 1)$-parity-check matrix*

$$H_f = \begin{pmatrix} 1 & \alpha & \alpha^2 & \dots & \alpha^{2^m - 2} \\ f(1) & f(\alpha) & f(\alpha^2) & \dots & f(\alpha^{2^m - 2}) \end{pmatrix} , \tag{1}$$

where each entry is viewed as a binary column vector of length m and α is a primitive element of $\mathbf{F}_{2^m}$. Then

(i) $\lambda_f = 2^{m-1}$ *if and only $\dim \mathcal{C}_f > 2^m - 1 - 2m$ or $\mathcal{C}_f^\perp$ contains the all-one vector.*

(ii) *If $\dim \mathcal{C}_f = 2^m - 1 - 2m$,*

$$\lambda_f = \max_{c \in \mathcal{C}_f^\perp, c \neq 0} |2^{m-1} - wt(c)| .$$

In particular, for odd m, f is AB if and only if for any non-zero codeword $c \in \mathcal{C}_f^\perp$,

$$2^{m-1} - 2^{\frac{m-1}{2}} \leq wt(c) \leq 2^{m-1} + 2^{\frac{m-1}{2}} .$$

(iii) f is APN if and only if the code C_f has minimum distance 5.

Tables 1 (resp. 2) give all known and conjectured values of exponents s (up to equivalence) such that the power function $x \mapsto x^s$ is APN (resp. AB). AB power permutations also correspond to pairs of maximum-length sequences with preferred crosscorrelation [23].

Table 1. Known and conjectured APN power functions x^s on $\mathbf{F}_{2^m}$ with $m = 2t + 1$

	exponents s	status
quadratic functions	$2^i + 1$ with $\gcd(i, m) = 1$ and $1 \leq i \leq t$	proven [10, 19]
Kasami's functions	$2^{2i} - 2^i + 1$ with $\gcd(i, m) = 1$ and $2 \leq i \leq t$	proven [14]
inverse function	$2^{2t} - 1$	proven [19, 1]
Welch's function	$2^t + 3$	proven [9]
Niho's function	$2^t + 2^{\frac{t}{2}} - 1$ if t is even	proven
	$2^t + 2^{\frac{3t+1}{2}} - 1$ if t is odd	[8]
Dobbertin's function	$2^{4i} + 2^{3i} + 2^{2i} + 2^i - 1$ if $m = 5i$	conjectured [8]

Table 2. Known AB power permutations x^s on $\mathbf{F}_{2^m}$ with $m = 2t + 1$

	exponents s	status
quadratic functions	$2^i + 1$ with $\gcd(i, m) = 1$ and $1 \leq i \leq t$	proven [10, 19]
Kasami's functions	$2^{2i} - 2^i + 1$ with $\gcd(i, m) = 1$ and $2 \leq i \leq t$	proven [14]
Welch's function	$2^t + 3$	proven [4, 3]
Niho's function	$2^t + 2^{\frac{t}{2}} - 1$ if t is even	proven
	$2^t + 2^{\frac{3t+1}{2}} - 1$ if t is odd	[12]

2.2 Weight divisibility of cyclic codes

We now give some properties of binary cyclic codes since the linear code C_f associated to a power function $f : x \mapsto x^s$ on $\mathbf{F}_{2^m}$ is a binary cyclic code of length $(2^m - 1)$ with two zeros. We especially focus on the weight divisibility of the duals of such codes.

Definition 1. *A linear binary code C of length n is cyclic if for all codewords $(c_0, \ldots, c_{n-1})$ in C, the vector $(c_{n-1}, c_0, \ldots, c_{n-2})$ is also in C.*

If each vector $(c_0, \ldots, c_{n-1}) \in \mathbf{F}_2^n$ is associated with the polynomial $c(X) = \sum_{i=0}^{n-1} c_i X$ in $\mathcal{R}_n = \mathbf{F}_2^n[X]/(X^n - 1)$, any binary cyclic code of length n is an ideal of $\mathcal{R}_n$. Since $\mathcal{R}_n$ is a principal domain, any cyclic code C of length n is generated by a unique monic polynomial g having minimal degree. This polynomial is called the generator polynomial of the code and its roots are the zeros of C. The defining set of C is then the set

$$I(C) = \{i \in \{0, \cdots, 2^m - 2\} | \, \alpha^i \text{ is a zero of } C\} \ .$$

where α is a primitive element of $\mathbf{F}_{2^m}$. Since C is a binary code, its defining set is a union of 2-cyclotomic cosets modulo $(2^m - 1)$, $Cl(a)$, where $Cl(a) = \{2^j a \bmod (2^m - 1)\}$. From now on the defining set of a binary cyclic code of length $(2^m - 1)$ is identified with the representatives of the corresponding 2-cyclotomic cosets modulo $(2^m - 1)$. The linear code C_f associated to the power function $f : x \mapsto x^s$ on $\mathbf{F}_{2^m}$ is defined by the following parity-check matrix:

$$H_f = \begin{pmatrix} 1 & \alpha & \alpha^2 & \cdots & \alpha^{2^m - 2} \\ 1 & \alpha^s & \alpha^{2s} & \cdots & \alpha^{(2^m - 2)s} \end{pmatrix} \ .$$

It then consists of all binary vectors c of length $(2^m - 1)$ such that $cH_f^T = 0$, i.e.

$$c(\alpha) = \sum_{i=0}^{2^m - 2} c_i \alpha^i = 0 \text{ and } c(\alpha^s) = \sum_{i=0}^{2^m - 2} c_i \alpha^{is} = 0 \ .$$

The code C_f is therefore the binary cyclic code of length $(2^m - 1)$ with defining set $\{1, s\}$.

Definition 2. *A binary code C is said 2^ℓ-divisible if the weight of any of its codewords is divisible by 2^ℓ. Moreover C is said exactly 2^ℓ-divisible if, additionally, it contains at least one codeword whose weight is not divisible by $2^{\ell+1}$.*

The following theorem due to McEliece reduces the determination of the exact weight divisibility of binary cyclic codes to a combinatorial problem:

Theorem 2. *[17] A binary cyclic code is exactly 2^ℓ-divisible if and only if ℓ is the smallest number such that $(\ell + 1)$ nonzeros of C (with repetitions allowed) have product 1.*

We now focus on primitive cyclic codes with two zeros and on the exact weight divisibility of their duals. We denote by $C_{1,s}$ the binary cyclic code of length $(2^m - 1)$ with defining set $Cl(1) \cup Cl(s)$. The nonzeros of the cyclic code $C_{1,s}^\perp$ are the elements α^{-i} with $i \in Cl(1) \cup Cl(s)$. Then $(\ell + 1)$ nonzeros of $C_{1,s}^\perp$ have product 1 if and only if there exist $I_1 \subset Cl(s)$ and $I_2 \subset Cl(1)$ with $|I_1| + |I_2| = \ell + 1$ and

$$\prod_{k \in I_1 \cup I_2} \alpha^{-k} = 1 \iff \sum_{k \in I_1 \cup I_2} k \equiv 0 \bmod (2^m - 1)$$

We consider both integers u and v defined by their 2-adic expansions: $u = \sum_{i=0}^{m-1} u_i 2^i$ and $v = \sum_{i=0}^{m-1} v_i 2^i$ where $u_i = 1$ if and only if $2^i s \bmod (2^m - 1) \in I_1$ and $v_i = 1$ if and only if $2^i \bmod (2^m - 1) \in I_2$. Then we have

$$\sum_{k \in I_1 \cup I_2} k \equiv \sum_{i=0}^{m-1} u_i 2^i s + \sum_{i=0}^{m-1} v_i 2^i \bmod (2^m - 1) \equiv 0 \bmod (2^m - 1)$$

The size of I_1 (resp. I_2) corresponds to $w_2(u) = \sum_{i=0}^{m-1} u_i$ which is the 2-weight of u (resp. v). McEliece's theorem can then be formulated as follows:

Corollary 1. *The cyclic code $C_{1,s}^{\perp}$ of length $(2^m - 1)$ is exactly 2^{ℓ}-divisible if and only if for all (u,v) such that $0 \leq u \leq 2^m - 1, 0 \leq v \leq 2^m - 1$ and*

$$us + v \equiv 0 \bmod (2^m - 1),$$

we have $w_2(u) + w_2(v) \geq \ell + 1$.

Since $v \leq 2^m - 1$, the condition $us + v \equiv 0 \bmod (2^m - 1)$ can be written $v = (2^m - 1) - (us \bmod (2^m - 1))$. This leads to the following equivalent formulation:

Corollary 2. *The cyclic code $C_{1,s}^{\perp}$ of length $(2^m - 1)$ is exactly 2^{ℓ}-divisible if and only if for all u such that $0 \leq u \leq 2^m - 1$,*

$$w_2(A(u)) \leq w_2(u) + m - 1 - \ell$$

where $A(u) = us \bmod (2^m - 1)$.

3 Characterization of almost bent functions

As previously seen the nonlinearity of a function from $\mathbf{F}_{2^m}$ into $\mathbf{F}_{2^m}$ is related to the weight distributions of some linear binary codes of length $(2^m - 1)$ and dimension $2m$. We here give some general results on the weight distributions of linear codes having these parameters. Our method uses Pless power moment identities [22] and some ideas due to Kasami [13, th. 13] (see also [5, th. 4]). The weight enumerator of a linear code C of length n is the vector $(A_0, \ldots, A_n)$ where A_i is the number of codewords of weight i in C.

Theorem 3. *Let C be a $[2^m - 1, 2^m - 2m - 1]$ linear binary code with minimum distance $d \geq 3$. Assume that the dual code $C^{\perp}$ does not contain the all-one vector $\mathbf{1} = (1, \cdots, 1)$. Let $A = (A_0, \cdots, A_{2^m - 1})$ (resp. $B = (B_0, \cdots, B_{2^m - 1})$) be the weight enumerator of $C^{\perp}$ (resp. C). Then we have*

(i) If w_0 is such that $A_w = A_{2^m - w} = 0$ for all $0 < w < w_0$, then

$$6(B_3 + B_4) \leq (2^m - 1) \left[(2^{m-1} - w_0)^2 - 2^{m-1} \right]$$

where equality holds if and only if $A_w = 0$ for all $w \notin \{0, w_0, 2^{m-1}, 2^m - w_0\}$.
(ii) If w_1 is such that $A_w = A_{2^m - w} = 0$ for all $w_1 < w < 2^{m-1}$, then

$$6(B_3 + B_4) \geq (2^m - 1) \left[(2^{m-1} - w_1)^2 - 2^{m-1} \right]$$

where equality holds if and only if $A_w = 0$ for all $w \notin \{0, w_1, 2^{m-1}, 2^m - w_1\}$.

Proof. The main part of the proof relies on the first Pless power moment identities [22]. The first four power moment identities on the weight distribution of the $[2^m - 1, 2m]$-code $C^{\perp}$ are:

$$\sum_{w=0}^{n} wA_w = 2^{2m-1}(2^m - 1),$$

$$\sum_{w=0}^{n} w^2 A_w = 2^{3m-2}(2^m - 1),$$

$$\sum_{w=0}^{n} w^3 A_w = 2^{2m-3}\left((2^m - 1)^2(2^m + 2) - 3!B_3\right),$$

$$\sum_{w=0}^{n} w^4 A_w = 2^{2m-4}\left(2^m(2^m - 1)(2^{2m} + 3 \cdot 2^m - 6) + 4!\left(B_4 - (2^m - 1)B_3\right)\right)$$

Let us consider the numbers $I_\ell = \sum_{w=1}^{2^m-1}(w - 2^{m-1})^\ell A_w$. Since for ℓ even

$$(w - 2^{m-1})^\ell = ((2^m - w) - 2^{m-1})^\ell \, ,$$

we have for any even ℓ:

$$I_\ell = \sum_{w=1}^{2^m-1}(w - 2^{m-1})^\ell A_w = \sum_{w=1}^{2^{m-1}-1}(w - 2^{m-1})^\ell(A_w + A_{2^m-w}) \, .$$

Note that the codeword of weight zero is not taken in account in the sum above. Recall that $C^{\perp}$ does not contain the all-one codeword. By using the four power moments, we obtain the following values for I_2 and I_4:

$$I_2 = 2^{2m-2}(2^m - 1)$$
$$I_4 = 2^{2m-2}\left[6(B_3 + B_4) + 2^{m-1}(2^m - 1)\right]$$

This implies

$$I(x) = I_4 - x^2 I_2 = \sum_{w=1}^{2^{m-1}-1}(w - 2^{m-1})^2\left((w - 2^{m-1})^2 - x^2\right)(A_w + A_{2^m-w})$$

$$= 2^{2m-2}\left[6(B_3 + B_4) + (2^m - 1)(2^{m-1} - x^2)\right]$$

The w-th term in this sum satisfies:

$$(w - 2^{m-1})^2\left((w - 2^{m-1})^2 - x^2\right) \begin{array}{l} < 0 \ \ \text{if } 0 < |2^{m-1} - w| < x \\ = 0 \ \ \text{if } w \in \{2^{m-1}, 2^{m-1} \pm x\} \\ > 0 \ \ \text{if } |2^{m-1} - w| > x \end{array}$$

This implies that, if $A_w = A_{2^m-w} = 0$ for all w such that $0 < w < w_0$, all the terms in $I(2^{m-1} - w_0)$ are negative. Then we have

$$6(B_3 + B_4) + (2^m - 1)\left[2^{m-1} - (2^{m-1} - w_0)^2\right] \leq 0$$

with equality if and only if all terms in the sum are zero. This can only occur when $A_w = 0$ for all $w \notin \{0, w_0, 2^{m-1}, 2^m - w_0\}$.

Similarly, if $A_w = A_{2^m - w} = 0$ for all w such that $w_1 < w < 2^{m-1}$, all the terms in $\mathcal{I}(2^{m-1} - w_1)$ are positive. Then we have

$$6(B_3 + B_4) + (2^m - 1)\left[2^{m-1} - (2^{m-1} - w_1)^2\right] \geq 0$$

with equality if and only if all terms in the sum are zero, $i.e.$ if $A_w = 0$ for all $w \notin \{0, w_1, 2^{m-1}, 2^m - w_1\}$. ◊

Let us now suppose that m is odd, $m = 2t + 1$. We give a necessary and sufficient condition on $f : \mathbf{F}_{2^m} \to \mathbf{F}_{2^m}$ to be almost bent.

Theorem 4. *Let m be an odd integer and let f be a function from $\mathbf{F}_{2^m}$ into $\mathbf{F}_{2^m}$ such that $\lambda_f \neq 2^{m-1}$. Then f is AB if and only if f is APN and the code $C_f^{\perp}$ defined in Theorem 1 is $2^{\frac{m-1}{2}}$-divisible.*

Proof. Let $(A_0, \cdots, A_{2^m-1})$ (resp. $(B_0, \cdots, B_{2^m-1})$) be the weight enumerator of $C_f^{\perp}$ (resp. C_f) and let w_0 be the smallest w such that $0 < w < 2^{m-1}$ and $A_w + A_{2^m - w} \neq 0$ for all $0 < w < w_0$. According to Theorem 1 (ii), f is AB if and only if $w_0 = 2^{m-1} - 2^{\frac{m-1}{2}}$. Since $\lambda_f \neq 2^{m-1}$, we deduce from Theorem 1 (i) that the code C_f has dimension $2^m - 2m - 1$ and that $C_f^{\perp}$ does not contain the all-one vector. Since the minimum distance of C_f is obviously greater than 3, Theorem 3 can be applied. The announced condition is sufficient: if $w_0 = 2^{m-1} - 2^{\frac{m-1}{2}}$ we have that $B_3 + B_4 = 0$ according to Theorem 3 (i). This means that C_f has minimum distance 5 ($i.e.$ f is APN). Moreover all nonzero weights of $C_f^{\perp}$ lie in $\{2^{m-1}, 2^{m-1} \pm 2^{\frac{m-1}{2}}\}$. The code $C_f^{\perp}$ is therefore $2^{\frac{m-1}{2}}$-divisible.

The condition is also necessary since, for any w such that $2^{m-1} - 2^{\frac{m-1}{2}} < w < 2^{m-1}$, both integers w and $2^{m-1} - w$ are not divisible by $2^{\frac{m-1}{2}}$. The condition on the divisibility of the weights of $C_f^{\perp}$ then implies that $A_w + A_{2^m - w} = 0$ for all w such that $2^{m-1} - 2^{\frac{m-1}{2}} < w < 2^{m-1}$. If f is APN, C_f does not contain any codeword of weight 3 and 4. The lower bound given in Theorem 3 (ii) (applied with $w_1 = 2^{m-1} - 2^{\frac{m-1}{2}}$) is then reached. It follows that the weight of every codeword in $C_f^{\perp}$ lies in $\{0, 2^{m-1}, 2^{m-1} \pm 2^{\frac{m-1}{2}}\}$ and therefore that f is AB. ◊

When f is a power function, $f : x \mapsto x^s$, the corresponding code C_f is the binary cyclic code $C_{1,s}$ of length $(2^m - 1)$ with defining set $\{1, s\}$. The weight divisibility of the corresponding dual code can therefore be obtained by applying McEliece's theorem, as expressed in Corollary 2. This leads to the following characterization of AB power functions:

Corollary 3. *Let $m = 2t + 1$. Assume that the power function $f : x \mapsto x^s$ on $\mathbf{F}_{2^m}$ has no affine component. Then f is AB on $\mathbf{F}_{2^m}$ if and only if f is APN on $\mathbf{F}_{2^m}$ and*

$$\forall u, \quad 1 \leq u \leq 2^m - 1, \quad w_2(A(u)) \leq t + w_2(u) \tag{2}$$

where $A(u) = us \bmod (2^m - 1)$.

Condition (2) is obviously satisfied when $w_2(u) \geq t+1$. Moreover, if $\gcd(s, 2^m - 1) = 1$ (*i.e.* if $x \mapsto x^s$ is a permutation), the condition also holds for all u such that $w_2(u) = t$. Using that

$$A(u2^i \bmod (2^m - 1)) = 2^i A(u) \bmod (2^m - 1),$$

we deduce that Condition (2) must only be checked for one element in each cyclotomic coset. Note that if u is the smallest element in its cyclotomic coset and $w_2(u) < t$, we have $u \leq 2^{m-2} - 1$. This result provides a fast algorithm for checking whether an APN power function is AB, and then for finding all AB power functions on $\mathbf{F}_{2^m}$. There are roughly $\frac{2^{m-1}}{m}$ cyclotomic representatives u such that $w_2(u) \leq t$ and each test requires one modular multiplication on m-bit integers and two weight computations. Condition (2) can then be checked with around 2^m elementary operations and at no memory cost.

The 2-weight of s obviously gives an upper bound on the weight divisibility of $\mathcal{C}_{1,s}^{\perp}$ (obtained for $u = 1$ in Corollary 2). Using this result, we immediately recover the condition on the degree of AB functions given in [5, Theorem 1] in the particular case of power functions.

Corollary 4. *Let m be an odd integer. If the power permutation $f : x \mapsto x^s$ is AB on $\mathbf{F}_{2^m}$, then*

$$\mathrm{degree}(f) = w_2(s) \leq \frac{m+1}{2} .$$

4 Power functions $x \mapsto x^s$ on $\mathbf{F}_2^m$ with $s = 2^{\frac{m-1}{2}} + 2^i - 1$

In his 1968 paper [11], Golomb mentioned a conjecture of Welch stating that for $m = 2t + 1$, the power function $x \mapsto x^s$ with $s = 2^t + 3$ is AB on $\mathbf{F}_{2^m}$. Niho [18] stated a similar conjecture for $s = 2^t + 2^{\frac{t}{2}} - 1$ when t is even and $s = 2^t + 2^{\frac{3t+1}{2}} - 1$ when t is odd. Note that all of these exponents s can be written as $2^t + 2^i - 1$ for some i. Since both Welch's and Niho's functions are APN [9,8], Corollary 3 leads to the following formulation of Welch's and Niho's conjectures:
Let $m = 2t + 1$ be an odd integer. For all u such that $1 \leq u \leq 2^m - 1$, we have

$$w_2((2^t + 2^i - 1)u \bmod (2^m - 1)) \leq t + w_2(u) \tag{3}$$

for the following values of i: $i = 2$, $i = t/2$ for even t and $i = (3t+1)/2$ for odd t. We proved that Condition (3) is satisfied in the Welch case ($i = 2$) [4,3]. More recently Xiang and Hollmann used this formulation for proving Niho's conjecture [12]. We here focus on all other values of s which can be expressed as $s = 2^t + 2^i - 1$ for some i. We prove that for almost all of these values $x \mapsto x^s$ is not AB on $\mathbf{F}_{2^m}$. This result is derived from both following lemmas which give an upper bound on the exact weight divisibility of $\mathcal{C}_{1,s}^{\perp}$.

Lemma 1. *Let $m = 2t+1$ be an odd integer and $s = 2^t + 2^i - 1$ with $2 < i < t-1$. Let $\mathcal{C}_{1,s}$ be the binary cyclic code of length $(2^m - 1)$ with defining set $\{1, s\}$. If 2^ℓ denotes the exact divisibility of $\mathcal{C}_{1,s}^{\perp}$, we have*

- *if $t \equiv 0 \bmod i$ and $i \neq t/2$, then $\ell \leq t - 1$,*
- *if $t \equiv 1 \bmod i$, then $\ell \leq t - i + 2$,*
- *if $t \equiv r \bmod i$ with $1 < r < i$, then $\ell \leq t - i + r$.*

Proof. Let $t = iq + r$ with $r < i$ and $A(u) = (2^t + 2^i - 1)u \bmod 2^m - 1$. McEliece's theorem (Corollary 2) implies that $C_{1,s}^{\perp}$ is at most 2^ℓ-divisible if there exists an integer $u \in \{0, \ldots, 2^m - 1\}$ such that $w_2(A(u)) = w_2(u) + 2t - \ell$. We here exhibit an integer u satisfying this condition for the announced values of ℓ.

- We first consider the case $r \neq 0$. Let $u = 2^t + 2^{r-1} \sum_{k=1}^{q} 2^{ik} + 1$. Then $w_2(u) = q + 2$ and we have

$$A(u) = 2^{2t} + 2^{t+r-1} \sum_{k=1}^{q} 2^{ik} + 2^{t+i} + (2^{t+i-1} - 2^{i+r-1}) + (2^i - 1) . \quad (4)$$

If $r > 1$, we have $t + i < t + r - 1 + ik \leq 2t - 1$ for all k such that $1 \leq k \leq q$. All terms in (4) are then distinct. It follows that

$$w_2(A(u)) = 1 + q + 1 + (t - r) + i = w_2(u) + t - r + i .$$

If $r = 1$, we obtain

$$A(u) = 2^{2t} + 2^t \sum_{k=2}^{q} 2^{ik} + 2^{t+i+1} + 2^{t+i-1} - 1 .$$

In this case

$$w_2(A(u)) = 1 + (q - 1) + 1 + (t + i - 1) = w_2(u) + t + i - 2 .$$

- Suppose now that $r = 0$ and $i \neq t/2$. Since $i < t$, we have $q > 2$. Let $u = 2^{t+i} + 2^{t+2} + 2^t + 2^{i+2} \sum_{k=0}^{q-2} 2^{ik} + 1$. Using that $i > 2$, we deduce that $i + 2 + ik \leq i(q - 1) + 2 \leq t - i + 2 < t$ for all $k \leq q - 2$. It follows that $w_2(u) = q + 3$. Let us now expand the corresponding $A(u)$:

$$A(u) = 2^{2t} + \sum_{k=0}^{q-3} 2^{t+2+(k+2)i} + 2^{t+2i} + 2^{t+i+3} - 2^{i+2} + 2^i + 2^{i-1} + 1 . \quad (5)$$

If $i > 2$, all values of k such that $0 \leq k \leq q - 3$ satisfy $t + 2i < t + 2 + (k+2)i < 2t$. We then deduce that, if $q > 2$, all the terms in (5) are distinct except if $i = 3$. It follows that, for any $i > 3$,

$$w_2(A(u)) = 1 + (q - 2) + 1 + (t + 1) + 3 = w_2(u) + t + 1 .$$

For $i = 3$, we have

$$A(u) = 2^{2t} + \sum_{k=0}^{q-3} 2^{t+3k+8} + 2^{t+7} - 2^5 + 2^3 + 2^2 + 1 .$$

In this case

$$w_2(A(u)) = 1 + (q - 2) + (t + 2) + 3 = w(u) + t + 1 .$$

◇

Lemma 2. *Let $m = 2t + 1$ be an odd integer $s = 2^t + 2^i - 1$ with $t + 1 < i < 2t$. Let $C_{1,s}$ be the binary cyclic code of length $(2^m - 1)$ with defining set $\{1, s\}$. If 2^ℓ denotes the exact divisibility of $C_{1,s}^\perp$, we have*

- *if $t + 1 < i < \frac{3t+1}{2}$, then $\ell \leq m - i$,*
- *if $\frac{3t+1}{2} < i < 2t - 1$, then $\ell \leq 2(m - i) - 1$,*
- *if $i = 2t - 1$, then $\ell \leq 3$.*

Proof. Let $A(u) = (2^t + 2^i - 1)u \bmod (2^m - 1)$. Exactly as in the proof of the previous lemma, we exhibit an integer $u \in \{0, \dots, 2^m - 1\}$ such that $w_2(A(u)) = w_2(u) + 2t - \ell$ for the announced values of ℓ. We write $i = t + j$ where $1 < j < t$.

- We first consider the case $t + 1 < i < \frac{3t+1}{2}$. Let $u = 2^t + 2^{j-1} + 1$. Then $w_2(u) = 3$ and

$$A(u) = 2^{2t} + 2^{t+2j-1} + 2^{t+j} + 2^{t+j-1} - 1 . \tag{6}$$

Since $j < \frac{t+1}{2}$, we have that $2t > t + 2j - 1$. All the terms in (6) are therefore distinct. We deduce

$$w_2(A(u)) = 3 + (t + j - 1) = w_2(u) + i - 1 .$$

- We now focus on the case $\frac{3t+1}{2} < i \leq 2t - 1$. Let $u = 2^t + 2^j + 1$. Then $w_2(u) = 3$ and

$$A(u) = 2^{2t} + 2^{t+j+1} - 2^{j-1} + 2^{2j-t-1} - 1 . \tag{7}$$

Since $\frac{t+1}{2} < j < t$, we have $0 < 2j - t - 1 < j - 1$. If $j \neq t - 1$, all the exponents in (7) are distinct. It follows that

$$w_2(A(u)) = 1 + (t + 2) + (2j - t - 1) = w_2(u) + 2(i - t) - 1 .$$

If $j = t - 1$, we have

$$A(u) = 2^{2t+1} - 2^{j-1} + 2^{2j-t-1} - 1 .$$

In this case

$$w_2(A(u)) = (2t + 1) - (t - j) = w_2(u) + 2t - 3 .$$

◇

From both lemma 1 and 2 we deduce the following theorem:

Theorem 5. *Let $m = 2t + 1$ be an odd integer and let $s = 2^t + 2^i - 1$ with $i \in \{1, \dots, 2t\}$. The only values of i such that $x \mapsto x^s$ is AB on $\mathbf{F}_{2^m}$ are $1, 2, \frac{t}{2}, t, t + 1, \frac{3t+1}{2}, 2t$ and maybe $t - 1$.*

Proof. If $i \notin \{1, 2, \frac{t}{2}, t - 1, t, t + 1, \frac{3t+1}{2}, 2t\}$, $C_{1,s}^\perp$ is not 2^t-divisible since the upper bounds given in both previous lemmas are strictly less than t. It follows from Theorem 4 that the corresponding power functions are not AB. Moreover $x \mapsto x^s$ is AB for $i \in \{1, 2, \frac{t}{2}, t, t + 1, \frac{3t+1}{2}, 2t\}$:

- $i = 1$ corresponds to a quadratic function,
- $i = 2$ corresponds to the Welch's function,
- $i = t$ corresponds to the inverse of a quadratic function since $(2^{t+1} - 1)(2^t + 1) \equiv 2^t \bmod 2^m - 1$.
- $i = t + 1$ corresponds to a Kasami's function since $2^t(2^{t+1} + 2^t - 1) \equiv 2^{2t} - 2^t + 1 \bmod 2^m - 1$.
- $i = 2t$ gives an s which is in the same 2-cyclotomic coset as $2^{t+1} - 1$.
- $i = \frac{t}{2}$ or $i = \frac{3t+1}{2}$ corresponds to the Niho's function. ◇

The only unresolved case is then $i = t - 1$. In accordance with our simulation results for $m \leq 39$ we conjecture that the dual of the binary cyclic code of length $(2^m - 1)$ with defining set $\{1, 2^t + 2^{t-1} - 1\}$ is exactly 2^t-divisible. For $m = 5$ and $m = 7$ the function $x \mapsto x^s$ for $s = 2^t + 2^{t-1} - 1$ is AB since it respectively corresponds to a quadratic function and to the Welch function. On the contrary it is known that this power function is not APN when 3 divides m since $C_{1,s}$ has minimum distance 3 in this case [7, Th. 5]. We actually conjecture that for any odd $m \geq 9$ the function $x \mapsto x^s$ with $s = 2^t + 2^{t-1} - 1$ is not APN on $\mathbf{F}_{2^m}$.

5   AB power functions on $\mathbf{F}_{2^m}$ when m is not a prime

We now focus on AB power functions on $\mathbf{F}_{2^m}$ when m is not a prime. We show that in this case the nonlinearity of $x \mapsto x^s$ on $\mathbf{F}_{2^m}$ is closely related to the nonlinearity of the power $x \mapsto x^{s_0}$ on $\mathbf{F}_{2^g}$ where g is a divisor of m and $s_0 = s \bmod (2^g - 1)$. We first derive an upper bound on the exact weight divisibility of $C_{1,s}^{\perp}$ from the exact weight divisibility of the code $C_{1,s_0}^{\perp}$ of length $(2^g - 1)$.

Proposition 3. *Let g be a divisor of m. Let $C_{1,s}$ be the binary cyclic code of length $(2^m - 1)$ with defining set $\{1, s\}$ and C_0 the binary cyclic code of length $(2^g - 1)$ with defining set $\{1, s_0\}$ where $s_0 = s \bmod (2^g - 1)$. Assume that $C_0^{\perp}$ is exactly 2^{ℓ}-divisible. Then $C_{1,s}^{\perp}$ is not $2^{\frac{m}{g}(\ell+1)}$-divisible.*

Proof. Let $s = s_0 + a(2^g - 1)$. We here use McEliece's theorem as expressed in Corollary 1. If $C_0^{\perp}$ is exactly 2^{ℓ}-divisible, there exists a pair of integers (u_0, v_0) with $u_0 \leq 2^g - 1$ and $v_0 \leq 2^g - 1$ such that

$$u_0 s_0 + v_0 \equiv 0 \bmod 2^g - 1 \text{ and } w_2(u_0) + w_2(v_0) = \ell + 1$$

Let us now consider both integers u and v defined by

$$u = u_0 \frac{2^m - 1}{2^g - 1} \text{ and } v = v_0 \frac{2^m - 1}{2^g - 1}$$

For $s = s_0 + a(2^g - 1)$, the pair (u, v) satisfies

$$us + v = u_0 a(2^m - 1) + \frac{2^m - 1}{2^g - 1}(u_0 s_0 + v_0) \equiv 0 \bmod (2^m - 1).$$

Since $\frac{2^m-1}{2^g-1} = \sum_{i=0}^{m/g-1} 2^{ig}$ and both u_0 and v_0 are less than $2^g - 1$, we have

$$w_2(u) + w_2(v) = \frac{m}{g}\left(w_2(u_0) + w_2(v_0)\right) = \frac{m}{g}(\ell + 1) .$$

We then deduce that $C_{1,s}^\perp$ is not $2^{\frac{m}{g}(\ell+1)}$-divisible.   ◇

We now derive a necessary condition on the values of the exponents which provide AB power functions.

Theorem 6. *Let m be an odd integer. The power function $x \mapsto x^s$ is not AB on $\mathbf{F}_{2^m}$ if there exists a divisor g of m with $g > 1$ satisfying one of the following conditions:*

1. $\exists i,\ 0 \le i < g,\ s \equiv 2^i \bmod (2^g - 1)$,
2. $s_0 = s \bmod (2^g - 1) \ne 2^i$ *and the dual of the cyclic code of length $(2^g - 1)$ with defining set $\{1, s_0\}$ is not $2^{\frac{g-1}{2}}$-divisible.*

Proof. Theorem 4 provide a necessary condition for obtaining an AB power function on $\mathbf{F}_{2^m}$: this function has to be APN and $C_{1,s}^\perp$ has to be $2^{\frac{m-1}{2}}$-divisible. When $s \equiv 2^i \bmod (2^g - 1)$, it is known [7] that the cyclic code $C_{1,s}$ has minimum distance 3. It follows that $x \mapsto x^s$ is not APN in this case. Suppose now that the dual of the cyclic code of length $(2^g - 1)$ with defining set $\{1, s_0\}$ is exactly 2^ℓ-divisible. According to the previous theorem we have that $C_{1,s}^\perp$ is not $2^{\frac{m}{g}(\ell+1)}$-divisible. If $C_{1,s}^\perp$ is $2^{\frac{m-1}{2}}$-divisible, it therefore follows that

$$\frac{m-1}{2} \le \frac{m}{g}(\ell + 1) - 1 .$$

This gives

$$\ell + 1 \ge \frac{g(m+1)}{2m} > \frac{g-1}{2}$$

since $(m + 1)g > m(g - 1)$. This implies that $C_0^\perp$ is $2^{\frac{g-1}{2}}$-divisible.   ◇

Example 1. We search for all AB power permutations on $\mathbf{F}_{2^{21}}$. We here use that the cyclic codes $C_{1,s_0}^\perp$ of length $(2^7 - 1)$ are at most 4-divisible when $s_0 \in \{7, 19, 21, 31, 47, 55, 63\}$ (and for their cyclotomic conjugates). Amongst the 42340 possible pairs of exponents (s, s^{-1}) such that $\gcd(s, 2^{21} - 1) = 1$ (up to equivalence), only 5520 satisfy both conditions expressed in Corollary 4 and Theorem 6. By testing the weight divisibility of the corresponding cyclic codes as described in Corollary 3 we obtain that only 20 such pairs correspond to a 2^{10}-divisible code $C_{1,s}^\perp$. The corresponding values of $\min(s, s^{-1})$ are:

$$\{3, 5, 13, 17, 33, 241, 257, 993, 1025, 1027, 1055, 3071, 8447\}$$
$$\cup \{171, 16259, 31729, 49789, 52429, 123423, 146312\} .$$

The exponents lying in the first set are known to provide AB functions (see Table 2). We finally check that the power functions corresponding to the second set of exponents are not APN.

We now exhibit another family of power functions which are not AB:

Proposition 4. *Let m be an odd integer. If there exists a divisor g of m such that s satisfies*

$$s \equiv -s_0 \bmod \frac{2^m - 1}{2^g - 1} \ \text{with} \ 0 < s_0 < \frac{2^m - 1}{2^g - 1} \ \text{and} \ w_2(s_0) \le \frac{1}{2}\left(\frac{m}{g} - 3\right)$$

then the power function $x \mapsto x^s$ is not AB on $\mathbf{F}_{2^m}$.

Proof. If the power function $x \mapsto x^s$ is AB on $\mathbf{F}_{2^m}$, we have that the dual of the cyclic code $C_{1,s}$ of length $(2^m - 1)$ with defining set $\{1, s\}$ is $2^{\frac{m-1}{2}}$-divisible. We here use McEliece's theorem as formulated in Corollary 2. Let $u = 2^g - 1$. Then we have

$$A(u) = us \bmod 2^m - 1 = (2^m - 1) - (2^g - 1)s_0 .$$

We obtain that $w_2(A(u)) = m - w_2((2^g - 1)s_0)$. Since $w_2((2^g - 1)s_0) \le g w_2(s_0)$, this implies that

$$w_2(A(u)) \ge m - g w_2(s_0)$$
$$\ge w_2(u) + m - g(w_2(s_0) + 1) > w_2(u) + \frac{m-1}{2}$$

when $w_2(s_0) \le \frac{1}{2}\left(\frac{m}{g} - 3\right)$. It follows that $C_{1,s}^{\perp}$ is not $2^{\frac{m-1}{2}}$-divisible. ◇

The third author conjectured that for $m = 5g$ the function $x \mapsto x^s$ with $s = 2^{4g} + 2^{3g} + 2^{2g} + 2^g - 1$ is APN on $\mathbf{F}_{2^m}$ [8]. The previous corollary implies:

Proposition 5. *Let m be an odd integer such that $m = 5g$. The power function $x \mapsto x^s$ with $s = 2^{4g} + 2^{3g} + 2^{2g} + 2^g - 1$ is not AB on $\mathbf{F}_{2^m}$.*

Proof. Since $s = \frac{2^{5g} - 1}{2^g - 1} - 2$, we apply the previous corollary with $s_0 = 2$ and $m/g = 5$ using that

$$w_2(s_0) = 1 = \frac{1}{2}\left(\frac{m}{g} - 3\right) .$$

◇

References

1. T. Beth and C. Ding. On almost perfect nonlinear permutations. In *Advances in Cryptology - EUROCRYPT'93*, number 765 in Lecture Notes in Computer Science, pages 65–76. Springer-Verlag, 1993.
2. E. Biham and A. Shamir. Differential cryptanalysis of DES-like cryptosystems. *Journal of Cryptology*, 4(1):3–72, 1991.
3. A. Canteaut, P. Charpin, and H. Dobbertin. Binary m-sequences with three-valued crosscorrelation: a proof of Welch's conjecture. Submitted.
4. A. Canteaut, P. Charpin, and H. Dobbertin. Couples de suites binaires de longueur maximale ayant une corrélation croisée à trois valeurs: conjecture de Welch. *Comptes Rendus de l'Académie des Sciences de Paris*, t. 328, Série I, pages 173–178, 1999.

5. C. Carlet, P. Charpin, and V. Zinoviev. Codes, bent functions and permutations suitable for DES-like cryptosystems. *Designs, Codes and Cryptography*, 15:125–156, 1998.

6. F. Chabaud and S. Vaudenay. Links between differential and linear cryptanalysis. In *Advances in Cryptology - EUROCRYPT'94*, number 950 in Lecture Notes in Computer Science, pages 356–365. Springer-Verlag, 1995.

7. P. Charpin, A. Tietäväinen, and V. Zinoviev. On binary cyclic codes with minimum distance $d = 3$. *Problems of Information Transmission*, 33(4):287–296, 1997.

8. H. Dobbertin. Almost perfect nonlinear power functions on $GF(2^n)$: the Niho case. *Information and Computation*, 1998. To appear.

9. H. Dobbertin. Almost perfect nonlinear power functions on $GF(2^n)$: the Welch case. *IEEE Transactions on Information Theory*, 1998. To appear.

10. R. Gold. Maximal recursive sequences with 3-valued recursive crosscorrelation functions. *IEEE Transactions on Information Theory*, 14:154–156, 1968.

11. S.W. Golomb. Theory of transformation groups of polynomials over $GF(2)$ with applications to linear shift register sequences. *Information Sciences*, 1:87–109, 1968.

12. H.D.L. Hollmann and Q. Xiang. A proof of the Welch and Niho conjectures on crosscorrelations of binary m-sequences. Submitted.

13. T. Kasami. Weight distributions of Bose-Chaudhuri-Hocquenghem codes. In *Proceedings of the conference on combinatorial mathematics and its applications*, pages 335–357. The Univ. of North Carolina Press, 1968.

14. T. Kasami. The weight enumerators for several classes of subcodes of the second order binary Reed-Muller codes. *Information and Control*, 18:369–394, 1971.

15. F.J. MacWilliams and N.J.A. Sloane. *The theory of error-correcting codes*. North-Holland, 1977.

16. M. Matsui. Linear cryptanalysis method for DES cipher. In *Advances in Cryptology - EUROCRYPT'93*, number 765 in Lecture Notes in Computer Science. Springer-Verlag, 1994.

17. R.J. McEliece. Weight congruence for p-ary cyclic codes. *Discrete Mathematics*, 3:177–192, 1972.

18. Y. Niho. *Multi-valued cross-correlation functions between two maximal linear recursive sequences*. PhD thesis, Univ. Southern California, 1972.

19. K. Nyberg. Differentially uniform mappings for cryptography. In *Advances in Cryptology - EUROCRYPT'93*, number 765 in Lecture Notes in Computer Science, pages 55–64. Springer-Verlag, 1993.

20. K. Nyberg. Linear approximation of block ciphers. In A. De Santis, editor, *Advances in Cryptology - EUROCRYPT'94*, number 950 in Lecture Notes in Computer Science. Springer-Verlag, 1994.

21. K. Nyberg and L.R. Knudsen. Provable security against differential cryptanalysis. In *Advances in Cryptology - CRYPTO'92*, number 740 in Lecture Notes in Computer Science, pages 566–574. Springer-Verlag, 1993.

22. V. Pless. Power moment identities on weight distributions in error-correcting codes. *Info. and Control*, 3:147–152, 1963.

23. D.V. Sarwate and M.B. Pursley. Crosscorrelation properties of pseudorandom and related sequences. *Proceedings of the IEEE*, 68(5):593–619, 1980.

24. V.M. Sidelnikov. On mutual correlation of sequences. *Soviet Math. Dokl.*, 12:197–201, 1971.

Imprimitive Permutation Groups and Trapdoors in Iterated Block Ciphers

Kenneth G. Paterson*

Hewlett-Packard Laboratories,
Filton Rd., Stoke Gifford,
Bristol BS34 8QZ, U.K.
kp@hplb.hpl.hp.com

Abstract. An iterated block cipher can be regarded as a means of producing a set of permutations of a message space. Some properties of the group generated by the round functions of such a cipher are known to be of cryptanalytic interest. It is shown here that if this group acts imprimitively on the message space then there is an exploitable weakness in the cipher. It is demonstrated that a weakness of this type can be used to construct a trapdoor that may be difficult to detect. An example of a DES-like cipher, resistant to both linear and differential cryptanalysis that generates an imprimitive group and is easily broken, is given. Some implications for block cipher design are noted.

1 Introduction

An iterated block cipher can be regarded as a means of producing a set of permutations of a message space by the repetition of simpler round functions. Properties of the groups generated by the round functions and by the actual encryptions of such a cipher have long been recognised as having cryptographic importance. For example, if either of these groups is "small" in size then the cipher may be regarded as having a weakness, since not every possible permutation of the message space can be realised by the cipher, [6,8]. Moreover, multiple encryption may offer little or no additional security if these groups are small. Attacks on ciphers whose encryptions generate small groups were given in [13].

Naturally, much attention has been devoted to groups associated with the DES algorithm. Early studies in [6] and [8] concentrated on the groups generated by a set of "DES-like functions", of which the actual round functions of DES form a subset. It was shown that these functions can generate the alternating group, a desirable property. Further work on this theme can be found in [26]. In [30] it was shown that the actual round functions of DES generate the alternating group. The question of whether the 2^{56} encryptions of the full DES algorithm themselves form a group, or generate a small group (see [13,23]), was answered

---

* This work was supported by The Royal Society through its European Science Exchange Programme and the Swiss National Science Foundation, and was performed whilst the author was visiting ETH Zurich.

in the negative in [5] and a lower bound of 10^{2499} was obtained in [4] for the size of this generated group. Thus the attacks of [13] are not applicable to DES.

However the ability of a cipher (or its round functions) to generate a large group does not alone guarantee security: an example of a weak cipher generating the symmetric group on the message space was given in [25]. The most that can be said is that a small group may lead to an insecurity.

Here we examine properties of the groups related to a block cipher more refined than simply their size. Consider the following statement of Wernsdorf [30] regarding the group generated by the round functions of DES:

"Since the generated alternating group $A_{2^{64}}$ is a large simple group and primitive on V_{64} [the message space] we can exclude several imaginable cryptanalytic 'shortcuts' of the DES algorithm."

In the next section we will formalise our discussion of the groups associated with iterated block ciphers and sketch the theory of primitive and imprimitive groups. Next, motivated by Wernsdorf's statement, we examine attacks on iterated block ciphers whose round functions generate imprimitive groups. Then we argue that these imprimitivity-based attacks enable a designer to build trapdoors into iterated block ciphers. We give an example of a 64-bit DES-like cipher having 32 rounds and an 80-bit key which is resistant to basic linear and differential cryptanalytic attacks but whose security is severely compromised by such an attack using 2^{32} chosen plaintexts. With a careful (and deliberately weak) choice of key-schedule and knowledge of the trapdoor, the cipher can be completely broken using only a few known plaintexts and 2^{41} trial encryptions. While the trapdoor in our example is not so well disguised, it can easily be made undetectable if the cipher design is not made public. We conclude by giving some implications of our work and ideas for future research.

We mention here the recent work of [28] in which block ciphers containing *partial* trapdoors are constructed: these give only partial information about keys and require rather large S-box components to be present in the cipher. Knowledge of the trapdoor allows an efficient attack based on linear cryptanalysis [21]. Unfortunately, the work of [32] shows that these trapdoors are either easily detected or yield only attacks requiring infeasible numbers of plaintext/ciphertext pairs. In contrast, our trapdoor can be inserted into a block cipher with very small S-boxes, reveals the entire key but is also detectable. In the language of [28], it is a *full*, but detectable, trapdoor. It is a moot point whether trapdoors that are both full and undetectable can be inserted in truly practical block ciphers.

2 Iterated Block Ciphers and their Groups

We begin by describing a model for *iterated block ciphers*. We will regard such a cipher as a set of invertible *encryption functions* mapping a set M, the message space, to itself, or equivalently as a subset of the symmetric group on M, denoted

S_M. We can then use notions from the theory of permutation groups to study such ciphers. The necessary algebraic background can be found in [29] or [31].

The encryption functions of a particular iterated block cipher are obtained by the composition of *round functions*, that is, a set of keyed invertible functions on M, which we denote by $\{R_k : M \to M, \ k \in K\}$. Here K is called the *round keyspace* and k a *round key*. In a t-round iterated block cipher, the encryption functions take the form

$$E_{k_1,\ldots,k_t} = R_{k_1} R_{k_2} \cdots R_{k_t}$$

where the k_i may be derived from a key from a (larger) session keyspace according to some key-scheduling algorithm, or may be independently chosen. So, the encryption of plaintext m under round keys $k_1, k_2, \ldots, k_t$ is

$$m E_{k_1,\ldots,k_t} = m R_{k_1} R_{k_2} \cdots R_{k_t}$$

(for the moment we denote all functions as acting on the right of their arguments, so that in a composition, functions are evaluated from left to right).

We write $G = < R_k : k \in K >$ for the group generated by the round functions, that is, the smallest subgroup of S_M containing each R_k. Similarly we write $G_t = < R_{k_1} \ldots R_{k_t} : k_i \in K >$ for the subgroup of S_M generated by the t-round encryptions with independent round keys. We say that G and the G_t *act* on the message space M. The groups G_t are hard to compute in practice, but we have the following result relating them to the group G generated by the round functions:

Theorem 1 ([12]). *With notation as above, G_t is a normal subgroup of G. Moreover the group generated by the t-round encryptions with round keys from a particular key-schedule is a subgroup of G_t.*

Example 1. DES (described in full in [7]) is essentially an iterated block cipher with $t = 16$ rounds, message space $M = V_{64}$, the vector-space of dimension 64 over $\mathbb{Z}_2$, and round keyspace $K = V_{48}$. The form taken by the round functions R_k of DES is:
$$m R_k = (l, r) R_k = (r, l \oplus f(r, k))$$
where $l, r \in V_{32}$ denote the left and right halves of message m and $f : V_{32} \times V_{48} \to V_{32}$. The group G generated by the round functions of DES is known to be the alternating group on V_{64}, denoted $A_{2^{64}}$, [30]. Since G is simple and G_{16} is normal in G, the group generated by DES with independent round keys is also $A_{2^{64}}$. The group generated by DES itself (with key-schedule as defined in [7]) is not known.

We will follow the exposition of [31], Sections 6 and 7 on imprimitive groups. Our presentation is necessarily compressed.

Let G be a group of permutations acting on a set M (the reader can imagine G and M to be as above). A subset Y of M is said to be a *block* of G if for every $g \in G$,

$$\text{either} \quad Yg = Y \quad \text{or} \quad Yg \cap Y = \emptyset.$$

Here Yg denotes the set $\{yg : y \in Y\}$. The sets M, $\emptyset$ and the singletons $\{y\}$ are blocks of every G acting on M. These are called the trivial blocks. The intersection of two blocks of G is also a block.

If Y is a block of G, then so is Yg for every $g \in G$. The set of distinct blocks obtained from a block Y in this way is called a *complete block system*. All blocks of such a system have the same size and if G is transitive on M, then every element of M lies in a block of the system. Thus, in this case, the blocks form a partition of M into disjoint sets of equal size.

Suppose now that G is transitive. Then G is said to be *imprimitive* (or act *imprimitively*) if there is at least one non-trivial block Y. We will then refer to a *complete non-trivial block system*. Otherwise, G is said to be *primitive*.

Let G act imprimitively on a finite set M and let Y be a block of G, with $|Y| = s$. Since G is transitive, there exist elements $1 = \tau_1, \tau_2, \ldots, \tau_r \in G$ such that the sets

$$Y_1 = Y\tau_1 = Y, Y_2 = Y\tau_2, \ldots, Y_r = Y\tau_r$$

form a complete non-trivial block system. Here, $|M| = rs$. Thus, for every $g \in G$, there exists a permutation $\bar{g}$ of $\{1, 2, \ldots, r\}$ such that

$$Y_i g = Y_{i\bar{g}}.$$

The set of $\bar{g}$ form a permutation group $\overline{G}$ on $\{1, 2, \ldots, r\}$ and the map $g \to \bar{g}$ is a group homomorphism from G onto $\overline{G}$.

3 Attacks Based on Imprimitivity

Suppose the group G generated by the round functions $R_k : M \to M$ of a t-round cipher acts imprimitively on M, and let $Y_1, \ldots, Y_r$ be a complete non-trivial block system for G. Suppose further that, given $m \in M$, there is a description of the blocks such that it is easy to compute the i with $m \in Y_i$ and that round keys $k_1, \ldots, k_t$ are in use.

Our basic attack is a chosen-plaintext attack whose success is independent of the number t of rounds in use.

3.1 Basic Attack

Suppose that we choose one plaintext m_i in each set Y_i and obtain the corresponding ciphertext c_i. Then the effect of $g = R_{k_1} R_{k_2} \ldots R_{k_t}$ on the blocks Y_i is determined. For by the imprimitivity of G,

$$c_i = m_i g \in Y_j \quad \Rightarrow \quad Y_i g = Y_j.$$

Now given any further ciphertext c, we compute l such that $c \in Y_l$. Then the plaintext m corresponding to c satisfies $m \in Y_{l\bar{g}^{-1}}$. Thus r chosen plaintexts determine that the message corresponding to any ciphertext must lie in a set of size $\frac{|M|}{r}$. Hence the security of the system is severely compromised. The plaintext m itself can be found by examining the set of meaningful messages in $Y_{k\bar{g}^{-1}}$.

Alternatively, the basic attack determines the permutation $\overline{g}$ of $\overline{G}$ corresponding to g: we can think of $\{1, \ldots, r\}$ as being the message space of a new cipher (where the encryption of i is $i\overline{g}$ for round keys $k_1, \ldots, k_t$) and regard our basic attack as simply obtaining all the plaintext/ciphertext pairs for a fixed set of round keys.

3.2 Key-Schedule Dependent Attack

Every choice of round keys $k_1, \ldots, k_t$ determines a corresponding permutation $\overline{g}$ of $\{1, 2, \ldots, r\}$. It is conceivable that there is an attack on the new cipher more efficient than exhaustively obtaining all the ciphertexts. Ideally such an attack would also obtain key information. As an important example, the round keys may be derived from a session key in such a way that $\overline{g}$ is wholly determined by only a part of the session key information. In practice, this information might take the form of the values of certain bits of the session key, or the value of linear expressions involving session key bits. We can think of $\overline{g}$ as being determined by keys from a reduced keyspace. Then it may be feasible to carry out an exhaustive search of the reduced keyspace using only a few known plaintext/ciphertext pairs to determine a unique reduced key. Given such session key information, it may then be possible to deduce the complete session key by another exhaustive search. We have a divide-and-conquer attack on the session key.

This latter attack is then closely related to the attacks of [27] and [9] on ciphers whose round functions possess linear factors and linear structures respectively. For example, when $M = V_n$ and the Y_i consist of a linear subspace U of V_n and its cosets, we have a special type of linear factor (as described in [27]) where the plaintext and ciphertext maps are equal and map coset $Y_i = U + a_i$ to a_i.

3.3 Multiple Block System Attack

In an extension of the basic attack, we make use of two or more complete nontrivial block systems.

Example 2. Using the notation of Example 1, we define an f function as follows: we divide the input r to the f function into two halves $r_1, r_2 \in V_{16}$ and define

$$f(r, k) = (f_1(r_1, k), f_2(r_2, k))$$

where $f_i : V_{16} \times K \to V_{16}$ are arbitrary. It was shown in [17] that the f_i can be chosen so that the iterated block cipher with round function $(l, r)R_k = (r, l \oplus f(r, k))$ is secure against linear and differential cryptanalysis. We model an attack based on two complete systems of imprimitivity: we write elements of V_{64} as (x_1, x_2, x_3, x_4) where $x_i \in V_{16}$ and define 2^{33} sets of size 2^{32}:

$$Y_{(x_1, x_3)} = (x_1, V_{16}, x_3, V_{16}), \quad x_1, x_3 \in V_{16}$$
$$Z_{(x_2, x_4)} = (V_{16}, x_2, V_{16}, x_4), \quad x_2, x_4 \in V_{16}.$$

Notice that

$$Y_{(x_1,x_3)}R_k = (x_3, V_{16}, x_1 \oplus f_1(x_3, k), V_{16}) = Y_{(x_3, x_1 \oplus f_1(x_3, k))}$$
$$Z_{(x_2,x_4)}R_k = (V_{16}, x_4, V_{16}, x_2 \oplus f_2(x_4, k)) = Z_{(x_4, x_2 \oplus f_2(x_4, k))}$$

so that the sets $\left\{Y_{(x_1,x_3)} : x_1, x_3 \in V_{16}\right\}$ and $\left\{Z_{(x_2,x_4)} : x_2, x_4 \in V_{16}\right\}$ form complete block systems for G, the group generated by the R_k. Moreover, for any x_1, x_2, x_3, x_4,

$$Y_{(x_1,x_3)} \cap Z_{(x_2,x_4)} = \{(x_1, x_2, x_3, x_4)\}.$$

Suppose we choose the 2^{32} plaintexts of the form (x_1, x_1, x_3, x_3) and obtain their encryptions. From this information we can recover permutations $\bar{g}_1$ and $\bar{g}_2$ of $V_{16} \times V_{16}$ such that for all x_1, x_2, x_3, x_4

$$Y_{(x_1,x_3)}g = Y_{(x_1,x_3)\bar{g}_1}, \qquad Z_{(x_2,x_4)}g = Z_{(x_2,x_4)\bar{g}_2}.$$

Given any further ciphertext (c_1, c_2, c_3, c_4) with corresponding message m we have

$$m \in Y_{(c_1,c_3)\bar{g}_1^{-1}} \cap Z_{(c_2,c_4)\bar{g}_2^{-1}},$$

a set of size one. Thus m can be found uniquely.

This attack is applicable to any cipher where the intersections of blocks from different systems can be computed and are "small".

4 A DES-like Cipher with a Trapdoor

Given the description of a set of round functions, it appears to be a difficult computational problem either to find a non-trivial complete block system for the corresponding group G or to disprove the existence of such a system. However the attacks above show that an iterated block cipher with an imprimitive group G is inherently weak if a complete block system is known.

It appears then that using a set of round functions which generate an imprimitive group (whose block system is not revealed) may lead to a block cipher containing a trapdoor that is difficult to detect. To give a convincing demonstration of this, we should build a set of round functions according to recognised principles. The individual components should satisfy relevant design criteria and we should also demonstrate the security of our cipher against known attacks. This is our objective in this section. We give a full design for such a block cipher, except for a key-schedule. In the next section we will describe how our round functions were designed to generate an imprimitive group and how the cipher can be broken.

4.1 Description of Round Function

Perhaps the most commonly used template in the design of a block cipher is the Feistel construction. In turn the most celebrated Feistel-type cipher is DES itself. With reference to example 1 and [7], the f function of DES consists of four components: we write $f(r, k) = PS(E(r) \oplus k)$ where

— the expansion phase, E, is a linear map from V_{32} to V_{48},

— k is the 48-bit round key, derived from a 56 bit session key,

— S denotes the operation of the S-boxes — eight carefully selected 6 bit to 4 bit functions, numbered $1, \ldots, 8$ operating in parallel on V_{48},

— P is a carefully selected bit permutation of V_{32}.

Our proposed block cipher consists of 32 repetitions of DES-like round functions:

$$(l, r) R_k = (r, l \oplus PS(E(r) \oplus k)).$$

Here E and P are as in the original DES, but the S-boxes are replaced by the boxes presented in the appendix. Our round keys k are also 48-bits and are derived from an 80-bit session key according to a key-scheduling algorithm which we leave unspecified. Any suitably strong schedule could be used (for example, we could expand the original DES schedule).

We note that the selection of S-boxes is critical to the security of DES. Numerous attacks have been made on versions of DES with modified S-boxes: see for example the early critique of DES in [11], the differential attacks on DES with modified S-boxes in [3] and the attack of [16] on the proposals of [14].

Each S-box in the appendix has the following properties, similar to those given in [5] for the DES S-boxes:

S1 Each S-box has six bits of input, four bits of output.

S2 The best linear approximation of an S-box (in the sense of [21], equation (3)) holds with probability p over all inputs, where $|p - \frac{1}{2}| \leq \frac{1}{4}$.

S3 Fixing the bits input to an S-box on the extreme left and on the extreme right at any two values, the resulting map from V_4 to V_4 is a permutation.

S4 If two inputs i, i' to an S-box differ in the pattern 000100 or 001000 (i.e. $i \oplus i' = 000100$ or 001000), then the corresponding outputs differ in at least one position.

S5 If two inputs i, i' to an S-box differ in the pattern 001100, then the corresponding outputs differ in at least one position.

S6 If two inputs i, i' satisfy $i \oplus i' = 11xy00$, where x and y are arbitrary bits, then the corresponding outputs differ in at least one position.

S7 For any non-zero input difference $i \oplus i'$ not equal to one of those specified in S4, S5, the number of ordered pairs i, i' leading to a given non-zero output difference is at most 16. For the input differences in S4 and S5, the corresponding maximum is 24.

S8 For any non-zero input difference $i \oplus i'$, the number of ordered pairs i, i' leading to an output difference of zero is at most 12.

S2 guarantees that the S-boxes are not too linear, while S3 ensures they are balanced. S4–S6 can be regarded as weak avalanche criteria. Thus our S-boxes automatically have some desirable features.

We also draw to the reader's attention the properties P1 to P3 of the P permutation noted in [5]. From left to right, we label the input bits to our S-boxes $p_1, p_2, p_3, p_4, p_5, p_6$ and the output bits q_1, q_2, q_3, q_4. We refer to bits p_3 and p_4 as *centre* bits and bits p_1, p_2, p_5, p_6 as *outer* bits.

P1 The four bits output from each S-box are distributed so that two of them affect centre bits, and the other two affect outer bits of S-boxes in the next round.

P2 The four bits output from each S-box affect six different S-boxes in the next round, no two affect the same S-box.

P3 For two S-boxes j, k, if an output bit from S-box j affects a centre bit of S-box k, then an output bit from S-box k cannot affect a centre bit of S-box j.

4.2 Security Against Linear and Differential Attacks

Here we estimate the resistance of our example to linear [21] and differential [24, 3] cryptanalysis.

We begin by estimating the complexity of a linear attack. By property S2 and Lemma 3 of [21], the best linear expression that is built up round-by-round and involves input bits to round 2, output bits from round 31, key bits and a linear approximation in *every* round will hold with approximate probability p_L where

$$|p_L - \frac{1}{2}| \leq 2^{29} \left(\frac{1}{4}\right)^{30} = 2^{-31}.$$

While a more delicate analysis may find linear characteristics not involving linear approximations in every round, it seems unlikely that these will have probability larger than the above bound on p_L (since this bound is calculated using the highest per-round probability). We make the rough assumption that a linear attack using Algorithm 2 of [21] would require at least 2^{62} known plaintexts.

The success of a basic differential attack depends on finding a high probability characteristic: a *t-round characteristic having probability p* is a sequence of differences

$$\Delta m_1, \Delta m_2, \ldots, \Delta m_{t-1}, \Delta m_t$$

such that if Δm_1 is the difference in plaintexts $m \oplus m'$ input to the first round, then the differences propagated to the inputs of subsequent rounds are $\Delta m_2, \ldots \Delta m_t$ with probability p, assuming independent round keys. In practice, at least a 29 round characteristic is needed to attack a 32 round iterated cipher. The number of plaintext input pairs required in a successful attack based on such a characteristic having probability p is at least $\frac{1}{p}$. Of particular importance are *iterative characteristics* where the output difference at the last round is equal to the initial input difference — such a characteristic can be concatenated with itself many times to form a longer characteristic. To provide practical security against a differential attack, we need to bound the probability of short iterative characteristics. For further details, see [3].

We say that an S-box j is *active* in round i of a characteristic if Δm_i involves a non-zero input difference to S-box j. We can use properties S3 to S6, P2 and P3 and arguments similar to those of [5] to show the following for our cipher:

Lemma 1. *If round i of a characteristic consists of two adjacent active S-boxes $j, j+1$ then either round $i-1$ or round $i+1$ (or both) has at least one active S-box. If round i of a characteristic has only one active S-box j, then either round $i-1$ or round $i+1$ (or both) has at least one active S-box.*

A 29 round characteristic having no rounds without active S-boxes must involve a total of at least 29 active S-boxes. Using S7 and assuming independence, we can bound the probability of such a pattern by $p \leq \left(\frac{24}{64}\right)^{29} = 2^{-41}$. We have found characteristics with probability close to this, but omit the details. An attractive pattern of differences (used in [3] to attack DES) involves active S-boxes on even numbered rounds and no active S-boxes on odd numbered rounds. From the above lemma, the active rounds must involve at least a pattern of 3 adjacent S-boxes. By property S8, we can bound the probability of a 29 round pattern of this type by $\left(\frac{12}{64}\right)^{42} = 2^{-101}$. One further pattern of differences that we consider involves no active S-boxes on every third round. Using P3 and the lemma above, we can show that such a characteristic must involve 3 or more active S-boxes on the two active rounds. The probability of such a characteristic over 29 rounds is, using S7, at most 2^{-41}. The analysis can be carried further, but it suffices to say that our cipher possesses a reasonable degree of resistance to differential cryptanalysis in its basic form. We note however that the our cipher is probably susceptible to more sophisticated attacks based on truncated [18] or impossible [19, 2] differentials.

5 Trapdoor Design

Each S-box in the appendix has the following property:

> By property P1, the combination of P followed by E moves two of the four outputs of the S-box (say q_i and q_j) so as to affect centre bits of S-boxes in the next round. These two outputs are dependent on every input bit, while the other two outputs depend only on the outer bits p_1, p_2, p_5, p_6 input to the S-box.

For example, P moves output bit q_3 of S-box 1 to position 23 in the output of the f function. After XORing with the left half and swopping, this position affects a centre bit, p_4, of S-box 6 in the next round. Thus q_3 depends on all six input bits to S-box 1.

¿From the property above, it follows that the output bits of the f function in positions $1, 4, 5, 8, \ldots, 29, 32$ depend only on round key bits and the f function inputs in the same positions, $1, 4, 5, 8, \ldots, 29, 32$ (these being the f function input bits which after E and key XOR become outer bits of S-boxes). We therefore have:

Lemma 2. *Label the 2^{16} distinct additive cosets of the 16 dimensional subspace*

$$U = \{(0, x_2, x_3, 0, 0, x_6, x_7, 0, \ldots, 0, x_{30}, x_{31}, 0) : x_i \in \mathbb{Z}_2\}$$

of V_{32} by $U \oplus a_1, \ldots, U \oplus a_{2^{16}}$. Then for every j and every round key k, there exists an l such that $PS(E(U \oplus a_j) \oplus k) \subseteq U \oplus a_l$.

Notice that for any subset W of subspace U, we have $U \oplus W = U$, so

$$(U \oplus a_i) \oplus PS(E(U \oplus a_j) \oplus k)) = U \oplus a_i \oplus a_l = U \oplus a_m$$

for some m. Therefore $(U \oplus a_i, U \oplus a_j)R_k = (U \oplus a_j, U \oplus a_m)$. It is easy to see that the R_k act transitively on V_{64} and we have

Lemma 3. *The 2^{32} subsets $(U \oplus a_i, U \oplus a_j)$ of V_{64} form a complete non-trivial block system for G, the group generated by the round functions of our cipher.*

The round functions of our cipher generate an imprimitive group where the blocks of a complete system are easily identified. Thus our cipher is susceptible to the basic attack described in Section 3 with 2^{32} chosen plaintexts. Suppose further that a key-schedule is chosen such that over the 32 rounds, only 40 bits of the 80-bit session key are involved in XORs with outputs of the E expansion which become outer bits of the S-boxes. Then, in the terminology of Section 3, the permutation $\bar{g}$ is determined by only half of the session key bits and an exhaustive attack on those bits can be successfully carried out with knowledge of a handful of plaintext/ciphertext pairs. The remaining 40 bits of session key can then also be found by exhaustive attack, the total complexity of the attack being around 2^{41} trial encryptions, well within the bounds of practicality. Notice that this attack depends crucially on the interaction between the system of imprimitivity and the key-schedule.

6 Discussion and Conclusions

We have considered attacks based on a property of a group associated with an iterated block cipher. The attacks motivate a new design criterion for iterated block ciphers: the group generated by the round functions should be primitive. Unfortunately this property seems to be hard to verify in practice. We note that DES and IDEA (probably, see [12]) do satisfy this property.

We have given an example of a cipher secure in some conventional senses but weak because of a deliberately inserted trapdoor. There are however some immediate criticisms that can be made of our example. Firstly, the S-boxes are incomplete (that is, not every output bit of the S-boxes depends on every input bit). This goes against a generally accepted design principle for S-boxes [1, 15, 22] and would arouse suspicion. A close examination of the S-boxes and their interaction with the P permutation would then reveal our trapdoor. Incompleteness in the S-boxes also leads to a block cipher where half of the ciphertext bits are independent of half of the plaintext bits. Thus our trapdoor is not so well hidden. Secondly and less seriously, our cipher's resistance to differential attacks is not as high as one might expect from a 32 round system.

Suppose however that our example cipher is not made public (for example, by using tamper-resistant hardware). We are then given a 64-bit iterated block cipher with 32 rounds and an 80-bit key and could be truthfully told by a panel of experts that it is secure against linear and differential attacks. The incompleteness noted above can be hidden by applying a suitable invertible output transformation to the ciphertexts. Because of the size of the message space and choice of output transformation, we would then be unlikely to be able to detect any block structure just by examining plaintext/ciphertext pairs. Yet our example cipher contains a trapdoor rendering the system completely insecure to anyone with knowledge of the trapdoor. Clearly in this situation, we must have complete faith in the purveyor of the block cipher.

We conclude by suggesting some avenues for further research.

The choice of trapdoor in our example was forced upon us by a combination of the E expansion, the round key XORing and the bitwise nature of the P permutation. Can "undetectable" trapdoors based on more complex systems of imprimitivity be inserted in otherwise conventional ciphers? It is easily shown that, in a DES-like cipher, any system based on a linear sub-space and its cosets leads to a noticeable regularity in the XOR tables of small S-boxes. It seems that we must look beyond the "linear" systems considered here, or consider other types of round function.

Our attention has been directed to block systems preserved by the group G, that is, on a per-round basis. It might also be interesting to look at the case where the round functions generate a primitive group, but the subgroup generated by the t-round cipher itself has a block structure. Attacks exploiting a block structure holding probablistically may also be powerful and worth examining. In this respect the thesis [10] is particularly relevant.

Acknowledgements

The author would like to thank Jim Massey for his encouragement during this research, and Lars Knudsen for patiently answering many questions and for his humour.

References

1. C.M. Adams and S.E. Tavares, "The structured design of cryptographically good S-boxes," *Journal of Cryptology*, **3**, 27–41,1990.
2. E. Biham, A. Biryukov and A. Shamir, "Cryptanalysis of Skipjack reduced to 31 rounds using impossible differentials," *Proceedings of EUROCRYPT'99*, LNCS, 1999.
3. E. Biham and A. Shamir, *Differential cryptanalysis of the Data Encrpytion Standard*, Springer-Verlag, New York, 1993.
4. K.W. Campbell and M. Wiener, "DES is not a group," *Proceedings of CRYPTO'92*, LNCS 740, 512–520, 1993.
5. D. Coppersmith, "The Data Encryption Standard (DES) and its strength against attacks," IBM Research Report, RC 18613, 1992.
6. D. Coppersmith and E. Grossman, "Generators for certain alternating groups with applications to cryptology," *SIAM Journal on Applied Mathematics*, **29**, 624–627, 1975.

7. *Data Encryption Standard*, National Bureau of Standards, Federal Information Processing Standards Publications No. 46, 1977.

8. S. Even and O. Goldreich, "DES-like functions can generate the alternating group," *IEEE Transactions on Information Theory*, **29**, 863–865, 1983.

9. J.-H. Evertse, "Linear structures in blockciphers," *Proceedings EUROCRYPT'87*, LNCS 304, 249–266, 1988.

10. C. Harpes, *Cryptanalysis of iterated block ciphers*, ETH Series in Information Processing, Ed. J. L. Massey, Hartung-Gorre Verlag, Konstanz, 1996.

11. M. Hellman, R. Merkle, R. Schroeppel, L. Washington, W. Diffie, S. Pohlig and P. Schweitzer, "Results of an initial attempt to cryptanalyze the NBS Data Encryption Standard," Information Systems Laboratory report, Stanford University, 1976.

12. G. Hornauer, W. Stephan and R. Wernsdorf, "Markov ciphers and alternating groups," Presented at Rump Session, EUROCRYPT'93, 1993.

13. B.S. Kaliski Jr., R.L. Rivest and A.T. Sherman, "Is the Data Encryption Standard a group? (Results of cycling experiments on DES)," *Journal of Cryptology*, **1**, 3–36, 1988.

14. K. Kim, "Construction of DES-like S-boxes based on boolean functions satisfying the SAC," *Proceedings of ASIACRYPT'91*, LNCS 739, 59–72, 1992.

15. B. Kam and G.I. Davida, "A structured design of substitution-permutation encryption networks," *IEEE Transactions on Computers*, **28**, 747–753, 1979.

16. L.R. Knudsen, "Iterative characteristics of DES and s^2-DES," *Proceedings of CRYPTO'92*, LNCS 740, 497–511, 1993.

17. L.R. Knudsen, "Practically secure Feistel ciphers," *Fast Software Encryption*, LNCS 809, 211-221, 1994.

18. L.R. Knudsen, "Applications of higher order differentials and partial differentials," *Fast Software Encryption*, LNCS 1008, 196-211, 1995.

19. L.R. Knudsen, "DEAL - A 128-bit Block Cipher," available online at http://www.ii.uib.no/ larsr/papers/deal.ps Revised May 15, 1998.

20. X. Lai, J.L. Massey and S. Murphy, "Markov ciphers and differential cryptanalysis," *Proceedings of EUROCRYPT'91*, LNCS 547, 17–38, 1991.

21. M. Matsui, "Linear cryptanalysis method for DES cipher," *Proceedings of EUROCRYPT'93*, LNCS 765, 386–397, 1994.

22. W. Meier and O. Staffelbach, "Nonlinearity criteria for cryptographic functions," *Proceedings of EUROCRYPT'89*, LNCS 434, 549–562, 1989.

23. J.H. Moore and G.J. Simmons, "Cycle structure of the DES with weak and semi-weak keys," *Proceedings of CRYPTO'86*, LNCS 263, 9–32, 1987.

24. S. Murphy, "The cryptanalysis of FEAL-4 with 20 chosen plaintexts," *Journal of Cryptology*, **2**, 145–154, 1990.

25. S. Murphy, K. Paterson and P. Wild, "A weak cipher that generates the symmetric group," *Journal of Cryptology*, **7**, 61–65, 1994.

26. J. Pieprzyk and X.-M. Zhang, "Permutation generators of alternating groups," *Proceedings of AUSCRYPT'90*, LNCS 453, 237–244, 1990.

27. J.A. Reeds and J.L. Manferdelli, "DES has no per round linear factors," *Proceedings of CRYPTO'84*, LNCS 196, 377–389, 1985.

28. V. Rijmen and B. Preneel, "A family of trapdoor ciphers," *Fast Software Encryption*, LNCS 1267, 139–148, 1997.

29. D.J.S. Robinson, *A course in the Theory of Groups*, Graduate Texts in Mathematics, Springer, New York, 1982.

30. R. Wernsdorf, "The one-round functions of the DES generate the alternating group," *Proceedings of EUROCRYPT'92*, LNCS 658, 99–112, 1993.

31. H. Wielandt, *Finite Permutation Groups*, Academic Press, New York and London, 1964.
32. H. Wu, F. Bao, R.H. Deng and Q.-Z. Ye, "Cryptanalysis of Rijmen-Preneel trapdoor ciphers," *Proceedings of ASIACRYPT'98*, LNCS 1514, 126–132, 1998.

Appendix

We present the S-boxes of our example block cipher in the same format as the DES S-boxes were presented in [7], that is each box is written as four rows of permutations:

S-box 1

```
 8  0 10  1  9  3 11  2  4 12  7 14  6 15  5 13
 9  5 10  7  8  4 11  6 14  1 13  0 12  2 15  3
14 10 15 11 12  9 13  8  1  5  2  7  0  4  3  6
11  5  9  4  8  6 10  7  1 14  0 12  3 15  2 13
```

S-box 2

```
 1 15  0 12  3 13  2 14  6  9  5  8  4 10  7 11
11  1 10  2  8  0  9  3  6 15  7 13  5 12  4 14
 1 14  3 12  0 15  2 13  8  6 10  4  9  5 11  7
 2  5  1  7  0  6  3  4 15  8 14  9 13 10 12 11
```

S-box 3

```
15 11 13  9 12 10 14  8  3  4  1  6  0  7  2  5
 0 14  1 12  2 15  3 13 10  6  8  5 11  7  9  4
14  1 13  2 15  0 12  3  8  7 11  6 10  5  9  4
 4 12  7 13  6 14  5 15 11  3  8  2  9  0 10  1
```

S-box 4

```
12  3  6  1  4 11 14  9  7  2 15 10  5  0 13  8
 5  3 15 11  7  9 13  1  6 10 14  8 12  0  4  2
 4  9 14 11 12  1  6  3  2  7  0 15 10 13  8  5
15  4  5 12 13 14  7  6  9 10 11  8  1  0  3  2
```

S-box 5

```
 1  6  4  7  0  2  5  3 13 10  8 14  9 15 12 11
 2  4  7  0  6  5  3  1  9 14 13 15  8 10 12 11
 0 13  4  9  1 12  5  8  7 15  6 10  2 11  3 14
11  2 15  7 14  3 10  6  1 13  4 12  5  8  0  9
```

S-box 6

```
 8  5 11  4  9  6 10  7  1 14  3 15  2 13  0 12
 7  3  6  0  4  1  5  2  9 14 11 13  8 12 10 15
 7  8  6 10  5  9  4 11  3 15  0 14  2 12  1 13
12  6 15  7 14  4 13  5  2 11  1  9  0  8  3 10
```

S-box 7

```
12  3 15  1 14  2 13  0 11  5 10  7  8  6  9  4
12  6 13  5 14  4 15  7  0  9  3 10  1  8  2 11
 1 12  3 14  2 13  0 15  9  7  8  4 11  6 10  5
11 14  9 15  8 13 10 12  4  1  7  3  5  2  6  0
```

S-box 8

```
12  5 10  7  8  3 14  1  6 11  0  9  4 15  2 13
11 12 13  8  9 10 15 14  2  3  0  1  6  5  4  7
 3  8  7 12  5 10  1 14  0 13  6 15  2  9  4 11
 5 13  3  9  1 11  7 15 10  0  8  6 12  4 14  2
```

On the Security of
Double and 2-Key Triple Modes of Operation

Helena Handschuh[1] and Bart Preneel[2]*

[1] Gemplus/ENST, France
helena.handschuh@gemplus.com
[2] Katholieke Universiteit Leuven, Dept. Electrical Engineering–ESAT
bart.preneel@esat.kuleuven.ac.be

Abstract. The DES has reached the end of its lifetime due to its too short key length and block length (56 and 64 bits respectively). As we are awaiting the new AES, triple (and double) encryption are the common solution. However, several authors have shown that these multiple modes are much less secure than anticipated. The general belief is that these schemes should not be used, as they are not resistant against attacks requiring 2^{64} chosen plaintexts. This paper extends the analysis by considering some more realistic attack models. It also presents an improved attack on multiple modes that contain an OFB mode and discusses practical solutions that take into account realistic constraints.

1   Introduction

Ever since the Data Encryption Standard [13] was adopted in the mid 1970s, the issue of its small key size has been raised. Nowadays a 56-bit key is clearly within the range of a dedicated exhaustive search machine [12, 29]. Already in 1979, Tuchman proposed the use of triple-DES with two or three keys [25]. Double encryption was rejected quickly because Merkle and Hellman showed that a meet-in-the-middle requires 'only' 2^{57} encryptions and a memory with 2^{56} 112-bit values [24]. Later van Oorschot and Wiener came up with a more practical version of this attack, that requires 2^{72} encryptions but only 16 Gbyte [27] (other trade-offs are available). In the 1980s, triple-DES became popular; for example double length master keys were used to encrypt single length DES session keys. The best known attack on 2-key triple-DES is also by van Oorschot and Wiener [26]; it requires 2^{120-t} encryptions and 2^t known plaintexts. This shows that 2-key triple-DES may provide increased strength against brute force key search.

For encryption of more than one block, a mode of operation has to be defined different from the ECB (Electronic CodeBook) mode. The ECB mode is vulnerable to a dictionary attack, where an opponent collects ciphertexts and

* F.W.O. postdoctoral researcher, sponsored by the Fund for Scientific Research, Flanders (Belgium).

corresponding plaintexts. The three other standard modes of operation are defined in FIPS 81 [14]: CBC (Cipher Block Chaining), CFB (Cipher FeedBack) and OFB (Output FeedBack). The limitation of CBC and CFB modes are the matching ciphertext attacks: after encrypting 2^{32} blocks, information starts to leak about the plaintext (see for example [18]). In the OFB mode, less information leaks, but the fact that the key stream has an expected period of 2^{63} blocks also provides some information on the plaintext. For a formal treatment of the modes of operation, see Bellare *et al.* [2].

In the early 1990s, modes for multiple encryption were analysed. The most straightforward solution is to replace DES by two-key triple-DES and to use this new block cipher in a 'standard' mode (known as 'outer-CBC' and 'outer-CFB' [16]). While for CFB and CBC mode this precludes exhaustive key search, the complexity of a matching ciphertext attack is still 2^{32} blocks, as this depends on the block length only. This motivated research on interleaved or combined modes, where the modes themselves are considered as primitives. Coppersmith analysed some early proposals for two-key triple-DES modes in [9,10]. The most straightforward solution is to iterate the CBC or CFB mode of a block cipher (known as 'inner-CBC' and 'inner-CFB'). However, Biham showed that these simple interleaved modes are vulnerable to a 2^{34} chosen ciphertext attack [4,5].

In [6], Biham systematically analyses all the double and triple 'interleaved' modes, where each layer consists of ECB, OFB, CBC, CFB and the inverses of CBC and CFB, denoted with CBC^{-1} and CFB^{-1} respectively. Note that there are 36 double encryption schemes and 216 triple encryption schemes. His main conclusion is that *"all triple modes of operation are theoretically not much more secure than a single encryption."* The most secure schemes in this class require 2^{67} chosen plaintexts or ciphertexts, 2^{75} encryptions, and 2^{66} storage (for example, scheme 208 in [6]).

Biham also proposes a small set of triple modes, where a single key stream is generated in OFB mode and exored before every encryption and after the last encryption [6]. The conjectured security is 2^{112} encryptions. He also proposes several quadruple modes with conjectured security level 2^{128} encryptions. However, at FSE'98 Wagner shows that if the attack model is changed to allow for chosen ciphertext/chosen *IV* attacks, the security of all but two of these modes can be reduced to 2^{56} encryptions and between 2 and 2^{32} chosen chosen-*IV* texts [28].

Coppersmith *et al.* propose the CBCM mode [11], which is a quadruple mode; this mode has been included in ANSI X9.52 [1]. However, Biham and Knudsen present an attack requiring 2^{65} chosen ciphertexts and memory that requires 2^{58} encryptions [7].

Many of these attacks are very intricate, but one cannot escape the conclusion that these are only 'certificational' attacks. In most environments, it is completely unthinkable to carry out a chosen plaintext or ciphertext attack with more than 2^{40} texts (e.g., on a smart card). Moreover, attacks that require a storage of 2^{56} 64-bit quantities are not feasible today. This does not imply that we do not recommend a conservative design. Our goal is to explore which schemes achieve a realistic security level today. For long term security, migration to AES (Advanced Encryption Standard) will provide a solution.

Our contribution. The goal of this paper is to develop a better understanding of the security of the simpler structures such as 2-key triple and double modes of operation. We show that for common applications where a known IV attack can be applied, these modes are scaringly close to being in the range of exhaustive search or at least susceptible to Merkle-Hellman's meet-in-the-middle attack [24]. We study double encryption schemes under different attack models (one of the two IV's known, and replay of IV). We also present a new attack on certain double modes (the cycle attack), that reduces the plaintext requirement from 2^{64} chosen plaintexts to about 2^{35} known plaintexts and memory, at the cost of an increased work factor for the analysis (2^{87} compared to 2^{58}); nevertheless we believe that this may be more realistic. Finally we compare some solutions for the cases where the integrity and/or secrecy of the IV's is protected. Depending on the setting, one of the following three modes is recommended : double OFB, CBC followed by CBC^{-1}, or the latter double mode masked with an OFB stream before each encryption and after the last.

The rest of the paper is organised as follows: the next section discusses the notation and the attack models for the IV's. Section 3 gives details on modes that can be broken by exhaustive search. Section 4 deals with modes that fall under the standard meet-in-the-middle attack (MITM) and Sect. 5 with modes that succumb to "narrow pipe" (the term "narrow pipe attack" is due to John Kelsey) or collision attacks. These three attacks are becoming more or less practical today because of the very low number of texts they require. In Sect. 6, we explain our new cycle attack and in Sect. 7 we compare several modes that provide a reasonable security level for current applications. Section 8 presents conclusions and open problems.

2 The Setting

In this section we introduce our notation and discuss the attack model in terms of control of the opponent over the IV.

2.1 Notation

We refer to Wagner's paper [28] for notation throughout this paper. The successive blocks of plaintext and ciphertext in every multiple mode are denoted by $P_0, P_1, P_2, \ldots$ and $C_0, C_1, C_2, \ldots$. The standard single modes (ECB, CBC, CFB, OFB, CBC^{-1}, and CFB^{-1}) are combined to double or two-key triple modes using the notation X/Y and X/Y/Z respectively, where X,Y,Z are one of the above modes. As usual, we assume that the underlying block cipher is "ideal" in the sense that the modes are attacked by generic methods, and not by differential [8] or linear cryptanalysis [23] for instance. We will be dealing exclusively with two keys K_1 and K_2. For two-key triple modes, K_1 is the key of the first and the last encryption components, and K_2 is the key of the middle decryption component. IV_1 and IV_2 are the initial values of the feedback and chaining modes, and for two-key triple encryption an additional IV_3 is required. Figure 1 contains an example of a 2-key triple mode.

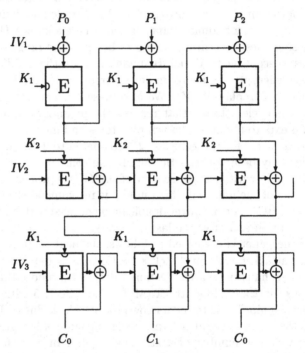

Fig. 1. The CBC/CFB/OFB mode

2.2 Models for the Initial Value

We would like to stress that Biham's attacks in [6] usually consider the initial values IV to be *unknown*, except for some of the modes that are very hard to cryptanalyse otherwise. This is the main reason why many attacks require a huge number plaintexts or ciphertexts (typically about 2^{66}). On the other hand, Wagner chose to use a security model in which the IV's may be *chosen* by the attacker. He mentions that his attacks may be converted into known IV attacks using slightly more IV's (about 2^{32}). One can also consider for certificational purposes the more artificial scenario where only one of the IV's is known.

We believe that for most applications known IV attacks are quite reasonable in the case of encryption as the IV's are chosen by the encryption box but have to be transmitted with the ciphertext in order to be decrypted by the other party. In several practical protocols the IV's are transmitted in the clear. We may also want to allow a kind of "chosen" IV attack (in a chosen ciphertext setting) in which the adversary does not know the actual value of the IV but is able to replay the same (possibly encrypted) IV a few times with different text queries. The result of our analysis is that under such threat models, basic double or triple modes are deeply flawed.

In Sect. 7 we will also recommend schemes for scenarios where the IV's are encrypted and/or where the integrity of the IV's can be protected.

3 Divide and Conquer Strategies

In [6], Biham analyses all 36 double modes (schemes 7 to 42) under the assumption that the IV's are unknown. We are interested in a stronger attack model, and would like to find out which schemes still have a 'reasonable' security level against practical attacks. Therefore we analyse double modes for which the best known attack (with unknown IV's) requires more than 2^{64} chosen texts. Biham lists 15 such modes.

We consider all of these modes under several known IV attacks and show that with a few known texts, their security drops down to the basic exhaustive search complexity of a 56-bit key.

3.1 Known IV_1 and IV_2 Attacks

Six modes are vulnerable to direct exhaustive search on each key, requiring only a handful plaintext/ciphertext pairs, about 2^{57} encryptions and no memory. These modes are: OFB/ECB, ECB/OFB, CBC^{-1}/OFB, OFB/CBC, OFB/CFB, and CFB^{-1}/OFB. Note that there are three different modes and their inverses. There is no IV on an ECB mode: we will denote this as $IV = 0$. As an example we show how to recover the two keys of the CBC^{-1}/OFB mode depicted in Fig. 2.

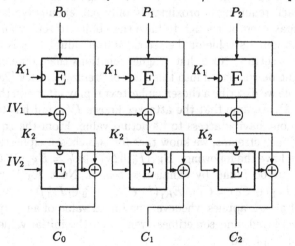

Fig. 2. The CBC^{-1}/OFB mode

The attack proceeds as follows. Choose a 3 block plaintext of the form (M, M, M) and get the corresponding ciphertext (C_0, C_1, C_2) as well as IV_2. Then from the structure of the mode it follows that $C_1 \oplus C_2 = E_{K_2}^2(IV_2) \oplus E_{K_2}^3(IV_2)$. Therefore we can exhaustively search for the key K_2 satisfying this relation. Once this key has been found, it is straightforward to recover K_1. If more than one key pair is found, a few additional plaintext/ciphertext pairs suffice to pick the right pair.

Another example is the $\text{CFB}^{-1}/\text{OFB}$ mode. Choose a message of the form (P_0, P_1) and encrypt it twice. Get the corresponding ciphertexts (C_0, C_1) and (C_0^*, C_1^*). The IV's will of course be different but the plaintext remains the same. Again, the relation between the two second ciphertext blocks is of the form: $C_1 \oplus C_1^* = E_{K_2}^2(IV_2) \oplus E_{K_2}^2(IV_2^*)$. Therefore we can first exhaustively search for K_2 and then for K_1.

Attacking the inverse modes requires mostly a chosen ciphertext attack where the IV's may either be chosen or just known to the attacker, depending on the context. The above modes can also be attacked under the assumption that only one of the IV's is known to the attacker. Typically, it can be shown that it suffices to know the initial value of the output feedback mode involved in every one of the six before-mentioned modes.

3.2 Replay Attacks

In this section we address a slightly different model of attack in which divide and conquer strategies may also apply. Here we assume that the attacker knows only one of the IV's, but is given the ability to replay the other IV without any knowledge of the actual value of it. In other words, one of the IV's may for instance be encrypted to offer more security. Then the ability to replay the same encrypted unknown IV together with the knowledge of the second initial value leads to an attack requiring approximately only one exhaustive key search. In some cases, it may even be enough to have the ability to replay an IV without any knowledge about its value or the second initial value. This is the case in a chosen ciphertext setting. Note that Wagner mentions that some of his chosen-IV attacks might be converted into this kind of "replay" attack [28].

As an example we describe a chosen ciphertext replay attack on the CBC/OFB mode (see Fig. 3). Assume that the attacker knows IV_1 and has the ability to replay IV_2 without having access to its actual value. From the equality of the two output feedback streams, we know that for two chosen ciphertexts (C_0, C_1) and (C_0^*, C_1^*) we have the following : $E_{K_1}(P_0 \oplus IV_1) \oplus C_0 = E_{K_1}(P_0^* \oplus IV_1^*) \oplus C_0^*$. Therefore K_1 can be found by exhaustive search. Next K_2 is recovered by $E_{K_2}(E_{K_1}(P_0 \oplus IV_1) \oplus C_0) = C_1 \oplus E_{K_1}(P_1 \oplus E_{K_1}(P_0 \oplus IV_1))$.

This type of attack applies whenever the initial value of an output feedback mode may be replayed, and sometimes even when the initial value of a cipher feedback mode is replayed.

4 Meet-in-the-Middle Attack

This attack requires only a handful of plaintext/ciphertext pairs, and about 2^{57} encryptions. The simple variant needs much more memory than the attacks of the

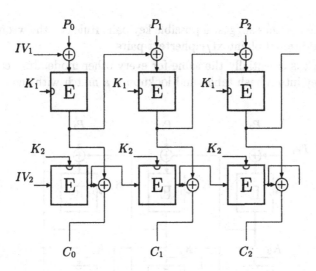

Fig. 3. The CBC/OFB mode

previous section, typically 2^{56} blocks. The latter requirement is currently hard to achieve. However, van Oorschot and Wiener show in [27] that such a standard meet-in-the-middle attack can be modified to work with a memory of 16 Gbyte, at the cost of 2^{72} encryptions; other trade-offs are possible. Their approach is based on cycle finding techniques using distinguished points. Therefore, when it comes to discussing threat models, we believe that a model in which about 2^{56} blocks have to be stored but only a few queries to the black box are needed is far more realistic than a scenario in which 2^{60} or more queries are made to the box (and possibly have to be stored anyway). We are focusing on attacks that require as few queries as possible.

4.1 Double Interleaved Modes

Again we make the assumption that both IV's are known to the attacker. It is easy to see that in this model, none of the 15 double modes can be more secure than the ECB/ECB mode. (Note that this does not hold for secret IV attacks, which are definitely more interesting from the cryptanalyst's point of view.) As explained in Sect. 3, six of these may also be attacked using exhaustive search on one key. Once again this proves that interleaved modes do not provide any additional security compared to standard encryption. In this particular setting, knowing only one of the IV's and possibly replaying it or the other one does not allow to mount a meet-in-the-middle attack.

As an example we show how an attack on CBC/CFB^{-1} proceeds (see Fig. 4). We always attack a single block message as in standard meet-in-the-middle attacks on two-key double encryption. Choose a fixed plaintext P_0 and get the corresponding ciphertext C_0. Then tabulate $E_{K_1}(IV_1 \oplus P_0) \oplus C_0$ for every possible value of the key K_1 (store the results in a hash table). Next compute every possible value of $E_{K_2}(IV_2)$ for every possible key K_2 and check for a match in the table. The matches suggest a possible key pair. Rule out the wrong key pairs with a few additional plaintext/ciphertext pairs.

The attack is essentially the same for every other mode. Just compute one half of the key into a hash table, and lookup for a match with the other half of the key.

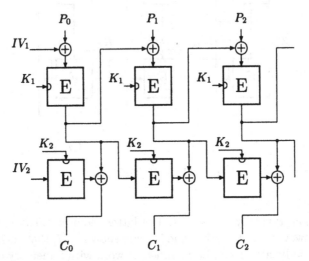

Fig. 4. The CBC/CFB^{-1} mode

4.2 Two-key Triple Interleaved Modes

We now address the case of some two-key triple interleaved mode, which is actually the idea that motivated our research in the first place. We were wondering whether two-key triple modes are as secure as standard two-key triple ECB encryption (the best attack on this scheme is the one by van Oorschot and Wiener discussed in Sect. 1).

The result of our investigation is that under a known IV attack, no such mode using a feedback mode on its inner layer is more secure than single encryption. Indeed, whenever a feedback mode involves the middle key, a mask is applied in between the two outer layers and can be computed into a hash table, while the outer layers may be computed on their own, and the exors of the results are looked up in the table. See Fig. 1 for a picture of the CBC/CFB/OFB mode.

Query the encryption of a single plaintext block P_0, and for every possible key K_2, compute $E_{K_2}(IV_2)$ into a hash table. Next compute $E_{K_1}(P_0 \oplus IV_1) \oplus E_{K_1}(IV_3) \oplus C_0$ for every possible key K_1 and look the matches up in the hash table. Rule out the wrong key pairs with some additional plaintext/ciphertext pair as usual.

5 Narrow Pipes and Collision Attacks

In this section we focus on threat models where one of the IV's is unknown to the attacker and show that some cipher block chaining modes fall under collision or "narrow pipe" attacks. This setting may not be usual at all but the goal here is to understand which are the minimum requirements to mount a collision attack on double interleaved modes. From the structure of these modes, it is easy to see that the weakness comes from the chaining mode itself. The complexity of this kind of attack is still quite acceptable as it requires only about 2^{32} plaintext/ciphertext pairs of a few blocks each, about 2^{57} encryptions and 2^{32} memory blocks.

We show how this attack works on the CFB/CBC^{-1} mode (see Fig. 5) when IV_1 is not known to the attacker. Randomly encrypt plaintexts of the form (P_0, P_1, M) where M is kept constant, and store the ciphertexts and associated IV_2 values. After about 2^{32} trials, a collision occurs on the exor value of the second block of the first encryption layer. This collision propagates through the cipher feedback of the first layer as well as through the plaintext chaining of the second layer to all the following ciphertext blocks. Therefore such a collision has most probably occurred when a collision is found on the third ciphertext block. Now write the equality of the colliding samples as:

$$D_{K_2}(C_0 \oplus IV_2) \oplus C_1 = D_{K_2}(C_0^* \oplus IV_2^*) \oplus C_1^*$$

and exhaustively search for the right key K_2. Once K_2 is found, find the first key by exhaustive search using the equation:

$$M \oplus D_{K_2}(C_2 \oplus D_{K_2}(C_1 \oplus D_{K_2}(C_0 \oplus IV_2))) = E_{K_1}(D_{K_2}(C_1 \oplus D_{K_2}(C_0 \oplus IV_2)))\ .$$

This technique applies to several modes making use of the CBC or CFB mode.

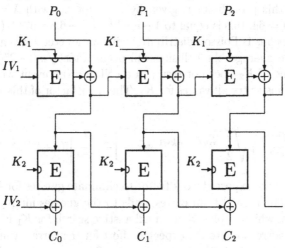

Fig. 5. The CFB/CBC^{-1} mode

6 Cycle Attacks

This attack is actually the dual of the narrow pipe attack. In this case we guess one of the keys (say, K_2) and peel off the corresponding layer. What remains is the output of an OFB-mode, which is in some sense a narrow pipe (64 bits). However, in this case, it is very *unlikely* that a collision will occur in a sequence of 2^{35} blocks (because the feedback function in OFB-mode is a permutation rather than an injective mapping). If a collision is observed, we know that our guess for the key K_2 was wrong. We will show that this attack requires about 2^{35} plaintext blocks, 2^{87} encryptions, and 2^{35} memory blocks (or 256 Gbyte).

This attack applies to the following double modes: CBC^{-1}/OFB, OFB/CBC, CFB^{-1}/OFB, and OFB/CFB, even if the *IV*'s are unknown; it represents a different trade-off than the attack by Biham (2^{64} chosen plaintexts, 2^{58} encryptions). The attack also applies to CBC/OFB, OFB/CBC^{-1}, CFB/OFB, and OFB/CFB^{-1} if one of the *IV*'s is known. If the mode of which the *IV* is known is not the OFB mode, then one has to choose the plaintext to be constant (for example, all zeroes after the 2nd block) in order to make the mode behave like the OFB mode.

Consider for example the OFB/CBC mode (see Fig. 6). The attack proceeds as follows. Collect a plaintext containing $\ell = 2^{34.7}$ blocks and the corresponding ciphertext. Guess K_2, and peel off the CBC mode. One can now compute a sequence of ℓ blocks that should be the output of the OFB mode. Therefore, if the guess for K_2 was correct, one does not expect to see a collision (the probability that a random starting point lies on an OFB cycle shorter than ℓ blocks is given by $\ell/2^{64}$, which is negligible in our case;[1] see for example Flajolet and Odlyzko [15]). If the guess for K_2 was wrong, the effect is that one obtains a random sequence of blocks, that contains with high probability a collision. For $\ell \approx \sqrt{2^n}$, this probability is given by $1 - \exp(-\lambda)$ with $\lambda = \ell^2/2^{n+1}$; for $\ell = 2^{34.7}$ and $n = 64$, this is equal to $1 - e^{-21.11} \approx 1 - 6.8 \cdot 10^{-10}$. (Note that the number of collisions is Poisson distributed with parameter λ given by the above expression.) On average, the collision will occur after $\sqrt{\pi/2} \cdot 2^{n/2}$ blocks [15]. If a wrong value of K_2 does not result in a collision (an event with probability $\exp(-\lambda)$), one has to try all values for K_1. The work factor of this attack is given by

$$\left(1 - exp\left[-\frac{\ell^2}{2^{n+1}}\right]\right) \sqrt{\frac{\pi}{2}} \cdot 2^{n/2} \cdot 2^{k-1} + exp\left[-\frac{\ell^2}{2^{n+1}}\right](\ell + 2^k)2^{k-1} + \ell + 2^{k-1} \ .$$

The first term is the expected work factor to eliminate guesses for K_2 that result in a collision. The second term corresponds to the guesses for K_2 for which no collision occurs, which implies that an exhaustive search for K_1 is required. The last two terms correspond to the expected effort for the correct value of K_2; they are negligible compared to the first two terms. The second term decreases with ℓ, and becomes negligible with respect to the first one if $\ell \geq 2^{34.7}$. The total

---

[1] Such a short cycle is easy to detect.

work factor is then approximately equal to

$$\sqrt{\frac{\pi}{8}} \cdot 2^{k+n/2} \approx 2^{87.3} .$$

At first sight, one might think that this attack also applies to the ECB/OFB and OFB/ECB modes. However, in this case a wrong key guess K_2^* means that we encrypt the OFB sequence in double DES (with the correct key K_2 and the wrong key guess K_2^* respectively). A double-DES encryption in ECB mode does not create collisions, which implies that it is not possible to distinguish between wrong and correct guesses.

The attack also applies to eight 2-key triple modes with OFB in the middle, where the first mode is CBC^{-1}, CFB^{-1}, or ECB and the last mode is CBC, CFB, or ECB (the only exception is the ECB/OFB/ECB mode). If the corresponding IV is known, the OFB mode is also allowed for the first or last encryption, the CBC^{-1} and CFB^{-1} are allowed for the last encryption, and CBC and CFB are allowed for the first encryption.

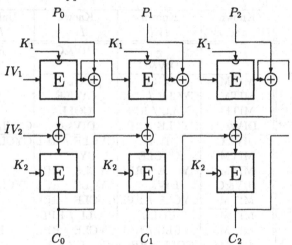

Fig. 6. The OFB/CBC mode

7 What's Left for Common Applications?

In this section we first summarise our results. Subsequently we look at which pragmatic solutions are available to designers who want a short-term solution with an acceptable security level.

7.1 Summarising Our Results

The results of the previous sections are summarised in Table 1. We will denote divide and conquer attacks as DIV&C, replay attacks as RPL, meet-in-the-middle attacks as MITM, collision attacks as COLL, and cycle attacks as CYCLE. We consider different known IV cases, as well as the case where no IV is known. The associated complexities are the following (known or chosen plaintexts/off-line computations/memory requirements):

- Divide and conquer or Replay attacks: $4/2^{57}/-$;
- Meet-in-the-middle attacks: $4/2^{57}/2^{56}$, $4/2^{66}/2^{40}$, or $4/2^{72}/2^{34}$;
- Collision attacks: $2^{32}/2^{57}/2^{32}$ (chosen plaintexts);
- Cycle attacks: $2^{35}/2^{87}/2^{35}$ (1 single plaintext, sometimes chosen; see Sect. 6).

Table 1 shows how vulnerable double modes can become if the attacker obtains information about the initial values or can manipulate these. We would like to stress that this is the case in many applications and that designers should make the right choices having these numbers in mind.

Table 1. Double modes under known/unknown IV attacks

Mode	Known IV_1 and IV_2	Known IV_1	Known IV_2	Unknown IV's
ECB/OFB	–	–	DIV&C	RPL
OFB/ECB	–	DIV&C	–	RPL
CBC/CBC^{-1}	MITM	COLL	COLL	
CBC/OFB	MITM	CYCLE / RPL	CYCLE	
CBC/CFB^{-1}	MITM	COLL / RPL	COLL	
CBC^{-1}/OFB	DIV&C	CYCLE / RPL	DIV&C	CYCLE / RPL
OFB/CBC	DIV&C	DIV&C	CYCLE / RPL	CYCLE / RPL
OFB/CBC^{-1}	MITM	CYCLE	CYCLE	
OFB/OFB	MITM	CYCLE / RPL	CYCLE / RPL	
OFB/CFB	DIV&C	DIV&C	CYCLE / RPL	CYCLE / RPL
OFB/CFB^{-1}	MITM	CYCLE / RPL	CYCLE / RPL	
CFB/CBC^{-1}	MITM	COLL	COLL / RPL	
CFB/OFB	MITM	CYCLE / RPL	CYCLE / RPL	RPL
CFB/CFB^{-1}	MITM	COLL / RPL	COLL / RPL	
CFB^{-1}/OFB	DIV&C	CYCLE / RPL	DIV&C	CYCLE / RPL

7.2 Discussion

An important question is: which solutions remain with a reasonable security level that require only two keys? This implies that we are not worried about attacks that require more than 2^{50} chosen plaintexts or ciphertexts, or that require a work factor of 2^{100} or more. The choice of these numbers is rather arbitrary; note however that it is easy to prevent attackers from having access to more than 2^{50} plaintext/ciphertext pairs by changing the keys more frequently, or by taking the system out of service early. However, once encrypted data is made public, an opponent can record it and wait 20 or 30 years (or even more) before he attempts to decipher it. We also assume that the keys are generated or derived in such a way that related key attacks are precluded [3].

We distinguish between four cases:

- if the IV's are encrypted and their integrity is protected by a MAC (which also should prevent replay), we recommend to use the simple OFB/OFB mode (scheme 28 in [6]). The best known attack described in [6] has complexity $2^{65}/2^{65}/2^{64}$; such an attack is not realistic in many environments. Note also that chosen-IV attacks are precluded by the use of the MAC algorithm. This mode provides no error propagation; if the authenticity of the information is a concern, it is recommended to calculate a MAC over the IV's and over the plaintext.

  As a MAC algorithm, MacDES could be used [20]; this algorithm extends the well known CBC-MAC with double-DES in the first and last encryption (but with different but related keys for the 2nd encryption). MacDES seems to provide high security at relatively low cost; forgery attacks are not feasible if the number of plaintexts encrypted with a single key is reduced to 2^{32} (or a little less), and the best known key recovery attack requires 2^{65} chosen text-MAC pairs, 2^{90} encryptions, 2^{55} MAC verifications, and 2^{37} bytes memory.

  Wagner discusses the use of encrypted and authenticated IV's and argues that *"adding this much complexity to the system may begin to test the limits of one's comfort zone,"* [28]. However, our point of view is that the currently known attacks on multiple modes tend to be very complex as well; moreover, MAC algorithms are probably better understood than encryption modes. It is of course important to apply appropriate key separation techniques (this may require additional evaluation).

- If the IV's are encrypted but their integrity is not protected by a MAC, we recommend to use the CBC/CBC^{-1} mode (scheme 15 in [6]). The best known attack described in [6] has complexity $2^{68}/2^{66}/2^{66}$. This mode seems to provide better security against IV replay attacks than the previous one. In order to simplify the scheme, one can choose $IV_1 = IV_2$.

- We do not recommend a double mode where the IV's are not encrypted but their integrity is protected. If follows from Table 1 that all these scheme succumb to a meet-in-the-middle attack that requires only a few plaintext/ciphertext pairs. For this case, we suggest the OFB[CBC,CBC^{-1}] mode proposed by Biham [6]; this notation means that one first applies the OFB mode, then CBC, then OFB (with the same key stream), then CBC^{-1} and finally OFB (again with the same key stream). Wagner asserts that his chosen-IV attacks do not apply to this scheme [28]. Our preliminary evaluation suggests that the security level of this mode is still sufficiently high even if the same key is used for the CBC and CBC^{-1} encryption.

- If the IV's are not encrypted and their integrity is not protected by a MAC, one could also use the previous scheme; however, we do not recommend this solution.

We understand that making such recommendations is a little risky; indeed, there are certificational attacks on these schemes (except for the last one), and in the past years significant progress has been made in the cryptanalysis of multiple modes. On the other hand, we believe that it is important to point out to the research community (and to practitioners) that for some of the schemes, we are not aware of any realistic attacks.

We also recall a number of other schemes that can serve as "reference points" (note that the major motivation for introducing new modes was precisely to avoid the drawbacks of the first two of them):

- 2-key triple-DES in outer-CBC mode: the main attacks here are a matching ciphertext attack and the van Oorschot-Wiener attack [26] with the following parameters: $2^t/2^{120-t}/2^t$.
- DESX in CBC mode [17]: the matching ciphertext attack applies as well; the security bound is $2^t/2^{119-t}/2^t$. A disadvantage is that this solution has a smaller margin to shortcut attacks (differential and linear cryptanalysis) than all double or triple modes.
- DEAL-128 in CBC mode [19]: this is certainly an interesting alternative. The best known attack on this cipher is $2^{70}/2^{121}/2^{67}$, where the texts are chosen plaintexts. A small disadvantage is the slow key schedule (6 DES encryptions). We believe that further research is necessary on this solution, as DEAL is a new block cipher rather than a mode (see also [22]).

Table 2 compares the efficiency of the solutions proposed. The security level corresponds to the best attack known. For DESX this is the security bound proved, but if the underlying block cipher is DES, shortcut attacks apply with a lower complexity (differential [8] and linear cryptanalysis [23]). If the IV's are encrypted, this requires 3 encryptions per IV (2-key triple encryption), except for DESX, where IV is encrypted using DESX. For the OFB/OFB scheme, it is assumed that the MAC algorithm is applied to both the IV's and the plaintext; this implies that this variant also provides guarantees on the message integrity. If the MAC is applied only to the IV's, the number of encryptions drops to $2t + 10$. Note that for the CBC/CBC^{-1} scheme a single IV is used. The MAC algorithm used is MacDES [20]; it requires $t + 2$ encryptions and requires that $t \geq 2$.

8 Conclusions and Open Problems

We have analysed the security of double and 2-key triple modes under the assumption that information on the IV's is available. Under this model, most of these schemes are practically insecure. This extends the work of Biham who has shown that these modes are theoretically insecure when the IV's are secret. We have also introduced a new attack, the cycle attack, that reduces the plaintext requirement for certain double and triple modes (at the cost of an increased number of off-line encryptions).

Table 2. Summary of properties of several schemes when encrypting a t-block plaintext

mode	encrypt IV's	authenticate IV's	number of encryptions	security
OFB/OFB	yes	yes	$3t + 10$	$2^{65}/2^{65}/2^{64}$
CBC/CBC^{-1}	yes	no	$2t + 3$	$2^{68}/2^{66}/2^{66}$
OFB[CBC/CBC^{-1}]	no	yes	$3t + 5$	$2/2^{112}/-$
2-key triple-DES outer-CBC	yes	no	$3t + 3$	$2^t/2^{120-t}/2^t$ 2^{32} Match. Ciph.
DESX in CBC	yes	no	$t + 1$	$2^t/2^{119-t}/2^t$ 2^{32} Match. Ciph.
DEAL in CBC	yes	no	$3t + 3$	$2^{70}/2^{121}/2^{67}$

We have also compared the security level and performance of a number of alternatives that offer a reasonable security level against attacks that require less than 2^{40} known or chosen texts. Some of these schemes seem to provide a simple solution that is easy to analyse, but we caution the reader against too much optimism. We leave it as an open problem to improve the attacks on the schemes listed in Table 2.

References

1. ANSI draft X9.52, *"Triple Data Encryption Algorithm Modes of Operation,"* Revision 6.0, 1996.
2. M. Bellare, A. Desai, E. Jokipii, P. Rogaway, "A concrete security treatment of symmetric encryption: Analysis of the DES modes of operation," *Proceedings of the 38th Symposium on Foundations of Computer Science*, IEEE, 1997.
3. E. Biham, "New types of cryptanalytic attacks using related keys," *EUROCRYPT'93, LNCS 765*, Springer-Verlag, 1994, pp. 398–409.
4. E. Biham, "On modes of operation," *Fast Software Encryption'93, LNCS 809*, Springer-Verlag, 1994, pp. 116–120.
5. E. Biham, "Cryptanalysis of multiple modes of operation," *ASIACRYPT'94, LNCS 917*, Springer-Verlag, 1994, pp. 278–292.
6. E. Biham, "Cryptanalysis of triple-modes of operation," *Technion Technical Report CS0885*, 1996.
7. E. Biham, L. R. Knudsen, "Cryptanalysis of the ANSI X9.52 CBCM mode," *EUROCRYPT'98, LNCS 1403*, Springer-Verlag, 1998, pp. 100–111.
8. E. Biham, A. Shamir, *"Differential Cryptanalysis of the Data Encryption Standard,"* Springer-Verlag, 1993.
9. D. Coppersmith, "A chosen-ciphertext attack on triple-DES modes," 1994.
10. D. Coppersmith, "A chosen-plaintext attack on 2-key inner triple DES CBC/EDE," 1995.
11. D. Coppersmith, D. B. Johnson, S. M. Matyas, "A proposed mode for triple-DES encryption," *IBM Journal of Research and Development*, Vol. 40, No. 2, 1996, pp. 253–262.

12. The Electronic Frontier Foundation, *"Cracking DES. Secrets of Encryption Research, Wiretap Politics & Chip Design,"* O'Reilly, May 1998.
13. FIPS 46, *"Data Encryption Standard,"* US Department of Commerce, National Bureau of Standards, 1977 (revised as FIPS 46-1:1988; FIPS 46-2:1993).
14. FIPS 81, *"DES Modes of Operation,"* US Department of Commerce, National Bureau of Standards, 1980.
15. P. Flajolet, A. M. Odlyzko, "Random mapping statistics," *EUROCRYPT'89*, *LNCS 434*, Springer-Verlag, 1990, pp. 329–354.
16. B. S. Kaliski, M.J.B. Robshaw, "Multiple encryption: Weighing security and performance," *Dr. Dobb's Journal*, January 1996, pp. 123–127.
17. J. Kilian, P. Rogaway, "How to protect DES against exhaustive key search, *CRYPTO'96, LNCS 1109*, Springer-Verlag, 1996, pp. 252–267.
18. L. R. Knudsen, *"Block Ciphers – Analysis, Design and Applications,"* PhD thesis, Aarhus University, Denmark, 1994.
19. L. R. Knudsen, *"DEAL: a 128-bit block cipher,"* AES submission, 1998.
20. L. Knudsen, B. Preneel, "MacDES: MAC algorithm based on DES," *Electronics Letters*, Vol. 34, No. 9, 1998, pp. 871–873,
21. S. Lucks, "Attacking triple encryption," *Fast Software Encryption'98, LNCS 1372*, Springer-Verlag, 1998, pp. 239–253.
22. S. Lucks, "On the security of the 128-bit block cipher DEAL," *Fast Software Encryption, LNCS*, L.R. Knudsen, Ed., Springer-Verlag, 1999.
23. M. Matsui, "Linear cryptanalysis method for DES cipher," *EUROCRYPT'93, LNCS 765*, Springer-Verlag, 1993, pp. 386–397.
24. R. C. Merkle, M. E. Hellman, "On the security of multiple encryption," *Communications of the ACM*, Vol. 24, No. 7, 1981, pp. 465–467.
25. W. Tuchman, "Hellman presents no shortcut solutions to the DES," *Spectrum*, Vol. 16, 1979, pp. 40–41.
26. P. C. van Oorschot, M. J. Wiener, "A known-plaintext attack on two-key triple encryption," *EUROCRYPT'90, LNCS 473*, 1990, pp. 318–325.
27. P. C. van Oorschot, M. J. Wiener, "Improving implementable meet-in-the-middle attacks by orders of magnitude," *CRYPTO'96, LNCS 1109*, 1996, pp. 229–236.
28. D. Wagner, "Cryptanalysis of some recently-proposed multiple modes of operation," *Fast Software Encryption'98, LNCS 1372*, Springer-Verlag, 1998, pp. 254–269.
29. M.J. Wiener, "Efficient DES key search," *Technical Report TR-244*, School of Computer Science, Carleton University, Ottawa, Canada, May 1994. Presented at the rump session of Crypto'93 and reprinted in W. Stallings, *Practical Cryptography for Data Internetworks*, IEEE Computer Society Press, 1996, pp. 31–79.

On the Construction of Variable-Input-Length Ciphers

Mihir Bellare[1] and Phillip Rogaway[2]

[1] Dept. of Computer Science & Engineering, University of California at San Diego,
9500 Gilman Drive, La Jolla, CA 92093 USA
mihir@cs.ucsd.edu www-cse.ucsd.edu/users/mihir/

[2] Dept. of Computer Science, Eng. II Bldg., One Shields Ave.,
University of California at Davis, Davis, CA 95616 USA
rogaway@cs.ucdavis.edu www.cs.ucdavis.edu/~rogaway/

Abstract. Whereas a block cipher enciphers messages of some one particular length (the blocklength), a variable-input-length cipher takes messages of varying (and preferably arbitrary) lengths. Still, the length of the ciphertext must equal the length of the plaintext. This paper introduces the problem of constructing such objects, and provides a practical solution. Our VIL mode of operation makes a variable-input-length cipher from any block cipher. The method is demonstrably secure in the provable-security sense of modern cryptography: we give a quantitative security analysis relating the difficulty of breaking the constructed (variable-input-length) cipher to the difficulty of breaking the underlying block cipher.

Keywords: Ciphers, Modes of Operation, Provable Security, Symmetric Encryption.

1 Introduction

This paper introduces the question of how to construct ciphers which operate on messages of varying lengths. Such a cipher, F, maps a key K and a plaintext M in $\{0,1\}^*$ (or M in some other set containing strings of various lengths) into a ciphertext $C = F_K(M)$ having the same length as M. Note that the length of M is not restricted to some fixed blocklength n, or even to some multiple of a blocklength. At the same time, being a cipher, F_K is a length-preserving permutation for which possession of K enables the efficient computation of both F_K and F_K^{-1}.

The ciphers we construct have a strong security property: we want that no efficient adversary can distinguish an oracle for $F_K(\cdot)$, for a random and secret K, from an oracle for a random length-preserving permutation $\pi(\cdot)$ (having the same domain as F_K). This is the (now customary) requirement for a block cipher (security in the sense of being a "pseudorandom permutation," or "PRP") originally suggested in [10, 4], and so it is the property we want for any variable-input-length cipher as well.

One could try to construct a variable-input-length cipher from scratch, in the confusion/diffusion tradition. But that approach is specialized and error-prone. Instead, we provide constructions which assume one already has in hand some underlying block cipher. We give a "mode of operation"—VIL mode (for "variable-input-length enciphering") which enciphers strings of arbitrary length (but at least n) using an n-bit block cipher.

We prove the soundness of VIL mode in the provable-security sense of modern cryptography: if the underlying block cipher is secure then so is the variable-input-length cipher we construct from it. VIL is actually more than one particular mode of operation; it is an approach for making a variable-input-length cipher that can be realized in many different ways.

WHY VARIABLE-INPUT-LENGTH CIPHERS? The obvious use of variable-input-length ciphers is to encrypt (ie, provide privacy protection) without any increase in message length. Suppose we'll be encrypting messages $M_1, M_2, \cdots$ where the lengths of these message may vary. We want to create ciphertexts $C_1, C_2, \cdots$ where $|C_i| = |M_i|$ and where ciphertext C_i hides everything about M_i (with respect to efficient computation) except for the length of M_i and which earlier plaintext, if any, equals M_i.

It is important to understand that the last sentence embodies a weaker notion of privacy than the customary one—semantic security, and its equivalent formulations [7, 3]. A semantically secure encryption computationally hides all information about M_i except for $|M_i|$—in particular, one does not allow to be leaked which earlier plaintext (if any) a given ciphertext corresponds to. But you pay a price for this added security—semantically secure encryption cannot possibly be length preserving. Thus length-preserving "encryption" (enciphering) embodies a tradeoff: shorter ciphertexts at the cost of an inferior security guarantee (and slower encryption/decryption).

Is this tradeoff a good one? If you don't know anything about how the encryption will be used, then we'd have to say no. But there are applications when the tradeoff *is* a good one. Let us give an example.

In networking applications a "packet format" may have been defined, this packet format having various fields, none of which were intended for cryptographic purposes. Now suppose a need arises to *add in* privacy features but, at the same time, it is no longer desirable (or feasible) to adjust the packet format. It cannot be lengthened by even one bit. Enciphering with a variable-input-length cipher leaves the packet size alone, and it leaves packets looking identical (after deciphering) to the way they looked before. This contributes to ease-of-acceptance, an easier migration path, and better code-reuse. These factors may outweigh the security consideration that we will be leaking which packets of a session are identical to which earlier ones.

As a second example, we may have *a priori* reason to believe that all the plaintexts $M_1, M_2, \cdots$ will be distinct. For example, each message may be known to contain a sequence number. In such a case the additional piece of information that secure encipherment leaks amounts to no information at all, and so here enciphering provides a way to achieve semantic security in a way that is both length-minimal and oblivious to the formatting conventions of each message (eg, where the sequence number appears in each message). This obliviousness contributes to the making of robust software; when message formats change the cryptography need not be adjusted. With typical length-minimal approaches this would not have been true.

Variable-input-length ciphers may prove to be useful tools for protocol design. As an example, Rivest put forward the idea of "strongly non-separable encryption" [23], wherein an adversary with a ciphertext C who guesses an encryption key K should have to invest $\Omega(|C|)$ time before obtaining information useful to verify if C was enciphered under K. Variable-input-length enciphering provides a simple way to provably achieve Rivest's goal.

THE DIFFICULTY. It is not so clear *how* to construct a secure variable-input-length cipher from a block cipher. We are making a stringent security requirement: we expect our ciphers to approximate a family of random permutations. In addition, we want them to be length-preserving permutations. This eliminates any hope of using conventional modes of operation. Consider, for example, using DES in CBC mode with a zero initialization vector (IV). For simplicity, assume the message length is a multiple of the blocklength.[1] This does *not* give a cipher that approximates a family of random permutation: if two plaintexts agree on blocks $1, \ldots, i$ then their ciphertexts agree on blocks $1, \ldots, i$, which is almost never true of a random permutation. To get around this one might try to make the IV some sort of hash of the message—but then how could one get a length-preserving construction?

OUR METHOD. We suggest simple and efficient ways for making variable-input-length ciphers from block ciphers. Our VIL mode of operation makes two passes over the message. In our preferred instantiation, the first pass computes some sort of CBC MAC over the message M, while the second pass encrypts M (in counter mode, for example) using the pass-one MAC as the IV. However, one cannot take the ciphertext C for M to be the pass-two ciphertext (including the IV), since this would be too long. Instead, we exploit a certain feature of the CBC MAC, which we call its "parsimoniousness." This enables us to drop one block from the pass-two ciphertext and *still* be able to recover the plaintext. (This is the main idea of our construction.) There are some technical matters that complicate things; see Section 2 and Fig. 1.

Our approach can be instantiated in many further ways; it actually encompasses many modes of operation. We describe VIL mode in terms of two specialized-tools: what we call a "parsimonious" pseudorandom function (PRF) and a "parsimonious" encryption scheme. Both of these tools can be constructed from block ciphers, and we show a few ways to do this. Thinking of VIL mode in these general terms not only provides versatility in instantiation, but, equally

---

[1] The difficult issue is not in dealing with messages of length not a multiple of the blocklength; there are well-known methods for dealing with this, like stream-cipher encrypting the short block and ciphertext stealing. See [13, Chapter 2] for a description of these techniques.

important, our proof of correctness is made much simpler by the added generality: what is irrelevant is out of sight, and what is relevant can be singled out and separately proved, in part by invoking known results [4, 21, 3].

RELATED WORK. There is a quite a lot of work on constructing block ciphers of one blocklength given block ciphers of another blocklength. Luby and Rackoff [10] consider the question of how to turn an n-bit to n-bit pseudorandom function (PRF) into a $2n$-bit to $2n$-bit block cipher. They show that three rounds of the Feistel construction suffices for this purpose, and that four rounds suffice to obtain a "super" PRP from a PRF. The paper has spawned much work, with [12, 22, 19, 20, 25] to name a few.

Naor and Reingold [15] provide a construction which extends a block cipher on n-bits to a block cipher on $N = 2ni$ bits, for any desired $i \geq 1$. A variation on their construction yields a cipher on $N = ni$ bits for any $i \geq 1$ [18]. It is unclear how to use these constructions for arbitrary N (meaning not necessarily a multiple of n) and across assorted input lengths.

Lucks [11] generalizes Luby-Rackoff to consider a three round unbalanced Feistel network, using hash functions for round functions. This yields a block cipher on any given length N by starting with a PRF of r bits to ℓ bits and another of ℓ bits to r bits where $r + \ell = N$. Of course this requires the availability of the latter primitives for given values of r, ℓ.

Anderson and Biham [1] provide two constructions for a block cipher (BEAR and LION) which use a hash function and a stream cipher. This too is an unbalanced Feistel network.

Some ciphers which are intended to operate on blocks of various lengths have been constructed from scratch. The CMEA (attacked by [24]) is an example.

A "forward-then-backwards" mode of operation is described in [8], under the names "Triple-DES Key Wrap" and "RC2 Key Wrap." While not length-preserving, a length-preserving variant is possible, and it might be a good cipher across messages of assorted lengths. See Section 5 for further discussion.

We have already mentioned Rivest's "strongly non-separable" encryption [23] and that variable-input-length enciphering provides one mechanism to achieve that goal.

The VIL mode of operation was invented in 1994 when the authors were at IBM [2]. No security analysis was provided at that time.

2 VIL Mode Example

In this section we describe one particular instantiation of VIL mode enciphering. For concreteness, let us start from DES, a map DES : $\{0,1\}^{56} \times \{0,1\}^n \rightarrow \{0,1\}^n$ where $n = 64$. Using this map we construct the function $F : \{0,1\}^{56 \times 3} \times \{0,1\}^{\geq 64} \rightarrow \{0,1\}^{\geq 64}$ for enciphering strings of length at least 64. (Extending to messages of length less than 64 will be discussed later.) Given a key $K = K1 \parallel K2 \parallel K3$, partitioned into three 56-bit pieces, and given a plaintext $M \in \{0,1\}^{\geq 64}$, form the ciphertext $C = F_K(M)$ as depicted in Fig. 1 and as specified here:

Algorithm $F_{K1 \| K2 \| K3}(M)$

(1) Let M_{prefix} be the first $|M| - n$ bits of M. Let M_{suffix} be the remaining bits.

(2) Let pad be a "1" followed by the minimum number of "0" bits such that $|M| + |pad|$ is divisible by 64.

(3) Partition $M_{\text{prefix}} \| pad \| M_{\text{suffix}}$ into 64-bit blocks $M_1 \cdots M_m$.

(4) Let $C_0 = 0^n$, and let $C_i = \text{DES}_{K1}(C_{i-1} \oplus M_i)$ for all $1 \le i \le m$.

(5) Let $\sigma = \text{DES}_{K2}(C_m)$.

(6) Let P be the first $|M| - n$ bits of
$$\text{DES}_{K3}(\sigma) \| \text{DES}_{K3}(\sigma + 1) \| \text{DES}_{K3}(\sigma + 2) \cdots .$$

(7) Let $C_{\text{prefix}} = P \oplus M_{\text{prefix}}$.

(8) Return ciphertext $C = \sigma \| C_{\text{prefix}}$.

The computation of C can be looked at as having two stages. In the first stage (Steps 1–5) we compute σ, which is some sort of CBC-MAC of M under the key $K1 \| K2$. In the second stage (Steps 6–7) we encrypt M, except for M's last 64 bits, under key $K3$. We use counter-mode encryption with an initialization vector of σ. The ciphertext is the MAC σ together with the encrypted prefix of M.

The MAC σ is not computed by the "basic" CBC-MAC, but some variant of it. Our constraints preclude using the CBC-MAC in its customary form. First we need to be able to properly handle messages of arbitrary length (the basic CBC-MAC is only secure on messages of some fixed length, this length being a multiple of the blocklength). But in addressing this issue we must ensure that given σ and an $|M| - 64$ bit prefix of M, we are able to reconstruct the last 64 bits of M. That this can be done can be seen in the following algorithm for computing $F^{-1}_{K1 \| K2 \| K3}(C)$. As before, $C \in \{0,1\}^{\ge 64}$ and $K1, K2, K3 \in \{0,1\}^{56}$. The existence of the following algorithm demonstrates that F is indeed a cipher.

Algorithm $F^{-1}_{K1 \| K2 \| K3}(C)$

(1) Let σ be the first 64 bits of C. Let C_{prefix} be the remaining bits.

(2) Let P be the first $|C_{\text{prefix}}|$ bits of
$$\text{DES}_{K3}(\sigma) \| \text{DES}_{K3}(\sigma + 1) \| \text{DES}_{K3}(\sigma + 2) \cdots .$$

(3) Let $M_{\text{prefix}} = P \oplus C_{\text{prefix}}$.

(4) Let pad be a "1" followed by the minimum number of "0" bits such that $|M_{\text{prefix}}| + |pad|$ is divisible by 64.

(5) Partition $M_{\text{prefix}} \| pad$ into 64-bit blocks $M_1 \cdots M_{m-1}$.

(6) Let $C_0 = 0^n$, and let $C_i = \text{DES}_{K1}(C_{i-1} \oplus M_i)$ for all $1 \le i \le m - 1$.

(7) Let $M_m = \text{DES}^{-1}_{K1}(\text{DES}^{-1}_{K2}(\sigma)) \oplus C_{m-1}$.

(8) Return $M = M_{\text{prefix}} \| M_m$.

The interesting step is Step 7, where one exploits the structure of (this version of) the CBC-MAC to compute the last block of plaintext.

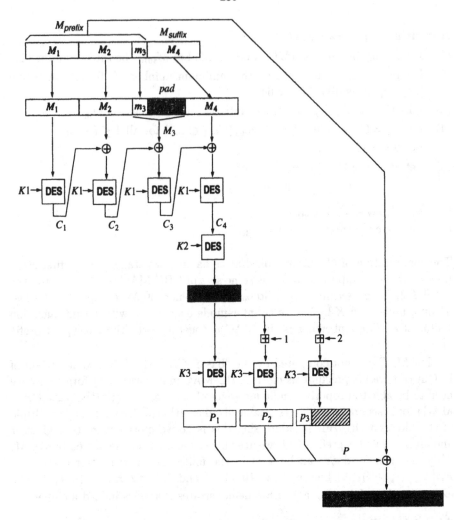

Fig. 1. *An example way to realize VIL-mode encipherment. Here we use the block cipher DES. In this example the message M to encipher is a few bits longer than 64×3 bits. The underlying key is $K = K1 \parallel K2 \parallel K3$. The ciphertext is $C = \sigma \parallel C_{\text{prefix}}$.*

We remark that standard methods, like setting $Ki = \text{DES}_K(i)[1..56]$, would allow $K1$, $K2$ and $K3$ to be derived from a single 56-bit key, in which case F would be a map $F : \{0,1\}^{56} \times \{0,1\}^{\geq 64} \to \{0,1\}^{\geq 64}$.

We also remark that that the domain can be extended to all of $\{0,1\}^*$ (that is, we can encipher strings of fewer than < 64 bits) using methods which we will later discuss. However, these methods have not been proven secure with desirable security bounds.

It should be kept in mind that the above example is just one way to instantiate VIL-mode encipherment. Both stages (the computation of σ and the encryption of M_{prefix}) can be accomplished in other ways. We now move towards these generalizations.

3 The General Approach

Towards the general description of VIL and its proof of correctness we now make some definitions.

PRELIMINARIES. A *message space* $\mathcal{M}$ is a nonempty subset of $\{0,1\}^*$ for which $M \in \mathcal{M}$ implies that $M' \in \mathcal{M}$ for all M' of the same length of M. A *ciphertext space* (or *range*) $\mathcal{C}$ is a nonempty subset of $\{0,1\}^*$. A *key space* $\mathcal{K}$ is a nonempty set together with a probability measure on that set. A *pseudorandom function* (PRF) with key space $\mathcal{K}$, message space $\mathcal{M}$ and range $\mathcal{C}$ is a set of functions $F = \{F_K \mid K \in \mathcal{K}\}$ where each $F_K : \mathcal{M} \to \mathcal{C}$. We usually write $F : \mathcal{K} \times \mathcal{M} \to \mathcal{C}$. We assume that $|F_K(M)|$ depends only on $|M|$. A *cipher* is a PRF $F : \mathcal{K} \times \mathcal{M} \to \mathcal{M}$ in which each $F_K : \mathcal{M} \to \mathcal{M}$ is a bijection. A *block-cipher* is a cipher $F : \mathcal{K} \times \{0,1\}^n \to \{0,1\}^n$. The number n is called the *blocklength*.

Let $\mathcal{M}$ be a message space and let $\ell : \mathsf{N} \to \mathsf{N}$ be a function. We define "reference" PRFs $\mathsf{Rand}(\mathcal{M}, \ell)$ and $\mathsf{Perm}(\mathcal{M})$. A random function $\rho \leftarrow \mathsf{Rand}(\mathcal{M}, \ell)$ is defined as follows: for each $M \in \mathcal{M}$, let $\rho(M)$ is a random string in $\{0,1\}^{\ell(|M|)}$. A random function $\pi \leftarrow \mathsf{Perm}_{\mathcal{M}}$ is defined as follows: for each number i such that $\mathcal{M}$ contains strings of length i, let π_i be a random permutation on $\{0,1\}^i$, and define $\pi(M) = \pi_i(M)$ where $i = |M|$.

We define security following [6], adapted to concrete security as in [4]. A *distinguisher* is a (possibly probabilistic) algorithm A with access to an oracle. Let A be a distinguisher and let $F = \{F_K \mid K \in \mathcal{K}\}$ be a PRF with key space $\mathcal{K}$ and $|F_K(M)| = \ell(|M|)$. Then we let

$$\mathrm{Adv}_F^{\mathrm{prf}}(A) = \Pr[K \leftarrow \mathcal{K} : A^{F_K(\cdot)} = 1] - \Pr[\rho \leftarrow \mathsf{Rand}(\mathcal{M}, \ell) : A^{\rho(\cdot)} = 1] \text{ and}$$
$$\mathrm{Adv}_F^{\mathrm{prp}}(A) = \Pr[K \leftarrow \mathcal{K} : A^{F_K(\cdot)} = 1] - \Pr[\pi \leftarrow \mathsf{Perm}(\mathcal{M}) : A^{\pi(\cdot)} = 1].$$

Define the functions $\mathrm{Adv}_F^{\mathrm{prf}}(t, q, \mu) = \max_A\{\mathrm{Adv}_F^{\mathrm{prf}}(A)\}$ and $\mathrm{Adv}_F^{\mathrm{prp}}(t, q, \mu) = \max_A\{\mathrm{Adv}_F^{\mathrm{prp}}(A)\}$ where the maximum is over all adversaries which run in time at most t and ask at most q oracle queries, these queries totaling at most μ bits. We omit the argument μ when $\mathcal{M}$ contains strings of just one length. Time is always understood to include the space for the description of the distinguishing algorithm. Throughout, if the distinguisher inquires as to the value of oracle f at a point $M \notin \mathcal{M}$ then the oracle responds with the distinguished point $\perp$. We assume there is a (simple) algorithm to decide membership in $\mathcal{M}$ and so we may assume adversaries do not make such queries.

PARSIMONIOUS PRF. Let $G : \{0,1\}^\kappa \times \mathcal{M} \to \{0,1\}^n$ be a PRF where $\mathcal{M}$ only includes strings of length at least n. Then G is said to be *parsimonious* if for all $K \in \mathcal{K}$ and all $M \in \mathcal{M}$, the last n bits of M are uniquely determined by the remaining bits of M, the key K, and $G_K(M)$. In other words, with a parsimonious PRF G, if you know K and receive the n-bit value $\sigma = G_K(M)$ then you don't need to receive *all* of M in order to know what it is: it is sufficient to get the $|M|-n$ bit prefix of M, M_{prefix}: from that you can recover the n missing bits by applying some function $\mathsf{Recover}_K(M_{\mathrm{prefix}}, \sigma)$ associated to the PRF.

EXAMPLES. The (basic) CBC-MAC is a parsimonious PRF. Assume a block cipher $E : \mathcal{K} \times \{0,1\}^n \to \{0,1\}^n$. Fix a constant $m \geq 1$. Consider the PRF $G : \mathcal{K} \times \{0,1\}^{nm} \to \{0,1\}^n$ defined by $G_K(M_1 \cdots M_m) = C_m$, where $C_0 = 0^n$ and $C_i = E_K(M_i \oplus C_{i-1})$ for $1 \leq i \leq m$. To recover M_m from K, $M_1 \cdots M_{m-1}$, and $\sigma = G_K(M_1 \cdots M_m)$, compute $C_0, C_1, \ldots, C_{m-1}$ by $C_0 = 0^n$ and $C_i = E_K(C_{i-1} \oplus M_i)$ and then, since $C_m = E_K(M_m \oplus C_{m-1})$, recover M_m as $M_m = E_K^{-1}(\sigma) \oplus C_{m-1}$. Note that it is crucial that we use the "full" CBC MAC (that is, the MAC is all of C_m, not a proper prefix). In [4] it is shown that the CBC MAC is secure whenever E is, in the sense that $\mathrm{Adv}_G^{\mathrm{prf}}(t, q) \leq \mathrm{Adv}_E^{\mathrm{prf}}(t', q') + 3q^2m^2 2^{-n-1}$ where $t' \approx t$ and $q' = qm$.

The computation of σ in the algorithm of Section 2 builds on the idea described above. We extend the CBC-MAC variant analyzed in [21] to domain $\{0,1\}^*$, doing this in a way that retains parsimoniousness (padding the second-to-last block instead of the last one). This CBC-MAC variant is once again secure. Let $G : \mathcal{K}^2 \times \{0,1\}^* \to \{0,1\}^n$ be the PRF obtained from the block cipher E by the method illustrated in Lines 1–5 in the description of Algorithm $F_{K1 \| K2 \| K3}(M)$ in Section 2 (where we had $E = $ DES). Then the results of [21] can be adapted to establish that that $\mathrm{Adv}_G^{\mathrm{prf}}(t, q, \mu) \leq 2 \cdot \mathrm{Adv}_E^{\mathrm{prf}}(t', q') + (\mu/n + q)^2 2^{-n} + 2^{-n}$ where $t' \approx t$ and $q' = \mu/n + q$.

PARSIMONIOUS ENCRYPTION. A parsimonious encryption scheme is a triple of algorithms $S = (\mathcal{K}, \mathcal{E}, \mathcal{D})$. Algorithm $\mathcal{K}$ returns a random element from the key space (which we likewise denote $\mathcal{K}$). Encryption algorithm $\mathcal{E} : \mathcal{K} \times \mathcal{M}$ takes a key $K \in \mathcal{K}$ and $M \in \mathcal{M}$, chooses a random IV $\leftarrow \{0,1\}^n$, and then encrypts the message M into a ciphertext $C = \mathrm{IV} \| C^*$, where $|C^*| = |M|$. The process is denoted $C \leftarrow \mathcal{E}_K(M)$, or $C \leftarrow \mathcal{E}_K(M; \mathrm{IV})$ when we regard IV as an explicitly given input to $\mathcal{E}$. The decryption algorithm has domain $\mathcal{K} \times \{0,1\}^*$ and, given $K \in \mathcal{K}$ and $C \in \{0,1\}^*$, $\mathcal{D}_K(C) = M$ whenever $C = \mathcal{E}_K(M; \mathrm{IV})$ for some $M \in \mathcal{M}$ and $\mathrm{IV} \in \{0,1\}^n$.

We define security following [3]. The idea is that an adversary cannot distinguish the encryption of text from the encryption of an equal-length string of garbage. Let $S = (\mathcal{K}, \mathcal{E}, \mathcal{D})$ be a parsimonious encryption scheme and let A be a distinguisher. Then

$$\mathrm{Adv}_A^{\mathrm{priv}}(S) = \Pr\left[K \leftarrow \mathcal{K} : A^{\mathcal{E}_K(\cdot)} = 1\right] - \Pr\left[K \leftarrow \mathcal{K} : A^{\mathcal{E}_K(\$^{|\cdot|})} = 1\right].$$

In the first experiment the oracle, given M, returns a random encryption of M under K, while in the second experiment it returns a random encryption of a random string of length $|M|$. Define $\mathrm{Adv}_S^{\mathrm{priv}}(t, q, \mu)$ to be $\max_A\{\mathrm{Adv}_S^{\mathrm{priv}}(A)\}$ where the maximum is over all adversaries who run in time at most t and ask at most q oracle queries, these totaling at most μ bits.

EXAMPLES. Common methods of symmetric encryption using a block cipher are parsimonious. For example, CBC-mode encryption with a random IV is parsimonious. Its domain is $\mathcal{M} = (\{0,1\}^n)^+$, where n is the blocklength of the underlying block cipher. The domain for CBC-mode encryption is easily enlarged to $\mathcal{M} = \{0,1\}^*$; for example, if the last "block" M_m of plaintext has length less

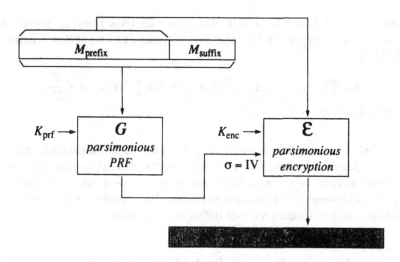

Fig. 2. *A general description of VIL mode. The ciphertext is $\sigma \parallel C_{\text{prefix}}$. The value σ is the output of the PRF G, the IV to the encryption scheme, and the first n bits of ciphertext.*

than the blocklength n then encrypt it as $C_m = E_K(C_{m-1})[1..|M_m|] \oplus M_m$. Alternatively, counter-mode encryption (with a random initial counter) is parsimonious and has domain $\{0,1\}^*$. This was the choice for Stage 2 in our example scheme of Section 2. The security of CBC-mode and counter-mode encryption are established in [3].

VIL: GENERAL SCHEME. We are now ready to give the general description of VIL mode. Let $\mathcal{M}'$ be a message space, let $n \geq 1$ be a number, and let $\mathcal{M} = \mathcal{M}'\{0,1\}^n$ (strings n-bits longer than strings in $\mathcal{M}$). Let $G : \mathcal{K}_{\text{prf}} \times \mathcal{M} \to \{0,1\}^n$ be a parsimonious PRF, and let $\text{Recover} : \mathcal{K}_{\text{enc}} \times \mathcal{M}' \times \{0,1\}^n \to \{0,1\}^n$ be its associated recovery algorithm. Let $\mathsf{S} = (\mathcal{K}, \mathcal{E}, \mathcal{D})$ be a parsimonious encryption scheme in which $\mathcal{E} : \mathcal{K}_{\text{enc}} \times \mathcal{M}' \to \mathcal{M}$. Then we construct the cipher $F = \text{VIL}[G, \mathsf{S}]$, where $F : \mathcal{K} \times \mathcal{M} \to \mathcal{M}$, by setting $\mathcal{K} = \mathcal{K}_{\text{prf}} \times \mathcal{K}_{\text{enc}}$ and defining:

Algorithm $F_{K_{\text{prf}} \parallel K_{\text{enc}}}(M)$	**Algorithm** $F^{-1}_{K_{\text{prf}} \parallel K_{\text{enc}}}(C)$
$M_{\text{prefix}} = M[1..|M| - n]$	σ be the first n bits of C
$\sigma = G_{K_{\text{prf}}}(M)$	$M_{\text{prefix}} = \mathcal{D}_{K_{\text{enc}}}(C)$
$C_{\text{prefix}} = \mathcal{E}_{K_{\text{enc}}}(M_{\text{prefix}}; \sigma)$	$M_{\text{suffix}} = \text{Recover}_{K_{\text{prf}}}(M_{\text{prefix}}, \sigma)$
return $C = \sigma \parallel C_{\text{prefix}}$	return $M = M_{\text{prefix}} \parallel M_{\text{suffix}}$

For a picture of the general scheme, see the Fig. 2.

4 Analysis

The following theorem says that F as constructed above is a secure variable-input-length cipher, as long as both G and S are secure.

Theorem 1. *Let $F = \text{VIL}[G, S]$ be the cipher obtained from the parsimonious PRF $G : \mathcal{K}_{\text{prf}} \times \mathcal{M} \to \{0,1\}^n$ and the parsimonous encryption scheme $S = (\mathcal{K}, \mathcal{E}, \mathcal{D})$. Then*

$$\text{Adv}_F^{\text{prp}}(t, q, \mu) \leq \text{Adv}_G^{\text{prf}}(t', q, \mu) + \text{Adv}_S^{\text{priv}}(t', q, \mu) + \frac{q^2}{2^n},$$

where $t' = t + O(qn + \mu)$.

PROOF. Let A be an adversary attacking F, and let t be its running time, q the number of queries it makes, and μ the total length of all its queries put together. We assume without loss of generality that A never repeats an oracle query. This is important to some of the claims made below. We consider various probabilities related to running A under various different experiments:

$$p_1 = \Pr[K \leftarrow \mathcal{K} : A^{F_K(\cdot)} = 1]$$
$$p_2 = \Pr[K_{\text{enc}} \leftarrow \mathcal{K}_{\text{enc}} \, ; \, g \leftarrow \text{Rand}(\mathcal{M}, n) : A^{\mathcal{E}_{K_{\text{enc}}}((\cdot)_{\text{prefix}}; g(\cdot))} = 1]$$
$$p_3 = \Pr[K_{\text{enc}} \leftarrow \mathcal{K}_{\text{enc}} \, ; \, A^{\mathcal{E}_{K_{\text{enc}}}((\cdot)_{\text{prefix}})} = 1]$$
$$p_4 = \Pr[K_{\text{enc}} \leftarrow \mathcal{K}_{\text{enc}} \, ; \, A^{\mathcal{E}_{K_{\text{enc}}}(\$^{|(\cdot)_{\text{prefix}}|})} = 1]$$
$$p_5 = \Pr[\pi \leftarrow \text{Perm}(\mathcal{M}) : A^{\pi(\cdot)} = 1]$$

Let us explain the new notation. In the experiment defining p_2, A's oracle, on query M, responds by encrypting the first $|M| - n$ bits of M using coins $IV = g(M)$. In the experiment defining p_3, A's oracle, on query M, responds by randomly encrypting the first $|M| - n$ bits of M. In the experiment defining p_4, A's oracle, on query M, responds by randomly encrypting a string of $|M| - n$ random bits.

Our goal is to upper bound $\text{Adv}_F^{\text{prp}}(A) = p_1 - p_5$. We do this in steps.

Claim. $p_1 - p_2 \leq \text{Adv}_G^{\text{prf}}(t', q, \mu)$.

Proof. Consider the following distinguisher D for G. It has an oracle for $g: \mathcal{M} \to \{0,1\}^n$. It picks $K_{\text{enc}} \leftarrow \mathcal{K}_{\text{enc}}$. It runs A, and when A makes oracle query M it returns $\mathcal{E}_{K_{\text{enc}}}(M_{\text{prefix}}; g(M))$ to A as the answer (where M_{prefix} is the first $|M| - n$ bits of M.) Finally D outputs whatever A outputs. Then

$$\Pr[K_{\text{prf}} \leftarrow \mathcal{K}_{\text{prf}} : D^{G_{K_{\text{prf}}}(\cdot)} = 1] = p_1$$
$$\Pr[g \leftarrow \text{Rand}(\mathcal{M}, n) : D^{g(\cdot)} = 1] = p_2$$

So $\text{Adv}_G^{\text{prf}}(D) = p_1 - p_2$. The claim follows.

Claim. $p_2 = p_3$.

Proof. The only difference between the experiment underlying p_2 and that underlying p_3 is that in the former, the IV used for encryption is a random function of M, while in the latter it is chosen at random by the encryption algorithm. These are the same as long as all the oracle queries are different, which is what we assumed about A.

Claim. $p_3 - p_4 \leq \text{Adv}_S^{\text{priv}}(t', q, \mu)$.

Proof. Consider the following adversary B for S that is given an oracle $\mathcal{O}$. It runs A, and when A makes oracle query M it returns $\mathcal{O}(M_{\text{prefix}})$ to A as the answer (where M_{prefix} is the first $|M| - n$ bits of M). Finally D outputs whatever A outputs. Then

$$\Pr[K_{\text{enc}} \leftarrow \mathcal{K}_{\text{enc}} : B^{\mathcal{E}_{K_{\text{enc}}}(\cdot)} = 1] = p_3$$
$$\Pr[K_{\text{enc}} \leftarrow \mathcal{K}_{\text{enc}} : B^{\mathcal{E}_{K_{\text{enc}}}(\$^{|\cdot|})} = 1] = p_4 .$$

So $\text{Adv}_B^{\text{priv}}(S) = p_3 - p_4$. The claim follows.

Claim. $p_4 - p_5 \leq q^2/2^n$.

Proof. Let $r = \Pr[h \leftarrow \text{Rand}(\mathcal{M}) : A^{h(\cdot)} = 1]$. We argue that $p_4 - r \leq q^2/2^{n+1}$ and also $r - p_5 \leq q^2/2^{n+1}$. The claim follows by the triangle inequality. It remains to prove the two subclaims.

The second subclaim, that $r - p_5 \leq q^2/2^{n+1}$, is of course clear; the statistical distance between a family of functions and a family of permutations is given by the collision probability under q queries. So consider the first subclaim, namely $p_4 - r \leq q^2/2^{n+1}$. This is true because the encryption scheme is parsimonious. The IV is chosen at random, and for each fixed IV, the map $\mathcal{E}_{K_{\text{enc}}}((\cdot)_{\text{prefix}}; IV)$ is a permutation on $\mathcal{M}$. Thus, $p_4 - r$ is the statistical distance between a family of permutations on $\mathcal{M}$ and a family of random functions on $\mathcal{M}$, which is again $q^2/2^{n+1}$ because all strings in $\mathcal{M}$ have length at least n.

Given these claims, we can complete the proof of the theorem by noting that

$$\text{Adv}_F^{\text{prp}}(A) = p_1 - p_5 = (p_1 - p_2) + (p_2 - p_3) + (p_3 - p_4) + (p_4 - p_5) . \quad \blacksquare$$

5 Comments and Open Problems

Our security bound for VIL mode enciphering degrades with q^2, as do the bounds for other common modes of operation. It would be interesting to find a method and analysis which had better quantitative security.

It would be desirable to have a good constructions for a *super* variable-input-length cipher (again, starting with a block cipher). Following [10], a super pseudorandom cipher F is one for which no reasonable adversary can do well at distinguishing a pair of oracles $(F_K(\cdot), F_K^{-1}(\cdot))$, for a random $K \in \mathcal{K}$, from a pair of oracles $(\pi(\cdot), \pi^{-1}(\cdot))$, for a random permutation $\pi(\cdot)$. This question has been investigated by Bleichenbacher and Desai, who point out that our VIL construction is not a super variable-input-length cipher, and they propose a construction for such a cipher [5].

We have focussed on the case in which the message length is at least the blocklength n of the underlying block cipher. For shorter messages of even length 2ℓ one can proceed as follows. First map the underlying enciphering key K into subkeys $(K_{\text{enc}}, K_{\text{prf}}, K_1, K_2, \ldots, K_\ell)$ using standard key-separation techniques.

Now when $|M| \geq n$, proceed according to VIL mode, using keys K_{enc} and K_{prf}. But when $|M| < n$ encipher M using an r-round Feistel network, keying the block-cipher-derived round function by $K_{|M|/2}$. We point out that while such an approach may work well in practice, the bounds one gets following [10] and its follow-on work will be very weak for our purposes, since these bounds degrade as the blocklength shrinks and we are here imagining a blocklength of just a few bits. Thus enciphering very short messages in a provably-good way remains open.

When this paper was presented at FSE '99, Mike Matyas described an alternative construction to encipher a message M: first, CBC-encrypt M (with zero IV) to get a ciphertext N; and then, to generate the ciphertext C, CBC-encrypt N, but starting from the its last black and working back towards the first block. A similar scheme is given in [8]. Ciphertext stealing can be used to handle inputs of length not a multiple of the blocklength. This sort of "forward-then-backwards" CBC sounds like an elegant approach, and it would be interesting to know if some version of it can be proven secure.

Acknowledgments

Many thanks to the anonymous reviewers of FSE'99, whose comments significantly improved our presentation. And thanks to Stefan Lucks and Ron Rivest for their comments on an earlier version of this work.

Mihir Bellare was supported by NSF CAREER Award CCR-9624439 and a Packard Foundation Fellowship in Science and Engineering. Phillip Rogaway was supported by NSF CAREER Award CCR-962540, and MICRO grants 97-150 and 98-129, funded by RSA Data Security, Inc., and ORINCON Corporation. Much of Phil's work on this paper was carried out while on sabbatical at Chiang Mai University, Thailand, hosted by the Computer Service Center, under Prof. Krisorn Jittorntrum and Prof. Darunee Smawatakul.

References

1. R. ANDERSON AND E. BIHAM, "Two practical and provably secure block ciphers: BEAR and LION." *Proceedings of the 3rd Fast Software Encryption Workshop*, Lecture Notes in Computer Science Vol. 1039, Springer-Verlag, 1996.

2. M. BELLARE AND P. ROGAWAY, "Block cipher mode of operation for secure, length-preserving encryption." US Patent #5,673,319, September 30, 1997. Filed February 6, 1995.

3. M. BELLARE, A. DESAI, E. JOKIPII AND P. ROGAWAY, "A concrete security treatment of symmetric encryption." *Proceedings of the 38th Symposium on Foundations of Computer Science*, IEEE, 1997.

4. M. BELLARE, J. KILIAN AND P. ROGAWAY, "The security of cipher block chaining." *Advances in Cryptology – Crypto 94 Proceedings*, Lecture Notes in Computer Science Vol. 839, Y. Desmedt ed., Springer-Verlag, 1994.

5. D. BLEICHENBACHER AND A. DESAI, "A construction of a super-pseudorandom cipher." Manuscript, February 1999.

6. O. GOLDREICH, S. GOLDWASSER AND S. MICALI, "How to construct random functions." *Journal of the ACM*, Vol. 33, No. 4, 210–217, 1986.

7. S. GOLDWASSER AND S. MICALI, "Probabilistic encryption." *Journal of Computer and System Sciences* Vol. 28, 270-299, April 1984.

8. R. HOUSLEY, "Cryptographic message syntax." S/MIME Working Group of the IETF, Internet Draft `draft-ietf-smime-cms-12.txt`. March 1999.

9. ISO/IEC 9797, "Information technology – Security techniques – Data integrity mechanism using a cryptographic check function employing a block cipher algorithm," International Organization for Standardization, Geneva, Switzerland, 1994 (second edition).

10. M. LUBY AND C. RACKOFF, "How to construct pseudorandom permutations from pseudorandom functions." *SIAM J. Computing*, Vol. 17, No. 2, April 1988.

11. S. LUCKS, "Faster Luby-Rackoff ciphers." *Proceedings of the 3rd Fast Software Encryption Workshop*, Lecture Notes in Computer Science Vol. 1039, Springer-Verlag, 1996.

12. U. MAURER, "A simplified and generalized treatment of Luby-Rackoff pseudorandom permutation generators." *Advances in Cryptology – Eurocrypt 92 Proceedings*, Lecture Notes in Computer Science Vol. 658, R. Rueppel ed., Springer-Verlag, 1992, pp. 239–255.

13. C. MEYER AND M. MATYAS, *Cryptography: A New Dimension in Data Security*. John Wiley & Sons, New York, 1982.

14. S. MICALI, C. RACKOFF AND R. SLOAN, "The notion of security for probabilistic cryptosystems." *SIAM J. Computing*, Vol. 17, No. 2, April 1988.

15. M. NAOR AND O. REINGOLD, "On the construction of pseudorandom permutations: Luby-Rackoff revisited." *Proceedings of the 29th Annual Symposium on Theory of Computing*, ACM, 1997.

16. National Bureau of Standards, FIPS PUB 46, "Data encryption standard." U.S. Department of Commerce, January 1977.

17. National Bureau of Standards, FIPS PUB 81, "DES modes of operation." U.S. Department of Commerce, December 1980.

18. S. PATEL, Z. RAMZAN AND G. SUNDARAM, "Towards making Luby-Rackoff ciphers optimal and practical." *Proceedings of the 6th Fast Software Encryption Workshop*, 1999.

19. J. PATARIN, "Improved security bounds for pseudorandom permutations." *Proceedings of the Fourth Annual Conference on Computer and Communications Security*, ACM, 1997.

20. J. PATARIN, "About Feistel schemes with six (or more) rounds." *Proceedings of the 5th Fast Software Encryption Workshop*, Lecture Notes in Computer Science Vol. 1372, Springer-Verlag, 1998.

21. E. PETRANK AND C. RACKOFF, "CBC MAC for real-time data sources." Manuscript, available at `http://philby.ucsd.edu/cryptolib.html`, 1997.

22. J. PIEPRZYK, "How to construct pseudorandom permutations from single pseudorandom functions." *Advances in Cryptology – Eurocrypt 90 Proceedings*, Lecture Notes in Computer Science Vol. 473, I. Damgård ed., Springer-Verlag, 1990 pp. 140–150.

23. R. RIVEST, "All-or-nothing encryption and the package transform." *Proceedings of the 4th Fast Software Encryption Workshop*, Lecture Notes in Computer Science Vol. 1267, Springer-Verlag, 1997.

24. D. Wagner, B. Schneier and J. Kelsey, "Cryptanalysis of the cellular message encryption algorithm." *Advances in Cryptology – Crypto 97 Proceedings*, Lec-

ture Notes in Computer Science Vol. 1294, B. Kaliski ed., Springer-Verlag, 1997, pp. 526–537.

25. Y. ZHENG, T. MATSUMOTO AND H. IMAI, "Impossibility results and optimality results on constructing pseudorandom permutations." *Advances in Cryptology – Eurocrypt 89 Proceedings*, Lecture Notes in Computer Science Vol. 434, J-J. Quisquater, J. Vandewille ed., Springer-Verlag, 1989.

Slide Attacks

Alex Biryukov*   David Wagner**

Abstract. It is a general belief among the designers of block-ciphers that even a relatively weak cipher may become very strong if its number of rounds is made very large. In this paper we describe a new generic known- (or sometimes chosen-) plaintext attack on product ciphers, which we call the *slide attack* and which in many cases is independent of the number of rounds of a cipher. We illustrate the power of this new tool by giving practical attacks on several recently designed ciphers: TREYFER, WAKE-ROFB, and variants of DES and Blowfish.

1 Introduction

As the speed of computers grows, fast block ciphers tend to use more and more rounds, rendering all currently known cryptanalytic techniques useless. This is mainly due to the fact that such popular tools as differential [1] and linear analysis [13] are statistic attacks that excel in pushing statistical irregularities and biases through surprisingly many rounds of a cipher. However any such approach finally reaches its limits, since each additional round requires an exponential effort from the attacker.

This tendency towards a higher number of rounds can be illustrated if one looks at the candidates submitted to the AES contest. Even though one of the main criteria of the AES was speed, several prospective candidates (and not the slowest ones) have really large numbers of rounds: RC6(20), MARS(32), SERPENT(32), CAST(48). This tendency is a reflection of a belief/empirical evidence that after some high number of rounds even a relatively weak cipher becomes very strong. It is supported by the example of DES, where breaking even 16 rounds is already a very hard task, to say nothing about 32–48 rounds (e.g. double- or triple-DES). Thus for the cryptanalyst it becomes natural to search for new tools which are essentially independent of the number of rounds of a cipher. The first step in this direction can be dated back to a 1978 paper by Grossman and Tuckerman [9], which has shown how to break a weakened Feistel cipher[3] by a chosen plaintext attack, independent of the number of rounds. We were also inspired by Biham's work on related-key cryptanalysis [2], and Knudsen's early work [12].

---

* Applied Mathematics Department, Technion - Israel Institute of Technology, Haifa, Israel 32000. Email: albi@cs.technion.ac.il
** University of California, Berkeley. Email: daw@cs.berkeley.edu
[3] An 8-round Feistel cipher with eight bits of key material per round used to swap between two S-boxes S_0 and S_1 in a Lucifer-like manner. A really weak cipher by modern criteria.

In this paper we introduce a new class of generic attacks which we call *slide attacks* together with a new set of cryptanalytic tools applicable to all product (mainly iterative) ciphers and even to any iterative (or recursive) process over the finite domain (stream ciphers, etc.). Such attacks apply as soon as the iterative process exhibits some degree of self-similarity and are in many cases independent of the exact properties of the iterated round function and of the number of rounds.

While the two other generic cryptanalytic attacks—differential and linear analysis—concentrate mainly on the propagation properties of the encryption engine (assuming a strong key-scheduling which produces independent subkeys), the degree of self-similarity of a cipher as studied by slide attacks is a totally different aspect. Depending on the cipher's design, slide attacks range from exploiting key-scheduling weaknesses to exploiting more general structural properties of a cipher. The most obvious version of this attack is usually easy to prevent by destroying the self-similarity of an iterative process, for example by adding iteration counters or fixed random constants. However more sophisticated variants of this technique are harder to analyze and to defend against.

We start by analyzing several block ciphers that decompose into r iterations of a single key-dependent permutation F_i. We call such ciphers *homogeneous*. This usually arises when the key-schedule produces a periodic subkey sequence, when $F_i = F_j$ for all $i \equiv j \mod p$ where p represents the period. In the simplest case, $p = 1$ and all round subkeys are the same. We call these attacks *self-related key attacks*, since they are essentially a special case of related-key attacks [2]. Note, however, that our attacks require only a known- (or sometimes chosen-) plaintext assumption and thus are much more practical than most related key attacks[4]. For the case of block ciphers operating on a n-bit block, the complexity of slide attacks (if they work) is usually close to $O(2^{n/2})$ known plaintexts. For Feistel ciphers where the round function F_j modifies only half of the block, there is also a chosen-plaintext variant which can often cut the complexity down to $O(2^{n/4})$ chosen texts.

A somewhat less expected observation is that schemes relying on key-dependent S-boxes are also vulnerable to sliding. In general, autokey ciphers and data-dependent transformations are potentially vulnerable to such attacks. We summarize our results in Table 1.

This paper is organized as follows. In Section 2, we describe the details of a typical slide attack, and in Section 3 we show how the attacks can be optimized for Feistel ciphers. We then proceed with an introductory example: a 96-bit DES variant with 64-rounds, which we call 2K-DES, Section 4. The next two sections are devoted to cryptanalysis of several concrete cipher proposals: Section 5 breaks TREYFER, a cipher published in *FSE'97*, and Section 6 analyzes stream cipher proposals based on WAKE presented at *FSE'97* and *FSE'98*. Finally, Section 7 shows slide attacks on ciphers with key-dependent S-boxes, focusing on a variant of Blowfish with zero round subkeys.

---

[4] However, Knudsen's early work on LOKI91 [12] showed how to use a related-key-type weakness to reduce the cost of exhaustive keysearch using only chosen plaintexts.

Cipher	(Rounds)	Key Bits	Our Attack	
			Data Complexity	Time Complexity
Blowfish[1]	(16)	448	2^{27}CP	2^{27}
Treyfer	(32)	64	2^{32}KP	2^{44}
2K-DES	(64)	96	2^{33}ACP	2^{33}
2K-DES	(64)	96	2^{32}KP	2^{50}
WAKE-ROFB	(k)	$32n$	2^{32}CR	2^{32}

[1] – Modified variant, without round subkeys. KP — known-plaintext, CP — chosen-plaintext, ACP — adaptive chosen-plaintext, CR — chosen-resynchronization (IV).

Table 1. Summary of our attacks on various ciphers.

2 A Typical Slide Attack

In Figure 1, we show the process of encrypting the n-bit plaintext X_0 under a typical product cipher to obtain the ciphertext X_r. Here X_j denotes the intermediate value of the block after j rounds of encryption, so that $X_j = F_j(X_{j-1}, k_j)$. For the sake of clarity, we often omit k by writing $F(x)$ or $F_i(x)$ instead of $F(x, k)$ or $F_i(x, k)$.

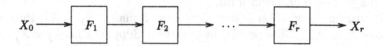

Fig. 1. A typical block cipher

As we mentioned before, the attack presented in this note is independent of the number of rounds of the cipher, since it views a cipher as a product of identical permutations $F(x, k)$, where k is a fixed secret key (here F might include more than one round of the cipher). Moreover its dependence on the particular structure of F is marginal. The only requirement on F is that it is very weak against known-plaintext attack with two plaintext-ciphertext pairs. More specifically, we call F a **weak** permutation if given the two equations $F(x_1, k) = y_1$ and $F(x_2, k) = y_2$ it is "easy" to extract the key k. This is informal definition since the amount of *easiness* may vary from cipher to cipher. We can show that 3 rounds of DES form a weak permutation[5]. One and a half round IDEA is also weak.

---

[5] For F = three rounds of DES, with DES keyschedule one may consider 4-bit output of specific S-box at the 1st and 3rd rounds. This gives a 4-bit condition on the 6 key bits entering this S-box at the 1st and on 6 bits entering this S-box at the 3rd round. Using similar observations it is possible to extract the full DES 56-bit key in time faster than that of one DES encryption.

We next show in Figure 2 how a slide attack against such a cipher might proceed. The idea is to "slide" one copy of the encryption process against another copy of the encryption process, so that the two processes are one round out of phase. We let X_0 and X_0' denote the two plaintexts, with $X_j = F_j(X_{j-1})$ and $X_j' = F_j(X_{j-1}')$. With this notation, we line up X_1 next to X_0', and X_{j+1} next to X_j'.

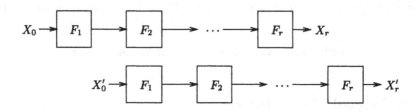

Fig. 2. A typical slide attack

Next, we suppose that $F_j = F_{j+1}$ for all $j \geq 1$; this is the assumption required to make the slide attack work. In this case, all the round functions are the same, so for the remainder of this section we will drop the subscripts and simply write F for the generic round transform.

The crucial observation is that if we have a match $X_1 = X_0'$, then we will also have $X_r = X_{r-1}'$. The proof is by induction. Suppose that $X_j = X_{j-1}'$. Then we may compute $X_{j+1} = F(X_j) = F(X_{j-1}') = F(X_{j-1}') = X_j'$, which completes the proof. Therefore, we call a pair (P, C), (P', C') of known plaintexts (with corresponding ciphertexts) a **slid pair** if $F(P) = P'$ and $F(C) = C'$.

With this observation in hand, the attack proceeds as follows. We obtain $2^{n/2}$ known texts (P_i, C_i), and we look for slid pairs. By the birthday paradox, we expect to find about one pair of indices i, i' where $F(P_i) = P_{i'}$, which gives us a slid pair.

Furthermore, slid pairs can often be recognized relatively easily. In general, we recognize slid pairs by checking whether it is possible that $F(P_i) = P_{i'}$ and $F(C_i) = C_{i'}$ both hold for some key. When the round function is *weak*, we are assured that this condition will be easy to recognize. Once we have found a slid pair, we expect to be able to recover some key bits of the cipher. If the round function is *weak*, we can in fact recover the entire key with not too much work. In general, we expect a single slid pair to disclose about n bits of key material; when the cipher's key length is longer than n bits, we may use exhaustive search to recover the remainder of the key, or we may alternatively obtain a few more slid pairs and use them to learn the rest of the key material.

Let us summarize the attack. For a cipher with n-bit blocks and repeating round subkeys, we need about $O(2^{n/2})$ known plaintexts to recover the unknown key. While a naive approach will require $O(2^n)$ work, much faster attacks are usually possible by exploiting the weaknesses in the F function. This technique applies to a very wide class of round functions.

3 Slide Attacks on Feistel Ciphers

In this section, we show how the slide attack can be optimized when it is applied to a Feistel cipher.

KNOWN-PLAINTEXT ATTACKS. In the case of Feistel ciphers, the round function $F((l, r)) = (r \oplus f(l), l)$ modifies only half of its input. Therefore, the condition $F(x) = x'$ can be recognized by simply comparing the left half of x against the right half of x', and this filtering condition eliminates all but $2^{-n/2}$ of the wrong pairs.

This improved filtering allows us to reduce the time complexity of attack under the known-plaintext threat model to $2^{n/2}$ known texts and $2^{n/2}$ offline work. We have a n-bit filtering condition on the potential slid pairs, for if (P_i, C_i) forms a slid pair with (P'_j, C'_j) then we have $F(P_i) = P'_j$ and $F(C_i) = C'_j$. Therefore, potential slid pairs can be identified using a lookup table (or sorted list) with $2^{n/2}$ entries: we sort the known text (P_i, C_i) based on the left halves of P_i and C_i, and for each j we look for a match with the right halves of P'_j and C'_j.

With this technique, we expect to find one good slid pair along with only one false alarm; false matches can be easily eliminated in a second phase. The slid pair gives us about n bits of information on the key; if this does not reveal all of the key material, we can look for a few more slid pairs or search over the remaining unknown key bits.

CHOSEN-PLAINTEXT ATTACKS. For Feistel ciphers, the data complexity can be reduced further to about $2^{n/4}$ texts when chosen plaintext queries are available. The key to the reduction in texts is the use of carefully-chosen structures. (This technique was first pioneered by Biham in his work on related-key cryptanalysis [2].) Fix an arbitrary $n/2$-bit value x. We choose a pool of $2^{n/4}$ plaintexts $P_i = (x, y_i)$ by varying over $2^{n/4}$ random values for y, and then choose a second pool of $2^{n/4}$ texts of the form $P'_j = (y'_j, x)$ by varying over another $2^{n/4}$ random choices for y'_j. This provides $2^{n/2}$ pairs of plaintexts, and a right pair occurs with probability $2^{-n/2}$ (namely, when $f(x) = y_i \oplus y'_j$), so we expect to find about one slid pair. This slid pair can be recognized using the $n/2$-bit filtering condition on the ciphertexts, and then we can use it to recover n bits of key material as before[6].

PROBABLE-PLAINTEXT ATTACKS. When plaintexts contain some redundancy, the data complexity of a known-plaintext slide attack can often be significantly reduced. Our techniques are derived from Biryukov and Kushilevitz's recent work on exploiting such plaintext redundancy in differential attack [4].

---

[6] Notice that if we deal with an unbalanced Feistel cipher, the effect of a chosen plaintext attack can be even greater. For example for a Skipjack-like construction with the same keyed permutation in all rounds, a chosen plaintext attack with only $2^{n/8}$ time and data is possible.

Consider first a very simple model: the plaintext source emits blocks where the four most significant bits of each byte are always zero, so that the resulting n-bit plaintexts have only $n/2$ bits of entropy. In this case, one can mount a slide attack with about $2^{3n/8}$ ciphertexts, which is midway between the data complexities of chosen-plaintext slide attacks ($2^{n/4}$ texts) and known-plaintext slide attacks ($2^{n/2}$ texts, for uniformly-distributed plaintexts).

The observation is that for any fixed value x that can occur as the left half of a plaintext, we expect to see about $2^{3n/8-n/4} = 2^{n/8}$ plaintexts of the form $P_i = (x, y_i)$, along with another $2^{n/8}$ plaintexts of the form $P_j' = (y_j', x)$. Each x gives about $2^{n/4}$ pairs of texts, and there are $2^{n/4}$ values for x. Assuming f behaves randomly, any such pair gives a $2^{-n/2}$ chance of forming a slid pair, so in total we expect to find about one slid pair among all the $2^{3n/8}$ ciphertexts.

This attack can even be converted to a ciphertext-only attack with a slight increase in complexity. Suppose the condition $f(u) = v, f(u') = v'$ uniquely identifies the key, and key recovery from u, u', v, v' takes $O(1)$ time. Then we can find the key with $2^{3n/8+1}$ ciphertexts and $O(2^{n/2})$ work. First, we note that the $n/2$-bit filtering condition on the ciphertexts gives a set of $2^{n/4+2}$ potential slid pairs, of which about four are correct (the rest are false matches). The list of potential slid pairs can be identified with $O(2^{3n/8})$ steps by hashing or sorting. Next, we make a guess at a correct slid pair C_i, C_j'. Third, for each remaining potential slid pair $C_{i'}, C_{j'}'$, we compute the key value suggested by the equations $F(C_i) = C_{i'}, F(C_j') = C_{j'}'$, and store this n-bit key value in a table. We search for collisions in this table (by hashing or sorting). If our guess at C_i, C_j' indeed gave a correct slid pair, the right key value will be suggested three times. On the other hand, the birthday paradox assures us that wrong key values will be suggested only with negligible probability. This yields an attack that takes $O(2^{n/2})$ time ($2^{n/4}$ guesses at C_i, C_j', performing $O(2^{n/4})$ operations per guess to build the table) and needs $2^{n/4+2}$ space and about $2^{3n/8+1}$ ciphertexts.

Of course, this is only an example. The exact complexity of the probable-plaintext and ciphertext-only slide attacks can vary widely: some plaintext distributions increase the complexity of slide attacks (or even render them impossible), while others reduce the complexity substantially. In general, the expected number of texts needed to find the first slid pair is approximately $2^{n/4}(\sum_x \Pr[r = x] \Pr[l = x])^{-1/2}$ (under heuristic assumptions on f), although the exact details of the attack will depend intimately on the distribution of the plaintexts.

4 Modified DES Example: 2K-DES

The following constitutes in our opinion a nice problem for a student crypto-course or an introductory crypto-textbook. Suppose one proposes to strengthen DES in the following way. One increases the number of rounds from 16 to 64, and extends the number of key-bits from 56 to 96 in the following simple way: given two independent 48-bit keys K_1, K_2 one uses K_1 in the odd rounds and K_2 in the even rounds instead of DES subkeys. This version is obviously immune to exhaustive search. The conventional differential and linear attacks probably will also fail due to the increased number of rounds. The question is: "Is this cipher more secure than DES?" Below we show two attacks on this cipher which use the symmetry of the key-scheduling algorithm and are independent of the number of rounds.

One very simple way to attack such cipher is as follows. For any known plaintext-ciphertext pair (P, C), decrypt ciphertext C one round under all possible 2^{32} outputs from the f function in the last round. For each of the 2^{32} resulting texts C', request the encryption $P' = E_K(C')$. This is equivalent to decryption all way back to the plaintext P and further by one more round to $F^{-1}(P, K_2) = P'$. Since F preserves 32 bits of its input, one can check a 32-bit filtering condition over P, P' to eliminate essentially all of the wrong guesses at C'. When we find a C', P' which survives the filtering condition, we can derive K_2 easily from the equations $F(P', K_2) = P$, $F(C', K_2) = C$ (here F includes the Feistel swap of the halves). This procedure leaves only the correct value of K_2 with high probability. Now K_1 can be found by exhaustive search; or, for a more efficient attack, we can peel off the first round using the known value of K_2, and repeat the attack once more on the resulting cipher to learn K_1. This simple attack uses one known-plaintext (P, C) pair, 2^{33} adaptive chosen plaintexts and 2^{33} time. A similar attack will actually work for any "almost"-symmetric key-scheduling; see also [3] for another example of this type of attack. Notice that if the number of rounds r is odd and key-scheduling is symmetric then double encryption with such a Feistel-cipher becomes an identity permutation.

This attack can be improved using the ideas of the present paper. By applying slide techniques, we can show that this cipher is much weaker than one would expect even when its number of rounds r is arbitrarily large, and that attacks are available even under the more practical known-plaintext threat model. For any fixed value of K_1, K_2 this cipher can be viewed as a cascade of $\frac{r}{2}$ identical fixed permutations. Thus given a pool of 2^{32} known plaintexts, one can recover all 96 bits of the secret key just by checking all the possible pairs in about $2^{63}/64 = 2^{57}$ naive steps (each step is equivalent to one 2K-DES encryption operation). Each pair of plaintexts (P, P^*) suggests 2^{16} candidates for K_1 and 2^{16} candidates for K_2 which are immediately checked against a pair of corresponding ciphertexts (C, C^*). Thus on the average after this process we are left with a few candidate 96-bit keys which can be further checked with trial encryption. Using a more sophisticated approach (ruling out many pairs simultaneously) it is possible to reduce the work factor considerably. For each plaintext we guess the left 24 bits of K_1, which allows us to calculate 16-bits of the S-box output and thus 16-bits of the possible related plaintext and 16-bits of related ciphertext. This gives a 32-bit condition on the possible related plaintext/ciphertext pair; then analyzing the pool of texts will take a total of $2^{24} \times 2^{32}/64 = 2^{50}$ steps.

5 TREYFER

In this section we apply slide attacks to cryptanalyze TREYFER, a block-cipher/MAC presented at FSE'97 by Gideon Yuval [10] and aimed at smart-card applications. It is characterized by a simple, extremely compact design (only 29 bytes of code) and a very large number of rounds (32). We show an attack on TREYFER that is independent of the number of rounds and exploits the simplicity of key-schedule of this cipher. It uses 2^{32} known-plaintexts and requires 2^{44} time for analysis.

Description of TREYFER

TREYFER is a 64-bit block cipher/MAC, with a 64-bit key, designed for a very constrained architectures (like a 8051 CPU with 1KB flash EPROM, 64 bytes RAM, 128 bytes EPROM and peak 1MHz instruction rate). The algorithm is as follows:

```
for(r=0; r < NumRounds; r++){
    text[8] = text[0];
    for(i=0; i<8; i++)
      text[i+1] = (text[i+1] + Sbox[(key[i]+text[i])%256])<<< 1;
      //rotate 1 left
    text[0] = text[8];
}
```

Here text is an eight-byte plaintext, key is an eight-byte key, S-box denotes an 8x8-bit S-box chosen at random, and NumRounds stands for 32 rounds. After 32 rounds of encryption text contains eight-byte ciphertexts. One of the motivations behind the design of this cipher was that in spite of the simplicity of the round function a huge number of rounds (32) will make any possible attack impractical.

As an aside (without any connection to our attack), we observe that TREYFER exhibits much weaker diffusion in the decryption direction: it takes two rounds for a one-byte difference to influence all eight bytes in the encryption direction, but it takes seven rounds in the decryption direction.

Our Attack on TREYFER

The idea of our attack is very similar to the related-key attacks [2, 12], however our attack is known-plaintext and not chosen-key like the attacks in [2].

In our attack we use the fact that due to hardware constraints the designers of TREYFER sacrificed a proper key-scheduling to make a more compact and faster cipher. Thus key-scheduling of TREYFER simply uses its 64-bit key K byte by byte. This is done exactly in the same fashion at each round.

However the simplicity of key-schedule causes TREYFER to be a cascade of 32 identical permutations! Thus suppose that two plaintexts P and P^* are encrypted by TREYFER to C and C^*. Denote the intermediate encrypted values after each round by $P_1, \ldots, P_{32}$, where $P_{32} = C$. Denote the round encryption function of TREYFER by F. Now, if two plaintexts are related by a one-round encryption as $F(P, K) = P^*$ then it must be that the same relation holds for the ciphertexts $F(C, K) = C^*$. Due to simplicity of the round function F, given a properly related pair the full 64-bit key K of TREYFER can be derived either from equation $F(P, K) = P^*$ or from equation $F(C, K) = C^*$. If P, P^* is a properly related pair both equations suggest the same value of the key. However if the pair is not properly related there is no reason for the two keys to be equal.

Thus on TREYFER with arbitrary number of rounds and with arbitrarily chosen S-box it is possible to mount an attack with about 2^{32} known plaintexts and in the time of 2^{44} offline TREYFER encryptions (performed on the attacker's computer and not on the slow smart-card processor). Due to the birthday paradox a pool of 2^{32} known plaintexts will contain a properly related pair with high probability. Thus a naive approach is to try all the possible 2^{63} pairs, and each time the two equations $F(P, K) = P^*$ and $F(C, K) = C^*$ suggest the same 64-bit key, check this candidate key with trial encryption. Since for each pair we perform 1/16 of the TREYFER encryption, the overall complexity of this naive attack is 2^{59} TREYFER encryptions, which is still faster than exhaustive search. However we can do better than that if for each plaintext we do $2^{16} = 2^8 \cdot 2^8$ guesses of the two subkeys k[7],k[0]. For each guess we arrive at a 32-bit condition on the possible co-related plaintext. Thus on the average only one out of 2^{32} plaintexts passes the 32-bit condition and it can be easily found in a sorted array of plaintexts. Then the newly formed pair is checked for the version of the full 64-bit key as it was done in a naive approach. The time required by the analysis phase of this attack is equivalent to $2^{16} \cdot 2^{32} \cdot \frac{1}{16} = 2^{44}$ TREYFER encryptions.

Thus we have shown an attack on TREYFER, with 2^{32} known plaintexts, 2^{44} time of analysis and 2^{32} memory. The interesting property of this attack is that it is independent of the number of rounds and of the exact choice of the S-box. This attack seems to be on the verge of practicality, due to very slow smart-card encryption (6.4 msec per block) and very slow communication wire (10KBPS) speed. However this task is easily parallelizable if an attacker obtains many smart-cards containing the same secret key. Once the attacker receives the data, the analysis can be done in a few days on an average computer.

It should be possible to make TREYFER immune to this attack by adding a more complex key-schedule[7].

6 Stream Ciphers, and WAKE-ROFB

It is also possible to mount slide attacks against stream ciphers. We show how to attack the re-synchronization mechanism used in WAKE-ROFB[8] [6], a recent WAKE variant proposed at *FSE'98*. Our attacks work only under restrictive assumptions on the IV selection and re-synchronization mechanism.

---

[7] Following the results of this paper round counters were introduced into the round function of TREYFER, as a counter-measure against such attacks [11].

[8] WAKE-ROFB is a refinement of a design originally proposed at *FSE'97* [5]. In this paper, we analyze only the *FSE'98* scheme; the *FSE'97* cipher's re-synchronization mechanism appears to protect it from slide attacks.

Note that this does not reflect poorly on the core of the WAKE-ROFB design; it merely shows that dealing with re-synchronization can be tricky, because it introduces the possibility of chosen-text attacks. (See also [8, 16, 5, 6].) In short, WAKE-ROFB is not broken. We point out these attacks merely to illustrate the intriguing theoretical possibility of applying slide attacks to stream ciphers.

WAKE-ROFB is a stream cipher with $32n$ bits of internal state, organized into n 32-bit words. The words are updated via a simple analogue of a non-linear feedback shift register, extended to operate on words instead of bits. Writing $R_1, \ldots, R_n$ for the state registers, WAKE-ROFB's state update function is defined as

$$R_1' \leftarrow R_{n-1} + F(R_n); \qquad R_j \leftarrow R_{j-1}; \qquad R_1 \leftarrow R_1'.$$

Here $F : \mathbf{Z}_2^{32} \to \mathbf{Z}_2^{32}$ is a bijective key-dependent nonlinear function. Every k-th time we step the register, we output the value of R_n as the next word of the key-stream. See Figure 3 for a pictorial illustration of the cipher.

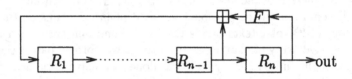

Fig. 3. The WAKE-ROFB stream cipher

The parameters k and n may be varied to suit performance and security needs. However, [6] suggests two concrete proposals: $(n, k) = (5, 8)$ and $(n, k) = (4, 4)$. For the $n = 5$ proposal, a concrete scheme for loading an initialization vector is proposed: the 64-bit IV (A, B) is loaded into the registers as $R_1 = R_4 = R_5 = A, R_2 = R_3 = B$, and then 8 words of output are generated and discarded. For the $n = 4$ proposal, no scheme for loading an IV was suggested.

Note that, to support re-synchronization, WAKE-ROFB is built around a mode of operation that is perhaps somewhat unusual for a stream cipher. Many published stream cipher constructions use a public feedback function and load their initial state from the key, and often no allowance is made for re-synchronization. In contrast, WAKE-ROFB is keyed solely by the choice of the key-dependent permutation F, and the initial state of the register is loaded from a publicly-known IV[9]. Re-synchronization in WAKE-ROFB is easily accomplished by choosing a new IV.

The main observation is that this construction can be viewed as roughly an unbalanced Feistel cipher (with round function F) that outputs one word

---

[9] But note that slide attacks do not always require knowledge of the initial state of the register. For instance, some of our attacks would still be possible even if the construction were modified to load the initial state of the register as e.g. the Triple-DES-CBC decryption of the IV under some additional keying material.

every k rounds. From this viewpoint, there is no round-dependence in the round transformation. Since Feistel ciphers with no round-dependence are susceptible to slide attacks, it seems natural to suspect that slide attacks may also prove useful against the WAKE-ROFB stream cipher. This is indeed the case.

First, as a warmup exercise, we note that when the attacker has full control over the initial state of the stream cipher, simple slide attacks are often available. The attack is the same as a chosen-plaintext slide attack on a Feistel cipher with constant round subkeys. We fix $r_1, \ldots, r_{n-1}$, and generate 2^{16} IV's of the form $IV_X = (r_1, \ldots, r_{n-1}, X)$ by varying X. We also generate 2^{16} IV's of the form $IV_Y = (Y, r_1, \ldots, r_{n-1})$ by varying Y. Note that if $r_{n-1} + F(X) = Y$, we will have a successful slide relation between the key-stream generated by IV_X and the key-stream generated by IV_Y. For such X, Y, the resulting internal states will be closely related: if we let $S_\alpha[t] = (R_{1,\alpha}[t], \ldots, R_{n,\alpha}[t])$ be the 32n-bit state generated from IV_α by stepping the cipher t times, then $S_Y[t] = S_X[t+1]$ for all t.

In many cases, this condition can be easily recognized, because the key-streams will be highly related to each other. For instance, for the $(n, k) = (4, 4)$ proposal, if we know the key-stream outputs from IV_X at times $jk, (j+1)k$ and the key-stream output from IV_Y at time jk, we can deduce one input-output pair for the F function for each time step; this property allows us to easily recognize slid pairs with about 8 known outputs for the F proposed in [6][10]. Analysis is apparently more difficult when $\gcd(n, k) = 1$, but attacks are still available (albeit with increased data requirements) by choosing $n \cdot 2^{32}$ IV's of the form $(Y, \ldots, Y, r, \ldots, r)$; the crucial observation is that $(r, \ldots, r)$ forms a slid pair with $(F(r)+r, r, \ldots, r)$, which forms a slid pair with $(F(r)+r, F(r)+r, r, \ldots, r)$, and so on.

We conclude that a slide attack may be possible with as few as 2^{17} streams (each containing at least 8 known outputs), when the attacker has full control over the initial state of the register. This situation might occur if, for instance, the IV-loading mechanism simply loaded the initial state of the register directly as the value of a n-word IV, since then an attacker would be able to control the initial state directly with a chosen-IV chosen-ciphertext attack. One corollary is that, to prevent slide attacks, the IV-loading mechanism must be carefully designed. Note that the WAKE-ROFB design precludes these attacks by explicitly specifying a resynchronization mechanism that allows only limited control over the initial state of the cipher.

Even when the attacker has no control over the initial state of the register, known-IV slide attacks may still be possible. By analogy to the standard known-

---

[10] This is because [6] constructs the T table from two 4×16-bit lookup tables, and by the birthday paradox after 7 observations of a 4-bit value we expect to see a collision or two. But even for more sophisticated constructions of the F function, the number of known outputs needed would not increase substantially. With a randomly generated T table, about 40 known outputs would suffice; even if the entire function F were chosen randomly, $2^{16.5}$–$2^{17.5}$ known outputs should be enough to detect slid pairs.

text attacks on block ciphers, we expect to find one successful slide relation after examining about $2^{32n/2}$ known text streams, and in some cases this might enable successful cryptanalysis of the cipher. One simple defense is to increase the size of the internal state enough so that the data requirements become infeasible.

Finally, we consider the concrete IV-loading scheme proposed in [6] for the $(n, k) = (5, 8)$ WAKE-ROFB cipher. There the 64-bit IV (A, B) is loaded into the registers as $(R_1, \ldots, R_5) = (A, B, B, A, A)$, and then 8 words of output are generated and discarded.

We note that a slide attack on this scheme is still possible, when 2^{32} chosen-IV queries are available. We obtain known key-stream output for the 2^{32} IV's of the form (A, A). This loads the initial state of the registers with $(R_1, \ldots, R_5) = (A, \ldots, A)$. Note that when $F(A) = 0$, we will have $R'_1 = A$, and so stepping the initial state $(A, \ldots, A)$ gives the state $(A, \ldots, A)$. In other words, for $A = F^{-1}(0)$, we obtain a cycle of period one. This can be easily recognized from a short stretch of known key-stream output, and allows allows us to obtain 32 bits of information on the key.

It is clear that the design of a secure IV-loading mechanism for WAKE-ROFB-like stream ciphers is non-trivial. Certainly running the cipher for $8k$ time steps and discarding the outputs helps stop some attacks, but as we have shown, it is not always sufficient.

Therefore, we propose the following design principle for such stream ciphers[11]:

> Whenever possible, the feedback function should
> include some form of round-dependence.

7 Key-Dependent S-boxes: A Variant of Blowfish

The following was inspired by a paper due to Grossman and Tuckerman [9] from 1978. In this section we show by using a more modern techniques that if the only strength of a cipher comes from key-dependent S-boxes (with no round dependence) then such cipher can be attacked easily using slide attacks. This shows that slide attacks are not restricted to ciphers with weak key-scheduling algorithms.

For an example of how this might work consider a cipher called Blowfish, which was designed by Bruce Schneier [14]. This is a Feistel cipher with 64-bit block, 16 rounds and up to 448 bits of the secret key. These are expanded into a table consisting of four S-boxes from 8 to 32 bits (4096 bytes total). S-boxes are key-dependent and unknown to the attacker. Also in each round a 32-bit subkey P_i is xored to one of the inputs. At the end two 32-bit subkeys P_{17} and P_{18} are xored to the output of a cipher. See Figure 4 for a picture of one round of Blowfish. So far no attacks are known on a full version of this cipher.

---

[11] Following the results of this paper, round counters were introduced into the resynchronization mechanism of WAKE-ROFB as a counter-measure against such attacks [7].

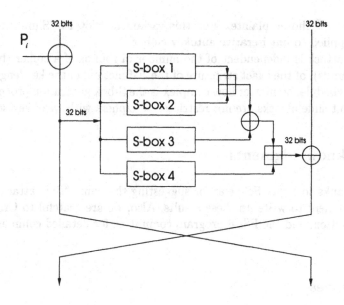

Fig. 4. One round of Blowfish.

The best previous result [15] is a differential attack on Blowfish with known S-boxes which can find the P_i array using 2^{8r+1} chosen plaintexts, where r stands for the number of rounds. For certain weak keys that generate bad S-boxes (1 out 2^{14} keys) the same attack requires 2^{4r+1} chosen plaintexts (still completely ineffective against 16-round Blowfish).

Assume that all the P_i's are equal to zero. In this case one may notice that all rounds of a cipher perform the same transformation which is data-dependent. Thus given a 32-bit input to the F-function the output of the F function is uniquely determined. Also only 16 bytes out of 4096 take part in each evaluation of the F-function. Thus one naive approach will be to fix a plaintext P, guess all these 128-bits of the key and partially encrypt P with the guessed keys one Feistel-round, and then perform a slide attack for P and for the guessed text. A less naive approach is to guess the 32-bit output of the F-function and thus obtain a correct encryption with one Feistel round in 2^{32} steps, checking if the guess was correct with a usual sliding technique. An even better approach is to encrypt two pools of chosen plaintexts (X, P_R) and (P_R, Y), where X and Y both receive 2^{16} random values and P_R is fixed. Thus with high probability there is an element (P_R, Y_i) in the second pool which is an exact one-round encryption of some element (X_j, P_R) from the first pool. Such pair can be easily detected by sliding considerations (especially if we repeat this experiment with the same value of P_R and other random values of X and Y).

Each slid pair provides us with about 64 bits of key-dependent S-box information (two equations for F-function). Thus with about 500 probes of this type it is possible to find all four S-boxes. Data for this attack can be packed into structures efficiently. Thus we have a very simple slide attack with only about

$2^9 \cdot 2^{18} = 2^{27}$ chosen plaintexts on this variant of Blowfish. Similar techniques can be applied to *any* iterative autokey cipher.

This attack is independent of the number of rounds of a cipher (be it 16 or 16000 rounds), of the exact structure of the F-function, of the key length, and of the key-schedule, no matter how complex is the S-box generation process[12]. This shows that slide attacks are not restricted to ciphers with weak key-scheduling.

8   Acknowledgments

Many thanks to Bruce Schneier for suggesting the name "slide attack", and for encouragement to write up these results. Also, we are grateful to Craig Clapp, Lars Knudsen, and the FSE6 program committee for detailed comments on the paper.

References

1. E. Biham, A. Shamir, *Differential Cryptanalysis of the Data Encryption Standard*, Springer-Verlag, 1993.
2. E. Biham, *New Types of Cryptanalytic Attacks Using Related Keys*, J. of Cryptology, Vol.7, pp.229–246, 1994.
3. E. Biham, A. Biryukov, N. Ferguson, L. R. Knudsen, B. Schneier, A. Shamir, *Cryptanalysis of Magenta*, Second AES Conference, 1999.
4. A. Biryukov, E. Kushilevitz, *From differential cryptanalysis to ciphertext-only attacks*, LNCS 1462, Advances in Cryptology—CRYPTO'98, pp.72–88, Springer-Verlag, 1998.
5. C. Clapp, *Optimizing a Fast Stream Cipher for VLIW, SIMD, and Superscalar Processors*, LNCS 1267, FSE'97 Proceedings, pp.273–287, Springer-Verlag, 1997.
6. C. Clapp, *Joint Hardware / Software Design of a Fast Stream Cipher*, LNCS 1373, FSE'98 Proceedings, pp.75–92, Springer-Verlag, 1998.
7. C. Clapp, *WAKE UPdate*, FSE'99 rump session, 1999.
8. J. Daemen, R. Govaerts, J. Vanderwalle, *Re-synchronization weaknesses in stream ciphers*, LNCS 765, Advances in Cryptology—EUROCRYPT'93, pp.159–169, Springer-Verlag, 1994.
9. E. K. Grossman, B. Tuckerman, *Analysis of a Weakened Feistel-like Cipher*, 1978 International Conference on Communications, pp.46.3.1–46.3.5, Alger Press Limited, 1978.
10. G. Yuval, *Reinventing the Travois: Encryption/MAC in 30 ROM Bytes*, LNCS 1267, FSE'97 Proceedings, pp.205–209, Springer-Verlag, 1997.
11. G. Yuval, *Private communication, August 1998*.
12. L. R. Knudsen, *Cryptanalysis of LOKI91*, LNCS 718, Advances in Cryptology—AUSCRYPT'92, pp.196–208, Springer-Verlag, 1993.
13. M. Matsui, *Linear Cryptanalysis Method of DES Cipher*, LNCS 765, Advances in Cryptology—EUROCRYPT'93, pp.386–397, Springer-Verlag, 1994.

[12] Notice also, that it is possible to find a 448-bit key which will force $P_1, ..., P_{14}$ to be zero; however, $P_{15}, .., P_{18}$ will remain uncontrolled.

14. B. Schneier, *Description of a New Variable-Length Key, 64-Bit Block Cipher (Blowfish)*, LNCS 809, FSE'94 Proceedings, pp.191–204, Springer-Verlag, 1994.
15. S. Vaudenay, *On the Weak Keys in Blowfish*, LNCS 1039, FSE'96 Proceedings, pp.27–32, Springer-Verlag, 1996.
16. D. Wagner, *Cryptanalysis of some recently-proposed multiple modes of operation*, LNCS 1373, FSE'98 Proceedings, pp.254–269, Springer-Verlag, 1998.

On the Security of CS-Cipher

Serge Vaudenay

Ecole Normale Supérieure — CNRS
Serge.Vaudenay@ens.fr

Abstract. CS-Cipher is a block cipher which has been proposed at FSE 1998. It is a Markov cipher in which diffusion is performed by multipermutations. In this paper we first provide a formal treatment for differential, linear and truncated differential cryptanalysis, and we apply it to CS-Cipher in order to prove that there exists no good characteristic for these attacks. This holds under the approximation that all round keys of CS-Cipher are uniformly distributed and independent. For this we introduce some new technique for counting active Sboxes in computational networks by the Floyd-Warshall algorithm.

Since the beginning of modern public research in symmetric encryption, block ciphers are designed with fixed computational networks: we draw a network and put some computation boxes on. The Feistel scheme [13] is a popular design which enables to make an invertible function with a random function. Its main advantage is that decryption and encryption are fairly similar because we only have to reverse the order of operations.

Another popular (and more intuitive) design consists of having a cascade of computational layers, some of which implement parallel invertible transformations. (People inappropriately call it the "SPN structure" as for Substitution Permutation Network, as opposed to Feistel schemes. Referring to Adams' Thesis [3], several Feistel schemes are also SPN ones.) For this we need two different implementations for encryption and decryption. Several such designs have been proposed to the Advanced Encryption Standard process: Serpent, Safer+, Rijndael and Crypton (see [2]). In this paper we focus on CS-Cipher [32] in order to investigate its security.[1]

The main general known attacks are Biham and Shamir's differential cryptanalysis [8] and Matsui's cryptanalysis [23, 24]. Over their variants, Knudsen's truncated differentials [18, 19] have been shown to be powerful against Massey's Safer block cipher [22], so we investigate it as well. In this paper we consider these attacks and we (heuristically) show that CS-Cipher is resistant against it. For this we use the well known active Sboxes counting arguments techniques.

Here we first recall what can be formally proven under the intuitive approximation that all round keys are uniformly distributed and independent for

---

[1] While this paper was presented, the owner of the CS-Cipher algorithm announced a "Challenge CS-Cipher": a 10000 euros award will be given to the first person who will decrypt a message encrypted with a key which has been purposely limited to 56 bits. This is basically an exhaustive search race. See http://www.cie-signaux.fr/.

differential and linear cryptanalysis. We contribute to a new similar analysis of truncated differential cryptanalysis. Then we apply these techniques to CS-Cipher. In particular we show how to count the minimal number of active Sboxes in a computational network with multipermutations by using some easy graph algorithms.

1 Previous Work

Public research on cryptography arose in the late 70s. On block ciphers, research has been paradoxically motivated by the Data Encryption Standard [1] controversial: the fact that the design rationales of DES was kept secret by the US government.

Originally the research community was focusing on the fascinating nonlinear properties of the DES Sboxes (and on the existence of a mythical hidden trapdoor). Nonlinear criterion has been investigated, and the possibility on how to achieve it (see Adams and Tavares [3, 4], Nyberg [27]).

Differential cryptanalysis has been invented by Biham and Shamir in the 90s [7], and a connection between the security against it and the nonlinearity of the Sboxes has been found (see Nyberg [28]). Later on the same link arose with Matsui's linear cryptanalysis [23, 24] (see Nyberg [29] and Chabaud-Vaudenay [9]).

Since then an important effort has been done in order to study the security of block ciphers against differential and linear cryptanalysis.

Lai and Massey first invented the notion of "Markov cipher" which enables to make a formal treatment on the security against differential cryptanalysis (see [21, 20]). This enables to formally prove some heuristic approximations used in this attack.

It was well known that the resistance against differential cryptanalysis depends on the minimal number of "active Sboxes" in a characteristic. (The bulk of Biham and Shamir's attack against DES is to find a characteristic with a number of active Sboxes as small as possible.)

In Heys and Tavares [16, 17] is defined the notion of "diffusion order" which enables to get lower bound on the number of active Sboxes in a substitution-permutation network. Similarly, Daemen [11] talks about "branch number". The question was also addressed by Youssef, Mister and Tavares [40]. These notions can be used together with the diffusion properties of the network. Namely, when we use "multipermutations" (see [33, 34]) we can compute these numbers. In particular, inspired by the notion of multipermutation, Daemen, Knudsen and Rijmen use an MDS code in the Square cipher [12] which has been used for two AES candidates: Rijndael and Crypton [2].

An alternate way to prove the security against differential and linear cryptanalysis is to use the Theorem of Nyberg and Knudsen [30, 31] (or a variant), which has been done by Matsui in the Misty cipher [25, 26]. We can also use the "decorrelation theory" [35–39] which has been used in order to create the Peanut and Coconut cipher families (see [15, 37]) and the DFC cipher [15] which is an AES candidate [2] (see [38, 5]). Both approachs provide provable security against differential and linear cryptanalysis (and not only a heuristic security).

2 Formal Treatment on Markov Ciphers

In this section we consider an r-round cipher

$$\text{Enc}(x) = (\rho_r \circ \ldots \circ \rho_1)(x)$$

in which each ρ_i round uses a subkey k_i. We assume that this is a Markov cipher with respect to the XOR addition law, which means, following Lai [20] that for any round i and any x, a and b, we have

$$\Pr_{k_i}[\rho_i(x \oplus a) \oplus \rho_i(x) = b] = \Pr_{k_i, X}[\rho_i(X \oplus a) \oplus \rho_i(X) = b]$$

where X is uniformly distributed. (Here $\oplus$ denotes the bitwise XOR operation.)

2.1 Preliminaries

For any p-to-q-bit function f, any p-bit a and any q-bit b, let us denote

$$\text{DP}^f(a, b) = \Pr_X[f(X \oplus a) \oplus f(X) = b] \qquad (1)$$

$$\text{LP}^f(a, b) = \left(2 \Pr_X[a \cdot X = b \cdot f(X)] - 1\right)^2. \qquad (2)$$

(Here $a \cdot x$ denotes the dot product of a and x: the sum modulo 2 of all $a_i x_i$.) It is well known that we have

$$\text{LP}^f(a, b) = 2^{-p} \sum_{x, y} (-1)^{(a \cdot x) + (b \cdot y)} \text{DP}^f(x, y) \qquad (3)$$

$$\text{DP}^f(a, b) = 2^{-q} \sum_{x, y} (-1)^{(a \cdot x) + (b \cdot y)} \text{LP}^f(x, y). \qquad (4)$$

For any random function F (or equivalently any function f which depends on a random parameter K) we consider the expected values over the distribution of F

$$\text{EDP}^F(a, b) = E_F(\text{DP}^F(a, b)) \qquad (5)$$

$$\text{ELP}^F(a, b) = E_F(\text{LP}^F(a, b)). \qquad (6)$$

Obviously, Equations similar to (3) and (4) hold for EDP and ELP.

2.2 Differential Cryptanalysis of Markov Ciphers

Biham and Shamir's original differential cryptanalysis (see [8]) is defined by a characteristic

$$\Omega = (\omega_0, \ldots, \omega_r) \tag{7}$$

and focus on the probabilistic event

$$E_\Omega : \{M_i \oplus M_i' = \omega_i; i = 0, \ldots, r / M_0 \oplus M_0' = \omega_0\}$$

where M_0 and M_0' are two different plaintexts and M_i and M_i' are the image of M_0 and M_0' respectively by

$$\rho_i \circ \ldots \circ \rho_1.$$

We let $\Delta M_i = M_i \oplus M_i'$.

Differential cryptanalysis uses the E_Ω event by looking at random pairs (M_0, M_0') such that $\Delta M_0 = \omega_0$ until E_Ω occurs. Thus we try n random pairs, the success rate is at most the probability that one out of the n pairs makes the E_Ω event occur. This probability is

$$1 - \left(1 - \Pr_{M_0, M_0'}[E_\Omega]\right)^n. \tag{8}$$

Thus the probability of success is less than $n \Pr[E_\Omega]$. The average probability of success (over the distribution of the key) is less than

$$n E_k \left(\Pr_{M_0, M_0'}[E_\Omega] \right).$$

Thus we need a number of trials of $p/E(\Pr[E_\Omega])$ in order to achieve an average probability of success at least p.

We define the following formal product

$$\mathrm{DP}(\Omega) = \prod_{i=1}^{r} \mathrm{DP}^{\rho_i}(\omega_{i-1}, \omega_i)$$

(which depends on the key) and

$$\mathrm{EDP}(\Omega) = \prod_{i=1}^{r} \mathrm{EDP}^{\rho_i}(\omega_{i-1}, \omega_i)$$

(which does not). We have the following result which is fairly similar to the treatment of Lai, Massey and Murphy [21].[2]

---

[2] The difference is that these authors assume the "principle of stochastic equivalence" which enables to remove the expectation over the distribution of the key. The proof is exactly the same.

Lemma 1. *If* Enc *is a Markov cipher and if the round keys* $k_1, \ldots, k_r$ *are uniformly distributed and independent, we have*

$$E_k \left(\Pr_{M_0, M_0'} [E_\Omega] \right) = \text{EDP}(\Omega).$$

Proof. Since Enc is a Markov cipher and that the keys are independent, from Lai [20] (see also [21]) we know that $\Delta M_0, \ldots, \Delta M_r$ is a Markov chain. Thus we have

$$E_k \left(\Pr_{M_0, M_0'} [E_\Omega] \right) = \prod_{i=1}^{r} \Pr_{M_0, M_0', k} [\Delta M_i = \omega_i / \Delta M_{i-1} = \omega_{i-1}, \ldots, \Delta M_0 = \omega_0]$$

$$= \prod_{i=1}^{r} \Pr_{M_0, M_0', k} [\Delta M_i = \omega_i / \Delta M_{i-1} = \omega_{i-1}]$$

$$= \prod_{i=1}^{r} \text{EDP}^{\rho_i} (\omega_{i-1}, \omega_i)$$

$$= \text{EDP}(\Omega).$$

$\square$

We thus have the following theorem.

Theorem 2. *Given a Markov cipher* Enc $= \rho_r \circ \ldots \circ \rho_1$ *for the XOR addition law which uses* r *independent round keys and any differential characteristic* $\Omega = (\omega_0, \ldots, \omega_r)$, *in order to achieve an average probability of success greater than* p *for a differential cryptanalysis we need a minimum number of trials of at least* $p \, (\text{EDP}(\Omega))^{-1}$. *This holds in the model were the probability of success of the differential cryptanalysis for a fixed key is given by Equation (8).*

We emphasis that this is a real formal theorem which does not relies on unproven assumptions.

2.3 Truncated Differential Cryptanalysis

In Biham and Shamir's original differential cryptanalysis, we have a given input difference ω_0 and we expect a given output difference ω_r when the computation follows a path of differences $\omega_1, \ldots, \omega_{r-1}$. It is sometimes useful to consider a multi-path with same ω_0 and ω_r. Actually, we have

$$\text{DP}^{\text{Enc}}(\omega_0, \omega_r) = \sum_{\omega_1, \ldots, \omega_{r-1}} \Pr_{M_0, M_0'} [E_{\omega_0, \ldots, \omega_r}]. \tag{9}$$

Thus, from Lemma 1, we obtain that

$$\text{EDP}^{\text{Enc}}(\omega_0, \omega_r) = \sum_{\omega_1, \ldots, \omega_{r-1}} \prod_{i=1}^{r} \text{EDP}^{\rho_i} (\omega_{i-1}, \omega_i). \tag{10}$$

In the original differential cryptanalysis we only consider the overwhelming term of this sum.

An alternative way is to consider a sub-sum of characteristics which correspond to the same pattern. For instance, Knudsen's truncated differentials [18] corresponds to the sum of all characteristics which predict some part of the differences, *i.e.* for which

$$\forall j \notin I_i \quad (\omega_i)_j = d_{i,j}.$$

In most of block ciphers, what makes the probability of a characteristic small is the differences $d_{i,j}$ of zero. We thus focus on the propagation of zero differences. (Actually, the attack on Safer by Knudsen and Berson [19] uses truncated differentials with zeroes.) Let us denote

$$\text{Supp}(\omega_i) = \{j; (\omega_i)_j \neq 0\}.$$

If we focus on characteristics in which

$$\forall i \quad \text{Supp}(\omega_i) = I_i \text{ and } \omega_i \in A_i$$

we can get a maximal probability with largest A_i sets. The multi-path sum is thus defined by $\Omega = (I_0, \ldots, I_r)$ and we consider the event

$$E_\Omega = \{\text{Supp}(\Delta M_i) = I_i; i = 1, \ldots, r/\text{Supp}(\Delta M_0) = I_0\}$$

in which $\Omega = (I_0, \ldots, I_r)$. We call Ω a "support characteristic".

Theorem 3. *Given a Markov cipher* $\text{Enc} = \rho_r \circ \ldots \circ \rho_1$ *for the XOR addition law which uses r independent round keys we consider a truncated differential cryptanalysis. We heuristically assume that there is an overwhelming support characteristic* $\Omega = (I_0, \ldots, I_r)$ *which is such that the probability of success of the differential cryptanalysis for a fixed key is given by Equation (8). The complexity of the attacks must be greater than*

$$p \left(\prod_{i=1}^r \Pr_{M_{i-1}, M'_{i-1}, k_i} [\text{Supp}(\Delta M_i) = I_i/\text{Supp}(\Delta M_{i-1}) = I_{i-1}] \right)^{-1}$$

in order to get an average probability of success greater than p, with the notations of Section 2.2.

2.4 Linear Cryptanalysis

Linear cryptanalysis is fairly similar to differential cryptanalysis. Here we consider a characteristic Ω associated with a set of linear approximations

$$(\omega_i \cdot M_i) \oplus (\omega_{i+1} \cdot M_{i+1}) \approx \alpha_i \cdot k_i.$$

The characteristic is not associated with a particular event, but corresponds to an (assumed) overwhelming term in the multi-path sum. We define the following formal product

$$LP(\Omega) = \prod_{i=1}^{r} LP^{\rho_i}(\omega_{i-1}, \omega_i)$$

(which depends on the key) and

$$ELP(\Omega) = \prod_{i=1}^{r} ELP^{\rho_i}(\omega_{i-1}, \omega_i).$$

We have the following result.

Lemma 4. *If* Enc *is a Markov cipher and if the round keys* $k_1, \ldots, k_r$ *are independent, we have*

$$ELP^{Enc}(\omega_0, \omega_r) = \sum_{\omega_1, \ldots, \omega_{r-1}} ELP(\omega_0, \ldots, \omega_r).$$

Proof. First, by Equations (3) and (10) we have

$$ELP^{Enc}(\omega_0, \omega_r) = 2^{-\ell} \sum_{u_0, \ldots, u_r} (-1)^{(\omega_0 \cdot u_0) + (\omega_r \cdot u_r)} \prod_{i=1}^{r} EDP^{\rho_i}(u_{i-1}, u_i)$$

where ℓ is the bit-length of the plaintext. If we now use Equation (4), after a few formal computation steps we obtain the result. □

Matsui's original linear cryptanalysis assumes that one characteristic in the sum is overwhelming, and the attack has a heuristic complexity equal to the inverse of $ELP^{Enc}(\omega_0, \omega_r)$. We can thus get a (heuristic) complexity lower bound by upper bounding $ELP(\Omega)$.

3 On the Security of CS-Cipher

3.1 Presentation of CS-Cipher

In this paper we use non standard notations for CS-Cipher which are better adapted for our treatment. We recall that the secret key is first transformed into a 64-bit subkey sequence $k^0, \ldots, k^8$. We also use two 64-bit constants c and c'. We let $k_0, \ldots, k_{24}$ denote the sequence

$$k^0, c, c', k^1, c, c', \ldots, k^7, c, c', k^8.$$

We thus consider a modified CS-Cipher which is denoted CSC* which is defined by a 1600-bit random key $k = (k_0, \ldots, k_{24})$ with a uniform distribution.

Let us denote

$$s_i(x) = x \oplus k_i$$

which is thus used to "randomize" the message block with a subkey.

We split the standard mixing function M into one linear transformation μ and two involutions P. The linear mapping μ takes two 8-bit inputs and produces two 8-bit outputs by

$$\mu(a,b) = (\varphi(a) \oplus b, R_l(a) \oplus b).$$

Here R_l is a circular rotation by one position to the left, and φ is the standard CS-Cipher operation defined by

$$\varphi(x) = (R_l(x) \wedge 55) \oplus x$$

where $\wedge$ denotes the bitwise AND operation and 55 is the 8-bit hexadecimal constant 01010101. For convenience we let μ^4 the linear mapping which takes eight 8-bit inputs and produces eight 8-bit outputs by four parallel μ operations

$$\mu^4(x_1,\ldots,x_8) = (\mu(x_1,x_2),\ldots,\mu(x_7,x_8)).$$

We let P denotes the standard CS-Cipher involution defined by a table lookup, and P^8 the application of eight parallel P computations:

$$P^8(x_1,\ldots,x_8) = (P(x_1),\ldots,P(x_8)).$$

We know let L_π denote the following permutation

$$L_\pi(x_1,\ldots,x_8) = (x_1,x_3,x_5,x_7,x_2,x_4,x_6,x_8).$$

We let

$$\rho_i = L_\pi \circ P^8 \circ \mu^4 \circ s_{i-1}$$

for $i = 1,\ldots,23$ and

$$\rho_{24} = s_{24} \circ L_\pi \circ P^8 \circ \mu^4 \circ s_{23}$$

One CS-Cipher block encryption is defined by

$$\text{Enc} = \rho_r \circ \ldots \circ \rho_1.$$

This way we can consider CSC* of being a 24-round cipher in which each round consists of one subkey offset, the μ^4 linear mixing function, the P^8 confusion boxes and the L_π permutation. Due to the s_i structure, it is obvious that CSC* is a Markov cipher.

3.2 Differential Cryptanalysis

We consider a differential characteristic $\Omega = (\omega_0,\ldots,\omega_{24})$ and we aim to upper bound EDP(Ω).

We compute each term of the product in EDP(Ω). Since s_i, L_π and μ^4 are linear, we let

$$\delta_i = \mu^4(\omega_{i-1}) \tag{11}$$

and

$$\delta_i' = (L_\pi)^{-1}(\omega_i). \tag{12}$$

δ_i and δ_i' are the input and output differences of the ith P^8 layer respectively. From the linearity of μ^4 and L_π and the parallelism of P^8 we obtain

$$\text{EDP}(\Omega) = \prod_{i=1}^{24} \prod_{j=1}^{8} \text{DP}^P((\delta_i)_j, (\delta_i')_j). \tag{13}$$

Since P is a permutation, the following assumption is necessary for having $\text{EDP}(\Omega) \neq 0$

$$\forall i \ \text{Supp}(\delta_i) = \text{Supp}(\delta_i'). \tag{14}$$

We say that a P-box corresponding to indices i, j is "active" if $(\delta_i)_j \neq 0$. We use the following definition.

Definition 5. *For any differential characteristic $\Omega = (\omega_0, \ldots, \omega_{24})$, we define the δ_is and δ_i's by Equations (11) and (12) respectively. We say that Ω is "consistent" if the property of Equation (14) holds. Let $\#\Omega$ denotes the number of indices i, j such that $(\delta_i)_j \neq 0$.*

We thus have the following result.

Lemma 6. *For any non-zero differential characteristic Ω we have*

$$\text{EDP}(\Omega) \leq (\text{DP}_{\max}^P)^{\#\Omega}$$

where $\text{DP}_{\max}^P = 2^{-4}$ and $\text{EDP}(\Omega) = 0$ if Ω is not consistent.

Proof. We start from Equation (13). If Ω is not consistent, we obviously have $\text{EDP}(\Omega) = 0$ since P is a permutation. For non active P-boxes, the probability is obviously 1. For active P-boxes (there are $\#\Omega$ of it), we upper bound the probability by

$$\text{DP}_{\max}^P = \max_{a \neq 0, b} \text{DP}^P(a, b)$$

which is equal to 2^{-4} for CS-Cipher by construction. □

We thus need to lower bound $\#\Omega$ for consistent differential characteristics. This paradigm is already well known in the literature: in order to protect against heuristic differential attacks, we need to make sure that all consistent characteristic have a large number of active nonlinear boxes. Actually, the original papers of Biham and Shamir focus on looking for differential characteristics with a minimal number of S-boxes (see [7]).

Thanks to the multipermutation property of μ, it is fairly easy to investigate the minimal number of active P-boxes in CS-Cipher. Actually, μ has the property that

1. μ is a permutation,
2. for all a, both outputs of $\mu(a, y)$ are permutations of y,

3. for all b, both outputs of $\mu(x, b)$ are permutations of x.

Thus, if exactly one input of μ is non-zero, then both outputs of μ are non-zero. If the two inputs of μ are non-zero, then at least one output of μ is non-zero. In other terms, the difference patterns around one μ box can only be one out of the six following patterns.

$$00 \to 00 \quad 0* \to ** \quad *0 \to ** \quad ** \to 0* \quad ** \to *0 \quad ** \to **.$$

(Stars mean any non-zero differences.) With the notations of the previous section, we recall that

$$\delta_{i+1} = (\mu^4 \circ L_\pi)(\delta_i').$$

Moreover we consider consistent characteristics, which means that $(\delta_i')_j$ is non-zero if and only if $(\delta_i)_j$ is non-zero. This enables to make rules for "non-zeroness" of the $(\delta_i)_j$.

Actually, we consider 8-bit vectors $I_i = \text{Supp}(\delta_i)$. From the previous arguments we can make a list of possible $I_i \to I_{i+1}$ transitions. (In total we have $6^4 = 1296$ rules.) To each possible I_i we associate its Hamming weight $\#I_i$. We can now make the graph of all possible I_is weighted by $\#I_i$ and in which each edge corresponds to a rule. Since $\#I_i$ is also equal to the number of non-zero entries in ω_i, finding out the minimal number of active P-boxes in a consistent differential characteristic corresponds to finding a path of length 24 edges with minimal non-zero weight in this graph, which is fairly easy, for instance by using the Floyd-Warshall algorithm [14] (see [10, pp. 558–565]). Its complexity is essentially cubic in time and quadratic in memory (in term of number of vertices, which is 256 here). Experiment shows that such a path has at least a total weight of 72. More precisely, the shortest non-zero weight for paths of given edge-length is given by the table below.

l	1	2	3	4	5	6	7	8	9	10	11	12	13	14	15	16	17	18	19	20	21	22	23	24
w	1	3	5	9	13	18	20	24	26	30	32	36	38	42	44	48	50	54	56	60	62	66	68	72

Thus, we obtain that for any differential characteristic Ω we have

$$\text{EDP}(\Omega) \leq 2^{-288}.$$

This makes CSC* provably resistant against the original differential cryptanalysis. Actually, six rounds of CSC* leads to an upper bound of 2^{-72}, which is already enough. This corresponds to two rounds of CS-Cipher instead of eight, so this suggests that **four rounds of CS-Cipher** are already secure against 2R differential attacks.

3.3 Linear Cryptanalysis

Linear cryptanalysis has a very similar treatment as was shown by Biham [6]. Actually, we have

$$\omega_{i-1} \cdot M_{i-1} = ({}^t(\mu^4)^{-1}(\omega_{i-1}) \cdot (\mu^4 \circ s_{i-1})(M_{i-1})) \oplus (\omega_{i-1} \cdot k_{i-1})$$

and

$$\omega_i \cdot M_i = {}^t L_\pi(\omega_{i+1}) \cdot (L_\pi)^{-1}(M_i)$$

thus we let

$$\delta_i = {}^t(\mu^4)^{-1}(\omega_{i-1}) \tag{15}$$

and

$$\delta_i' = {}^t L_\pi(\omega_i). \tag{16}$$

As for differential cryptanalysis, we have the following result.

Definition 7. *For any linear characteristic $\Omega = (\omega_0, \ldots, \omega_{24})$, we define the δ_is and δ_i's by Equations (15) and (16) respectively. We say that Ω is "consistent" if the property of Equation (14) holds. Let $\#\Omega$ denotes the number of indices i, j such that $(\delta_i)_j \neq 0$.*

We thus have the following result.

Lemma 8. *For any non-zero linear characteristic Ω we have*

$$\mathrm{ELP}(\Omega) \leq (\mathrm{LP}_{\max}^P)^{\#\Omega}$$

where $\mathrm{LP}_{\max}^P = 2^{-4}$ and $\mathrm{ELP}(\Omega) = 0$ if Ω is not consistent.

Here the relation between the δ_is and the δ_i's is

$$\delta_{i-1}' = {}^t(\mu^4 \circ L_\pi)(\delta_i)$$

which is equivalent to

$$\delta_i = (({}^t\mu^{-1})^4 \circ L_\pi)(\delta_{i-1}')$$

instead of

$$\delta_i = (\mu^4 \circ L_\pi)(\delta_{i-1}')$$

as for differential cryptanalysis. Obviously, ${}^t\mu^{-1}$ has the same multipermutation property than μ, thus the "non-zeroness" rules for the δ_is and δ_i's are the same. We thus obtain that

$$\mathrm{ELP}(\Omega) \leq 2^{-288}.$$

This makes CSC* heuristically resistant against the original linear cryptanalysis.

3.4 Support Characteristics

Here we aim to upper bound the probabilities of the support characteristics for CSC*. One problem is that the propagation of non-zero differences through the P-boxes has no unusual cases. For this we concentrates on unusual propagations through the μ boxes.

Here the characteristic $\Omega = (I_0, \ldots, I_{24})$ defines exactly which inputs and outputs of the μ-boxes are non-zero. The probability of the characteristic is non-zero only if the number of non-zero input-output of any μ-box is in $\{0, 3, 4\}$. With these rules we can make the graph of all possible $I_i \to I_{i+1}$ transitions. The problem is to weight it.

The more interesting probabilities correspond to the case where two inputs of a μ-box are non-zero, and one output is zero. Let us denote μ_1 and μ_2 the two outputs. We thus consider the two probabilities

$$\Pr_{X,X',Y,Y'}[\mu_j(X \oplus X', Y \oplus Y') = 0/X \neq X', Y \neq Y']$$

for $j = 1$ and $j = 2$. Due to the linearity of μ, this is equal to

$$\Pr_{X,Y}[\mu_j(X,Y) = 0/X \neq 0, Y \neq 0]$$

which is 2^{-8} from the multipermutation properties of μ.

One problem is the vertex $I = \{1,\ldots,8\}$, because all transitions towards it have weight 0. Intuitively, if we go through this vertex, we loose all information, and the final probability is actually meaningless, because it is smaller than the probability of the same external characteristic for a truly random cipher. For instance, if we have the support characteristic $\Omega = (I,\ldots,I_{24})$ in which $I_i = \{1,\ldots,8\}$, we obtain

$$\Pr_{M_0,M_0',k}[E_\Omega] \leq \Pr_X[\text{Supp}(X) = I_{24}]$$

so the "signal" of the support characteristic will vanish against the "noise" of natural behavior. Thus we remove this vertex from the graph.

We can now weight the edges of the graph by the total number of 2-1 transitions in the four μ-boxes: each $I_i \to I_{i+1}$ edge defines four transitions though a μ-box, so we can count the ones with no zero-input and one zero-output. Then we can look for the path with length 24 and minimal weight. The experiment shows that the minimal weight is 22. Actually, for any length $\ell \geq 2$, the minimal weight is $\ell - 2$ is obtained, for instance, by iterating the path

$$\{1,3\} \to \{1,2,5,6\} \to \{1,3\}$$

which has weight 2 (thus probability 2^{-16}). For instance, the path

$$\{1,3\} \to \{1,2,5,6\} \to \{1,3\} \to \ldots \to \{1,2,5,6\} \to \{1,3,6,8\}$$

of even length ℓ has weight $\ell - 2$.

Thus the probability of a support characteristic on 24 rounds is less than $(2^{-8})^{22} = 2^{-176}$. Actually ten rounds of CSC* leads to an upper bound of 2^{-64}. This corresponds to 3.33 rounds of CS-Cipher. So we believe that these properties make 5.33 **rounds of CS-Cipher** heuristically resistant against any multi-path differential characteristics. Eight rounds is therefore a comfortable safety margin.

One open problem is the resistance against the recent impossible differential cryptanalysis. In this paper we investigated differential characteristics with overwhelming behavior. The question now is how to address characteristics with unexpected low probabilities.

4 Conclusion

We have shown that CSC* admits no differential or linear characteristic with average probability greater than 2^{-288}, and no support characteristic with an average probability greater than 2^{-176}. We believe that these results hold for CS-Cipher as well, which makes it heuristically secure against differential, linear, truncated, and other related differential cryptanalysis. The question on the impossible differentials issue remains open though, as well as more general attacks.

Whereas ciphers similar than CS-Cipher use linear diffusion layers for mixing all pieces of a message in each round (for instance the four AES candidates Safer+, Serpent, Rijndael, Crypton), CS-Cipher uses a nonlinear diffusion primitive: the μ operation which is mixed with two non linear P-boxes. This enables to achieve a stronger design at a minimal cost (both μ and P have quite efficient implementations). It also illustrates that we can use general multipermutations and not only MDS codes: large linear layers are nice presents for the attacker.

References

1. *FIPS 46*, Data Encryption Standard. U.S. Department of Commerce — National Bureau of Standards, National Technical Information Service, Springfield, Virginia. *Federal Information Processing Standard Publication 46*, 1977.
2. *CD-ROM "AES CD-1: Documentation"*, National Institute of Standards and Technology (NIST), August 1998. Documentation for the First Advanced Encryption Standard Candidate Conference.
3. C. M. Adams. *A Formal and Practical Design Procedure for Substitution-Permutation Network Cryptosystems.*, Ph.D. Thesis of Queen's University, Kingston, Ontario, Canada, 1990.
4. C. M. Adams, S. E. Tavares. Designing s-boxes Resistant to Differential Cryptanalysis. In *Proceedings of 3rd Symposium on the State and Progress of Research in Cryptography*, pp. 386–397, Rome, Italy, 1994.
5. O. Baudron, H. Gilbert, L. Granboulan, H. Handschuh, R. Harley, A. Joux, P. Nguyen, F. Noilhan, D. Pointcheval, T. Pornin, G. Poupard, J. Stern, S. Vaudenay. DFC Update. In Proceedings from the Second Advanced Encryption Standard Candidate Conference, National Institute of Standards and Technology (NIST), March 1999.
6. E. Biham. On Matsui's Linear Cryptanalysis. In *Advances in Cryptology EUROCRYPT'94*, Perugia, Italy, Lectures Notes in Computer Science 950, pp. 341–355, Springer-Verlag, 1995.
7. E. Biham, A. Shamir. Differential Cryptanalysis of DES-like Cryptosystems. In *Advances in Cryptology CRYPTO'90*, Santa Barbara, California, U.S.A., Lectures Notes in Computer Science 537, pp. 2–21, Springer-Verlag, 1991.
8. E. Biham, A. Shamir. *Differential Cryptanalysis of the Data Encryption Standard*, Springer-Verlag, 1993.
9. F. Chabaud, S. Vaudenay. Links Between Differential and Linear Cryptanalysis. In *Advances in Cryptology EUROCRYPT'94*, Perugia, Italy, Lectures Notes in Computer Science 950, pp. 356–365, Springer-Verlag, 1995.

10. T. H. Cormen, C. E. Leiserson, R. L. Rivest. *Introduction to Algorithms*, Mc Graw Hill, 1990.
11. J. Daemen. *Cipher and Hash Function Design — Strategies based on Linear and Differential Cryptanalysis*, Doctoral Dissertation, Katholieke Universiteit Leuven, 1995.
12. J. Daemen, L. R. Knudsen, V. Rijmen. The Block Cipher Square. In *Fast Software Encryption*, Haifa, Israel, Lectures Notes in Computer Science 1267, pp. 149–165, Springer-Verlag, 1997.
13. H. Feistel. Cryptography and Computer Privacy. *Scientific American*, vol. 228, pp. 15–23, 1973.
14. R. W. Floyd. Algorithm 97 (SHORTEST PATH). In *Communications of the ACM*, vol. 5, p. 345, 1962.
15. H. Gilbert, M. Girault, P. Hoogvorst, F. Noilhan, T. Pornin, G. Poupard, J. Stern, S. Vaudenay. Decorrelated Fast Cipher: an AES Candidate. Submitted to the Advanced Encryption Standard process. In *CD-ROM "AES CD-1: Documentation"*, National Institute of Standards and Technology (NIST), August 1998.
16. H. M. Heys. *The Design of Substitution-Permutation Network Ciphers Resistant to Cryptanalysis*, Ph.D. Thesis of Queen's University, Kingston, Ontario, Canada, 1994.
17. H. M. Heys, S. E. Tavares. Substitution-Permutation Networks Resistant to Differential and Linear Cryptanalysis. *Journal of Cryptology*, vol. 9, pp. 1–19, 1996.
18. L. R. Knudsen. Truncated and Higher Order Differentials. In *Fast Software Encryption*, Leuven, Belgium, Lectures Notes in Computer Science 1008, pp. 196–211, Springer-Verlag, 1995.
19. L. R. Knudsen, T. A. Berson. Truncated Differentials of SAFER. In *Fast Software Encryption*, Cambridge, United Kingdom, Lectures Notes in Computer Science 1039, pp. 15–26, Springer-Verlag, 1996.
20. X. Lai. *On the Design and Security of Block Ciphers*, ETH Series in Information Processing, vol. 1, Hartung-Gorre Verlag Konstanz, 1992.
21. X. Lai, J. L. Massey, S. Murphy. Markov Ciphers and Differential Cryptanalysis. In *Advances in Cryptology EUROCRYPT'91*, Brighton, United Kingdom, Lectures Notes in Computer Science 547, pp. 17–38, Springer-Verlag, 1991.
22. J. L. Massey. SAFER K-64: a Byte-Oriented Block-Ciphering Algorithm. In *Fast Software Encryption*, Cambridge, United Kingdom, Lectures Notes in Computer Science 809, pp. 1–17, Springer-Verlag, 1994.
23. M. Matsui. Linear Cryptanalysis Methods for DES Cipher. In *Advances in Cryptology EUROCRYPT'93*, Lofthus, Norway, Lectures Notes in Computer Science 765, pp. 386–397, Springer-Verlag, 1994.
24. M. Matsui. The First Experimental Cryptanalysis of the Data Encryption Standard. In *Advances in Cryptology CRYPTO'94*, Santa Barbara, California, U.S.A., Lectures Notes in Computer Science 839, pp. 1–11, Springer-Verlag, 1994.
25. M. Matsui. New Structure of Block Ciphers with Provable Security against Differential and Linear Cryptanalysis. In *Fast Software Encryption*, Cambridge, United Kingdom, Lectures Notes in Computer Science 1039, pp. 205–218, Springer-Verlag, 1996.
26. M. Matsui. New Block Encryption Algorithm MISTY. In *Fast Software Encryption*, Haifa, Israel, Lectures Notes in Computer Science 1267, pp. 54–68, Springer-Verlag, 1997.
27. K. Nyberg. Perfect Nonlinear *S*-Boxes. In *Advances in Cryptology EUROCRYPT'91*, Brighton, United Kingdom, Lectures Notes in Computer Science 547, pp. 378–385, Springer-Verlag, 1991.

28. K. Nyberg. Differentially Uniform Mapping for Cryptography. In *Advances in Cryptology EUROCRYPT'93*, Lofthus, Norway, Lectures Notes in Computer Science 765, pp. 55–64, Springer-Verlag, 1994.
29. K. Nyberg. Linear Approximation of Block Ciphers. In *Advances in Cryptology EUROCRYPT'94*, Perugia, Italy, Lectures Notes in Computer Science 950, pp. 439–444, Springer-Verlag, 1995.
30. K. Nyberg, L. R. Knudsen. Provable Security against a Differential Cryptanalysis. In *Advances in Cryptology CRYPTO'92*, Santa Barbara, California, U.S.A., Lectures Notes in Computer Science 740, pp. 566–574, Springer-Verlag, 1993.
31. K. Nyberg, L. R. Knudsen. Provable Security against a Differential Cryptanalysis. *Journal of Cryptology*, vol. 8, pp. 27–37, 1995.
32. J. Stern, S. Vaudenay. CS-Cipher. In *Fast Software Encryption*, Paris, France, Lectures Notes in Computer Science 1372, pp. 189–205, Springer-Verlag, 1998.
33. S. Vaudenay. On the Need for Multipermutations: Cryptanalysis of MD4 and SAFER. In *Fast Software Encryption*, Leuven, Belgium, Lectures Notes in Computer Science 1008, pp. 286–297, Springer-Verlag, 1995.
34. S. Vaudenay. *La Sécurité des Primitives Cryptographiques*, Thèse de Doctorat de l'Université de Paris 7, Technical Report LIENS-95-10 of the Laboratoire d'Informatique de l'Ecole Normale Supérieure, 1995.
35. S. Vaudenay. A cheap Paradigm for Block Cipher Security Strengthening. Technical Report LIENS-97-3, 1997.
36. S. Vaudenay. Provable Security for Block Ciphers by Decorrelation. In *STACS 98*, Paris, France, Lectures Notes in Computer Science 1373, pp. 249–275, Springer-Verlag, 1998.
37. S. Vaudenay. Feistel Ciphers with L_2-Decorrelation. To appear in SAC'98, LNCS.
38. S. Vaudenay. The Decorrelation Technique Home-Page. URL:http://www.dmi.ens.fr/~vaudenay/decorrelation.html
39. S. Vaudenay. Resistance Against General Iterated Attacks. (To appear in Eurocrypt' 99.)
40. A. M. Youssef, S. Mister, S. E. Tavares. On the Design of Linear Transformations for Substitution Permutation Encryption Networks. Presented at SAC'97.

Interpolation Attacks of the Block Cipher: SNAKE

Shiho Moriai[1]*, Takeshi Shimoyama[2]*, and Toshinobu Kaneko[3]

[1] NTT Laboratories
1-1 Hikari-no-oka, Yokosuka, 239-0847 Japan
e-mail: shiho@isl.ntt.co.jp
[2] Fujitsu Laboratories LTD.
4-1-1, Kamikodanaka Nakahara-ku Kawasaki, 211-8588 Japan
e-mail: shimo@flab.fujitsu.co.jp
[3] Science University of Tokyo
2641 Yamazaki, Noda, Chiba, 278-8510 Japan
e-mail: kaneko@ee.noda.sut.ac.jp

Abstract. This paper presents an efficient interpolation attack using a computer algebra system. The interpolation attack proposed by Jakobsen and Knudsen was shown to be effective for attacking ciphers that use simple algebraic functions. However, there was a problem that the complexity and the number of pairs of plaintexts and ciphertexts required for the attack can be overestimated. We solve this problem by first, finding the actual number of coefficients in the polynomial (or rational expression) used in the attack by using a computer algebra system, and second, by finding the polynomial (or rational expression) with fewest coefficients by choosing the plaintexts. We apply this interpolation attack to the block cipher SNAKE proposed by Lee and Cha at JW-ISC'97. In the SNAKE family there are two types of Feistel ciphers, SNAKE(1) and SNAKE(2), with different round functions. Both of them use the inverse function in Galois Field $GF(2^m)$ as S-box. We show that when the block size is 64 bits and $m = 8$, all round keys are recovered for SNAKE(1) and SNAKE(2) with up to 11 rounds. Moreover, when the block size is 128 bits and $m = 16$, all round keys are recovered for SNAKE(1) with up to 15 rounds and SNAKE(2) with up to 16 rounds.

1 Introduction

Since two powerful cryptanalyses on block ciphers, differential cryptanalysis[1] and linear cryptanalysis[6], were presented, some new block ciphers with provable security against these cryptanalyses have been proposed. On the other hand, Jakobsen and Knudsen raised the alarm that some of them are easy to cryptanalyze by algebraic attacks such as higher order differential attack and interpolation attack[3]. These attacks are effective for attacking ciphers that use simple algebraic functions. For example, there is the 6-round prototype Feistel cipher presented in [8], called the cipher $\mathcal{KN}$. It uses the cubing function in $GF(2^{33})$

---

* Most part of this work was done while the authors were with TAO, or Telecommunications Advancement Organization of Japan.

in the round function, and was broken by the higher order differential attack exploiting the low degree of polynomial expression over GF(2). A variant of the cipher, called the cipher $\mathcal{PURE}$, which uses the cubing function in $GF(2^{32})$ as the round function, was broken by the interpolation attack up to 32 rounds by exploiting the low degree of polynomial expression over $GF(2^{32})$. Moreover, a slightly modified version of the cipher SHARK[9], which uses the inverse function in $GF(2^8)$ as S-box, was broken up to 5 rounds by an interpolation attack exploiting the low degree of rational expression over $GF(2^8)$.

The principle of the interpolation attack is that, roughly speaking, if the ciphertext is represented as a polynomial or rational expression of the plaintext with N coefficients, the polynomial or rational expression can be constructed using N pairs of plaintexts and ciphertexts. Since N determines the complexity and the number of pairs required for the attack, it is important to find as small N as possible.

This paper shows two solutions to find a tighter upper bound of N. The first problem is that generally it is difficult to find the actual number of coefficients in the polynomial or rational expression. In [3] Jakobsen and Knudsen estimated it from the degree of the polynomial or rational expression. However, this method often overestimates it when we use a multivariate polynomial or rational expression, in particular. As the solution to this problem, we compute the actual polynomial or rational expression by using a computer algebra system and find the number of coefficients. The second problem is the number of coefficients (or the degree) of the polynomial or rational expression varies with the plaintexts chosen. If we use a computer algebra system, it is easy to compute the number of coefficients of the polynomial or rational expression in a few variables. We can find the polynomial or rational expression with the fewest coefficients by choosing the plaintexts.

We apply this interpolation attack to the block cipher SNAKE proposed by Lee and Cha at JW-ISC'97[5]. This cipher is not a prototype cipher and we don't modify it to simplify the cryptanalysis. The cipher SNAKE is a Feistel cipher with provable resistance against differential and linear cryptanalysis. In [5], it is also claimed that SNAKE is resistant against higher order differential attack and interpolation attack, though the rationale was not discussed enough. SNAKE(1) and SNAKE(2) have different round functions. To put it concretely, the structure of the round function is the same, the substitution-permutation network (SPN). Both of them use the same number of S-boxes in the round function, the function used as the S-box is the same, e.g., the inverse function in $GF(2^m)$, but only the diffusion layer is different.

We apply to the cipher SNAKE the interpolation attack using *rational expressions*. If we represent the cipher SNAKE as a polynomial, the attack becomes impractical with only a few rounds, since the number of coefficients in the polynomial increases to the upper bound of the number of pairs we can obtain. This is because the degree of the inverse function in $GF(2^m)$ in polynomial expression is very high as follows: $f(x) = x^{-1} = x^{2^m-2}$. Using a computer algebra system, we find the rational expression with the fewest coefficients by choosing the plaintexts. As a result, both of the SNAKE ciphers with many rounds are broken. When the block size is 64 bit and $m = 8$, all round keys are recovered for SNAKE(1) and SNAKE(2) with up to 11 rounds. Moreover, when the block size is 128 bit and $m = 16$, all round keys are recovered for SNAKE(1) with up to 15 rounds and SNAKE(2) with up to 16 rounds.

This paper is organized as follows. In Section 2, we give a summary of the interpolation attack. Section 3 describes the specifications of the cipher SNAKE. In Sections 4 and 5, we apply the interpolation attack to the cipher SNAKE with blocksize 64 bits and 128 bits, respectively. In Section 6, we discuss some problems and make concluding remarks.

2   The Interpolation Attack

In this section, we describe the outline of the interpolation attack proposed by Jakobsen and Knudsen in [3] and explain the notations used in this paper. The target of the attack is an iterated cipher with block size $2n$ bits and R rounds. We denote a plaintext by x and a ciphertext by y. Let x be the concatenation of u subblocks $x_i \in \mathrm{GF}(2^m)$, where $2n = m \times u$. We define y similarly.

$$x = (x_u, x_{u-1}, \ldots, x_1) \in \mathrm{GF}(2^m)^u, \quad x_i \in \mathrm{GF}(2^m)$$
$$y = (y_u, y_{u-1}, \ldots, y_1) \in \mathrm{GF}(2^m)^u, \quad y_j \in \mathrm{GF}(2^m)$$

Moreover, we denote the i-th round key by $k^{(i)}$ and let the length of $k^{(i)}$ be l bits. Similarly let $k^{(i)}$ be the concatenation of t subblocks $k_j^{(i)}$, where $l = m \times t$.

$$k^{(i)} = (k_t^{(i)}, k_{t-1}^{(i)}, \ldots, k_1^{(i)}) \in \mathrm{GF}(2^m)^t \quad k_j^{(i)} \in \mathrm{GF}(2^m)$$

2.1   Global deduction

If the key is fixed to k, a ciphertext subblock $y_j \in \mathrm{GF}(2^m)$ can be expressed as a polynomial in plaintext subblocks $\{x_u, x_{u-1}, \ldots, x_1\}$ as follows:

$$y_j = f_{jk}(x_u, x_{u-1}, \ldots, x_1) \in \mathrm{GF}(2^m)[x_u, x_{u-1}, \ldots, x_1],$$

where $\mathrm{GF}(2^m)[X]$ is the polynomial ring of $X = \{x_u, \ldots, x_1\}$ over $\mathrm{GF}(2^m)$. If the number of coefficients in $f_{jk}(x_u, x_{u-1}, \ldots, x_1)$ is N, the attacker can construct $f_{jk}(x_u, x_{u-1}, \ldots, x_1)$ from different N pairs of plaintexts and ciphertexts. If we define $\deg_{x_i} f_{jk}$ as the degree of $f_{jk}(x_u, x_{u-1}, \ldots, x_1)$ with respect to x_i, N is estimated as follows.

$$N \leq \prod_{1 \leq i \leq u} (\deg_{x_i} f_{jk} + 1) \tag{1}$$

Note that N can be overestimated when u is large and the polynomial is sparse.

Once the attacker constructs $f_{jk}(x_u, x_{u-1}, \ldots, x_1)$, (s)he can encrypt any plaintext into the corresponding ciphertext for key k, without knowing the key. This attack is called *global deduction* by Knudsen[4,3]. Similarly, by swapping ciphertexts and plaintexts, once the attacker can construct $x_i = f'_{ik}(y_u, y_{u-1}, \ldots, y_1)$ $\in \mathrm{GF}(2^m)[y_u, y_{u-1}, \ldots, y_1]$, (s)he can decrypt any ciphertext into the corresponding plaintext for key k, without knowing the key.

2.2 Instance deduction

If some subblocks of plaintexts are fixed to some values as e.g., $x = (0, \ldots, 0, x_1)$, a ciphertext subblock $y_j \in \mathrm{GF}(2^m)$ can be expressed as a polynomial as follows:

$$y_j = f_{jk}(x_1) \in \mathrm{GF}(2^m)[x_1].$$

In this case, $f_{jk}(x_1)$ is a polynomial in one variable x_1. Generally, there are fewer coefficients in $f_{jk}(x_1)$ than in global deduction. Therefore, the attacker can construct $f_{jk}(x_1)$ from fewer chosen plaintexts and ciphertexts. Let N be the number of coefficient and let $\deg_{x_1} f_{jk} = d$, and N is estimated as $N \leq d+1$. Once the attacker can construct $f_{jk}(x_1)$ from N pairs of plaintexts and ciphertexts, (s)he can encrypt a subset of all plaintexts, e.g., $x = (0, \ldots, 0, x_1)$, $^{\forall}x_1 \in \mathrm{GF}(2^m)$, into the corresponding ciphertexts for key k, without knowing the key. This attack is called *instance deduction* by Knudsen[4, 3]. Similarly, by swapping ciphertexts and plaintexts, the attack where a subset of all ciphertexts are decrypted into the corresponding plaintexts is possible.

2.3 Key recovery

The attacker recovers the last round key as follows. We denote the output of the $(R-1)$-th round by $\tilde{y} = (\tilde{y}_u, \tilde{y}_{u-1}, \ldots, \tilde{y}_1) \in \mathrm{GF}(2^m)^u$. A ciphertext subblock $\tilde{y}_j \in \mathrm{GF}(2^m)$ can be expressed as a polynomial in $\{x_u, x_{u-1}, \ldots, x_1\}$ as follows:

$$\tilde{y}_j = \tilde{f}(x_u, x_{u-1}, \ldots, x_1) \in \mathrm{GF}(2^m)[x_u, x_{u-1}, \ldots, x_1].$$

Let N' be the number of coefficients in $\tilde{f}(x_u, x_{u-1}, \ldots, x_1)$. On the other hand, $\tilde{y}_j$ can be also expressed using the ciphertext y and the last round key $k^{(R)}$. Therefore, if N' pairs of plaintexts x and ciphertexts y are available, the attacker can construct $\tilde{f}(x_u, x_{u-1}, \ldots, x_1)$ using $\tilde{y}_j$ which is computed using y and a guessed $k^{(R)}$.

$$\tilde{f}(x_u, x_{u-1}, \ldots, x_1) = \tilde{y}_j(y, k^{(R)}) \tag{2}$$

If Eq. (2) holds for another plaintext/ciphertext pair, the guessed $k^{(R)}$ is correct with high probability. From the procedure above, the last round key is recovered from any $N'+1$ pairs of plaintexts and ciphertexts. The average of the required complexity for recovering the last round key is $(N'+1)2^{l'-1}$, where l' is the number of last round key bits effective in Eq. (2). Repeating similar procedures, the attacker can find all round keys.

In the above, we showed only how to recover the last round key in the case of the global deduction attack, or known plaintext attack. Similarly the instance deduction attack, or chosen plaintext attack is also possible. In the instance deduction attack, the attacker can only use chosen plaintexts and ciphertexts, but fewer pairs are required than in the global deduction attack.

2.4   Meet-in-the-middle approach

The meet-in-the-middle approach in the interpolation attack was introduced by Jakobsen and Knudsen[3], which is effective for some attacks on block ciphers.

We denote the output of a certain internal round by $z = (z_u, z_{u-1}, \ldots, z_1) \in GF(2^m)^u$. A subblock of z, $z_j \in GF(2^m)$ can be expressed as a polynomial in $\{x_u, x_{u-1}, \ldots, x_1\}$ as follows:

$$z_j = f(x_u, x_{u-1}, \ldots, x_1) \in GF(2^m)[x_u, x_{u-1}, \ldots, x_1]$$

On the other hand, z_j can be also expressed as a polynomial in $\{\tilde{y}_u, \tilde{y}_{u-1}, \ldots, \tilde{y}_1\}$ as follows:

$$z_j = g(\tilde{y}_u, \tilde{y}_{u-1}, \ldots, \tilde{y}_1) \in GF(2^m)[\tilde{y}_u, \tilde{y}_{u-1}, \ldots, \tilde{y}_1].$$

Note that $\tilde{y}_j$ can be computed from the ciphertext y and a guessed $k^{(R)}$.

Therefore, Eq. (3) is constructed by guessing $k^{(R)}$.

$$f(x_u, x_{u-1}, \ldots, x_1) = g(\tilde{y}_u, \tilde{y}_{u-1}, \ldots, \tilde{y}_1) \tag{3}$$

The number of pairs required for constructing Eq. (3) is computed as follows. If f and g are represented as polynomials, the required number of pairs is

$$(\# \text{ of coefs. in } f) + (\# \text{ of coefs. in } g).$$

If f and g are represented as rational expressions $f = \frac{f_1}{f_2}$ and $g = \frac{g_1}{g_2}$, where $f_2 \neq 0$ and $g_2 \neq 0$, it is

$$((\# \text{ of coefs. in } f_1) - 1) \times (\# \text{ of coefs. in } g_2)$$
$$+ (\# \text{ of coefs. in } f_2) \times ((\# \text{ of coefs. in } g_1) - 1).$$

Note that we subtract 1's because we can fix one of the coefficients in the rational expression to a certain value, e.g., 1. The attacker can judge whether $k^{(R)}$ is correct or not by examining if Eq. (3) holds for another plaintext/ciphertext pair.

3   SNAKE

The cipher SNAKE is a Feistel cipher, which has two types, SNAKE(1) and SNAKE(2), with different round functions. The general form is SNAKE(i)(m, s, w, r), where

i – (= 1 or 2) the type of SNAKE described in the below,
m – the size of input and output of the S-box in bit,
s – the number of S-boxes used in the round function,
w – block size in bit ($w = 2sm$),
r – the number of rounds.

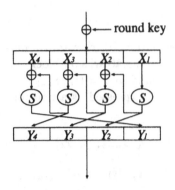

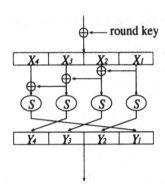

Fig. 1. Round function of SNAKE(1)   **Fig. 2.** Round function of SNAKE(2)

Figures 1 and 2 show the round functions of SNAKE(1) and SNAKE(2) for $s = 4$, which were demonstrated in [5]. For the S-box in the round function, the inverse function $S(x) = x^{-1}$ in $\mathrm{GF}(2^m)$ is used, because differential probability and linear probability of $S(x)$ are 2^{2-m} when m is even. In this paper we define the S-box as follows, though the output for input 0 is not defined in [5].

$$S(x) = \begin{cases} x^{-1} \text{ in } \mathrm{GF}(2^m) & x \neq 0 \\ 0 & x = 0 \end{cases}$$

Since SNAKE(i)(8, 4, 64, 16) is given as an example in [5], we apply the interpolation attack to it in Section 4. Moreover, we also apply the interpolation attack to a 128-bit variant, SNAKE(i)(16, 4, **128**, 16) in Section 5, since in [5] it is claimed that one of merits of the cipher SNAKE is that its encrypting data block length (=block size) is flexible.

4   Interpolation Attack of SNAKE(i)(8, 4, 64, r)

4.1   Rational expression over GF(2^8) of SNAKE(i)(8, 4, 64, r)

In this section, we attack SNAKE(i)(8, 4, 64, r) using the interpolation attack. If we represent the cipher SNAKE as a polynomial, the attack becomes impractical with only a few rounds, since the number of coefficients in the polynomial increases to the upper bound of the number of pairs we can obtain. Therefore, we represent SNAKE as a rational expression over GF(2^8).

Let the plaintext block and the ciphertext block be as follows.

$$x = (x_8, x_7, \ldots, x_1) \in \mathrm{GF}(2^8)^8, \quad x_i \in \mathrm{GF}(2^8)$$
$$y = (y_8, y_7, \ldots, y_1) \in \mathrm{GF}(2^8)^8, \quad y_j \in \mathrm{GF}(2^8)$$

We denote the i-th round key by

$$k^{(i)} = (k_4^{(i)}, k_3^{(i)}, k_2^{(i)}, k_1^{(i)}) \in \mathrm{GF}(2^8)^4, \quad k_j^{(i)} \in \mathrm{GF}(2^8).$$

Moreover, we denote the upper half (32 bits) of the output of the r-th round by

$$z^{(r)} = (z_4^{(r)}, z_3^{(r)}, z_2^{(r)}, z_1^{(r)}) \in \mathrm{GF}(2^8)^4, \quad z_j^{(r)} \in \mathrm{GF}(2^8).$$

Global deduction. In the global deduction, we represent a ciphertext subblock as a rational expression over $\mathrm{GF}(2^8)$ in $\{x_8, x_7, \ldots, x_1\}$. First of all, we show that the round functions of SNAKE(1) and SNAKE(2) can be represented as simple rational expressions as follows:

SNAKE(1)

SNAKE(2)

$$Y_2 = \frac{1}{X_1}$$

$$Y_3 = \frac{1}{X_2 + \frac{1}{X_1}}$$

$$Y_4 = \frac{1}{X_3 + \frac{1}{X_2 + \frac{1}{X_1}}}$$

$$Y_1 = \frac{1}{X_4 + \frac{1}{X_3 + \frac{1}{X_2 + \frac{1}{X_1}}}}$$

$$Y_2 = \frac{1}{X_1}$$

$$Y_3 = \frac{1}{X_1 + X_2}$$

$$Y_4 = \frac{1}{X_1 + X_2 + X_3}$$

$$Y_1 = \frac{1}{X_1 + X_2 + X_3 + X_4},$$

where variables $X_i, Y_j \in \mathrm{GF}(2^8)$ are shown in Figures 1 and 2.

Next, we extend the expressions of the round function to the entire cipher. In a Feistel cipher, there are XORs between 32-bit data in each round. These operations are regarded as four additions on $\mathrm{GF}(2^8)$. We'd like to find the rational expression over $\mathrm{GF}(2^8)$ of each subblock of the output of the r-th round, $z_j^{(r)} = \frac{f_{j1}^{(r)}}{f_{j2}^{(r)}}$, where $f_{j1}^{(r)}, f_{j2}^{(r)} (\neq 0) \in \mathrm{GF}(2^8)[x_8, \ldots, x_1, k_4^{(1)}, \ldots, k_1^{(1)}, \ldots, k_4^{(r)}, \ldots, k_1^{(r)}]$.

We use the computer algebra system Risa/Asir[7] to compute the rational expressions. It usually takes much time and space complexity to find them since the number of variables and the degree increases as the number of rounds increases. However, it is possible to find the rational expressions of the cipher SNAKE with only a few rounds. We show the *actual* numbers of coefficients in the rational expressions in Table 1. The number of coefficients we find here is very important and useful for evaluating the tighter upper bound of the complexity and the number of p/c pairs in the key-recovery attack that uses the meet-in-the-middle approach (see Section 5).

For estimating the number of coefficients in the rational expressions of SNAKE with more rounds, we use the following two techniques.

- decrease the number of variables by representing each round key $k_j^{(r)}$ as $\kappa^i \in \mathrm{GF}(2^8)$, i.e., a monomial in κ, where $\kappa \in \mathrm{GF}(2^8)$ and i is randomly chosen from $\mathrm{GF}(2^8) \setminus \{0, 255\}$.
- estimate the upper bound of the number of coefficients using Eq. (1), since it is easy to find the degree of the rational expression with respect to each variable.

Table 1. # of coef. in rational exp. over $GF(2^8)$ of SNAKE(1) and SNAKE(2) (global deduction)

	SNAKE(1)				SNAKE(2)			
$z_4^{(1)}, z_3^{(1)}, z_2^{(1)}, z_1^{(1)}$	$\frac{(12)}{(8)}$,	$\frac{(6)}{(4)}$,	$\frac{(3)}{(2)}$,	$\frac{(24)}{(16)}$	$\frac{(5)}{(4)}$,	$\frac{(4)}{(3)}$,	$\frac{(3)}{(2)}$,	$\frac{(6)}{(5)}$
$z_4^{(2)}, z_3^{(2)}, z_2^{(2)}, z_1^{(2)}$	$\frac{(432)}{(352)}$,	$\frac{(108)}{(88)}$,	$\frac{(40)}{(32)}$,	$\frac{(1760)}{(1540)}$	$\frac{(85)}{(72)}$,	$\frac{(34)}{(27)}$,	$\frac{(14)}{(10)}$,	$\frac{(198)}{(185)}$

Note) (# of coefs. in the numerator)/(# of coefs. in the denominator)

We show the degrees of the rational expressions over $GF(2^8)$ with respect to each variable in Table 2. Since for every subblock of every round $z_j^{(r)} \in GF(2^8)$, the rational expressions of SNAKE(1) and SNAKE(2) are of the same degree with respect to each variable, we put them together in one table, Table 2.

Instance deduction. In the instance deduction, we fix some subblocks of the plaintexts $x = (x_8, x_7, \ldots, x_1)$ to a certain value. For example, we fix $\{x_7, \ldots, x_1\}$ to $\{0, \ldots, 0\}$, and represent a ciphertext subblock as a rational expression over $GF(2^8)$ in x_8. If the number of coefficients in this rational expression in x_8, denoted by N, does not exceed $2^8 = 256$, we can construct the rational expression using N pairs of chosen plaintexts and ciphertexts. Therefore, it is desirable to find chosen p/c pairs such that the required number of pairs is as small as possible.

Chosen plaintexts useful for attacking SNAKE(1). We decided to find the rational expression with the fewest coefficients from the rational expressions in one variable. The reason for this is as follows. Let α and β be the numbers of variables. For the rational expression of a subblock $z_j^{(r)}$, if $\alpha > \beta$, the minimum value of the number of coefficients in the rational expression in α variables is larger than that in β variables.

It is easy to compute the rational expressions in one variable for all possible chosen plaintexts, since there are only 2^8 combinations. Our experimental results show that when we choose plaintexts s.t. $(x_8, 0, \ldots, 0)$ the number of coefficients in the rational expression in x_8 is the smallest for SNAKE(1). Table 3 shows the degrees of the rational expressions over $GF(2^8)$ when we choose plaintexts s.t. $(x_8, 0, \ldots, 0)$ and $(0, x_7, 0, \ldots, 0)$, respectively. The figures in brackets are the numbers of coefficients in the numerator or denominator polynomials. From Table 3, we can see that these rational expressions are dense, or all coefficients are nonzero. Note that the degrees with respect to x_8 and x_7 in Table 2 are not always equivalent to those in Table 3, though you may conjecture that they are equivalent.

Chosen plaintexts useful for attacking SNAKE(2). For SNAKE(2), if we choose plaintexts s.t. $(x_8, x_8, 0, \ldots, 0)$, the degree of the rational expression in x_8 falls as Table 4 shows. This is because the input to the leftmost S-box in the 2-nd round function becomes constant. Our experimental results show that the plaintexts

Table 2. Degrees of rational exp. over $GF(2^8)$ of SNAKE(1) and SNAKE(2) (global deduction)

	SNAKE(1)	SNAKE(2)
$z_4^{(1)}, z_3^{(1)}$	1,0,0,0,0,1,1,1 / 0,0,0,0,0,1,1,1	0,1,0,0,0,0,1,1 / 0,0,0,0,0,0,1,1
$z_2^{(1)}, z_1^{(1)}$	0,0,1,0,0,0,0,1 / 0,0,0,0,0,0,0,1	0,0,0,1,1,1,1,1 / 0,0,0,0,1,1,1,1
$z_4^{(2)}, z_3^{(2)}$	0,1,1,1,2,1,2,3 / 0,1,1,1,1,1,1,2	0,0,1,1,1,2,1,2 / 0,0,1,1,1,1,1,2
$z_2^{(2)}, z_1^{(2)}$	0,0,0,1,1,1,2,1 / 0,0,0,1,1,1,1,1	1,1,1,1,1,2,3,5 / 1,1,1,1,1,2,3,4
$z_4^{(3)}, z_3^{(3)}$	2,1,2,3,3,6,7,9 / 1,1,2,3,3,6,7,9	1,2,1,2,2,3,6,7 / 1,1,1,2,2,3,6,7
$z_2^{(3)}, z_1^{(3)}$	1,1,2,1,1,2,3,6 / 1,1,1,1,1,2,3,6	1,2,3,5,6,7,9,12 / 1,2,3,4,6,7,9,12
$z_4^{(4)}, z_3^{(4)}$	3,6,7,9,11,13,20,28 / 3,6,7,9,10,13,20,28	2,3,6,7,8,11,13,20 / 2,3,6,7,8,10,13,20
$z_2^{(4)}, z_1^{(4)}$	1,2,3,6,7,8,11,13 / 1,2,3,6,7,8,10,13	6,7,9,12,13,20,28,39 / 6,7,9,12,13,20,28,38
$z_4^{(5)}, z_3^{(5)}$	11,13,20,28,31,45,59,81 / 10,13,20,28,31,45,59,81	8,11,13,20,22,31,45,59 / 9,10,13,20,22,31,45,59
$z_2^{(5)}, z_1^{(5)}$	7,8,11,13,14,22,31,45 / 7,8,10,13,14,22,31,45	13,20,28,39,45,59,81,112 / 13,20,28,38,45,59,81,112
$z_4^{(6)}, z_3^{(6)}$	31,45,59,81,92,125,177,244 / 31,45,59,81,91,125,177,244	22,31,45,59,67,92,125,177 / 22,31,45,59,67,91,125,177
$z_2^{(6)}, z_1^{(6)}$	14,22,31,45,52,67,92,125 / 14,22,31,45,52,67,91,125	45,59,81,112,125,177,244,255 / 45,59,81,112,125,177,244,255
$z_4^{(7)}, z_3^{(7)}$	92,125,177,244,255,255,255,255 / 91,125,177,244,255,255,255,255	67,92,125,177,199,255,255,255 / 67,91,125,177,199,255,255,255
$z_2^{(7)}, z_1^{(7)}$	52,67,92,125,139,199,255,255 / 52,67,91,125,139,199,255,255	125,177,244,255,255,255,255,255 / 125,177,244,255,255,255,255,255

Note) Let $\deg_{x_i} f$ be the degree of f with respect to x_i, and the degrees in Table 2 are shown as follows.

$$\frac{\deg_{x_8} f_{j1}^{(r)}, \deg_{x_7} f_{j1}^{(r)}, \deg_{x_6} f_{j1}^{(r)}, \deg_{x_5} f_{j1}^{(r)}, \deg_{x_4} f_{j1}^{(r)}, \deg_{x_3} f_{j1}^{(r)}, \deg_{x_2} f_{j1}^{(r)}, \deg_{x_1} f_{j1}^{(r)}}{\deg_{x_8} f_{j2}^{(r)}, \deg_{x_7} f_{j2}^{(r)}, \deg_{x_6} f_{j2}^{(r)}, \deg_{x_5} f_{j2}^{(r)}, \deg_{x_4} f_{j2}^{(r)}, \deg_{x_3} f_{j2}^{(r)}, \deg_{x_2} f_{j2}^{(r)}, \deg_{x_1} f_{j2}^{(r)}}$$

s.t. $(x_8, x_8, 0, \ldots, 0)$ bring about the rational expression in one variable of the fewest coefficients for SNAKE(2). The plaintexts s.t. $(0, x_7, x_7, 0, \ldots, 0)$ bring about the second fewest one.

4.2 Key recovery

In this subsection, we demonstrate how to recover the last round key by taking a simple example of a chosen plaintext attack of SNAKE(2) with 9 rounds, i.e. SNAKE(2)(8, 4, 64, 9), (see also Figure 3 in Appendix). If we choose plaintexts s.t. $x = (x_8, x_8, 0, \ldots, 0)$, the second subblock from the right of the output of the 7-th round, $z_2^{(7)} \in GF(2^8)$, is represented as the rational expression $z_2^{(7)} = \frac{f_1(x_8)}{f_2(x_8)}$, where both $f_1(x_8)$ and $f_2(x_8)$ have 16 coefficients (see Table 4). Therefore, if $16 + 15 = 31$ pairs of plaintexts s.t. $x = (x_8, x_8, 0, \ldots, 0)$ and corresponding ciphertexts are given, we can construct the rational expression. The attack equation is as follows.

$$\frac{f_1(x_8)}{f_2(x_8)} = y_6 + S(y_1 + k_1^{(9)}) \tag{4}$$

Table 3. Degrees of rational exp. over $GF(2^8)$ of SNAKE(1).

when $x = (x_8, 0, \ldots, 0)$

$z_4^{(1)}, z_3^{(1)}, z_2^{(1)}, z_1^{(1)}$	$\dfrac{1\,(2)}{0\,(1)}$,	$\dfrac{0\,(1)}{0\,(1)}$,	$\dfrac{0\,(1)}{0\,(1)}$,	$\dfrac{0\,(1)}{0\,(1)}$
$z_4^{(2)}, z_3^{(2)}, z_2^{(2)}, z_1^{(2)}$	$\dfrac{0\,(1)}{0\,(1)}$,	$\dfrac{0\,(1)}{0\,(1)}$,	$\dfrac{0\,(1)}{0\,(1)}$,	$\dfrac{0\,(1)}{1\,(2)}$
$z_4^{(3)}, z_3^{(3)}, z_2^{(3)}, z_1^{(3)}$	$\dfrac{2\,(3)}{1\,(2)}$,	$\dfrac{1\,(2)}{1\,(2)}$,	$\dfrac{1\,(2)}{1\,(2)}$,	$\dfrac{1\,(2)}{1\,(2)}$
$z_4^{(4)}, z_3^{(4)}, z_2^{(4)}, z_1^{(4)}$	$\dfrac{3\,(4)}{3\,(4)}$,	$\dfrac{2\,(3)}{2\,(3)}$,	$\dfrac{1\,(2)}{1\,(2)}$,	$\dfrac{5\,(6)}{6\,(7)}$
$z_4^{(5)}, z_3^{(5)}, z_2^{(5)}, z_1^{(5)}$	$\dfrac{11\,(12)}{10\,(11)}$,	$\dfrac{8\,(9)}{8\,(9)}$,	$\dfrac{7\,(8)}{7\,(8)}$,	$\dfrac{13\,(14)}{13\,(14)}$
$z_4^{(6)}, z_3^{(6)}, z_2^{(6)}, z_1^{(6)}$	$\dfrac{31\,(32)}{31\,(32)}$,	$\dfrac{22\,(23)}{22\,(23)}$,	$\dfrac{14\,(15)}{14\,(15)}$,	$\dfrac{44\,(45)}{45\,(46)}$
$z_4^{(7)}, z_3^{(7)}, z_2^{(7)}, z_1^{(7)}$	$\dfrac{92\,(93)}{91\,(92)}$,	$\dfrac{67\,(68)}{67\,(68)}$,	$\dfrac{52\,(53)}{52\,(53)}$,	$\dfrac{125\,(126)}{125\,(126)}$

Note) degrees with respect to x_8

when $x = (0, x_7, 0, \ldots, 0)$

$z_4^{(1)}, z_3^{(1)}, z_2^{(1)}, z_1^{(1)}$	$\dfrac{0\,(1)}{0\,(1)}$,	$\dfrac{1\,(2)}{0\,(1)}$,	$\dfrac{0\,(1)}{0\,(1)}$,	$\dfrac{0\,(1)}{0\,(1)}$
$z_4^{(2)}, z_3^{(2)}, z_2^{(2)}, z_1^{(2)}$	$\dfrac{0\,(1)}{1\,(2)}$,	$\dfrac{0\,(1)}{0\,(1)}$,	$\dfrac{0\,(1)}{0\,(1)}$,	$\dfrac{0\,(1)}{1\,(2)}$
$z_4^{(3)}, z_3^{(3)}, z_2^{(3)}, z_1^{(3)}$	$\dfrac{1\,(2)}{1\,(2)}$,	$\dfrac{2\,(3)}{1\,(2)}$,	$\dfrac{1\,(2)}{1\,(2)}$,	$\dfrac{2\,(3)}{2\,(3)}$
$z_4^{(4)}, z_3^{(4)}, z_2^{(4)}, z_1^{(4)}$	$\dfrac{5\,(6)}{6\,(7)}$,	$\dfrac{3\,(4)}{3\,(4)}$,	$\dfrac{2\,(3)}{2\,(3)}$,	$\dfrac{6\,(7)}{7\,(8)}$
$z_4^{(5)}, z_3^{(5)}, z_2^{(5)}, z_1^{(5)}$	$\dfrac{13\,(14)}{13\,(14)}$,	$\dfrac{11\,(12)}{10\,(11)}$,	$\dfrac{8\,(9)}{8\,(9)}$,	$\dfrac{20\,(21)}{20\,(21)}$
$z_4^{(6)}, z_3^{(6)}, z_2^{(6)}, z_1^{(6)}$	$\dfrac{44\,(45)}{45\,(46)}$,	$\dfrac{31\,(32)}{31\,(32)}$,	$\dfrac{22\,(23)}{22\,(23)}$,	$\dfrac{58\,(59)}{59\,(60)}$
$z_4^{(7)}, z_3^{(7)}, z_2^{(7)}, z_1^{(7)}$	$\dfrac{125\,(126)}{125\,(126)}$,	$\dfrac{92\,(93)}{91\,(92)}$,	$\dfrac{67\,(68)}{67\,(68)}$,	$\dfrac{177\,(178)}{177\,(178)}$

Note) degrees with respect to x_7

The last round key $k_1^{(9)}$ is recovered as follows. For 31 plaintext/ciphertext pairs, we compute the right side of Eq. (4) guessing $k_1^{(9)}$. Thus all the coefficients in $\frac{f_1(x_8)}{f_2(x_8)}$ are determined. If the constructed Eq. (4) holds for the 32-nd pair of plaintext and ciphertext, we can judge that the guessed $k_1^{(9)}$ is correct with high probability. Since $k_1^{(9)}$ is 8 bits, the average of the required complexity of this attack is about $32 \times 2^8 \times \frac{1}{2} \sim 2^{12}$ times the computation of an S-box. Note that the required complexity for constructing the rational expression is negligible.

We apply similar key-recovery attacks to SNAKE with several rounds. We show some best attacks in Table 5, for which I mean that there is trade-off relations between the required number of p/c pairs and the complexity. The complexity is measured by the times of computation of the round function. In the column of strategy we show the attack strategies using simple symbols.

For example, the strategy "$7i + 1k$" means that the key-recovery attack uses the *instance deduction of 7-round* and recovers the last round key (m bits) as Figure 3 shows. The strategy "$7i + 2k$" means that the key-recovery attack uses the *instance deduction of 7-round* and recovers the last round key ($4m$ bits) and a subblock of the key of the second round from the bottom (m bits). The strategy "$11i + 2g + 1k$" means that the key-recovery attack uses the meet-in-the-middle

Table 4. Degrees of rational expression over $GF(2^8)$ of SNAKE(2)

when $x = (x_8, x_8, 0, \ldots, 0)$

$z_4^{(1)}, z_3^{(1)}, z_2^{(1)}, z_1^{(1)}$	$\dfrac{1\ (2)}{0\ (1)},$	$\dfrac{1\ (2)}{0\ (1)},$	$\dfrac{0\ (1)}{0\ (1)},$	$\dfrac{0\ (1)}{0\ (1)}$
$z_4^{(2)}, z_3^{(2)}, z_2^{(2)}, z_1^{(2)}$	$\dfrac{0\ (1)}{1\ (2)},$	$\dfrac{0\ (1)}{0\ (1)},$	$\dfrac{0\ (1)}{0\ (1)},$	$\dfrac{0\ (1)}{0\ (1)}$
$z_4^{(3)}, z_3^{(3)}, z_2^{(3)}, z_1^{(3)}$	$\dfrac{1\ (2)}{0\ (1)},$	$\dfrac{1\ (2)}{0\ (1)},$	$\dfrac{0\ (1)}{0\ (1)},$	$\dfrac{1\ (2)}{1\ (2)}$
$z_4^{(4)}, z_3^{(4)}, z_2^{(4)}, z_1^{(4)}$	$\dfrac{2\ (2)}{3\ (4)},$	$\dfrac{1\ (2)}{1\ (2)},$	$\dfrac{1\ (2)}{1\ (2)},$	$\dfrac{1\ (2)}{1\ (2)}$
$z_4^{(5)}, z_3^{(5)}, z_2^{(5)}, z_1^{(5)}$	$\dfrac{4\ (5)}{3\ (4)},$	$\dfrac{3\ (4)}{2\ (3)},$	$\dfrac{1\ (2)}{1\ (2)},$	$\dfrac{7\ (8)}{7\ (8)}$
$z_4^{(6)}, z_3^{(6)}, z_2^{(6)}, z_1^{(6)}$	$\dfrac{13\ (14)}{14\ (15)},$	$\dfrac{9\ (10)}{9\ (10)},$	$\dfrac{8\ (9)}{8\ (9)},$	$\dfrac{14\ (15)}{14\ (15)}$
$z_4^{(7)}, z_3^{(7)}, z_2^{(7)}, z_1^{(7)}$	$\dfrac{35\ (36)}{34\ (35)},$	$\dfrac{25\ (26)}{24\ (25)},$	$\dfrac{15\ (16)}{15\ (16)},$	$\dfrac{52\ (53)}{52\ (53)}$
$z_4^{(8)}, z_3^{(8)}, z_2^{(8)}, z_1^{(8)}$	$\dfrac{105\ (106)}{106\ (107)},$	$\dfrac{76\ (77)}{76\ (77)},$	$\dfrac{60\ (61)}{60\ (61)},$	$\dfrac{139\ (140)}{139\ (140)}$

Note) degrees with respect to x_8

Table 5. Interpolation attacks of SNAKE(i)(8, 4, 64, r)

SNAKE(1)				
#rounds(r)	#pairs	complexity	chosen plaintexts	strategy
9	59	2^{37}	$(x_8, 0, \ldots, 0)$	$6i + 1g + 1k$
	106	2^{14}	$(x_8, 0, \ldots, 0)$	$7i + 1k$
10	106	2^{46}	$(x_8, 0, \ldots, 0)$	$7i + 2k$
	211	2^{39}	$(x_8, 0, \ldots, 0)$	$7i + 1g + 1k$
11	211	2^{47}	$(x_8, 0, \ldots, 0)$	$7i + 1g + 2k$

SNAKE(2)				
#rounds(r)	#pairs	complexity	chosen plaintexts	strategy
9	32	2^{12}	$(x_8, x_8, 0, \ldots, 0)$	$7i + 1k$
10	32	2^{43}	$(x_8, x_8, 0, \ldots, 0)$	$7i + 2k$
	63	2^{38}	$(x_8, x_8, 0, \ldots, 0)$	$7i + 1g + 1k$
	122	2^{14}	$(x_8, x_8, 0, \ldots, 0)$	$8i + 1k$
11	122	2^{46}	$(x_8, x_8, 0, \ldots, 0)$	$8i + 2k$

approach where the *instance deduction of* 11-*round* and the *global deduction of* 2-*round* are used, and recovers the last round key ($4m$ bits) as Figure 4 shows.

5 Interpolation Attack of SNAKE(i)(16, 4, 128, r)

We apply the interpolation attack to a 128-bit variant, SNAKE(i)(16, 4, 128, r). When the block size is 128 bits and the size of input and output of the S-box is 16 bits, the maximum number of available p/c pairs for the attacker increases compared with the case when the block size is 64 bits. Thus, some attacks become possible that would be impractical when the block size was 64 bits.

For example, we demonstrate the interpolation attack of SNAKE(2) with 15 rounds, i.e. SNAKE(2)(16, 4, 128, 15) (see also Figure 4 in Appendix). If we choose plaintexts s.t. $x = (x_8, x_8, 0, \ldots, 0)$, the second subblock from the

Table 6. Degrees of rational exp. over $\text{GF}(2^{16})$ of SNAKE(1)

when $x = (x_8, 0, \ldots, 0)$

$z_4^{(8)}, z_3^{(8)}, z_2^{(8)}, z_1^{(8)}$	$\frac{275}{275}$,	$\frac{199}{199}$,	$\frac{139}{139}$,	$\frac{380}{381}$
$z_4^{(9)}, z_3^{(9)}, z_2^{(9)}, z_1^{(9)}$	$\frac{811}{810}$,	$\frac{587}{587}$,	$\frac{433}{433}$,	$\frac{1119}{1119}$
$z_4^{(10)}, z_3^{(10)}, z_2^{(10)}, z_1^{(10)}$	$\frac{2414}{2414}$,	$\frac{1751}{1751}$,	$\frac{1258}{1258}$,	$\frac{3330}{3331}$
$z_4^{(11)}, z_3^{(11)}, z_2^{(11)}, z_1^{(11)}$	$\frac{7151}{7150}$,	$\frac{5176}{5176}$,	$\frac{3764}{3764}$,	$\frac{9873}{9873}$
$z_4^{(12)}, z_3^{(12)}, z_2^{(12)}, z_1^{(12)}$	$\frac{21227}{21227}$,	$\frac{15388}{15388}$,	$\frac{11131}{11131}$,	$\frac{29294}{29294}$
$z_4^{(13)}, z_3^{(13)}, z_2^{(13)}, z_1^{(13)}$	$-$,	$-$,	$\frac{33059}{33059}$,	$-$

Note) degrees with respect to x_8

Table 7. Degrees of rational exp. over $\text{GF}(2^{16})$ of SNAKE(2)

when $x = (x_8, x_8, 0, \ldots, 0)$

$z_4^{(9)}, z_3^{(9)}, z_2^{(9)}, z_1^{(9)}$	$\frac{310}{309}$,	$\frac{224}{223}$,	$\frac{154}{154}$,	$\frac{433}{433}$
$z_4^{(10)}, z_3^{(10)}, z_2^{(10)}, z_1^{(10)}$	$\frac{916}{917}$,	$\frac{663}{663}$,	$\frac{493}{493}$,	$\frac{1258}{1258}$
$z_4^{(11)}, z_3^{(11)}, z_2^{(11)}, z_1^{(11)}$	$\frac{2724}{2723}$,	$\frac{1975}{1974}$,	$\frac{1412}{1412}$,	$\frac{3764}{3764}$
$z_4^{(12)}, z_3^{(12)}, z_2^{(12)}, z_1^{(12)}$	$\frac{8067}{8068}$,	$\frac{5839}{5839}$,	$\frac{4257}{4257}$,	$\frac{11131}{11131}$
$z_4^{(13)}, z_3^{(13)}, z_2^{(13)}, z_1^{(13)}$	$\frac{23951}{23950}$,	$\frac{17363}{17362}$,	$\frac{12543}{12543}$,	$\frac{33059}{33059}$

Note) degrees with respect to x_8

right of the output of the 11-th round, $z_2^{(11)} \in \text{GF}(2^{16})$, is represented as the rational expression $z_2^{(11)} = \frac{f_1(x_8)}{f_2(x_8)}$. According to Table 7, $\deg_{x_8} f_1 = 1412$ and $\deg_{x_8} f_2 = 1412$. On the other hand, $z_2^{(11)}$ is also represented using $\tilde{y}$, which can be computed from y and a guessed $k^{(15)}$: $z_2^{(11)} = \frac{g_1(\tilde{y})}{g_2(\tilde{y})}$. Using the meet-in-the-middle approach, we have the attack equation as follows.

$$\frac{f_1(x_8)}{f_2(x_8)} = \frac{g_1(\tilde{y}(y, k^{(15)}))}{g_2(\tilde{y}(y, k^{(15)}))} \tag{5}$$

From Table 1, the numbers of coefficients in g_1 and g_2 are 14 and 10, respectively. The numbers of coefficients in f_1 and f_2 are estimated to be at most 1413. Therefore, the required number of p/c pairs for constructing Eq. (5) is at most $(14 - 1) \times (1413 - 1) + 10 \times 1413 \sim 2^{15}$ for a guessed $k^{(15)}$. Since $k^{(15)}$ is 64 bits, the average of the required complexity of this attack is at most $2^{15} \times 2^{64} \times \frac{1}{2} \sim$ about 2^{78} times of computation of the round function.

If we didn't know the actual numbers of coefficients in g_1 and g_2, we would estimate them to be 48 and 32, respectively, from Eq. (1) and the degrees of $z_2^{(2)}$ in Table 1. Then, the attack would be considered as impossible because the required number of pairs exceeds 2^{16}.

We applied similar key-recovery attacks to SNAKE with the blocksize of 128 bits with several rounds. Similarly to Section 4, we show some best attacks in Table 9. As a practical attack of SNAKE(2)(16, 4, 128, 16), we give the attack

Table 8. Degrees of rational expression over GF(2^{16}) of SNAKE(2)

when $x = (x_8, x_8 + x_7, x_7, \ldots, 0)$

$z_4^{(1)}, z_3^{(1)}, z_2^{(1)}, z_1^{(1)}$	$\frac{1,0}{0,0}$,	$\frac{1,1}{0,0}$,	$\frac{0,1}{0,0}$,	$\frac{0,0}{0,0}$
$z_4^{(2)}, z_3^{(2)}, z_2^{(2)}, z_1^{(2)}$	$\frac{0,0}{1,0}$,	$\frac{0,0}{0,1}$,	$\frac{0,0}{0,0}$,	$\frac{0,0}{0,0}$
$z_4^{(3)}, z_3^{(3)}, z_2^{(3)}, z_1^{(3)}$	$\frac{1,1}{0,1}$,	$\frac{1,1}{0,0}$,	$\frac{0,1}{0,0}$,	$\frac{1,1}{1,1}$
$z_4^{(4)}, z_3^{(4)}, z_2^{(4)}, z_1^{(4)}$	$\frac{2,1}{3,1}$,	$\frac{1,2}{1,3}$,	$\frac{1,1}{1,1}$,	$\frac{1,2}{1,2}$
$z_4^{(5)}, z_3^{(5)}, z_2^{(5)}, z_1^{(5)}$	$\frac{4,7}{3,7}$,	$\frac{3,4}{2,3}$,	$\frac{1,3}{1,2}$,	$\frac{7,8}{7,8}$
$z_4^{(6)}, z_3^{(6)}, z_2^{(6)}, z_1^{(6)}$	$\frac{13,14}{14,14}$,	$\frac{9,13}{9,14}$,	$\frac{8,9}{8,9}$,	$\frac{14,22}{14,22}$
$z_4^{(7)}, z_3^{(7)}, z_2^{(7)}, z_1^{(7)}$	$\frac{35,52}{34,52}$,	$\frac{25,35}{24,34}$,	$\frac{15,25}{15,24}$,	$\frac{52,67}{52,67}$
$z_4^{(8)}, z_3^{(8)}, z_2^{(8)}, z_1^{(8)}$	$\frac{105,139}{106,139}$,	$\frac{76,105}{76,106}$,	$\frac{60,76}{60,76}$,	$\frac{139,199}{139,199}$
$z_4^{(9)}, z_3^{(9)}, z_2^{(9)}, z_1^{(9)}$	$\frac{310,433}{309,433}$,	$\frac{224,310}{223,309}$,	$\frac{154,224}{154,223}$,	$\frac{433,587}{433,587}$
$z_4^{(10)}, z_3^{(10)}, z_2^{(10)}, z_1^{(10)}$	$\frac{916,1258}{917,1258}$,	$\frac{663,916}{663,917}$,	$\frac{493,663}{493,663}$,	$\frac{1258,1751}{1258,1751}$
$z_4^{(11)}, z_3^{(11)}, z_2^{(11)}, z_1^{(11)}$	$\frac{2724,3764}{2723,3764}$,	$\frac{1975,2724}{1974,2723}$,	$\frac{1412,1975}{1412,1974}$,	$\frac{3764,5176}{3764,5176}$
$z_4^{(12)}, z_3^{(12)}, z_2^{(12)}, z_1^{(12)}$	$\frac{8067,11131}{8068,11131}$,	$\frac{5839,8067}{5839,8068}$,	$\frac{4257,5839}{4257,5839}$,	$\frac{11131,15388}{11131,15388}$
$z_4^{(13)}, z_3^{(13)}, z_2^{(13)}, z_1^{(13)}$	$\frac{23951,33059}{23950,33059}$,	$\frac{17363,23951}{17362,23950}$,	$\frac{12543,17363}{12543,17362}$,	$\frac{33059,45602}{33059,45602}$
$z_4^{(14)}, z_3^{(14)}, z_2^{(14)}, z_1^{(14)}$	$\frac{-}{}$,	$\frac{-}{}$,	$\frac{37316,51441}{37316,51441}$,	$-$

Note) degrees with respect to x_8 and x_7

which requires $< 2^{32}$ p/c pairs and complexity of 2^{47} times the computation of the round function. It uses the chosen plaintexts s.t. $x = (x_8, x_8 + x_7, x_7, 0, \ldots, 0)$. This brings about the rational expression in two variable of the fewest coefficients for SNAKE(2).

6 Discussion and Concluding Remarks

Division by 0. Here we discuss a problem in the interpolation attack using rational expressions, which wasn't pointed out in [3]. The problem is that we can't always construct correct rational expressions if at least one of the inputs of S-boxes are 0 in the encryption process. We can detect this by comparing the degree of the constructed rational expression with that in Table 2 etc. The degree often gets higher. If this happens, we may construct the rational expression again using different pairs of plaintexts and ciphertexts. In this case the required number of p/c pairs can be estimated by the cryptanalysis with probabilistic nonlinear relations shown by Jakobsen [2]. This is based on Sudan's algorithm for decoding Reed-Solomon codes beyond the error-correction diameter. If we apply Jakobsen's result to this problem, when the rational expression holds with probability μ, the attack is possible with $\mathcal{N} = \frac{N}{\mu^2}$ p/c pairs in time polynomial in $\mathcal{N}$, where N is the number of coefficients in the rational expression. The probability μ is equal to the probability with which none of the inputs of S-boxes are zero in the encryption process. Therefore, $\mu = \left(\frac{2^m - 1}{2^m}\right)^{4r}$ for SNAKE(i)($m, 4, 8m, r$), if we assume every input of the S-box is random and independent. For example,

Table 9. Interpolation attacks of SNAKE(i)$(16, 4, 128, r)$

SNAKE(1)				
#rounds(r)	#pairs	complexity	chosen plaintexts	strategy
13	2^{13}	2^{28}	$(x_8, 0, \ldots, 0)$	$11i + 1k$
14	2^{15}	2^{30}	$(x_8, 0, \ldots, 0)$	$12i + 1k$
15	2^{15}	2^{94}	$(x_8, 0, \ldots, 0)$	$12i + 2k$
	2^{16}	2^{79}	$(x_8, 0, \ldots, 0)$	$12i + 1g + 1k$
SNAKE(2)				
#rounds(r)	#pairs	complexity	chosen plaintexts	strategy
13	2^{11}	2^{74}	$(x_8, x_8, 0, \ldots, 0)$	$10i + 1g + 1k$
	2^{12}	2^{27}	$(x_8, x_8, 0, \ldots, 0)$	$11i + 1k$
14	2^{14}	2^{29}	$(x_8, x_8, 0, \ldots, 0)$	$12i + 1k$
15	2^{14}	2^{93}	$(x_8, x_8, 0, \ldots, 0)$	$12i + 2k$
	2^{15}	2^{30}	$(x_8, x_8, 0, \ldots, 0)$	$13i + 1k$
16	2^{15}	2^{94}	$(x_8, x_8, 0, \ldots, 0)$	$13i + 2k$
	2^{32}	2^{47}	$(x_8, x_8 + x_7, x_7, 0, \ldots, 0)$	$14i + 1k$

the attack for SNAKE(i)$(8, 4, 64, 11)$ is possible with $\mathcal{N} = \frac{N}{\mu^2} \sim 1.411N$ p/c pairs in time polynomial in $\mathcal{N}$, and the attack for SNAKE(2)$(16, 4, 128, 16)$ is possible with $\mathcal{N}' = \frac{N'}{\mu^2} \sim 1.002N'$ p/c pairs in time polynomial in $\mathcal{N}'$.

Diffusion layer. It is the plain diffusion layer that makes the interpolation attack on the cipher SNAKE(2) easier. The diffusion layer of the cipher SNAKE(2) keeps the outputs of some subblocks *constant* for some chosen plaintexts. We have to consider this in designing the diffusion layer.

Concluding remarks. We presented an efficient interpolation attack using a computer algebra system. We succeeded in attacking the block cipher SNAKE efficiently – with smaller complexity and fewer p/c pairs – 1) by finding the actual number of coefficients in the rational expression used in the attack and 2) by finding the rational expression with the fewest coefficients by choosing the plaintexts. We found some attacks feasible which we would consider as impossible by the interpolation attack described in [3]. When we evaluate the resistance of a block cipher to the interpolation attack, it is necessary to apply the interpolation attack described in this paper.

We showed that when the block size is 64 bits and $m = 8$, all round keys are recovered for SNAKE(1) and SNAKE(2) with up to 11 rounds. Moreover, when the block size is 128 bits and $m = 16$, all round keys are recovered for SNAKE(1) with up to 15 rounds and SNAKE(2) with up to 16 rounds.

References

1. E.Biham and A.Shamir, "Differential Cryptanalysis of DES-like Cryptosystems," Journal of Cryptology, Volume 4, Number 1, pp.3–72, Springer-Verlag, 1991.

2. T.Jakobsen, "Cryptanalysis of Block Ciphers with Probabilistic Non-Linear Relations of Low Degree," Advances in Cryptology – CRYPTO'98, Lecture Notes in Computer Science 1462, pp.212–222, Springer-Verlag, 1998.
3. T.Jakobsen and L.R.Knudsen, "The Interpolation Attack on Block Ciphers," Fast Software Encryption, FSE'97, Lecture Notes in Computer Science 1267, pp.28–40, Springer-Verlag, 1997.
4. L.R.Knudsen, "Block Ciphers – Analysis, Design and applications," phD thesis, Aarhus University, Denmark, 1994.
5. C.Lee and Y.Cha, "The Block Cipher : SNAKE with Provable Resistance against DC and LC attacks," In Proceedings of 1997 Korea-Japan Joint Workshop on Information Security and Cryptology (JW-ISC'97), pp.3–17, 1997.
6. M.Matsui, "Linear Cryptanalysis Method for DES Cipher," Advances in Cryptology – EUROCRYPT'93, Lecture Notes in Computer Science 765, pp.386–397, Springer-Verlag, 1994.
7. M.Noro and T.Takeshima, "Risa/Asir – a computer algebra system," Proceedings of ISSAC'92, pp.387–396, ACM Press, 1992.
8. K.Nyberg and L.R.Knudsen, "Provable Security Against a Differential Attack," Journal of Cryptology, Volume 8, Number 1, pp.27–37, Springer-Verlag, 1995.
9. V.Rijmen, J.Daemen, B.Preneel, A.Bosselaers, and E.De Win, "The cipher SHARK," Fast Software Encryption, FSE'96, Lecture Notes in Computer Science 1039, pp.99–112, Springer-Verlag, 1996.

Appendix

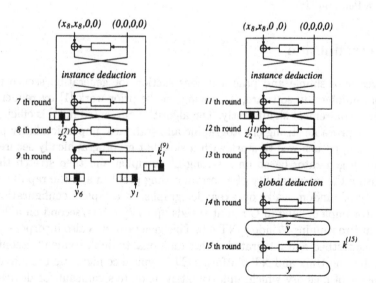

Fig. 3. A chosen plaintext attack of SNAKE(2)(8,4,64,9)

Fig. 4. A chosen plaintext attack of SNAKE(2)(16,4,128,15)

High-Speed Pseudorandom Number Generation with Small Memory

William Aiello[1], S. Rajagopalan[2], and Ramarathnam Venkatesan[3]

[1] ATT Labs – Research, Florham Park, NJ, U.S.A. aiello@research.att.com[†]
[2] Telcordia Technologies, 445 South Street, Morristown, NJ 07960, U.S.A.
sraj@research.telcordia.com
[3] Microsoft Research, One Microsoft Way, Redmond, WA, U.S.A.
venkie@microsoft.com[†]

Abstract. We present constructions for a family of pseudorandom generators that are very fast in practice, yet possess provable strong cryptographic and statistical unpredictability properties. While such constructions were previously known, our constructions here have much smaller memory requirements, e.g., small enough for smart cards, etc. Our memory improvements are achieved by using variants of pseudorandom functions. The security requirements of this primitive are a weakening of the security requirements of a pseudorandom function. We instantiate this primitive by a keyed secure hash function. A sample construction based on DES and MD5 was found to run at about 20 megabits per second on a Pentium II.

1 Introduction

We present a simple and practical construction for generating secure pseudo random numbers in software, improving on the prior work [1] by reducing the memory requirement significantly. The algorithm presented in [1] is efficient and possesses provable strong cryptographic and statistical unpredictability properties. The approach was to start with a slow but cryptographically secure pseudorandom generator based on a strong block cipher and then stretch the outputs using the intractability of a certain coding problem and the rapidly mixing property of random walks on expander graphs. In a typical configuration, this generator implemented in C ran at speeds up to 70 Mbits/second on a 200MHz PentiumPro running WindowsNT 4.0. This generator was also incorporated into an IPSec testbed and integrated with a high quality duplex video teleconferencing system on Unix and NT platforms. This typical configuration required 16 to 32 Kbytes of memory which, unfortunately, is quite significant for devices with a limited amount of memory such as smart cards or cell-phones.

Our improvement here is achieved by replacing the stretching mechanism in [1] by using what we call *random-input pseudorandom (family of) functions* (RI-PRF) or *hidden-input pseudorandom (family of) functions* (HI-PRF). These

---

[†] Work done while at Telcordia.

functions accept *random* inputs and map them into *longer* pseudorandom outputs. The former allows the adversary to see the random inputs while the latter does not. Hence their security requirements are weaker than usual pseudorandom functions (PRF) that must map *adversarially and adaptively* chosen inputs into pseudorandom outputs. The existence of a RI-PRF is equivalent to the existence of a PRF (and both are equivalent to the existence of a one-way function by [11] and [13]). However, while every PRF is also a RI-PRF, not every RI-PRF is a PRF. For example, consider the following simple modification to a PRF. On input 0, the modified function always outputs zero. Such a modified function can obviously be distinguished from a random function with one query chosen by the adversary. However, the modified function remains a RI-PRF.

We suggest that RI-PRF's can be instantiated in practice by well known secure hash functions such as MD5, and SHA-1. The current attacks against these hash functions ([6], [7], [18], [20]) do not contradict their being secure RI-PRF's.

We note that secure hash functions have been used to construct different primitives. For example, [4] construct PRF's on arbitrary length inputs from PRF's on fixed length inputs which they instantiated by well-known compression functions. [3] construct a message authentication code (an unpredictable PRF family) from well-known compression functions. [17] have independently explored several variations of the PRF model given by varying the requirement between predictability and indistinguishability, and varying the query model from adaptively chosen to random. While our RI-PRF model is the same as one of their variations, our HI-PRF model is new.

Our implementation in C using MD5 and DES ran at 28 to 40 Mbits/sec on a 233 MHz PentiumII running Windows NT 4.0. The memory requirement ranges from 128 Bytes to 3 KBytes. The algorithm can be adapted for encrypting packets that are sent across a network and may be received out of order.

2   The Generator G_{vra}

In [1], a generator named VRA ("Video Rate Algorithm") was presented. We will denote this generator by G_{vra} and briefly recall its construction for purposes of comparison. The generator presented in this paper is denoted G and described in the next section. In addition, we will present some improvements to G_{vra} itself in this paper in section 5.4.

G_{vra} has parameters (n, k, L). It starts with a short preprocessing step when it runs a slow but secure generator, denoted by G_0, the output of which is subsequently stretched to a much longer output during the run of the algorithm in a way many desirable properties are preserved. The secure generator G_0 may be based on a one way permutation (OWP) or block cipher. The computational cost of the preprocessing step is amortized over a long output. The outputs of $z_1, z_2, \ldots, z_m$ are each L bits long. The overall generator needs $(n + 1)L$ bits of memory and it takes roughly k simple machine operations like shift, exclusive-or and table look-up to generate each machine word-sized block. The relevant security parameter is $\binom{n}{k}$ where n and k can be chosen so that $\binom{n}{k}$ is large enough to be considered infeasible (e.g. 2^{60}) and $\frac{1}{\binom{n}{k}}$ negligible. Note here that n is not the length of the seed input to the strong generator. Also, n and k can be varied within certain bounds to provide a smooth time-space tradeoff.

2.1 Construction of G_{vra}

The approach in [1] is to begin with a few bits from a high quality source with cryptographic properties. The algorithm "stretches" these bits to a much longer sequence while maintaining many desirable properties.

The generator G_{vra} has a simple description. First, let us assume we are given a possibly slow but perfect or cryptographically secure generator G_0 (it was shown in [1] how to construct one from a strong cipher such as DES or Triple-DES). Let $x \leftarrow G_0(\cdot)$ denote that x is assigned a random string of length $|x|$ by making a call to G_0 and obtaining the next block of random bits of appropriate length. Below, we use a d-regular expander graph with 2^L nodes each labeled with a L-bit string. Since the graph is d-regular, it can be edge-colored with colors $\{1, \ldots, d\}$. For any node y, $1 \le r \le d$, let $neighbor(y, r)$ denote the neighbor of y reached by traversing the edge colored r. G_{vra} has two processes P_0 and P_1 each producing a sequence of L-bit numbers. Here $\oplus$ stands for bitwise exclusive-or of strings of equal length. $A[i]$ denotes the i-th row of matrix A. p is a probability parameter $\in [0, \frac{1}{2}]$.

Initialization for both processes
    P_0 : $A \leftarrow G_0(\cdot), A \in \{0,1\}^{n \times L}$.
    P_1 : $y_0 \leftarrow G_0(\cdot), y_0 \in \{0,1\}^L$.
On-line steps for $i := 1, 2, \ldots$ do
    P_0 : $c_1, \ldots, c_k \leftarrow G_0(\cdot), c_j \in \{0, 1, \ldots, n-1\}, c_j$ distinct
        $x_i := \oplus_{j=1}^{k} A[c_j], x_i \in \{0,1\}^L$
    P_1 : $b \leftarrow G_0, b \in \{0,1\}^{\lceil \log \frac{1}{p} \rceil}$.
        if ($b = 00 \ldots 0$) $y_i := y_{i-1}$ [i.e., stay at the same node with probability p]
        else $r \leftarrow G_0, r \in \{1, \ldots, d\}, y_i := neighbor(y_{i-1}, r)$ [i.e., move to a random neighbor]
Output $z_i := x_i \oplus y_i$.

Note that for process P_1, the random walk on an expander, the computation of each neighbor of a node must be both efficiently computable and require small memory. The Gabber-Galil [9] expander, defined below, is the most efficient in computation and memory of all known expanders. The neighbors of (x, y) are $(x, x + 2y + \{0,1,2\})$ and $(2x + y + \{0,1,2\}, y)$ where x and y are $\ell = L/2$ bit strings and arithmetic is done $\mod 2^\ell$.

The generator thus stretches $k\lceil \log n \rceil + \lceil \log d \rceil + \lceil \log \frac{1}{p} \rceil$ bits (all logs are binary) to L bits. For example, for the setting ($n = 256, k = 6, d = 6, L = 512, p = \frac{1}{2}$) the stretch factor is approximately 10. The properties of the generator are detailed in [1].

2.2 The Large Memory Requirement of $\mathbf{G_{vra}}$

Note that $\mathbf{G_{vra}}$ requires a matrix A of $n \times L$ random bits. A typical setting for achieving high speed and reasonable security is $n = 256$ and $L = 1024$ [1], i.e., an A of size 32 Kbytes which is significant and may result in two difficulties. First, the memory requirement may be unacceptable to small devices such as cell phones, handheld computing devices, and even low-end set-top boxes. On platforms such as smart cards, a realistic size for available memory is about 1Kbyte. Second, the cache architecture on modern CISC CPUs such as i86xx is such that data structures that do not fit in a cache page suffer from high page swap penalties. $\mathbf{G_{vra}}$ suffers from this problem as the random row accesses to the matrix A cannot be effectively pipelined. The survey in [21] recommends that tables should not be larger than 4Kbytes. Furthermore, for applications such as e-commerce transactions which require both high speed and semantic security (i.e. every bit must be unpredictable to the adversary even if all the other bits are known), the proof in [8] shows that the memory requirement of $\mathbf{G_{vra}}$ is much larger. There seems to be no easy way to configure $\mathbf{G_{vra}}$ with small memory and achieve high security.

In the following section, we show how to reduce the memory requirement to about 1Kbyte while still achieving high security and reasonable speed. We do so by introducing a new primitive called a *random-input pseudorandom function*.

3 Construction and Properties of the Generator G

As in the case of $\mathbf{G_{vra}}$, our approach is to begin with a few pseudorandom bits from a high quality source with strong cryptographic properties and "stretch" these bits to a much longer sequence while maintaining security properties. For this we will use an additional assumption. To begin with, we consider using a pseudorandom function (PRF) [11]. However, as we will see, we do not need the full security of a PRF. We will be able to use a length-increasing function with a weaker security requirement which we call a *random-input pseudorandom function*. Whereas in the case of a PRF, its outputs must appear to be random to a computationally bounded adversary even when the adversary makes adaptive queries to the function, for a length-increasing random-input pseudorandom function (RI-PRF) we only require that the outputs appear to be random to a computationally bounded adversary when the inputs are chosen at random. The expectation is that weaker security requirements for a random-input pseudorandom function may be traded off for greater efficiency.

Next we will describe our construction of a pseudorandom generator $\mathbf{G}$ assuming the availability of a RI-PRF. In Section 4.2 we formally define RI-PRF's and suggest implementations.

3.1 The Construction of G

Our generator is a simple modification of $\mathbf{G_{vra}}$. $\mathbf{G}$ takes parameters ℓ, m_1, m_2, and n. As before, we assume we have a cryptographically strong PRG G_0. We also assume that we are given a random-input pseudorandom function family with parameters l, m_1 and m_2, $f : \{0,1\}^l \times \{0,1\}^{m_1} \to \{0,1\}^{m_2}, m_2 > m_1$. We write $f_K(x) \equiv f(K, x)$. The parameter n is typically less than 10. Let $L = nm_2$. The P_1 process for $\mathbf{G}$ is exactly the same as that for $\mathbf{G_{vra}}$.

A simple description of $\mathbf{P_0}$ is as follows. In the pre-processing step, randomly choose n keys of length l for the n random-input pseudorandom functions. On each on-line step, choose a random input of length m_1 and feed it to each of the RI-PRF's. x_i is the concatenation of all the outputs of the n functions.

We describe the new $\mathbf{P_0}$ process formally below.

Initialization $\mathbf{P_0}$: $K_1, K_2, \ldots, K_n \leftarrow G_0(\cdot), |K_i| = \ell.$
On-line steps for $i := 1, 2, \ldots$ **do**
$\quad \mathbf{P_0} :$ $B \leftarrow G_0(\cdot), B \in \{0,1\}^{m_1}.$
$\qquad x_i := f_{K_1}(B) \circ \cdots \circ f_{K_n}(B).$

As in $\mathbf{G_{vra}}$, the i-th output of $\mathbf{G}$ is $z_i := x_i \oplus y_i$ where y_i is the ith output of P_1.

Clearly, the memory requirement of P_0 is $\leq n \times \ell + m_1$ bits (not counting the internal memory requirements of f which is used as a blackbox). In a prototypical implementation using MD5, $m_2 = 128$ $m_1 = 64$, $\ell = 512 - 64$. Typically $n = 4$ and hence the memory needed is about 0.5Kbyte. In the on-line steps, the generator thus stretches $m_1 + \lceil \log \frac{1}{p} \rceil + \lceil \log d \rceil$ bits to L bits where $L = n \times m_2$. For example, for the setting $(n = 4, d = 6, l = 448, m_1 = 64, m_2 = 128, p = \frac{1}{2})$ the stretch factor is approximately 8.

Outline: In section 4, we give definitions and conventions used in this paper we show that the process $\mathbf{P_0}$ has strong security properties. In section 5 we describe the properties of the full generator. In section 5.3, we describe some variations in the construction of $\mathbf{G}$ and $\mathbf{G_{vra}}$ and their usefulness in specific scenarios.

4 Definitions and Notations

4.1 Preliminaries

For any string $x \in \{0,1\}^*$, let $|x|$ be its length and let $\circ$ denote the concatenation operator. We first define strong one-way permutations. Let $f : \{0,1\}^* \to \{0,1\}^*$ be a length-preserving function that is easy (e.g. polynomial time) to compute. f is a permutation if it is one-to-one as well. Let $T : \mathbb{N} \to \mathbb{N}$ and $\epsilon : \mathbb{N} \to [0,1]$. The security of f is $(T(n), \epsilon(n))$ if the following statement is true for infinitely many n. For a given n, for all probabilistic adversaries A that run for time $\leq T(n)$, $\text{Prob}[A(f(x)) \in f^{-1}(f(x))] \leq \epsilon(n)$ where the probability is taken over the input $x \in \{0,1\}^n$ and the coin-flips of A. f is said to be a "strong" one-way function if it has security $(n^{O(1)}, n^{-\omega(1)})$, where $\omega(1)$ is any function on integers that goes to infinity asymptotically. For ease of exposition, whenever n is understood, we will use T and ϵ in place of $T(n)$ and $\epsilon(n)$, respectively.

A pseudorandom generator g accepts a short random seed x of length, say n, and produces a sequence of bits $g(x) = b_1, b_2, \ldots, b_m$ for some $m > n$. g is defined to have bit security $(T_b(n), \epsilon_b(n))$ if, for any $i, 1 \leq i \leq m$, any probabilistic algorithm that is given $b_1, \ldots, b_{i-1}$, after running for time $\leq T_b$ cannot predict b_{i+1} with probability $> \frac{1}{2} + \epsilon_b{}^1$. Analogously, a pseudorandom *sequence* $b_1, \ldots, b_l$ is defined to have security (T_s, ϵ_s) if any probabilistic algorithm, after running for time T_s cannot distinguish $b_1 \ldots b_l$ from l truly random bits with probability $> \frac{1}{2} + \epsilon_s$. Yao [22] showed that the bit security of a generator and the security of any l bits of its output are tightly related: $\frac{T_s}{\epsilon_s} \geq \frac{T_b}{l\epsilon_b}$. g is *cryptographically strong* (or simply strong) if its security is such that whenever $T_b(n)$ is feasible $\epsilon_b(n)$ is negligible. Hence, if g is strong, no efficient algorithm can distinguish g from a random source with better than negligible probability.

Goldreich and Levin [12] gave a construction for a PRG using any one-way permutation such that the bit security of the generator is nearly the same as the security of the underlying one-way function. In [1], a similar construction for a PRG is given for any cipher (which is secure in an appropriately defined model) such that the bit security of the generator is nearly that of the cipher. In our construction of G given in section 3 we assume that G_0 is such a strong generator.

4.2 Pseudorandom Functions

Pseudorandom functions were defined in [11]. They presented a construction that makes as many calls as the input length to a PRG that doubles the input length. Recently, a more economical construction based on the Decisional Diffie-Hellman assumption was given in [16]. However, all constructions whose security is reducible to the security of well-known number theoretic problems are too slow for many applications. In situations which require an efficient PRF, a keyed cryptographic hash function or a block cipher (with Merkle's construction which destroys the invertibility) are often used. Rather than the security of the PRF being reduced to that of a well known problem, it is simply be asserted on the strength of empirical evidence. In such situations it seems prudent to try as much as possible to reduce the security requirements of the cryptographic primitive whose security is being asserted. This is the approach we take here.

Let us first recall the definition of a PRF. Traditionally, PRF's are used as length-preserving functions but we will allow the general version here. A function family with parameters (k, m_1, m_2) family $\mathcal{F}$ is a collection of efficiently computable functions f_K mapping m_1-bits to m_2 bits indexed by $K \in \{0,1\}^k$. Given the string K one can easily compute the function f_K. We will assume that the parameters of the family can be increased suitably and without any bound.

Definition 1 (Security of Prf) *A pseudorandom function family $\mathcal{F}$ has security (T, U, δ) if, for every valid m_1, no probabilistic adversary $\mathcal{A}$ given access to*

---

[1] Bit security of g has also been defined as $s_b = \frac{T_b}{\epsilon_b}$ (see,e.g., [14]) but we prefer the two-parameter model as it is more transparent.

an oracle of $f_K \in_{random} \mathcal{F}_{m_1}$ running in time T and making at most U queries to the oracle, can distinguish the oracle from a random function oracle with probability (over the adversary's coin flips and choice of K) $> \delta$.

We observe that a slight generalization of the classical definition of a PRF family is to allow the polynomially bounded adversary access to many instances f_{K_i} (the number is determined adaptively by the adversary) where the adversary does not know any of the K_i's but can query any f_{K_i} at the cost of a query each. Next, we define a weaker notion of PRF that we suggest is useful and perhaps more tenable. This notion was independently proposed as *random-challenge pseudorandom* function in [17]. A function family is *random-input pseudorandom* (RI-PRF) if the adversary has to distinguish a member of this family from a truly random one on random queries. That is, the adversary does not adaptively choose the queries as in the definition of a pseudorandom function but rather random query points are chosen for her. More formally, the adversary sees a sequence $(x_1, f_K(x_1)), \ldots, (x_u, f_K(x_u))$ where each x_i is chosen uniformly at random from $\{0,1\}^{m_1}$ and the key $K \in \{0,1\}^l$ is chosen uniformly and is unknown to the adversary.

Definition 2 (Security of RI-PRF family) *A function family $\mathcal{F}$ is random-input pseudorandom with security (T, U, δ) if for every valid m_1, no probabilistic adversary $\mathcal{A}$ given access to a random-input oracle of $f \in_{random} \mathcal{F}_{m_1}$ running in time T and seeing at most U can distinguish U input-output pairs for f_K from U input-output pairs for a truly random function where the input queries are random with probability (over the adversary's coin flips, and choice of K and x_i's) $> \delta$.*

One can trivially get a strong PRG g from a RI-PRF and a pseudorandom source (or a long enough seed). g uses the pseudorandom source to select a random member of the RI-PRF family and an intial random input. Iteratively, for every successive block of pseudorandom bits to be output, g flips as many bits as the input length of the RI-PRF and outputs these bits as well as the value of the RI-PRF on that input. One can stop here and use this construction for a strong generator if one can find concrete functions that are efficient in practice and can be modeled as RI-PRF's with good security. However, the RI-PRF assumption may be too strong for some concrete functions and we would like to weaken the assumption of security further. To this end, we first note that the security of a RI-PRF is at least as much or higher if the input was hidden from the adversary. We call such a function a *hidden-input pseudorandom* (HI-PRF). More formally, we define an HI-PRF family as follows.

Definition 3 (Security of HI-PRF Family) *A function family $\mathcal{F}$ is hidden-input pseudorandom with security (T, U, δ) if for every valid m_1, no probabilistic adversary $\mathcal{A}$ given access to a random-input oracle of $f \in_{random} \mathcal{F}_{m_1}$ running in time T and seeing at most U can distinguish U outputs of f_K from U outputs of a truly random function where the input queries are random and unknown with probability (over the adversary's coin flips, and choice of K and x_i's) $> \delta$.*

A further variation on HI-PRF is when the random inputs are chosen without replacement. Note that drawing with or without replacement for RI-PRF is an inessential distinction since the adversary can see when an input is repeated.

4.3 PRF's vs RI-PRF's vs HI-PRF's vs PRG's

Any RI-PRF or HI-PRF is a one-way function as is clear from the definition. Thus, the notions of PRF, RI-PRF, HI-PRF, and PRG are equivalent in terms of their existence to that of one-way functions. Nevertheless, we show that there exists a function which is an HI-PRF but not a RI-PRF, and another that is a RI-PRF but not a PRF.

First, let us assume we are given a pseudorandom function f from n bits to n bits. Note that the simple function $F_K(x) := (x, f_K(x))$ is an HI-PRF from n bits to $2n$ bits. However, it is not a RI-PRF since the input, seen by the adversary, and output are obviously correlated. A RI-PRF which is not a PRF can be constructed as follows using a standard two-round Feistel network: $F_{K_1,K_2}(x,y) = (z, f_{K_2}(z) \oplus x)$ where $z = f_{K_1}(x) \oplus y$. This function is not a PRF since, for inputs (x, y_1) and (x, y_2), $z_1 \oplus z_2 = y_1 \oplus y_2$, and thus the adversary who can choose these inputs can easily distinguish this function from a random one. However, for random choices for x and y, using ideas of [19] we can show that the outputs are indistinguishable from random if f is a PRF.

Following the comment after Definition 1, we note that the model of security for RI-PRF and HI-PRF can be generalized (as in the case of PRF's) to allow multiple independent instantiations that an adversary can query. Secondly, we note that any function that is a RI-PRF is an HI-PRF. The distinguishing probability for an adversary who does not see the inputs in the HI-PRF model may be significantly lower than when she can see the inputs in the RI-PRF model for the same function. Finally, note that an HI-PRF which is not length increasing is trivial (the identity function is one).

Note that a secure HI-PRF family is equivalent to a PRG whose outputs on correlated seeds are indistinguishable from random when the seeds are of the form $K \circ r_i$ where K is random but fixed and the r_i's are random and independent. However, we can distinguish HI-PRF's from PRG's as follows. As before, let us say that we have a HI-PRF family whose members are indexed with $k = |K|$ bits and that we have n independent instantiations of this family. Then, in i iterations, for an input of $k \cdot n + i \cdot m_1$ random bits, we get $i \cdot n \cdot m_2$ output bits. In order to compare similar things, let us consider a PRG which takes n seeds of m_1 bits each and outputs $i \cdot n \cdot m_2$ bits in i iterations. The difference between the two is that the HI-PRF construction uses an extra $n \cdot k$ bits which may make a difference in their security in the following sense. There may exist functions whose security is lower when used as a PRG (i.e. without the extra $n \cdot k$ random bits input) as compared to HI-PRF's.

To make this concrete, consider the example of MD5 with $n = 1$, $i = 2$, and $m_1 = 64$ (implying $k = 448 = 512 - 64$. The difference between the two modes is as follows: in the case of the PRG, in each iteration we use MD5 with m_1 random bits and a fixed pad known to the adversary of length k . Contrast this with the HI-PRF mode of using MD5 where the k pad bits are chosen at random and are fixed and secret from the adversary. At each iteration, we run MD5 on m_1 random bits and this pad. It is quite conceivable that the bits output by MD5 in the second mode are much more secure than in the first.

[15] define a *pseudorandom synthesizer* as a function whose outputs cannot be distinguished from random even when the adversary knows the outputs on a matrix of inputs generated as a cross-product of two lists of random values. Our construction may be seen as a one-dimensional case of a synthesizer where one of the two inputs is held constant while the other varies over a random list.

4.4 Security of G

Note that from the construction of **G** and the definition of security of HI-PRF, if G_0 is a secure PRG and if $F_{K_1,\ldots,K_n}(x) := f_{K_1}(x) \circ \cdots \circ f_{K_n}(x)$ is a secure HI-PRF, then **G** is a secure PRG. In the next lemma we will show that if f is a secure RI-PRF then F is a secure RI-PRF. It follows immediately that F is also a secure HI-PRF.

Lemma 1 *If f_K, with K chosen at random, is a secure RI-PRF with security (T, U, ϵ) then $f_{K_1} \circ \ldots \circ f_{K_n}$ with $K_1, \ldots, K_n$ chosen at random is a RI-PRF with security (T', U, ϵ') where $T'/\epsilon' \leq nT/\epsilon$.*

Proof Sketch Define D_n to be the input/output sequence given by the composite construction. That is, one input/output pair looks like $r, f_{K_1}(r), \ldots, f_{K_n}(r)$ where r is random. Define D_0 to the the input/output sequence given by n truly random functions, i.e., one input/output pair looks like $r, R_1, \ldots, R_n$ where all the values are random. More generally, let D_i be the input/output sequence defined by the following input/output pairs: $r, f_{K_1}(r), \ldots, f_{K_i}(r), R_{i+1}, \ldots, R_n$, where $R_{i+1}, \ldots, R_n$, and r are random. Using a standard argument initiated in [22], one can show that if there is an adversary distinguishing D_0 from D_n with probability ϵ' then there is some i such that the same adversary can distinguish between D_{i-1} and D_i with probability ϵ'/n. This adversary can then be used to build an adversary distinguishing (with the same probability) sequences whose input/output pairs are given by $r, f_K(r)$, for r random, from sequences whose input/output pairs are given by r, R where both r and R are random. □

4.5 Random-Input Pseudorandom Functions from Hash Functions

As noted earlier, when "provable" PRF's are often too slow in software one resorts to constructions based on cryptographic hash-functions like MD5 and SHA-1 under the assumption that they behave like PRF's. As noted above milder security assumptions are preferable. We use the compression function of secure hash function here. These have considerably longer input buffers than the output. We limit the attackers ability in choosing the inputs, by fixing a substantial portion of the input buffer with a random string so that in effect the compression function on the remainder of the input acts as a length-increasing function.

Definition 4 (RI-PRF's from secure compression functions) *A family $\mathcal{F}_{m_1}$ of RI-PRF's $h : \{0,1\}^{l+m_1} \to \{0,1\}^{m_2}$ where $m_1 < m_2$, is defined as follows. Let $Mix(\cdot)$ be a length preserving function that is easy to compute. and let K be randomly chosen from $\{0,1\}^l$. Then, $f_K : \{0,1\}^{m_1} \to \{0,1\}^{m_2}$ is defined as $f_K(x) := h(Mix(K \circ x))$.*

One may choose Mix reflecting the beliefs about the security of the hash function. Examples of $Mix(K,x)$ are $(K \circ x)$, $(x \circ K)$, $(lefthalf(x) \circ K \circ righthalf(x))$ etc. A successful attack on such RI-PRF's must work for most random choices of K by the user (*not* the attacker's random choices). Our current knowledge of attacks on MD5 and SHA-1 suggest that it is reasonable to assume that their compression functions yield suitable RI-PRF's. Even if this assumption proves to be false, the construction of generator still holds as long as there exists a single efficient RI-PRF.

4.6 The Feedback Construction

An alternative method for $\mathbf{P}_0$ to get the m_1-bit inputs is by feeding back some of the output rather than by getting them from G_0. The output length in each iteration then becomes $nm_2 - m_1$. In this section, we analyze the various ways in which output bits can be fed back into the input so that the construction can be iterated. For clarity, let us set $n = 1$, i.e. there are no multiple instantiations of the underlying function. The following discussion also holds for polynomially many independent instantiations of the underlying function. To be more concrete, one can imagine that the function family is instantiated using a hash function like MD5 where the index is simply the random bits used in the pad. However, the arguments hold in general. First, let us consider the simplest variant g_1 of the generator. Let $(y)_{\leftarrow j}$ and $(y)_{\rightarrow j}$ be, respectively, the first and last j bits of a string y. Then, g_1 can described as follows: at the i-th step ($i > 0$), output $y_i := f_K((y_{i-1})_{\leftarrow m_1})$ with y_0 being a random seed of m_1 bits. If f_K is a member of a RI-PRF family, g_1 is a strong generator. Because an HI-PRF derived from a RI-PRF by hiding the input is at least as and perhaps much more secure, we can claim that the following generator g_2 has the same or more securitythan g_1. At the i-th iteration, $y_i := f_K((y_{i-1}))_{\leftarrow m_1}$; if i is the last iteration, output y_i, else output $(y_i)_{\rightarrow(m_2-m_1)}$.

Finally, we can show that the following generator g_3 has higher security than g_2 under the assumption that we have access to a pseudorandom source g_0 whose security is higher than the security of f_K. g_3 can be described simply as: at the i-th step, g_0 outputs a random x_i of length m_1 and g_3 outputs $f_K(x_i)$. Let ϵ be the probability of distinguishing these m_1 feedback bits from random. It can be shown by induction that after t iterations, the probability of distinguishing these m_1 feedback bits is now only bounded by $t\epsilon$. Thus, the security of t outputs of the alternative $\mathbf{P}_0$ is degraded by this amount. Let us compare this to using G_0 instead of truly random bits for t outputs of the standard $\mathbf{P}_0$, suppose that the security of m_1 bits of G_0 is ϵ'. It can be shown that the security of t outputs of $\mathbf{P}_0$ is degraded by $t\epsilon'$. Thus, whenever G_0 is more secure than the feedback bits of $\mathbf{P_0}$, using G_0 will result in a more secure (albeit, potentially slower) generator. The G_0 we will use in our implementations is based on a strong cipher such as DES and possibly much more secure than any m_1 bits of the $\mathbf{P_0}$.

5 Properties of G

5.1 Dealing with Birthday Collisions

As shown in the previous section the process $\mathbf{P_0}$ in-and-of-itself produces a cryptographically strong pseudorandom sequence. However, in practice, when actually setting the parameters so that $\mathbf{P_0}$ is very fast, the value of m_1 is relatively small so as to reduce the load on the strong pseudorandom generator. However, in such a case, m_1 may not be large enough to avoid birthday collisions. By the birthday paradox, in $\approx \sqrt{2^{m_1}}$ steps, some x_i is quite likely to repeat, which would help to distinguish outputs of $\mathbf{P_0}$ from a truly random sequence of comparable length. A similar problem occurred in [1]. The solution we propose here is the same as for $\mathbf{G_{vra}}$. In parallel with $\mathbf{P_0}$ we preform a random walk $\mathbf{P_1}$ and then take the bitwise xor of the two outputs as the output of the generator $\mathbf{G}$. This is precisely the generator described in Section 2.

The intuition behind this construction is as follows. For a random walk on an expander of 2^L nodes, the probability that the walk is at the same node that it was t steps ago is very small, say $2^{-c \cdot t}$ for some $c > 0$. Hence for large enough t this probability is small and offers a good "long range" decorrelation properties, while in the short range, an output of $\mathbf{P_1}$ can easily repeat. However, the probability that $\mathbf{P_0}$ returns in t steps is negligible for small t ("in the short range") and as mentioned above in the long range the choice m_1 may make the output repeat. The idea is that by xoring the two processes, the probability of return will be relatively small for all values of t.

Before we quantify these remarks, we observe that adding $\mathbf{P_1}$ to $\mathbf{P_0}$ did not weaken the cryptographic security of $\mathbf{P_0}$. Indeed, if we are given a distinguisher D for $\mathbf{G}$ we can attack $\mathbf{P_0}$ as follows: Generate $\mathbf{P_1}$ of suitable lengths independently and xor it with the output of $\mathbf{P_0}$. Now D will distinguish this from random strings; however this would be impossible if $\mathbf{P_0}$ were purely random.

5.2 Return Time for G

A generator is said to enter a cycle of period M after a transient period of M_0 steps, if $z_i = z_{i+M}$ for all $i > M_0$, for some M_0. It is desirable for a PRG to have large cycle length M, since it gives an upper bound on the maximum number of useful outputs that can be obtained from $\mathbf{G}$ with a single seed. A generator with security $(T(n), s(n))$ cannot, *on average*, have cycle length substantially smaller than $T(n)(1 - \epsilon(n))$ since one can distinguish the generator's output from random sequences with certainty in time proportional to the cycle length. However, this does not preclude the generator from having small cycle lengths on some small fraction of inputs (seeds). In this section, we show that the probability that **G** repeats an input is very small. Note that repeating an earlier output is necessary but not sufficient for a generator to be in a cycle. Using the theory of random walks on expanders, [1] showed that the probability of $\mathbf{G_{vra}}$ repeating its starting point is negligible. In fact, it is smaller than either the probability that P_0 repeats or the probability that P_1 repeats. A similar result holds for the probability that **G** repeats its starting point (or any other point for that matter) and is given in the lemmas below. To state the lemma we let $V(m)$ and $W(m)$ be the probability that P_0 and P_1 repeat after m steps.

Lemma 2 *The probability that* **G** *repeats its first output at the m-th step, for $m \geq 2$,*

$$V(m)W(m) \leq R(m) := Prob[Z_m = Z_1] \leq min(V(m), 2^{-L} + \bar{\lambda}_2^m(1 - 2^{-L}))$$

where the probability is over the choice of inputs to $\mathbf{P_0}$ *and the random walk at each step. Moreover, $\bar{\lambda}_2$ is the second largest eigenvalue of the expander graph in P_1 in absolute value.*

The following lemma gives a lower bound on $W(m)$ in terms the degree of the expander.

Lemma 3 (Alon-Boppana) *The probability $W(m)$ of return of* $\mathbf{P_1}$ *in m steps is bounded below as:*

$$Prob[Y_m = Y_1] \geq md^{-m}p^{m-1}(1 - p)\rho(m - 1) \text{ for odd } m > 3$$
$$\geq d^{-m}p^m\rho(m) \qquad \text{for even } m > 2$$

where p is the probability of staying at the same node, $\rho(2r) = \frac{1}{r}\binom{2r-2}{r-1}d(d-1)^{r-1}$, $r \geq 2$. (It is easy to compute $W(m)$ exactly for $m = 1, 2, 3$.)

Random walks on expander graphs have other strong statistical properties. For example, they generate a sequence of numbers that are statistically almost as good as random and independent numbers for use in Monte-Carlo estimations as was shown by Gillman [10]. That is, the mean of any bounded function over the node values can be estimated with an error which decreases exponentially with the number of samples. This was generalized in [1] to the case when the random walk node label was xored with the output of the $\mathbf{P_0}$ given in that paper and it extends to our case with **G** .

5.3 Alternate Ways to Avoid Birthday Repeats

Note that the security is not independent of m_2. Indeed, after $2^{m_1/2}$ input-output pairs, some output is likely to repeat whereas for a true random source this does not happen until $2^{m_2/2}$ outputs. This is taken care of by the $\mathbf{P_1}$ process. However, the $\mathbf{P_1}$ process can be difficult to handle for small devices since it involves arithmetic modulo large numbers. We suggest some new ways of avoiding the birthday attack without using P_1.

The essential idea is that the birthday collisions $\mathbf{P_0}$ works in time $2^{m_1/2}$. This is because we have fixed l bits of the input. However the RI-PRF may have significantly more security than $2^{m_1/2}$. We can exploit this additional security by modifying the construction as follows. Some number of bits, say m_3, of the m_2 output bits are fed back and only $m_2 - m_3$ bits are output. These bits are temporarily stored until enough bits are accumulated to form a new $n \times l$ matrix A of key values. It takes $\lceil nl/m_3 \rceil$ rounds to compute this new A. After this new A has been computed, the key values for the random-input pseudorandom functions are given by this A. Since $\lceil nl/m_3 \rceil$ is much less than $2^{m_1/2}$, the birthday attack is thwarted. In fact, it can be shown that the security of the scheme can be reduced to syntactically weaker security requirements for the RI-PRF since the adversary is only given $\lceil nl/m_3 \rceil$ queries per random key with which to distinguish the outputs of the function from random. We should also note that the bits for generating the new A need not be feedback bits alone. It may be desirable for some or all of these bits to come from G_0. The decision about where to get the new bits of A depends on the details of the security limitations of G_0 and the random-input pseudorandom function.

One need not wait until all of the bits of the new A are ready before incorporating some of these bits into the new keys. In fact, the feedback bits could be used as new bits for the key values of the next round. That is, at each on-line step, we output the value of a new function $f_K : \{0,1\}^{m_1} \to \{0,1\}^{m_2}$ where K changes slightly at each step. For the MD5 construction, m_3 could be 32, and the buffer is "rotated" right with the extra 32 bits appended to the buffer. Heuristically, this appears to be a better scheme than that above since the keys change at every step, but we are not able to prove this formally.

5.4 Variations on $\mathbf{G_{vra}}$

A similar idea to the above for reducing birthday collisions can be used for $\mathbf{G_{vra}}$. The $n \times L$ matrix A can be interpreted as a linear array. The feedback bits can be appended to the linear array to form a new linear array from 1 to $n \times L + m_3$. A new matrix can be fashioned from the linear array from locations m_3 to $n \times L + m_3$. Alternatively, each row of A can be "rotated" right using some of the feedback bits.

We also suggest some changes to $\mathbf{G_{vra}}$ that make it more suitable to a larger set of applications. Recall that the matrix A is completely filled in the pre-processing step with random bits. As noted earlier, this may be a large cost for some applications. The case of inadequate memory has been addressed with G . Here we provide a solution for applications that occasionally need only a short string of pseudorandom bits or need to amortize the overhead of the preprocessing step. For example, if the number of bits needed is much less than $n/k \times L$, then some rows of A will not be used. For this scenario, we offer the following alternative. We do not fill A in the pre-processing step. Instead, each row has a "filled" bit which indicates whether that row has been initialized or not. In each on-line step, we first generate the random choice of rows. For every row thus chosen, we first check the "filled" bit for that row and if it is not set, we go ahead and generate the random bits of the row. Thus, only those rows that will actually be used will be filled in A.

6 Implementation

In this section, we present the results of our sample implementation on a Pentium II 233 Mhz workstation Windows NT 4.0 with Visual C++ 5.0. The algorithm was implemented entirely in C with no heroic attempts being made for optimization. In order to implement the generator, we have to choose instances of a strong pseudorandom generator and a RI-PRF. For the strong generator, we chose two examples: first, we used the outputs of single DES in OFB mode. We also implemented the Goldreich-Levin generator based on Triple DES in OFB mode. For comparison, we also implemented the strong generator using "alleged" RC4. For the RI-PRF implementation, we chose MD5 and SHA-1. These choices constrain the parameters of our implementation of G as follows. In the case of MD5, the input buffer is of length 512 bits and the hashed output is 128 bits long. For n parallel instances of MD5, the memory requirement is around $512n$ bits. For small devices one can take $n \leq 8$ with a memory requirement ranging from 64 to 512 bytes. We chose $m_1 = 64$, which is the block length of DES.

We used the public domain implementations of DES and MD5/SHA-1. The raw speeds of MD5 and SHA-1 were about 45Mbits/sec and 32 Mbits/sec, respectively. The raw speed of DES in OFB mode was found to be 25 Mbits/sec. The raw speed of the Goldreich-Levin generator based on Triple DES was 10 Mbits/sec. For comparison, RC4 ran at about 64 Mbits/second on this platform. The following paragraph summarizes the speeds for various combinations of our generator parameters using DES or RC4 as the initial generator G_0.

Here we summarize the speeds in Mbits/sec of our implementations for various values of n. In all cases, the strong generator was DES in OFB mode, and the P_1 process was used. We observed that the P_1 process slows down the generator by about 10% for the parameter values tested. The Goldreich-Levin slowed down the generator by approximately 20%. We also noted that for higher values of n the speeds continued to increase but the memory requirement for P_0 was more than 1Kbyte. The speeds for $n = 1, 2, 4, 8$ for MD5 were, respectively, $23, 30, 35, 38$ Mbits/s. The corresponding figures for SHA-1 were $21, 25, 27, 28$ Mbits/s respectively. For comparison we report the speed of G when using the RC4 as G_0. When $n = 8$, G ran at 41 Mbits/sec and 32 Mbits/sec using MD5 and SHA-1, respectively. Although RC4 is much faster than DES, it does not improve the speed of G significantly. The conclusion is that the factor limiting the speed of G is the hash function: MD5 and SHA-1.

References

1. W. Aiello, S. Rajagopalan, R. Venkatesan. "Design of Practical and Provably Good Random Number Generators," *J. Algorithms* **29**, (1998) 358-389. Appeared previously in *5th Annual ACM-SIAM Symp. Disc. Alg.* (1995) 1-8.

2. N. Alon, "Eigenvalues and expanders," *Combinatorica* **6** (1986) 83-96.
3. M. Bellare, R. Canetti, H. Krawczyk, "Keying Hash Functions for Message Authentication," *Proceedings of Crypto '96*, 1-15.
4. M. Bellare, R. Canetti, H. Krawczyk, "Pseudorandom functions revisited: The Cascade Construction and its Concrete Security," *Proceedings of the 37th Symposium on Foundations of Computer Science*, 1996.
5. M. Blum, S. Micali, "How to Generate Cryptographically Strong Sequences of Pseudorandom Bits," *Proceedings of FOCS* (1982); *SIAM J. Computing*, **13** (1984) 850-864.
6. B. den Boer, A. Bosselaers, "Collisions for the compression function of MD5," *Proceedings of Eurocrypt '93*, 293-304, 1994.
7. H. Dobbertin, "The Status of MD5 After a Recent Attack," *CryptoBytes* v2 No.2 (Summer 1996).
8. J.-B. Fischer, J. Stern, "An efficient pseudorandom generator provably as secure as syndrome decoding," in *Proceedings of EUROCRYPT96* (1996) 245-255.
9. O. Gabber, Z. Galil, "Explicit constructions of linear-sized superconcentrators," *J. Comput. Sys. Sci.* **22** (1981).
10. D. Gillman, "A Chernoff bound for random walks in expander graphs," *Proceedings of FOCS* (1993).
11. O. Goldreich, S. Goldwasser, and S. Micali, "On the cryptographic applications of random functions," in *Proceedings of CRYPTO 84* (1984) 276-288.
12. O. Goldreich, L.A. Levin, "Hard Core Bit For Any One Way Function," *Proceedings of STOC* (1990); *J. Symbolic Logic* **58** (1993) 1102-1103.
13. J. Hastad, R. Impagliazzo, L.A. Levin, M. Luby, "Pseudorandom Generation From One-Way Functions, *Proceedings of STOC* (1989) 12-24; "Pseudorandom Generators under Uniform assumptions," *Proceedings of STOC* (1990) 395-404.
14. M. Luby, "Pseudorandomness and its Cryptographic applications" *Princeton Univ Press*, 1996.
15. M. Naor, O. Reingold, "Synthesizers and their application to the parallel construction of Pseudorandom Functions," *Proceedings of FOCS*, (1995) 170-181.
16. M. Naor, O. Reingold, "Number-Theoretic Constructions of Efficient Pseudorandom Functions," *Proceedings of FOCS*, (1997) 458-467.
17. M. Naor, O. Reingold, "From Unpredictability to Indistinguishability: A simple construction of Pseudorandom Functions from MACs," *Proceedings of Crypto'98*, 267-282.
18. P. van Oorschot, M. Wiener, "Parallel collision search with application to hash functions and discrete logarithms," in *Proceedings of 2nd ACM Conference on Computer and Communication Security*, 1994.
19. J. Patarin, "New Results on Pseudorandom Permutation Generators Based on the DES Scheme," *Proceedings of Crypto'91*, (1991) 301-312.
20. M. J. B. Robshaw, "On Recent Results for MD2, MD4 and MD5," *RSA Laboratories Bulletin* No. 4 (November 12, 1996).
21. B. Schneier, D. Whiting, "Fast Software Encryption: Designing Encryption Algorithms for Optimal Software Speed on the Intel Pentium Processor," *Fast Software Encryption Workshop* (1997) 242-259.
22. A.C. Yao, "Theory and Applications of Trapdoor Functions," *Proceedings of FOCS* (1982) 80-91.

SOBER Cryptanalysis

Daniel Bleichenbacher and Sarvar Patel
{bleichen,sarvar}@lucent.com

Bell Laboratories
Lucent Technologies

Abstract. SOBER is a new stream cipher that has recently been developed by Greg Rose for possible applications in wireless telephony [3]. In this paper we analyze SOBER and point out different weaknesses. In the case where an attacker can analyze key streams generated for consecutive frames with the same key we present an attack, that in our implementation requires less than one minute on a 200Mhz Pentium.

1 Overview and Motivation

Encryption schemes that are used in wireless telephony have to meet rather difficult constraints. The schemes have to encrypt rather large amounts of data, but mobile stations often have very limited computational power. Hence the encryption scheme must be quite efficient. Simple schemes, however, are under a big risk of being insecure.

In this paper we analyze the stream cipher SOBER, which was developed by Greg Rose [3]. An improved version of SOBER [4] has recently been submitted for a TIA (Telecommunications industry association) standard. The goal of the TIA standards process is to replace ORYX and CMEA, for which weaknesses have been discovered [6, 5].

The outline of the paper is as follows. Section 2 describes the notation used in this paper. We review SOBER in Section 3. Section 4 analyzes SOBER under the assumption that an attacker knows the first 4 bytes of 64 key streams all generated with the same key and the frame numbers 0 through 63. This attack is the most severe attack described in our paper, since it requires only 256 bytes of known key stream and is very efficient. Our implementation often finds the key in less than a minute on 200 Mhz Pentium. That is we reduce the time complexity from 2^{128} for a brute force search to about 2^{28}. Section 5 analyzes SOBER under the more restrictive assumption that an attacker knows only one key stream rather than several as assumed before. Section 6 describes a weakness in the key setup procedure. In particular, we show that using an 80 bit key instead of a 128 bit key can considerably simplify cryptanalysis. In Section 7 we show how to find keys that produce no output. While this is not a severe flaw in SOBER, such keys might be used for a denial of service attack in certain protocols.

2 Notation, Underlying Mathematical Structure and Basic Operations

Most of our cryptanalysis in this paper is based on heuristic arguments. For example, we often assume that certain values are uniformly distributed. We will call statements based on heuristic arguments *claims* as opposed to statements that are rigorously provable, which are usually called *theorems*. However, we have verified our claims if possible with computer experiments.

SOBER uses operations over the ring $\mathbb{Z}/(256)$ and the field GF_{2^8} and mixes these operations. Hence, the computations depend heavily on the exact representation of elements in these structures.

The field GF_{2^8} is represented as $\mathrm{GF}_2[x]/(x^8 + x^6 + x^3 + x^2 + 1)$. Addition and multiplication over GF_{2^8} will be denoted by $\oplus$ and $\otimes$ respectively. The symbol '+' will denote addition over the ring $\mathbb{Z}/(256)$ and '$\wedge$' will denote the bitwise logical AND. Elements in $\mathbb{Z}/(256)$ and GF_{2^8} can both be represented with one byte. An implicit conversion ϕ takes place when an element of GF_{2^8} is used for an operation over $\mathbb{Z}/(256)$. This conversion ϕ can be defined by

$$\phi(\sum_{i=0}^{7} c_i x^i) = \sum_{i=0}^{7} c_i 2^i \text{ where } c_i \in \{0,1\},$$

i.e. the coefficients of polynomials in $\mathrm{GF}_2[x]/(x^8 + x^6 + x^3 + x^2 + 1)$ are interpreted as bits of the binary representation of integers in the interval $[0, 255]$. For the rest of the paper will use ϕ and ϕ^{-1} as implicit conversions between GF_{2^8} and $\mathbb{Z}/(256)$ when necessary, e.g. we can use the constants 141 and 175 to represent the polynomials $x^7 + x^3 + x^2 + 1$ and $x^7 + x^5 + x^3 + x^2 + 1$ respectively.

3 Description of SOBER

SOBER is a stream cipher having a key length up to 128 bits. A stream cipher generally transforms a short key into a key stream, which is then used to encrypt the plaintext. In particular, the ciphertext is usually the bitwise XOR of the key stream and the plaintext. A key stream must not be used to encrypt two plaintexts, since the knowledge of two ciphertexts encrypted with the same key stream would allow to extract the XOR of the two plaintexts. SOBER has a feature, called frames, that allows us to use the same key multiple times without generating the same key stream. This is very useful in applications where a lot of small messages have to be encrypted independently. In particular the key stream generator has two input parameters, namely the key and the frame number. The frame number is not part of the key. It may be just a counter, and is sent to the receiver in clear or is known to him. Hence we have to assume that the frame number is known to an attacker too.

The main reason to chose a linear feedback shift register over GF_{2^8} instead of a LFSR over GF_2 was efficiency [3]. In this paper we consider the security of the cipher. Therefore we will not describe implementation details.

3.1 LFSR

SOBER is based on a linear feedback shift register of degree 17 over GF_{2^8} producing a sequence s_n that satisfies the recurrence relation

$$s_{n+17} = (141 \otimes s_{n+15}) \oplus s_{n+4} \oplus (175 \otimes s_n). \tag{1}$$

During the key and frame setup this recurrence relation is slightly modified to add the key and frame number into the state of the LFSR. In particular the following relation is used.

$$s_{n+17} = (141 \otimes s_{n+15}) \oplus s_{n+4} \oplus (175 \otimes (s_n + a_n)) \tag{2}$$

The value a_n depends on either the key or the frame number and will be described in the next two sections.

3.2 Key setup

A key consists of 4 to 16 bytes, $K_0, \ldots, K_{\ell-1}$, where ℓ denotes the length of the key in bytes. The LFSR is initialized to the first 17 Fibonacci numbers, i.e.

$$s_0 = s_1 = 1$$
$$s_n = s_{n-1} + s_{n-2} \quad (\text{mod } 256) \text{ for } 2 \leq n \leq 16$$

Then each byte of the key is added to the lowest byte of the LFSR, before the LFSR is cycled, i.e. $a_n = K_n$, so that

$$s_{n+17} = (141 \otimes s_{n+15}) \oplus s_{n+4} \oplus (175 \otimes (s_n + K_n)) \text{ for } 0 \leq n \leq \ell - 1. \tag{3}$$

Next, we set $a_\ell = \ell$ and $a_n = 0$ for $\ell < n \leq 40$ and compute the state $(s_{40}, \ldots, s_{56})$ of the register. This concludes the setup of the key.

  Setting $a_\ell = \ell$ guarantees that the state of the LFSR after the initialization is unique for all keys. The key setup procedure is an almost linear operation. In particular, there exists a 17×18 matrix M independent of the key, such that

$$\begin{pmatrix} s_{40} \\ s_{41} \\ \vdots \\ s_{56} \end{pmatrix} = M \begin{pmatrix} 1 \\ s_0 \oplus (s_0 + a_0) \\ s_1 \oplus (s_1 + a_1) \\ \vdots \\ s_{16} \oplus (s_{16} + a_{16}) \end{pmatrix}. \tag{4}$$

3.3 Frame setup

In some application the same key is used to produce more than one key stream. In order to achieve this a frame number f is used to generate a different key stream for each time the key is used. A frame number is a 32-bit integer. It is added in 11 steps to the LFSR. In particular the n-th step adds the bits $3n,\ldots,3n+7$ to the lowest register of the LFSR and cycles the LFSR afterwards. Hence

$$s_{n+17} = (141 \otimes s_{n+15}) \oplus s_{n+4} \oplus (175 \otimes (s_n + a_n)) \quad \text{for } 40 \leq n \leq 50$$

where $a_n = \lfloor f/8^{n-40} \rfloor \bmod 256$.

The values $s_i : 58 \leq i \leq 96$ are computed with (1). The frame initialization is finished as soon as the state $(s_{80}, \ldots, s_{96})$ is computed.

3.4 Computation of the key stream

The sequence v_n is computed in a non-linear way from s_n as follows:

$$v_n = (s_n + s_{n+2} + s_{n+5} + s_{n+12}) \oplus (s_{n+12} \wedge s_{n+13})$$

Assume that the stream cipher is in a state n, i.e. represented by $(s_n, \ldots, s_{n+16})$. Then the cipher produces the key stream as follows: n is incremented by 1 and v_n is stored in a special register called the *stutter control register*. Hence, v_{81} is the first stutter control byte if a frame number is used. The stutter control register is used to generate 0 to 4 bytes of the key stream as follows: First the stutter control register is divided into 4 bit pairs. For each of these bit pairs, starting with the least significant bits the following is done based on the value of the 2 bits:

bit pair	Action taken
00	Increment n by 1. (No output is produced.)
01	Output the key stream byte $105 \oplus v_{n+1}$ and increment n by 2.
10	Output the key stream byte v_{n+2} and increment n by 2.
11	Output the key stream byte $150 \oplus v_{n+1}$ and increment n by 1.

4 Analysis of the Frames

In this section, we analyze the situation where an attacker knows different key streams generated with one key, but different frame numbers. We might regard the frame number as a part of the key. Hence, the attack described in this section could be classified as an related-key attack. Biham introduced this type of attack and applied it to various ciphers in [1]. We use a the fact that different frames are strongly related to derive an efficient differential attack [2] based on this relation. It is the most serious attack presented in this paper, since both the number of necessary known plaintext bytes and the number of necessary operations to recover the key are small. In particular, we show the following result:

Claim 1. *Given the first 4 bytes of key stream for 64 frames generated with the same key and the frame numbers 0 through 63. Then we expect to find the key in about $c2^{28}$ steps, where c is the number of steps in the innermost loop.*

Due to the nature of the attack the time complexity can vary and is hard to examine, because the attack is based on a search tree, whose size depends on given input parameter. Our attack is based on the assumption that the values of the first stutter byte are uniformly distributed, and hence that all 4 values for the first 2-bits occur with about the same frequency. We will for example assume that at least 24 out of 64 bit pairs have the value 01 or 11. If that condition is not met, we can run the algorithm again with a lower threshold, and hence a larger tree to search. To verify that our assumptions are reasonable we have implemented the attack. Recovering the key often requires less than minute on a 200Mhz Pentium. We also found that the algorithm indeed shows the expected behavior.

Before we describe the attack, we will define some notations and point out some properties of the frame initialization that will be helpful for the attack.

In order to distinguish the state of LFSR produced with different frame numbers f we will denote the nth value in the sequence s for f by

$$s_n(f).$$

The differential of two such sequences will be denoted by $\Delta_n(f_1, f_2)$, i.e.

$$\Delta_n(f_1, f_2) := s_n(f_1) \oplus s_n(f_2).$$

The j-th byte of the key stream for frame f will be denoted by

$$p_j(f).$$

The 6 least significant bits of the frame number are used twice during the frame setup. They are added to s_{40} and s_{41} during the computation of s_{57} and s_{58}. Therefore, if f_1 and f_2 differ only in the 6 least significant bits, and the attacker can guess s_{40} and s_{41} then he can easily compute $\Delta_n(f_1, f_2)$ for all $n \geq 0$ by

$$\Delta_n(f_1, f_2) = 0 \text{ for } 0 \leq n \leq 56$$
$$\Delta_{n+17}(f_1, f_2) = (175 \otimes (s_n + a_n(f_1)) \oplus (s_n + a_n(f_2))) \text{ for } n = 40, 41$$
$$\Delta_{n+17}(f_1, f_2) = (175 \otimes \Delta_n(f_1, f_2)) \oplus \Delta_{n+4}(f_1, f_2) \oplus$$
$$(141 \otimes \Delta_{n+15}(f_1, f_2)) \text{ for } n \geq 42$$

We can now give a short description of our attack. First we guess s_{40} and s_{41} and compute the Δ's. Then we guess certain well chosen bits of the internal state of the LFSR for the frame 0. Based on these guesses and the precomputed Δ's we compute the corresponding bits for the LFSR state of the other frames. These bits are then used to compute possible output bytes. We don't know the state of the stutter byte, hence we cannot predict with certainty what an output byte should look like. Therefore, we will use a probabilistic approach, i.e. we reject our guess if considerably less output bytes coincide with our prediction than we would expect for a correct guess. Otherwise we extend our guess with a few more bits and test again. This can be repeated recursively until we have either found a reason to reject that guess or we know enough information about the LFSR state to compute the key. We will now give a more detailed description of the attack.

Step 1: Guessing s_{40} and s_{41}. First we guess the values s_{40} and s_{41}. Next, we compute the values for $\Delta_n(0, f)$ for $82 \leq n \leq 99$ and $0 \leq f \leq 63$.

Different pairs of values of s_{40} and s_{41} may lead to equal values for all $\Delta_n(0, f)$. Since we will only need the Δ's but not s_{40} and s_{41} we can use this fact to improve the algorithm. In particular the most significant bit of s_{40} has no influence on $\Delta_n(0, f)$. Moreover, the $s_{40} = 0$ and $s_{40} = 64$ give the same Δ's. Hence, it is sufficient to chose s_{40} satisfying $1 \leq s_{40} \leq 127$. Two values for s_{41} are equivalent if either their 3 least significant bits are all zero or if their $k > 3$ least significant bits are equal and the k-th least significant bit is zero. It follows, that it is sufficient to chose s_{41} among the following set:

$$\{0, 1, 2, 3, 4, 5, 6, 7, 9, 10, 11, 12, 13, 14, 15,$$
$$25, 26, 27, 28, 29, 30, 31, 57, 58, 59, 60, 61, 62, 63,$$
$$121, 122, 123, 124, 125, 126, 127, 249, 250, 251, 252, 253, 254, 255\}$$

Step 2: Guessing $s_{82}(0), s_{84}(0), s_{87}(0), s_{94}(0)$ and $s_{95}(0)$. Now we would like to guess the values for $s_{82}(0), s_{84}(0), s_{87}(0), s_{94}(0)$ and $s_{95}(0)$. In order to improve the efficiency, we will start with guessing only the two least significant bits of each byte. We test that guess and if the guess looks promissing then we extend it recursively by guessing the next least significant bits and test again.

Testing is done as follows. Assume that we have guessed the k least significant bits of $s_{82}(0), s_{84}(0), s_{87}(0), s_{94}(0)$ and $s_{95}(0)$. This allows us to compute the k least significant bits of

$$s_n(f) = s_n(0) \oplus \Delta_n(0, f)$$

for $n \in \{82, 84, 87, 94, 95\}$. We can now compute the k least significant bits of

$$v_{82}(f) = (s_{82}(f) + s_{84}(f) + s_{87}(f) + s_{94}(f)) \oplus (s_{94}(f) \wedge s_{95}(f))$$

With probability $1/4$ the two least significant bits of the first stutter byte v_{81} is 01 and with the same probability it is 11. Hence, with probability $1/4$ each the first output byte $p_1(f)$ for frame f is either $v_{82}(f) \oplus 105$ or $v_{82}(f) \oplus 150$. Now, we count the number of frames f for which the k least significant bits of $p_1(f)$ and either $v_{82}(f) \oplus 105$ or $v_{82}(f) \oplus 150$ are equal. We would expect to find about 32 matches on average, if we have guessed the bits for $s_{82}(0), s_{84}(0), s_{87}(0), s_{94}(0)$ and $s_{95}(0)$ correctly. In our experiments, we rejected the values for s whenever we found less than 24 matches. The correct solution should be rejected by mistake with a probability less than 3%.

After having guessed and checked all 8 bits, usually only few, typically less than 100 possibilities for the tuple $(s_{82}(0), s_{84}(0), s_{87}(0), s_{94}(0), s_{95}(0))$ remain.

We also know the values for the Δ's and have partial knowledge about $s_{40}(0)$ and $s_{41}(0)$. Consequently, the most time consuming part of the analysis is already done.

Steps 3.1 – 3.4: Guessing more of the LFSR state. Next, we extend each of these tuples by using a similar method involving $v_{83}(f), v_{84}(f), v_{85}(f)$ and $v_{86}(f)$. In step $3.i$ $(1 \leq i \leq 4)$ we guess the unknown values out of $s_{82+i}(0), s_{84+i}(0), s_{87+i}(0), s_{94+i}(0)$ and $s_{95+i}(0)$. Then we compute $v_{82+i}(f)$ and compare these values to the known key stream. This comparison of $v_{82+i}(f)$ with the key stream slightly more complex than before, since we have to decide, which byte of the key stream we should use for comparison. Generally, we assume that if there was a match with $v_{82+j}(f)$ for $j < i$ that the corresponding byte was indeed generated using $v_{82+j}(f)$. We will use the following rules in our algorithm:

- If a test $p_j(f) = v_i(f) \oplus x$ where $x \in \{0, 105, 150\}$ was successful then we use $p_{j+1}(f)$ for the next comparison with $v_{i+1}(f)$ otherwise we use $p_j(f)$ and $v_{i+1}(f)$.
- If $p_j(f) = v_i(f) \oplus 105$ then we will not test $v_{i+1}(f)$, since SOBER skips one byte after generating output of the form $v_i(f) \oplus 105$.
- A test $p_j(f) = v_i(f)$ will only be performed if the last test was not successful.

Step 4: Recovering the key At this point we know all the bytes $s_i(0)$ for $82 \leq i \leq 98$ with exception of $s_{92}(0)$ and $s_{93}(0)$. Usually, the previous steps narrow the possibilities to a few hundred cases. Hence we can easily just test each case with all possible values for $s_{92}(0)$ and $s_{93}(0)$. For each combination we compute $s_i(0)$ for $i = 81, 80, \ldots, 16$ using

$$s_i(0) = (175^{-1} \otimes (s_{i+17}) \oplus (141 \otimes s_{i+15}) \oplus s_{i+4}).$$

Finally, we recover the $i - th$ key byte by

$$K_i = 175^{-1} \otimes (s_{i+4} \oplus (141 \otimes s_{i+15})) \oplus s_{i+17}) - s_i.$$

Remember, that s_i for $0 \leq i \leq 16$ is equivalent to the i-th Fibonacci number. We may now do some further test such as decrypting the whole message to check whether we have found the correct key.

A very rough analysis

It is hard to analyze this algorithm analytically. However, we roughly estimate it's complexity as follows. We have to guess s_{40} (7 bits) and s_{41} (5.4 bits) and the 2 least significant bits of $s_{82}(0), s_{84}(0), s_{87}(0), s_{94}(0)$ and $s_{95}(0)$ (10 bits) before we can make the first test in step 2. Each test has to compare with 64 frames. Hence, so far we have a time complexity of approximately $2^{7+5.4+10+6}$, which is slightly more than 2^{28}. Our experiments show that the first test cuts enough nodes in the search tree that the remaining tree is almost negligible. Hence this rough analysis gives an approximation for the actual runtime of the algorithm.

5 Analysis of the Cipher Stream

In this section we analyze the nonlinear output of SOBER and investigate in how difficult it is to compute the internal state of the LFSR given the key stream of the cipher. In particular, we will now show the following result:

Claim 2. *Assume, that 17 consecutive key stream bytes $p_1, \ldots, p_{17}$ are known. Assume further that these bytes are generated from two stutter control bytes and that the value of the first byte is 10111110_2 and the second one is 01010101_2. Then it is possible to find the internal state of the LFSR in $c2^{72}$ steps, where c is a small constant denoting the number of steps for the innermost loop.*

Let the first stutter byte be v_n. To simplify notation we'll use $t_i = s_{n+i}$. From the assumption on the stutter control register the following is known:

$$(t_0 + t_2 + t_5 + t_{12}) \oplus (t_{12} \wedge t_{13}) \equiv 10111110_2 \pmod{256} \tag{5}$$

$$(t_2 + t_4 + t_7 + t_{14}) \oplus (t_{14} \wedge t_{15}) \equiv p_1 \pmod{256} \tag{6}$$

$$(t_3 + t_5 + t_8 + t_{15}) \oplus (t_{15} \wedge t_{16}) \equiv (p_2 \oplus 10010110_2) \pmod{256} \tag{7}$$

$$(t_4 + t_6 + t_9 + t_{16}) \oplus (t_{16} \wedge t_{17}) \equiv (p_3 \oplus 10010110_2) \pmod{256} \tag{8}$$

$$(t_6 + t_8 + t_{11} + t_{18}) \oplus (t_{18} \wedge t_{19}) \equiv p_4 \pmod{256} \tag{9}$$

$$(t_7 + t_9 + t_{12} + t_{19}) \oplus (t_{19} \wedge t_{20}) \equiv 01010101_2 \pmod{256} \tag{10}$$

$$(t_8 + t_{10} + t_{13} + t_{20}) \oplus (t_{20} \wedge t_{21}) \equiv p_5 \oplus 01101001_2 \pmod{256} \tag{11}$$

$$(t_{10} + t_{12} + t_{15} + t_{22}) \oplus (t_{22} \wedge t_{23}) \equiv p_6 \oplus 01101001_2 \pmod{256} \tag{12}$$

The algorithm works as follows. First we guess the 9 bytes

$$t_0, t_4, t_5, t_6, t_{12}, t_{13}, t_{15}, t_{22} \text{ and } t_{23}.$$

We can use these equations to solve for more values t_i as follows:

use equation   to compute

(1) $t_{17} = (141 \otimes t_{15}) \oplus t_4 \oplus (175 \otimes t_0)$

(6) $t_2 = (p_1 \oplus (t_{14} \wedge t_{15})) - (t_4 + t_7 + t_{14}) \pmod{256}$

(12) $t_{10} = (p_6 \oplus 01101001_2 \oplus (t_{22} \wedge t_{23})) - (t_{12} + t_{15} + t_{22}) \pmod{256}$

(1) $t_{19} = (141 \otimes t_{17}) \oplus t_6 \oplus (175 \otimes t_2)$

(1) $t_{21} = (141^{-1} \otimes (t_{23}) \oplus t_{10} \oplus (175 \otimes t_6))$

(1) $t_8 = t_{21} \oplus (141 \otimes t_{19}) \oplus (175 \otimes t_4)$

(11) t_{20} (see below)

(1) $t_9 = t_{22} \oplus (141 \otimes t_{20}) \oplus (175 \otimes t_5)$

(10) $t_7 = (01010101_2 \oplus (t_{19} \wedge t_{20})) - (t_9 + t_{12} + t_{19}) \pmod{256}$

(6) t_{14} (see below)

(8) t_{16} (see below)

(7) $t_3 = (p_2 \oplus 10010110_2 \oplus (t_{15} \wedge t_{16})) - (t_5 + t_8 + t_{15}) \pmod{256}$

(1) $t_{18} = 141^{-1} \otimes (t_{20} \oplus t_7 \oplus (175 \otimes t_3))$

(1) $t_1 = 175^{-1} \otimes ((141 \otimes t_{16}) \oplus t_5 \oplus t_{18})$

(9) $t_{11} = (p_4 \oplus (t_{18} \wedge t_{19})) - (t_6 + t_8 + t_{18}) \pmod{256}$

(1) $t_{24}, t_{25}, \ldots$

We have now enough information to compute the corresponding key stream and compare it to $p_7, \ldots, p_{16}$. If all the values are equal then we output $t_0, \ldots, t_{16}$ as possible candidate for the internal state of the LFSR. Solving most of these equations is easy, since the equations are either linear over GF_{2^8} or $\mathbb{Z}/(256)$. The only non-linear equations are the equations (6),(8), and (11). These equations have the form

$$(A + X) \oplus (X \wedge B) = C,$$

where A, B, C are given and X is unknown. There are 2^{24} possible combinations for A, B and C, hence it is feasible to precompute the set of solutions of all equations and store the result. Then solving these non-linear equations requires only table look-ups. Moreover, there are totally 2^{24} solutions for the 2^{24} equations. Hence, we expect one solution on average for each of the equations (6),(8), and (11). Therefore we may assume that testing each guess for the 9 bytes $t_0, t_4, t_5, t_6, t_{12}, t_{13}, t_{15}, t_{22}$ and t_{23} takes a constant number c of steps and thus the whole algorithms needs about $c2^{72}$ steps.

If we know enough key stream then we can repeat the attack above for all tuples of 17 consecutive key stream bytes. Since a stutter byte is used for 3 key stream bytes on average, it follows that $n + 17$ consecutive key stream bytes contain on average $n/3$ sequences of 17 bytes of key stream where the first byte was generated with a new stutter bytes. The probability that such a sequence was generated starting with the two stutter bytes 10111110_2 and 01010101_2 is 2^{-16}.

Claim 3. *There exists an algorithm that given $n + 16$ consecutive key stream bytes of SOBER, can find the internal state of the LFSR in $cn2^{72}$ steps, with probability about $1 - (1 - 2^{-16})^{n/3}$. where c denotes the number of steps for performing the innermost loop of our algorithm.*

Hence, we expect to find the internal state of SOBER after examining about $n = 3 \cdot 2^{16}$ bytes using about $c2^{89.6}$ steps on average. Respectively, after $c2^{89.1}$ steps we have found the key with probability $1/2$. Even though, this is still a huge number, the security of SOBER is nonetheless much lower than what we would expect from a cryptosystem with 128 bit keys.

Remarks. Variants of the attack described in this section are possible and hence an attacker would have some flexibility. First, it can be noticed that the bytes $p_7, \ldots, p_{17}$ are only used in the last step of the attack to distinguish correct guesses of the LFSR state from wrong guesses. This differentiation would also be possible if other bytes than $p_7, \ldots, p_{17}$ are known. Additionally, statistical information on the values $p_7, p_8, \ldots$ would be already sufficient to complete the attack.

The algorithm we have described is based on the assumption that we can find key stream bytes $p_1, \ldots$ produced with two stutter bytes being 10111110_2 and 01010101_2. These values have the property that the resulting system of equations is easily solvable. However, they are chosen somewhat arbitrarily from a set of equally well suited values. Other values would lead to a different system of equations, with a different method to solve. For simplicity we haven't described any such alternative attacks here. It should, however, be noted that these alternatives could possibly be used to reduce the number of necessary key stream bytes.

6 Analysis of the Key Setup

In this section, we analyze the key setup. During the key setup a key of length 40 bit to 128 bit is expanded into an initial state of the LFSR register. Not all 2^{136} states of the LFSR are therefore possible. Hence a desirable property of the key setup would be that the knowledge of the key setup procedure is not helpful for cryptanalysis. However, we show that SOBER leaves the LFSR in a state that can be easily described and that this information is helpful for cryptanalysis.

In the following we will restrict ourselves to the analysis of the key setup for 80 bit keys, since this key size is often recommended for application that do not require high security. Similar, attacks can be found for other key sizes too.

Claim 4. *Given 12 consecutive bytes of known plaintext and corresponding ciphertext encrypted with an unknown 80 bit key. Then it is possible to find the key in about $c2^{68}$ operations with probability 9/16.*

The idea behind the attack is as follows: The attacker guesses 4 bits of the first stutter byte. This will give him two equations such as the ones described used in Section 5, if the two bit pairs are different from 00. This happens with probability 9/16. Then he can guess 8 bytes of the internal state of the LFSR, such that he can compute 2 more bytes. The remaining state of the LFSR can now be found by using Equation (4). Finally, the solution has to be verified by computing more key stream bytes and comparing it to some known plaintext.

7 Weak Keys

In this section, we describe how to find keys that generate no key stream. We will call them *weak keys*.

After the key and frame setup it can happen that the LFSR contains only 0's. In that case, all non-linear output bytes and therefore all stutter bytes are equal to zero. Hence the stream cipher will loop forever without generating a single byte of key stream.

The probability that this event occurs is very low, i.e., for a randomly chosen key and frame number this will occur only with probability 2^{-136}.

The existence of such keys is no risk of privacy. However, the party that choses the keys might use this weakness to initiate a denial of service attack against another party. Generally, we recommend to check for such a state of the LFSR. One possible countermeasure is to reinitialize the stream cipher with a different frame number (e.g. $2^{32} - 1$. This would be sufficient countermeasure, since at most one frame for every key can show this behavior.)

Claim 5. *There exists an efficient algorithm that given a frame number f, finds a key K, if such a key exists, such that the LFSR is in the zero state after initializing the key K and the frame number f. The probability that such a key exists for a randomly chosen frame number is larger than $1/256$.*

Assume that we are given a frame number f and that we are looking for a key k such that the LFSR after the initialization is in the zero state. Since each of the steps during the initialization of the frame number is linear, these steps can easily be reversed. Next, we try to find the corresponding key. For simplicity, we are only interested in 128-bit keys. Given the state after the initialization of the key (i.e. n=40), the state of the LFSR after step n=17 can be computed by reversing the effect of cycling the register and hence $s_{17}, \ldots, s_{33}$ can be computed. Since $s_0, .., s_{16}$ are also known, we can now easily compute the i-th key K_i byte from

$$((175 \otimes (s_i + K_i)) \oplus s_{i+4} \oplus (141 \otimes s_{i+15})) = s_{i+17}.$$

Finally we have to check, whether adding the keylength 16 to s_{16} and cycling the register would produce the correct value for s_{33}. We may assume that this will be the case with probability $1/256$. The runtime of this algorithm is negligible. A few pairs of keys and corresponding frame numbers are given below.

key	frame
85FA3E93F1993225E71B13EFC0811DAC	114
34149FED30DEAC25D4FB89A0F0551DA7	12F
FA1F9189BEE0A2128BA818165B83F86E	240
376DA8DCF4632B0FD4A3EB745E3DB584	291
8A7F49B63524B10FE78371BB4E09B57F	2AE
956F2E347D8CC9F50F14C978C68E740B	530
237DE6F06CE5BAEBD58040767F00D31A	5BE
C7DC7B5B6FAFFCF1CFADB819493C4D77	63F
5EE4BB2970166108F78CFE33374CAE94	7E5

8 Conclusion

We have shown different flaws in SOBER. We have implemented the most serious attack and shown that we can often recover the key in less than 1 minute on a Pentium/200Mhz. Greg Rose has developed a newer, still unpublished version of SOBER[4]. This version is based on commissioned cryptanalysis by Codes & Ciphers Ltd. This work is unpublished, but partially mentioned in [4]. It seems that similar attacks to those described in Section 5 and Section 6 have been known found independently to our analysis. This new version of SOBER takes countermeasures against these attack. Moreover, these countermeasures seem to avoid the attack in Section 4 in this paper, though further analysis is still necessary.

References

1. E. Biham. New types of cryptanalytic attacks using related keys. In T. Helleseth, editor, *Advances in Cryptology — EUROCRYPT'93*, volume 765 of *Lecture Notes in Computer Science*, pages 398–409, Berlin, 1994. Springer Verlag.
2. E. Biham and A. Shamir. *A Differential Cryptanalysis of the Data Encryption Standard*. Springer-Verlag, 1993.
3. G. Rose. A stream cipher based on linear feedback over $GF(2^8)$. In C. Boyd and E. Dawson, editors, *ACISP'98, Australian Conference on Information Security and Privacy*, volume 1438, page Lecture Notes in Computer Science. Springer Verlag, July 1998.
4. G. Rose. SOBER: A stream cipher based on linear feedback over GF(2^8). (preprint), 1999.
5. D. Wagner, B. Schneier, and J. Kelsey. Cryptanalysis of the cellular message encryption algorithm. In B. S. Kaliski, editor, *CRYPTO'97*, volume 1294 of *Lecture Notes in Computer Science*, pages 526–537. Springer Verlag, 1997.
6. D. Wagner, L. Simpson, E. Dawson, J. Kelsey, W. Millan, and B. Schneier. Cryptanalysis of ORYX. In *Fifth Annual Workshop on Selected Areas in Cryptography, SAC'99*, 1998.

Author Index

Lecture Notes in Computer Science

For information about Vols. 1–1548
please contact your bookseller or Springer-Verlag

Vol. 1592: J. Stern (Ed.), Advances in Cryptology – EUROCRYPT '99. Proceedings, 1999. XII, 475 pages. 1999.

Vol. 1593: P. Sloot, M. Bubak, A. Hoekstra, B. Hertzberger (Eds.), High-Performance Computing and Networking. Proceedings, 1999. XXIII, 1318 pages. 1999.

Vol. 1594: P. Ciancarini, A.L. Wolf (Eds.), Coordination Languages and Models. Proceedings, 1999. IX, 420 pages. 1999.

Vol. 1595: K. Hammond, T. Davie, C. Clack (Eds.), Implementation of Functional Languages. Proceedings, 1998. X, 247 pages. 1999.

Vol. 1596: R. Poli, H.-M. Voigt, S. Cagnoni, D. Corne, G.D. Smith, T.C. Fogarty (Eds.), Evolutionary Image Analysis, Signal Processing and Telecommunications. Proceedings, 1999. X, 225 pages. 1999.

Vol. 1597: H. Zuidweg, M. Campolargo, J. Delgado, A. Mullery (Eds.), Intelligence in Services and Networks. Proceedings, 1999. XII, 552 pages. 1999.

Vol. 1598: R. Poli, P. Nordin, W.B. Langdon, T.C. Fogarty (Eds.), Genetic Programming. Proceedings, 1999. X, 283 pages. 1999.

Vol. 1599: T. Ishida (Ed.), Multiagent Platforms. Proceedings, 1998. VIII, 187 pages. 1999. (Subseries LNAI).

Vol. 1601: J.-P. Katoen (Ed.), Formal Methods for Real-Time and Probabilistic Systems. Proceedings, 1999. X, 355 pages. 1999.

Vol. 1602: A. Sivasubramaniam, M. Lauria (Eds.), Network-Based Parallel Computing. Proceedings, 1999. VIII, 225 pages. 1999.

Vol. 1603: J. Vitek, C.D. Jensen (Eds.), Secure Internet Programming. X, 501 pages. 1999.

Vol. 1605: J. Billington, M. Diaz, G. Rozenberg (Eds.), Application of Petri Nets to Communication Networks. IX, 303 pages. 1999.

Vol. 1606: J. Mira, J.V. Sánchez-Andrés (Eds.), Foundations and Tools for Neural Modeling. Proceedings, Vol. I, 1999. XXIII, 865 pages. 1999.

Vol. 1607: J. Mira, J.V. Sánchez-Andrés (Eds.), Engineering Applications of Bio-Inspired Artificial Neural Networks. Proceedings, Vol. II, 1999. XXIII, 907 pages. 1999.

Vol. 1609: Z. W. Raś, A. Skowron (Eds.), Foundations of Intelligent Systems. Proceedings, 1999. XII, 676 pages. 1999. (Subseries LNAI).

Vol. 1610: G. Cornuéjols, R.E. Burkard, G.J. Woeginger (Eds.), Integer Programming and Combinatorial Optimization. Proceedings, 1999. IX, 453 pages. 1999.

Vol. 1611: I. Imam, Y. Kodratoff, A. El-Dessouki, M. Ali (Eds.), Multiple Approaches to Intelligent Systems. Proceedings, 1999. XIX, 899 pages. 1999. (Subseries LNAI).

Vol. 1612: R. Bergmann, S. Breen, M. Göker, M. Manago, S. Wess, Developing Industrial Case-Based Reasoning Applications. XX, 188 pages. 1999. (Subseries LNAI).

Vol. 1613: A. Kuba, M. Šámal, A. Todd-Pokropek (Eds.), Information Processing in Medical Imaging. Proceedings, 1999. XVII, 508 pages. 1999.

Vol. 1614: D.P. Huijsmans, A.W.M. Smeulders (Eds.), Visual Information and Information Systems. Proceedings, 1999. XVII, 827 pages. 1999.

Vol. 1615: C. Polychronopoulos, K. Joe, A. Fukuda, S. Tomita (Eds.), High Performance Computing. Proceedings, 1999. XIV, 408 pages. 1999.

Vol. 1617: N.V. Murray (Ed.), Automated Reasoning with Analytic Tableaux and Related Methods. Proceedings, 1999. X, 325 pages. 1999. (Subseries LNAI).

Vol. 1619: M.T. Goodrich, C.C. McGeoch (Eds.), Algorithm Engineering and Experimentation. Proceedings, 1999. VIII, 349 pages. 1999.

Vol. 1620: W. Horn, Y. Shahar, G. Lindberg, S. Andreassen, J. Wyatt (Eds.), Artificial Intelligence in Medicine. Proceedings, 1999. XIII, 454 pages. 1999. (Subseries LNAI).

Vol. 1621: D. Fensel, R. Studer (Eds.), Knowledge Acquisition Modeling and Management. Proceedings, 1999. XI, 404 pages. 1999. (Subseries LNAI).

Vol. 1622: M. González Harbour, J.A. de la Puente (Eds.), Reliable Software Technologies – Ada-Europe'99. Proceedings, 1999. XIII, 451 pages. 1999.

Vol. 1625: B. Reusch (Ed.), Computational Intelligence. Proceedings, 1999. XIV, 710 pages. 1999.

Vol. 1626: M. Jarke, A. Oberweis (Eds.), Advanced Information Systems Engineering. Proceedings, 1999. XIV, 478 pages. 1999.

Vol. 1627: T. Asano, H. Imai, D.T. Lee, S.-i. Nakano, T. Tokuyama (Eds.), Computing and Combinatorics. Proceedings, 1999. XIV, 494 pages. 1999.

Col. 1628: R. Guerraoui (Ed.), ECOOP'99 - Object-Oriented Programming. Proceedings, 1999. XIII, 529 pages. 1999.

Vol. 1629: H. Leopold, N. García (Eds.), Multimedia Applications, Services and Techniques - ECMAST'99. Proceedings, 1999. XV, 574 pages. 1999.

Vol. 1631: P. Narendran, M. Rusinowitch (Eds.), Rewriting Techniques and Applications. Proceedings, 1999. XI, 397 pages. 1999.

Vol. 1632: H. Ganzinger (Ed.), Automated Deduction – Cade-16. Proceedings, 1999. XIV, 429 pages. 1999. (Subseries LNAI).

Vol. 1633: N. Halbwachs, D. Peled (Eds.), Computer Aided Verification. Proceedings, 1999. XII, 506 pages. 1999.

Vol. 1634: S. Džeroski, P. Flach (Eds.), Inductive Logic Programming. Proceedings, 1999. VIII, 303 pages. 1999. (Subseries LNAI).

Vol. 1636: L. Knudsen (Ed.), Fast Software Encryption. Proceedings, 1999. VIII, 317 pages. 1999.

Vol. 1638: A. Hunter, S. Parsons (Eds.), Symbolic and Quantitative Approaches to Reasoning and Uncertainty. Proceedings, 1999. IX, 397 pages. 1999. (Subseries LNAI).

Vol. 1639: S. Donatelli, J. Kleijn (Eds.), Application and Theory of Petri Nets 1999. Proceedings, 1999. VIII, 425 pages. 1999.

Vol. 1653: S. Covaci (Ed.), Active Networks. Proceedings, 1999. XIII, 346 pages. 1999.